IMAGERY, MEMORY AND COGNITION
Essays in Honor of Allan Paivio

Edited by
JOHN C. YUILLE
University of British Columbia

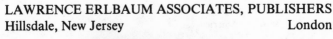
LAWRENCE ERLBAUM ASSOCIATES, PUBLISHERS
1983   Hillsdale, New Jersey   London

Lawrence Erlbaum Associates, Inc., Publishers
365 Broadway
Hillsdale, New Jersey 07642

Library of Congress Cataloging in Publication Data
Main entry under title:

Imagery, memory, and cognition.

   Includes bibliographical references and indexes.
   1. Imagery (Psychology)—Addresses, essays, lectures.
2. Memory—Addresses, essays, lectures.   3. Cognition—
Addresses, essays, lectures.   4. Paivio, Allan—Addresses,
essays, lectures.   I. Yuille, John C.
BF367.I463   1982   153   82-13859
ISBN 0-89859-215-1

Printed in the United States of America
10   9   8   7   6   5   4   3   2   1

Contents

243531

Preface

The 14 chapters in this volume are based upon presentations made to a conference held at the University of Western Ontario in June, 1981. The primary purpose of that conference was to mark the 10th anniversary of the publication of Allan Paivio's text, *Imagery and Verbal Processes*, and to acknowledge the continuing contribution that Paivio is making to imagery research and theory. His landmark book has been the major publication in the field of imagery, and during the last decade Paivio's theorizing and research have dominated the investigation of imaginal processes. The most appropriate fashion in which to honor the achievements and activities of Paivio was to hold a conference on current developments in imagery research and theory. The conference participants were 14 active researchers in the field from Canada and the United States. In addition, the conference attracted a number of observers.

The conference participants reflect, as much as his published work, on Paivio's influence on the field of imagery research. All participants are former associates of Paivio. Twelve completed Masters and/or Ph.D. degrees in Paivio's laboratory (over a period of 15 years) while d'Agostino was his colleague and coworker. The fact that all of these people continue to be active researchers in the imagery field is indicative of the model that Paivio has been for all of us. He continues to be a source of encouragement for all who have been privileged to work with him. Two conference participants, Desrochers and te Linde, recently completed their graduate training with Paivio, and reflect his continuing capacity to encourage and develop fine experimental psychologists.

In noting the considerable number of Paivio's academic offspring, it is appropriate to mention that, at the conference, we learned something about Paivio's (and hence our own) academic roots. Dan Yarmey supplied the conference with a

TABLE 1
Geneological Tree of Paivio and his Students

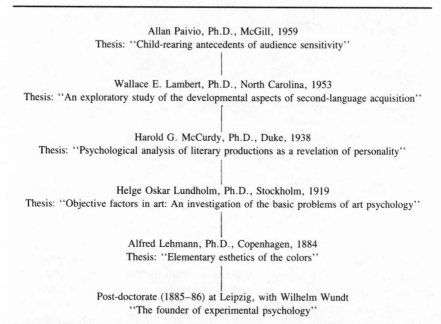

Allan Paivio, Ph.D., McGill, 1959
Thesis: "Child-rearing antecedents of audience sensitivity"

Wallace E. Lambert, Ph.D., North Carolina, 1953
Thesis: "An exploratory study of the developmental aspects of second-language acquisition"

Harold G. McCurdy, Ph.D., Duke, 1938
Thesis: "Psychological analysis of literary productions as a revelation of personality"

Helge Oskar Lundholm, Ph.D., Stockholm, 1919
Thesis: "Objective factors in art: An investigation of the basic problems of art psychology"

Alfred Lehmann, Ph.D., Copenhagen, 1884
Thesis: "Elementary esthetics of the colors"

Post-doctorate (1885–86) at Leipzig, with Wilhelm Wundt
"The founder of experimental psychology"

synopsis of the history of academic advisors in Paivio's "geneological" tree. With thanks to Professors Thom Herrmann and Ian Lubek of the University of Guelph, a modified version of this information is provided in Table 1. Each entry indicates the thesis title, university where it was completed, and the year of completion for successive advisors. Paivio can trace a path through four generations of psychologists to Wundt's laboratory; while the ability to trace ones roots to a founding laboratory is not too surprising in such a young discipline, the titles of the theses provide rich food for thought concerning how successive generations of researchers influence one another.

The contents of this volume reflect the diverse areas in cognitive psychology in which imagery is being investigated. They also indicate the breadth of application of dual-coding theory. The problem areas range from individual differences in imagery, through memory and problem solving, to language and emotions. Paivio has always encouraged his students to be critical and demanding of theoretical developments. He has been rewarded for his encouragement in the present instance by a variety of critical, as well as supportive, comments about his model. In a number of the chapters, the reader will find proposals for the expansion and/or modification of the dual-coding position.

Although the chapters vary in approach and area of interest, there is considerable overlap of topics. The overlap that does exist is reflected in the sequencing of the chapters. The first two chapters, by Ernest and by Katz, concern the difficult topic of individual differences in imagery. Ernest proposes a new model for dealing with this research that incorporates recent insights into cortical laterality. Katz has generated an interactionist model that views imagery as one possible, adaptive method of accommodation. These two chapters form a complementary set dealing with individual differences.

A second set of chapters (Chapters 3–8) is primarily research oriented, and concerned with the role of imagery in memory and in problem solving. In Chapter 3, Madigan provides a comprehensive review of picture memory research. This is followed by the presentation of typically "tight" research by Begg, on the effect of imagery instructions on verbal learning. The next two chapters deal with the currently popular research paradigm of semantic decisions. John te Linde (Chapter 5) presents some unpublished data concerning picture/word effects in semantic decisions. The role of both bilingualism and French unilingualism in this type of task is discussed in Chapter 6 (Desrochers & Petrusic). This is the only chapter in this volume that includes a contribution from someone who has not worked with Paivio. While Petrusic did not participate in the June, 1981 conference, he is a coauthor with Desrochers. Since completing his graduate work with Paivio, Desrochers has been working at Carleton University in Petrusic's laboratory.

The memory section of the book is completed by the chapters of d'Agostino (7) and Yarmey (8). the former looks at color memory, the latter examines self-image. The subsequent three chapters relate to the memory topic, but are distinguished by a greater concern with theoretical issues. Bleasdale (Chapter 9) discusses associative relations among words, including bilingual networks (this complements the experimental findings of Desrochers & Petrusic). Bleasdale proposes some additions to dual-coding theory, as does Clark in the following chapter (Chapter 10). Clark's examination of representational memory is in the context of the current, heated debate about analogue vs. amodal forms of representation. Marschark (Chapter 11) completes this section with an integration of findings from a number of paradigms. He calls for a broadening of dual-coding theory to accommodate amodal codes.

The final section of the text contains three chapters which have a primary theoretical emphasis. Each of them deals directly with the success, or lack of success, of dual-coding theory. Yuille (Chapter 12) suggests that there is a crisis in imagery theories in general, and that major changes in both research strategy and theory are required. Rogers (Chapter 13) echos Yuille's concern, emphasizing the inability of dual-coding theory to incorporate emotions as a type of code. Rogers proposes that a number of research findings demand a triple coding model (images, verbal processes, and emotions). The final contribution (Chapter 14) is by Paivio. It is appropriate that he would have the last word in such a volume, and the nature of his contribution is sufficient justification for the conference and for this book. Paivio has taken this opportunity to examine how he thinks dual-coding theory has fared in the last decade. This is the first time, since his 1971 text, that he has evaluated his model against all of the relevant evidence. His review of the variety of paradigms in which dual-coding theory has been tested provides impressive evidence of the viability of his theory. He demonstrates that dual-coding theory has no rivals in predicting and explaining research outcomes.

Many people contributed to the academic and social success of the imagery conference. There are some individuals who merit special appreciation. Ted Rowe's musical gifts charmed us on a number of occasions, and, together with the Sheik, provided one of the highlights of the conference. Our appreciation is extended to Professor William McClelland, Department of Psychology Chairman at the University of Western Ontario, for his moral and financial support. We all thank Al and Kay Paivio for their kind hospitality. Finally, our thanks to the staff of Spencer Hall for making our conference a pleasant and trouble-free one.

1
Spatial-Imagery Ability, Sex Differences, and Hemispheric Functioning

Carole H. Ernest
Trent University

The central theme of the research I am reporting evolved from a study that Al Paivio and I did when I was a graduate student in his lab. In that study (Paivio & Ernest, 1971) we asked the following question: Are high imagers more accurate than low imagers in their visual recognition of nonverbal stimuli such as pictures and geometric forms, particularly if these stimuli are presented to the right hemisphere of the brain? In other words, is high visual imagery ability associated with superior right hemispheric functioning?

The question was a theoretically important one for two reasons. First, Paivio's (1971) dual-coding approach to memory and cognition distinguished two independent but interconnected symbolic processing systems, a verbal system and a nonverbal or imagery system. The verbal system was viewed as being specialized for dealing with relatively abstract information, such as language, whereas the specialization of the imagery system was processing concrete-perceptual information, such as nonverbal objects or events (see Paivio, 1978a, and this volume, for recent discussions of the assumptions underlying dual-coding theory). We viewed imagery *ability* as the individual differences counterpart of the imagery symbolic system. And we defined visual imagery ability primarily in terms of psychometric tests of spatial ability, tests such as the revised Minnesota Paper Form Board test (MPFB; Likert & Quasha, 1941) and Space Relations of the Differential Aptitude Test battery (Bennett, Seashore, & Wesman, 1947). Both of these tests are measures of spatial visualization, requiring individuals to manipulate two-dimensional figural information mentally in three-dimensional space. Our choice of *visualization* tests to index imagery ability, as distinct from other forms of spatial functioning (see Barratt, 1953; Ekstrom, French, Harman, & Dermen, 1976; Guilford, 1967; McGee, 1979), was influenced by Barratt's

1

(1953) factor analytic study in which he concluded that "imagery is an important component in the solution of those tasks that involve the 'mental' manipulation of spatial relations" (pp. 160–161; more recently, see Carpenter & Just, in press).

A second reason why the question was important theoretically was because Paivio's two symbolic systems seemed to have their counterparts in the neuro-psychological literature on lateralization of brain function. Studies using brain-damaged populations (e.g., Paterson & Zangwill, 1944; Penfield & Roberts, 1959; Sperry & Gazzaniga, 1967) as well as normal individuals (e.g., Kimura, 1961, 1964; Kimura & Durnford, 1974) suggested that the left hemisphere of the brain is specialized for verbal/linguistic/analytic functions whereas the special skills associated with the right hemisphere pertain to nonverbal/spatial information processing as well as global/holistic modes of analysis.

Thus, it seemed reasonable to expect that people who have enhanced spatial-imaginal skills should excel in a task that requires the visual recognition of nonverbal stimuli when such stimli are presented initially to the right hemisphere of the brain. No differences between high and low spatial-imagers might be anticipated when these stimuli are presented to the left hemisphere, that is, the verbal hemisphere. Nor indeed, we speculated, should the imagery groups differ in their recognition of verbal stimuli, such as single letters.

The program of research discussed in this chapter began with essentially the same question. But it also answered some questions I didn't realize I was asking. This research is interpreted within a framework (or model) of hemispheric functioning for high and low spatial-imagers. In its simplest form, this framework suggests essentially two things. It suggests that although high spatial-imagers do excel in their perceptual processing of nonverbal information relative to low imagers, this superiority does *not* appear to be exclusive to the right hemisphere of the brain. Rather, high spatial-imagers seem to be "bilater-lized" for spatial processing. Secondly, individual differences in spatial-imagery ability must be examined within the context of sex differences. Male and female high spatials do not always behave similarly, nor do male and female low spatials. Instead, the sexes within these two ability groups appear to differ in an unexpected fashion in the "lateralization" of their *verbal* functions.

My intention is to discuss several unpublished studies which evolved from the question posed above; to propose and elaborate an organizational framework which seems to encompass most of the experimental findings reported here; and, finally, to speculate on what relevance the proposed framework may have to the more general cognitive functioning of high and low spatial-imagers, particularly in the areas of learning and memory.

But first, the present approach is placed in broader perspective by reviewing selectively relevant literature in three independent but interrelated areas of en-quiry: imagery and perception; cognitive abilities from an information processing perspective; and individual differences in cerebral lateralization. These areas are viewed as independent because they evolved from different "motivations." They are viewed as interrelated because all three postulate the existence of two coding or processing systems—a verbal/analytic system and a spatial/holistic system.

THREE PERSPECTIVES

Imagery and Perception. The notion that imagery and perception tap similar underlying processes is explicit in Paivio's dual-coding theory (1971, 1978a, 1978b) as well as in other theoretical and empirical statements in the literature (e.g., Brooks, 1968; Hebb, 1968; Segal & Fusella, 1970). Hebb (1968), for example, postulates three levels of cell assembly activity. The actual perception of an object, he proposes, involves the activation of first-order as well as higher-order assemblies, whereas a memory image "may consist only of second- and higher-order assemblies, without the first-order ones that would give it the completeness and vividness of perception [1968, p. 473]." And Paivio (1978b) has suggested that the representational units of the image system ("imagens") may be viewed as perceptual isomorphs or analogs, whereas those of the verbal system ("logogens"; Morton, 1969) are assumed to be discrete entities "only arbitrarily related to perceptual information [p. 379]."

Possibly the first evidence that spatial-imagery *ability* and perception may be functionally related emerged unexpectedly in a study on incidental learning (Ernest & Paivio, 1971a, Expt. 2). The orienting task required written identification of briefly-exposed pictures or words; this was followed by an unexpected free recall task. Surprisingly, high imagers excelled in picture identification but not in concrete or abstract word identification. This differential pattern of imagery-picture and imagery-word effects was subsequently pursued in a series of studies employing different recognition paradigms and procedures (Ernest, 1972, 1979, 1980; Paivio & Ernest, 1971). The paradigms were recognition threshold, recognition latency, and visual half-field—all of which involved a clear speed component, either with respect to stimulus presentation or response requirements. Timed, but relatively unspeeded, paper-and-pencil tests requiring the identification of fragmented pictures and fragmented words were also used. Procedural differences included the presentation of pictures and words in heterogeneous lists, as homogeneous blocks in a within-subjects design, or as homogeneous lists in a between-subjects design, or as homogeneous lists in a between-subjects design. The sought-after differential pattern of picture/word effects emerged most unambiguously using the latter experimental design, that is, homogeneous list presentation to independent groups of high and low imagers (Ernest, 1979, Expt. 4, as well as Ernest & Paivio, 1971a, Expt. 2). The only occasion when imagery ability was not clearly associated with superior picture recognition, even under these circumstances, was in the threshold paradigm. Here, imagery differences occurred only for pictures relatively low in familiarity (Ernest, 1979, Expt. 2).

From these studies it seems reasonable to conclude that the cognitive skills involved in the solution of spatial manipulation tests—skills such as encoding and storing figural segments and mentally constructing a complete figure or gestalt from these segments—are also involved in the identification of figural information under speeded or reduced cue conditions. Clearly, however, the conditions for observing such a relationship are not easily determined. Stimulus mode per se seems to be less the source of inconsistency than the context within which stimuli are presented. Contexts that permit the "expected" processing strategy to be primed—"expected" meaning congruent with stimulus mode— appear to yield most unambiguously the imagery ability-picture/word effects first observed, serendipitously, in the incidental learning study. In other words, imagery ability-picture effects emerge when a nonverbal/spatial processing strategy is primed, presumably because such a strategy can be used more effectively by high than by low spatial-imagers. Imagery ability-word effects do *not* emerge when a verbal/linguistic processing strategy is primed, presumably because high and low imagers are comparable with respect to their competence with this strategy.

The view that context can modify one's processing strategy is not new, of course. Indeed, context effects are of interest in their own right and have attracted the attention of many investigators in recent years (e.g., Godden & Baddeley, 1980; Stanovich & West, 1979). They represent a phenomenon that must be reckoned with—at a minimum from the perspective of choice of experimental design (see also Poulton, 1975).

Also relevant to a discussion of spatial-imagery ability and perception is evidence that high spatial-imagers can generate images to words more quickly than can low imagers (Ernest & Paivio, 1971b). This finding is compatible with evidence from recent studies contrasting high and low imagers in speed of mental comparisons (e.g., Paivio, 1978c, d). In mental comparisons tasks (Moyer, 1973), individuals are presented two words, for example, and must decide which one of the pair has more, or less, of a given attribute. Typically, the more similar are the item pairs in a given attribute, such as size, the more difficult is the decision; that is, response times are longer. This has been labeled the "symbolic distance" effect by Moyer and Bayer (1976). Paivio (1975) has assumed that performance on such tasks requires the generation of long-term memory representations of the named items via the imagery system, with these perceptual analogs then mentally contrasted with respect to the relevant attribute.

Pertinent here are those studies concerned with intrinsic or defining attributes of objects. In one study (Paivio, 1978c), for example, high and low spatial-imagers were required to decide which of two digitally-presented clock times formed the smaller angle. Both ability groups demonstrated the typical symbolic distance effect; more importantly, high imagers were significantly faster in two of three "mental clocks" experiments, although the trend was the same in all three. A similar trend emerged when the defining attribute of shape was involved and the stimuli were word pairs (Paivio, 1978d).

These findings have been confirmed in a group-administered version of the "mental clocks" task as well as a size comparisons task where the dependent measure was number correct within a specified time period. Paivio and Harshman (see Paivio, 1980) report significant correlations between Space Relations and the accuracy measures for both tasks. Interestingly, verbal processes, as reflected in Inference Test and (to a lesser degree) Word Fluency scores, were also significantly implicated in performance on these tasks.

This discussion of imagery ability and its relation to perceptual processing has been brief and selective. It has concentrated on imagery ability as defined by spatial manipulation tasks and has omitted some of the interesting work of others on the same topic but approached from the perspective of individual differences in visual imagery *vividness* (e.g., Finke, 1980; Marks, 1973, in press). Nevertheless, it has served the purpose of affirming the relationship between perception and imagery—the latter from an individual differences perspective; of inferring a relationship between strategy and ability; and of suggesting that both spatial and verbal skills may contribute to performance on tasks presented in the verbal mode (see also Ernest, 1980). Some of these points are elaborated in the following section.

Cognitive Abilities From an Information Processing Perspective.   The last few years have witnessed an encouraging and exciting new development both for differential and for cognitive psychology. The information processing paradigms and theoretical frameworks emerging from cognitive psychology are providing valuable new insights into the meaning of individual variation in cognitive abilities (e.g., Carpenter & Just, in press; Carroll, 1976; Hunt, Lunneborg, & Lewis, 1975), and recognition is increasing of the importance of individual difference variables in the construction and modification of theories of cognitive functioning (e.g., Hunt, Frost, & Lunneborg, 1973; Morton & Patterson, 1980; Underwood, 1975). Cronbach (1957, 1975) must be pleased!

The abilities most commonly investigated from an information processing perspective, and which are directly relevant here, are verbal ability and, more recently, spatial ability (e.g., Carpenter & Just, in press; Cooper & Regan, in press; Hunt, 1980; Hunt et al., 1975). Just as there is more than one type of spatial ability (e.g., Guilford, 1967; see also McGee, 1979), verbal ability similarly cannot be viewed as a single ability. The most common verbal factor emerging from factor analytic studies is a "vocabulary" factor. Besides word knowledge, this factor taps reading comprehension and knowledge of the rules of one's language (see Carroll, 1979). "Fluency" is a more difficult verbal factor to interpret. Measured by word generation-type tests, it seems to reflect "facility in calling up isolated words and unrelated ideas; facility in utilizing learned associations in . . . semantic memory'' (Carroll, 1979, p. 21), and so on. Both of these verbal factors are relevant in the context of the present chapter.

"Vocabulary" most clearly reflects verbal ability as defined by Hunt and his associates (see Hunt et al., 1975). With the orienting view of the individual as an information processor, they have demonstrated that individuals high in verbal ability are particularly skilled in rapidly retrieving highly overlearned material from long-term memory (e.g., Posner, Boies, Eichelman, & Taylor's, 1969, identity *vs* name matching task), in storing order information in short-term memory (e.g., Wickens', 1970, release-from-PI paradigm), and in comprehending simple negative (relative to affirmative) sentences (e.g., Clark & Chase's, 1972, sentence-picture verification task). Their sentence "comprehension" study, and particularly the sentence-picture verification task, is important to a discussion of *spatial* ability and its information processing correlates. In this task, individuals are presented a sentence such as "The STAR is above the PLUS." This is followed by either $^+_*$ or $^*_+$ to which they must respond "true" or "false" by pressing the appropriate of two keys. The dependent measures in the Hunt et al. (1975) study were reaction times for sentence reading (or comprehension) and for verification.

One explanation of the processes underlying performance on this task emphasizes linguistic processes, suggesting that the sentences and the pictures are translated into internal representations that assume abstract propositional form (see Carpenter & Just, 1975). But this task is similar to one described by Rosenfeld (1967)—a same-different reaction time (RT) task in which a figure and a verbal description of that figure were successively presented. Rosenfeld examined different types of coding hypotheses as explanations of performance on this task. Predictions based on the hypothesis that words-are-translated-into-representations-of-objects were most strongly supported. The Clark–Chase task similarly seems to lend itself to the use of *nonverbal* (i.e., spatial-imaginal) encoding stragegies, as Paivio's mental comparisons task also do.

Indeed, when MacLeod, Hunt, and Mathews (1978) examined spatial as well as verbal ability differences in the sentence-picture task, they found that spatial ability predicted RTs as well as verbal ability. Further, individuals whose data poorly fit predictions based on a linguistic model of performance proved to have significantly higher spatial ability scores than "well-fit" individuals. The two groups' verbal ability scores did not differ. "Poorly-fit" individuals took longer in the comprehension stage of the task (i.e., the sentence-to-picture conversion stage) but *less* long in the verification stage.

In general, the performance of "poorly-fit" subjects was consistent with a pictorial or visual-imaginal model of sentence verification whereas "well-fit" subjects were consistent with a linguistic model. Correlational analyses further revealed that verbal ability was the best predictor of reaction times for those following a linguistic model; it was spatial visualization ability for those following a visual-imaginal model.

A follow-up study (Mathews, Hunt, & MacLeod, 1980) replicated and extended these findings in several important respects using subjects selected as high or low in spatial ability (but average in verbal ability). However, it failed to confirm clearly the MacLeod et al. (1978) conclusion that strategy choice seems to be predictable from measured abilities. That is, "well fit" and "poorly fit" groups did use a linguistic and pictorial strategy, respectively, as reflected, for example, in longer comprehension times and shorter verification times by the "poorly-fit" subjects. But the "pictorial strategy" group did not consist predominantly of high spatials. It included approximately the same proportion of high and low spatial individuals. Mathews et al. (1980) speculated that their subject sampling procedures may account for this discrepancy, that is, their requirement that all subejcts have average verbal ability scores. On the other hand, the use of over 2-year-old spatial test scores to identify high and low-spatial subjects may also have been a contributing factor. Mathews et al. (1980) point out that a median split of a concurrently-administered spatial visualization test resulted in a high-low classification of subjects which was not exactly the same as that based on the older test scores. Spatial ability differences emerged more clearly in subsequent analyses when recent test scores were used to classify individuals into high-low spatial groups. Unfortunately, however, the strategy choice-ability relationship was not directly reexamined with this new grouping.

A particularly important inclusion in the Mathews et al. (1980) study was a strategy *instruction* variable. Differences between high and low spatials were evident when subjects were instructed to use a pictorial strategy, but not when a linguistic strategy was required. Furthermore, all individuals, regardless of their spatial ability, acquired a linguistic strategy with ease. Low spatials, however, did have some difficulty in following instructions and adopting a pictorial strategy. This was reflected, in part, in their significantly shorter comprehension RTs, relative to high spatials, *and* longer verification RTs. That is, "low spatials either formed a hasty, impoverished image during the comprehension time, or . . . they gave up part way through the transformation [p. 545]."

The same general pattern of findings was recently reported by Sternberg and Weil (1980) using three-term series problems such as "If A is taller and B, and B is taller than C, who is tallest?". This syllogistic reasoning task has similarly been the subject of theoretical debate with respect to the nature of the processes underlying solution times (e.g., Huttenlocher's, 1968, spatial-imagery model *vs* Clark's, 1969, linguistic model). Sternberg and Weil (1980) obtained evidence for their mixed model; that is, that both linguistic and spatial processes are involved. This was reflected in the significant and independent contributions of both verbal and spatial abilities to performance.

They also found clear evidence for an ability-strategy relationship. Their strategy measure was not based on the strategy subjects were instructed to use since, they point out, subjects do not always (for whatever reason; see Mathews et al., 1980) follow instructions. Instead, it was based on the strategy subjects *actually* used, as determined by a mathematical modeling procedure. Under these circumstances, verbal scores (but not spatial scores) were highly correlated with performance for those whose solution latencies fit a linguistic model; spatial (but not verbal) scores were highly correlated with performance for the spatial-model group; and both spatial and verbal scores were significantly correlated with latencies in the mixed-model group.

Two conclusions, particularly relevant to the present discussion, seem warranted. First, *general* models of cognitive functioning may prove to be oversimplications of reality. Individual differences must be considered because all individuals do not approach the same task in the same way. Secondly, a relationship exists between ability and strategy. That is, "the effectiveness of a given strategy . . . depends on one's pattern of abilities" (Sternberg & Weil, 1980, p. 234) and one's choice of strategy may be predictable from a knowledge of psychometrically-tested abilities (see MacLeod et al., 1978; Mathews et al., 1980).

Individual Differences in Cerebral Lateralization.   Of considerable interest over the past few years has been the question of individual and group differences in the extent to which the left and right hemispheres of the brain are specialized, respectively, for linguistic and spatial processing. Discussion has focused on whether hemispheric lateralization (particularly left hemisphere specialization for verbal functions) characterizes right-handers more than left-handers (see Hicks & Kinsbourne, 1978; Levy, 1974), good readers more than poor readers (see Kinsbourne & Hiscock, 1978; Young & Ellis, 1981), field independents more than field dependents (see Garrick, 1978; Zoccolotti & Oltman, 1978), late maturers more than early maturers (Waber, 1976), adults more than children (see Kinsbourne & Hiscock, 1977), young adults more than old adults (Borod & Goodglass, 1980), and males more than females (see Bryden, 1979; McGlone, 1980; Witelson, 1976). It is to the question of sex-related differences in brain asymmetry that we now turn.

Interest in this area has stemmed from evidence that, by adolescence, the sexes apparently differ in certain cognitive abilities. Males typically demonstrate superior spatial manipulation skills (see Harris, 1978; Maccoby & Jacklin, 1974) and females excel in linguistic tasks such as verbal fluency (Maccoby & Jacklin, 1974; see, however, Fairweather, 1976, and Macaulay, 1978). Speculation concerning the sources or determinants of these differences has led to an examination of sex differences in brain organization.

My concern here is not with sex differences in cerebral organization per se—a concern that would have to encompass a discussion of anatomical, clinical, electrophysiological, and other types of investigations (see McGlone, 1980). It is with noninvasive behavioral investigations of the question, such as those using the visual half-field (and dichotic listening) paradigms. (Note, however, that McGlone bases her conclusions primarily on the latter types of investigation, as well as clinical studies.) The findings here have recently been reviewed by Bryden (1979) and McGlone (1980). They conclude that when sex differences are found, males tend to be more lateralized for verbal *and* spatial functions than females. The evidence is not strong, however, and "more is known of sex differences in language representation than those in spatial representation" (McGlone, 1980, p. 226). This conclusion is consistent with the view (e.g., Levy, 1969, 1974) that bilateral representation of language interferes with spatial processing, which is presumed to be the province of the right hemisphere. Thus, the poorer spatial skills of females.

McGlone's acknowledgment that within-sex variation may be greater than between-sex variation (see Harshman, Remington, & Krashen, 1974, cited in McGlone, 1980) suggests that other individual differences factors must be considered. Bryden (1979), for example, has suggested that males and females may use different strategies in performing so-called lateralization tasks. Certainly there is evidence from other sources that the sexes differ in their approach to the same task (e.g., Allen & Hogeland, 1978; Freedman & Rovegno, 1981; Kail, Carter, & Pellegrino, 1979; McGlone, 1981; Tapley & Bryden, 1977). Bryden (1980), and others (e.g., Kinsbourne & Hiscock, 1977; Young & Ellis, 1981), have clearly argued that asymmetries in performance on hemispheric tasks may be reflections of attention (see Kinsbourne, 1970) and strategy choices (see Bryden's commentary in McGlone, 1980) rather than "true" differences in brain specialization. Indeed, the susceptibility of the visual half-field paradigm to such influences was demonstrated in the Paivio and Ernest (1971) study. A right visual field (RVF) effect for letter recognition did not emerge in this study when the analysis

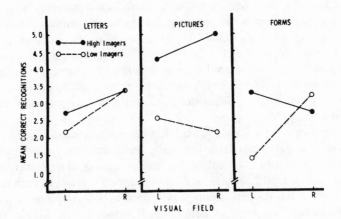

FIG. 1.1.   First list recognition accuracy scores as a function of imagery ability, stimulus attribute, and visual field. (From Paivio and Ernest, 1971. *Perception and Psychophysics*, 1971, *10*, 429–432. Reproduced with permission of the Psychonomic Society).

included letter data from all subjects; that is, when these stimuli were the first, second, or third lists received by different subjects. (Recall that the other two stimulus lists were pictures and geometric forms.) It was when first-list data only were analyzed—that is, when any priming or carry-over effects from other stimulus types were avoided—that the expected RVF effect for letter identification occurred (see Fig. 1.1, left panel). These considerations are pertinent, of course, to any investigation where individual or group comparisons are of interest, such as those mentioned at the beginning of this section, and including the current examination of individual differences in spatial ability.

Summary.   These three areas of enquiry address several issues and problems that are clearly pertinent to an investigation of the relatively simple (or simple-minded) question posed earlier. That is, are high spatial-imagers more accurate in their visual recognition of nonverbal (but not verbal) stimuli, particularly if these stimuli are presented via the left visual field to the right hemisphere of the brain. The most central issues involve the relationship among abilities (spatial and verbal), sex differences, and strategy use (imaginal and linguistic). These are addressed in the studies to follow through methodological controls (e.g., verbal ability), statistical analysis (e.g., sex differences), and *post hoc* analyses and/or questionnaires (e.g., strategies).

THE PRESENT STUDIES

Preliminary.   The results of four unpublished studies will be discussed. Two studies required the identification of words (Study 1) and pictures (Study 2), and two were nonidentification or matching studies using pictures (Study 3) and random shapes (Study 4) as stimuli. The order in which these studies is presented reflects an assumed progression in the demands made on a spatial-imaginal processing system, or, conversely, an attenuation in the linguistic processing requirements of the tasks. Accordingly, spatial-imagery ability effects should be conspicuously absent in the Word study and conspicuously present in the Random Shapes study.

A common strategy was used in the selection of subjects and conduct of these studies. At least 100 (paid) Trent University undergraduates—mostly Introductory Psychology students—completed an imagery and verbal test battery on each of three occasions representing three different academic years. In each instance, high (or low) spatial-imagery ability was defined as achieving scores above (or below) the mean of the group on *both* Space Relations and the MPFB. Because fewer males than females volunteered, attempts to select an equal number of males and females within each spatial-imagery group were not always realized. Verbal ability, as defined by verbal fluency measures, was controlled across the Imagery-Sex groups for each experiment described. Verbal fluency scores were based either on the total number of words generated to four concrete and four abstract words (see Paivio, 1971) or on the Word Beginnings and Endings Test (Ekstrom et al., 1976).

Of the 110 subjects selected for these studies (32–40 per study with some subjects participating in more than one study), three were left-handed for writing (Annett, 1970); none of these, however, reported familial sinistrality (see Zurif & Bryden, 1969). All three were low-spatial males. All subjects but three endorsed at least eight of the 12 items in Annett's handedness questionnaire as right-handed items. No subjects reported uncorrected visual defects.

All studies were conducted using a 3-channel Harvard tachistoscope (Gerbrands Model 3-TB-1). Subjects were tested individually with each session preceded by several practice items. Stimulus presentation was unilateral—that is, either to the LVF or RVF—except for the Words study where presentation was bilateral. Standard counterbalancing procedures with respect to stimuli and visual field of presentation were carried out within each Imagery-Sex group.

All stimuli were positioned approximately 1.9 cm from central fixation and viewed from a distance of 80 cm. The letters constituting the word stimuli were 5mm high. The maximum height and/or width of the pictures was 2.5 cm; for random shapes it was approximately 3.5 cm.

Attempts to ensure central fixation prior to stimulus presentation included regular reminders to subjects throughout each testing session (see Bryden & Rainey, 1963) as well as permitting subjects to control stimulus onset through the use of a hand switch held in the dominant hand. Both accuracy data and verbal response times were collected in some studies. However, emphasis here is placed on accuracy.

Study 1: Word Identification

The only evidence bearing on the question of the lateralization of linguistic functions in high and low spatial-imagers comes from the Paivio and Ernest (1971) study where single letters were presented. High and low spatial-imagers did not differ in overall accuracy and both ability groups shown the typical RVF effect for letter identification (see Fig. 1.1, left panel). There was no interaction. Since a RVF effect for verbal material tends to be stronger for words than for single letters (see Young & Ellis, 1981), the present study allowed a more stringent examination of visual field effects for verbal stimuli in these two ability groups by using words as the linguistic material.

Twenty concrete and high-imagery words (CW) and 20 abstract and low-imagery words (AW) were selected (unpublished norms for over 2000 words; Paivio's lab). All were 5-letter nouns and were selected in pairs such that one concrete word matched one abstract word as closely as possible in Throndike-Lorge frequency (Thorndike & Lorge, 1944), Kučera-Francis frequency (Kučera & Francis, 1967), and printed familiarity (unpublished norms; Paivio's lab). The abstract words were randomly paired, as were their concrete word counterparts. The bilateral presentation procedure was based on that described by Schmuller and Goodman (1979) whereby a central arrow on the stimulus card dictates to subjects the required order of responding, as well as ensuring fixation. Thus, *both* words are to be identified but are counted as correct only if the noted order of report is honored. (A more lenient scoring procedure, ignoring order of report, did not yield substantially different results from those reported here.) In the present study, a "Don't Know" (DK) response was permitted, thus allowing for a "WORD-DK" response, for example, or "DK-WORD." Exposure duration was 40 ms for all subjects and only those achieving at least 25% accuracy for CW or AW identification, regardless of order of report, were included in the analysis.

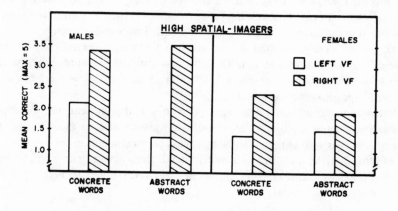

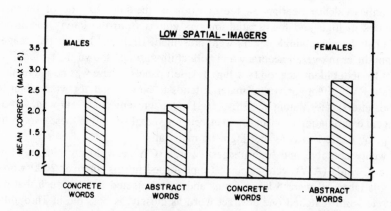

FIG. 1.2. Mean correct word identifications as a function of spatial-imagery ability, sex, visual field, and word imagery (Study 1).

The results for the 16 high and 16 low spatial-imagers (sexes equally represented) yielded a strong RVF effect for word identification and clearly no main
effect for spatial-imagery ability. However, a highly significant 3-way interaction involving Ability, Sex, and Field emerged which, in turn, was qualified by a
4-way interaction that included Word Imagery (see Fig. 1.2). (It should be noted
that neither of these interactions was qualified by the Order-of-Report factor,
which will not be discussed at the present time.)

With respect to the 3-way interaction, a RVF effect for word identification
was clearly apparent for high-spatial males (Hi-M) and low-spatial females
(Lo-F). (All subjects but one, a low-spatial female, showed a RVF advantage.) The
significance of the RVF effect was confirmed in separate ANOVAs of their
respective data. A RVF effect was less apparent and, indeed, *not* significant for
high-spatial females (Hi-F). It was absent completely for low-spatial males
(Lo-M).

Thus, high and low spatials are comparable with respect to overall accuracy in
word identification (cf. Ernest, 1979; Ernest & Paivio, 1971a), as are the sexes.
However, the sexes *within* the ability groups do seem to differ in the ''lateralization'' of their linguistic functions. Male and female high-spatials are not similarly left-hemisphere lateralized for language, nor are male and female low-
spatials. Indeed, low-spatial males appear to be bilateralized. (38% showed a
RVF advantage and 50% a LVF advantage.) The results for high-spatial females
are more ambiguous. Although the absence of a significant RVF effect suggests
''bilateralization,'' a RVF superiority was evident for all but one subject. Nevertheless, the left hemisphere advantage for the remaining subjects was somewhat
weaker (in absolute terms) than that for high-spatial males and low-spatial
females, in that order. Larger sample sizes in future should help to clarify their
language-dominance status. Other evidence to be reported below, however,
suggests that high-spatial females may indeed be more similar ''linguistically'' to
low-spatial males than to the other two subject groups.[1]

The two subject groups demonstrating significant RVF effects—high-spatial
males and low-spatial females—also showed a weaker RVF effect for concrete
words than for abstract words (see Fig. 1.2). This was most clearly evident for
high-spatial males. A stronger RVF effect for AW than for CW is not surprising
since it has been reported elsewhere in the literature (e.g., Ellis & Shepherd,
1974; Hines, 1976; Marcel & Patterson, 1978; see also Ley & Bryden, in press).
However, these data suggest that a Word Imagery-Visual Field interaction may

---

[1]For ease of discussion, the terms ''lateralized'' and ''bilateralized'' or ''nonlateralized'' are used
throughout this chapter to refer to hemispheric specialization (or lack of it) as inferred from visual
field results. It is recognized, however, as noted earlier and in the Concluding Remarks section of this
chapter, that visual field effects may reflect other than ''true'' (i.e., neurological) differences in
hemispheric specialization.

be specific to certain subject groups. High-spatial males, in particular, seem to be using *right*-hemispheric functions for processing concrete words, with their left hemispheres similarly efficient in concrete and abstract word identification.

Study 2: Picture Identification

The Paivio and Ernest (1971) study affirmed the superiority of high spatial-imagers in picture identification, but there was no suggestion that this superiority was exclusive to the right hemisphere of the brain (see Fig. 1.1, center panel). Indeed, ability differences were greater under RVF presentation conditions, that is, in the *left* hemisphere, with high imagers showing a slight bias in favor of the RVF and low imagers a bias in favor of the LVF, or right hemisphere. The present study sought to replicate this portion of that study for several reasons. The sample size was small, making an analysis of sex differences unfeasible; all stimuli were presented twice—once to each visual field—adding a potential memory component to the task (see Hardyck, Tzeng, & Wang, 1978; but see Schmuller, 1980); and the pictures used were all easily labeled. Ease of label retrieval clearly might inhibit right hemisphere involvement or, conversely, encourage left hemisphere processing of the pictures. It might also provide a potential advantage for high spatial-imagers who have been shown to be faster in picture naming than low imagers (Ernest, 1972).

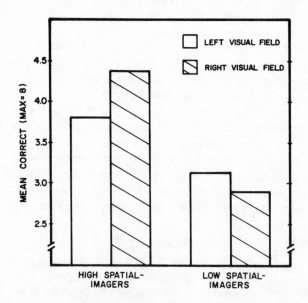

FIG. 1.3.   Mean correct picture identifications as a function of spatial-imagery ability and visual field of presentation (Study 2).

In the present study (Ernest, 1982a), 20 high and 20 low spatial-imagers (8 males and 12 females in each group) were presented 32 outline drawings of pictures, once only, and for 30 ms, to the left or right visual field. The pictures were selected to vary in their verbal codability. They were selected in pairs such that the two members of a pair were matched as closely as possible on the frequency of their verbal labels (Thorndike & Lorge, 1944), picture familiarity, and labeling consistency (at least 75%); they differed, however, in the latency with which they could be be labeled (LLAT) (unpublished norms, Paivio's lab). Short LLAT was defined as < 1.70 sec, long LLAT as > 1.75 sec.

Only a portion of the results will be mentioned here. With respect to sex differences—there were none; nor were there any interactions with gender. High spatial-imagers again significantly excelled in picture identification and a trend emerged for imagery ability and field of presentation to interact. This interaction, illustrated in Fig. 1.3, parallels precisely the trend obtained in the 1971 study. That is, the superiority of high imagers in picture processing is not exclusive to the right hemisphere of the brain; it obtains to *both* hemispheres with greater facilitation, in fact, occurring in the left hemisphere. Imagery ability did not interact with the verbal codability (LLAT) factor, even though this factor had a dramatic effect on performance. It seems, then, that the picture processing skills of high spatial-imagers are *not* exclusive to easy-to-label pictures.

Study 3: Picture Matching

This study minimized further the verbal processing component in picture recognition by eliminating the requirement of verbal identification. The task was one of picture matching or picture recognition memory. The same easy-to-label and difficult-to-label pictures were used as in the previous study and the subjects were those who had participated in the Word Identification experiment. The present study was conducted several weeks following completion of the Word study.

Exposure duration was 20 ms and presentation was to the left or right visual field. One second following stimulus presentation, an array of four pictures was presented tachistoscopically. One was the target item and the remaining three were lures that had been selected to be structurally similar to the target. The subjects' task was to indicate verbally the *location* of the target item using the response system of top-left, top-right, bottom-left, or bottom-right.

Accuracy was extremely high in this study, averaging 86% for high spatials and 88% for low spatials. Clearly, there was no main effect for spatial-imagery ability. There was, however, for LLAT. That is, easy-to-label pictures were more accurately matched than difficult-to-label pictures despite the fact that labeling was not a requirement of this task. This codability effect was specific to two subject groups, however, as reflected in a significant interaction involving Ability, Sex, and LLAT and separate analyses of the four subject groups' data.

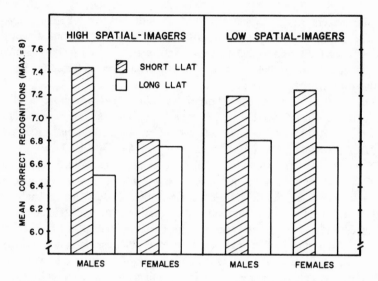

FIG. 1.4.   Mean correct picture matches as a function of spatial-imagery ability, sex, and picture codability (Study 3).

Figure 1.4 identifies these groups as high-spatial males and low-spatial females, the same groups most left-hemisphere lateralized for language in the Word Study.

The same (significant) interaction emerged when verbal response times (RT) were analyzed using subjects' median response latencies for correctly matched pictures. Figure 1.5 shows that matching times were faster for easy-to-label (i.e., short LLAT) pictures for all four subject groups, but the inhibiting effect of difficult-to-label pictures is more apparent in the case of high-spatial males and low-spatial females.

Although the high-low spatial groups did not differ in accuracy, as already noted, high spatial-imagers did tend to respond more *quickly* (p = .07). There was no suggestion of an interaction with visual field of presentation, however. Thus, response times proved to be sensitive to spatial-imagery ability differences under circumstances of near-ceiling performance, but the picture processing capabilities of high spatial-imagers again were not exclusive to the right hemisphere of the brain.

Study 4: Random Shapes Matching

A more rigorous examination of the question concerning superior right hemispheric functioning was attempted using the random shapes generated by Vanderplas and Garvin (1959). These stimuli do not have agreed-upon verbal labels

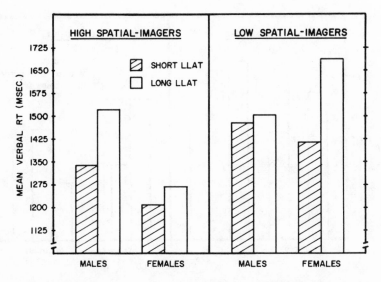

FIG. 1.5.   Mean verbal response times for correct picture matches as a function of spatial-imagery ability, sex, and picture codability (Study 3).

as do the pictures used in the previous two studies. But they do differ with respect to their association value (AV). Association value is defined by Vanderplas and Garvin as the percentage of subjects giving a ''content'' or a YES response to each shape during a 3-sec exposure. A ''content'' response is a one-or two-word naming response; a YES response was given if the shape reminded subjects of some object or situation but they had insufficient time to name it. Association value was varied in the present study within approximately the same range of high and low values for 6-point (low complexity), 12-point (medium complexity), and 24-point (high complexity) random shapes.

Eighteen high imagers (9 males, 9 females) and 20 low imagers (6 males, 14 females) participated. None had participated in previous studies. The shapes were presented unilaterally, for 30 ms, in a mixed sequence; that is, the Complexity factor was not blocked. Four sec later a single shape appeared for several seconds at fixation. The subject's task was to respond SAME or DIFFERENT. The ''different'' items (50% of the trials) were of the same complexity as the target items, and were constructed to resemble the target. The dependent measure was the number of correct responses (SAME + DIFFERENT).

Accuracy levels were 74%, 73%, and 69% for low, medium, and high complexity shapes, respectively. Although Complexity per se was not a significant factor in recognition accuracy, Imagery Ability was (see Fig. 1.6). However, Ability was involved in interaction effects that differed for the three complexity levels.

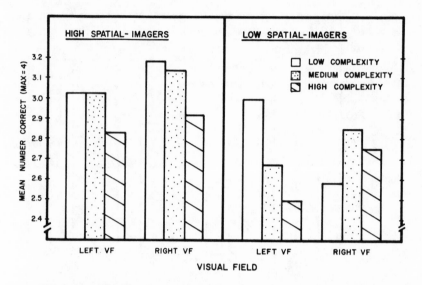

FIG. 1.6.   Mean correct matches for random shapes of low (6-point), medium (12-point), and high (24-point) complexity as a function of spatial-imagery ability and visual field of presentation (Study 4).

Low Complexity Shapes.   Spatial-imagery ability significantly predicted recognition accuracy when simple 6-point shapes were presented, but an interaction with field-of-presentation qualified this effect. Figure 1.6 clearly shows that the superiority of high imagers is specific to RVF presentation. The pattern of effects is remarkably similar to that previously reported for pictures (e.g., Paivio & Ernest, 1971, and Study 2 here). That is, high imagers show a slight "preference" for RVF-presentation (or left hemisphere reception) whereas low imagers clearly, in this instance, favor the *right* hemisphere for simple shapes recognition. (65% of low spatials showed a LVF advantage; 15% favored the RVF, and 20% showed no visual field preference. Percentages for high spatials were 39%, 39%, and 22%, respectively.) The discrepancy between spatial-imagery groups is again, then, particularly with respect to left hemispheric functioning. Consistent with the "picture" studies, there were no interactions with gender.

Medium Complexity Shapes.   With respect to 12-point shapes, high spatial-imagery ability was again associated with significantly higher accuracy scores. But no interactions with Imagery Ability emerged. The 12-point shapes analysis was the only one in which AV had a significant (positive) effect on performance. Association value did not interact with any other factor, however.

High Complexity Shapes.   The Ability factor was *unrelated* to accuracy in the case of 24-point shapes. However, the interaction of Imagery, Sex, and Field was marginally significant (p = .06; see Fig. 1.7). Two patterns are evident here. First, high-spatial males and low-spatial females are (again) "behaving" similarly, as are high-spatial females and low-spatial males. More importantly, the sexes within the *low*-spatial group are noticeably different in their performance. Males tend to find complex shapes easier to match if first they access the right hemisphere, as both sexes did when the shapes were simple. (50% showed this advantage; 33% showed a left-hemisphere advantage.) The reverse is the case for females. (64% of females showed a RVF advantage, the same percentage showing a *LVF* advantage for 6-point shapes. 21% favored a LVF presentation for 24-point shapes.) This suggests that females may now be utilizing a different—perhaps a linguistic—processing strategy.

Evidence that this may be so emerged from a correlational analysis in which Associational Fluency (FLU) scores were correlated with accuracy scores for 6-, 12-, and 24-point shapes *within* the male and female samples. (Recall that the sexes do not differ in fluency.) For low-spatial females, the correlations were essentially zero between FLU and LVF (or right hemisphere) performance for all three levels of complexity. For RVF (or left hemisphere) performance, however, the correlation was significant and positive only in the case of 24-point shapes. The pattern for low-spatial males was somewhat different, with a tendency towards positive correlations between FLU and LVF performance reaching significance for 24-point shapes. Thus, highly complex shapes did seem to evoke a different processing strategy in females, one which could have been verbal in nature.

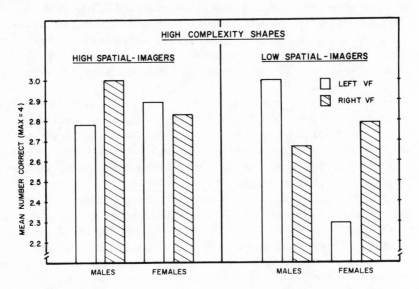

FIG. 1.7.   Mean correct matches of high complexity (24-point) random shapes as a function of spatial-imagery ability, sex, and visual field of presentation (Study 4).

It is difficult to contrast the results obtained in this study with random shapes studies reported in the literature (e.g., Dee & Fontenot, 1973; Fontenot, 1973; Hannay, 1976; Hannay, Rogers, & Durant, 1976). This is because the published studies are sometimes inconsistent with respect to differential visual field effects for simple and more complex shapes. The present results do affirm Hannay's point, however, that subject characteristics such as spatial ability and sex differences must be considered in such studies (Hannay, 1976; Hannay, Rogers, & Durant, 1976).

The correlational analysis carried out within Imagery-Sex groups raises the broader question of differential strategy "implementation" in high- and low-spatial males and females and, importantly, whether strategies other than those associated with one's spatial ability (particularly in the case of high spatials) may be accounting for the results obtained in this and previous studies. Such questions will be raised again in the course of presenting a framework of hemispheric functioning for high and low spatial-imagers which encompasses the data from these studies.

A FRAMEWORK OF HEMISPHERIC FUNCTIONING

The question Al Paivio and I began with 10 years ago seemed relatively straightforward. The answer to that question clearly is not. My expectations in pursuing the question had not been quite so naive as to assume that because verbal ability was controlled, and because both males and females were selected as high and low spatials, that sex differences and verbal processing factors would not play some role in perceptual recognition. Our own work, as well as an examination of the learning and memory literature (see Ernest, 1977), dictated otherwise. Nevertheless, I had not anticipated the Imagery-Sex-Linguistic pattern that emerged here.

The results of the four studies are summarized in Table 1.1. The framework within which these results will be interpreted and discussed is illustrated in Fig. 1.8. This framework of hemispheric functioning postulates the existence of four distinct Imagery-Sex/Linguistic groups. The sexes within each spatial-imagery group are represented as relatively consistent with respect to spatial functions. That is, high-spatial imagers, regardless of their sex, are viewed as bilateralized for spatial functions. Low spatial-imagers, on the other hand, are viewed as right-hemisphere dominant for such functions. The sexes within, and across, the spatial-imagery groups are not consistent, however, with respect to hemispheric specialization of linguistic functions. High-spatial males and low-spatial females are most clearly left hemispheric dominant. High-spatial females are represented as "weakly" left hemisphere lateralized, and low-spatial males as most clearly bilateralized for language. The bases for this characterization will now be briefly reviewed and supplemented, where possible, by additional evidence.

TABLE 1.1
Summary of Significant Effects and Trends

Effects	Study 1: Word Naming	Study 2: Picture Naming	Study 3: Picture Matching	Study 4: Random Shape Matching		
				6-Point	12-Point	24-Point
ABILITY	NOT SIGNIFICANT (NS)	SIGNIFICANT (SIG)	NS: Accuracy MARG. SIG[a]: Latency	SIG	SIG	NS
SEX	NS	NS	NS	NS	NS	NS
FIELD	SIG	NS	NS	NS	NS	NS
ABILITY X FIELD	MARG SIG RVF effect stronger in Hi than Lo; see interactions below, however	TREND Hi—RVF trend; Lo—LVF trend. Greatest difference in RVF	NS	SIG Hi—RVF trend; Lo—strong LVF effect. Difference in RVF only	NS	NS
SEX X FIELD	NS	NS	NS	NS	NS	NS
ABILITY X SEX X FIELD	SIG Hi-M and Lo-F: RVF effect; Hi-F and Lo-M no RVF effect	NS	NS	NS	NS	MARG. SIG Hi-M and Lo-F: RVF better; Hi-F and Lo-M: LVF better. But interaction primarily due to sex differences in Lo group.
ABILITY X SEX X FIELD X WORD IMAGERY	SIG Hi-M and Lo-F: weaker RVF effects for CW than AW	NOT RELEVANT (NR)	NR	NR		NR

(continued)

21

TABLE 1.1 (Continued)

Effects	Study 1: Word Naming	Study 2: Picture Naming	Study 3: Picture Matching	Study 4: Random Shape Matching		
				6-Point	12-Point	24-Point
CODABILITY OF NONVERBAL STIMULI (i.e., LLAT and AV)	NR	SIG	SIG	NS	SIG	NS
ABILITY X SEX X CODABILITY	NR	NS	SIG Hi-M and Lo-F more affected by codability factor than Hi-F and Lo-M	NS	NS	NS

[a]MARGINALLY SIGNIFICANT (p ≤ .07).

HIGH SPATIAL-IMAGERS

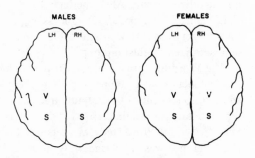

LOW SPATIAL-IMAGERS

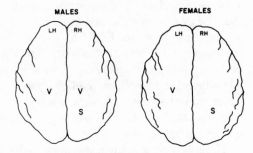

FIG. 1.8. Proposed framework of hemispheric functioning for males and females of high and low spatial-imagery ability.

Specialization of Linguistic Functions. The designation just described for the specialization of language functions evolved primarily from the Word Identification study. In this study a significant RVF effect for language processing emerged only for high-spatial males and low-spatial females; thus, their designation as left hemisphere dominant for language. Low-spatial males emerged most clearly as bilateralized. Their LVF and RVF performance in the Word study were essentially identical. Most difficult to designate are high-spatial females. The absence of a significant RVF effect for word identification suggests that they are not as lateralized as high-spatial males and low-spatial females. But neither are they as bilateralized as low-spatial males. Nevertheless, they do have certain linguistic behaviors in common with low-spatial males (see following), and so are viewed here as more similar in language dominance to low-spatial males than to the other two subject groups.

Thus, two "linguistic" groups that cross spatial and sex boundaries are proposed. One group is lateralized (i.e., Hi-M and Lo-F), the other is not (i.e., Hi-F and Lo-M). Some of the evidence that supports this dichotomy comes from the studies reported here. Possibly the strongest is the fact that the lateralized linguistic group shows evidence of verbally processing pictures in the Picture Matching study (see Figs. 1.4 and 1.5). Little evidence of such processing emerged for the nonlateralized group. Also, the lateralized group is consistent in its tendency to right-hemisphere (spatially?) process high-imagery/concrete words relative to low-imagery/abstract words (see Fig. 1.2). This tendency is not present in the nonlateralized linguistic group.

The Word Identification study revealed another characteristic common to the two subject groups comprising each linguistic group. The lateralized group showed no evidence of perceptual trace decay as defined by first *versus* second report data. The nonlateralized did; that is, the second of two words to be identified in the Word study was reported less accurately than the first, although the difference was significant only in the case of low-spatial males.

Specialization of Spatial Functions.   The designation of high spatial-imagers as bilateralized for spatial processing is based on the remarkable consistency they show in their visual field performance across different types of nonverbal material. For picture identification (see Figs. 1.3 and 1.1, center panel) and random shapes recognition (see Fig. 1.6)—as well as geometric forms identification in the Paivio and Ernest (1971) study (see Fig. 1.1, right panel)—high spatials perform equally well regardless of the hemisphere initially stimulated. Although a bias favoring the RVF, or *left* hemisphere, emerged in several instances, it was never marked—except in its consistency. In fact, when only high spatials' data from the random shapes study were analyzed, the RVF superiority did not emerge as significant.

Nevertheless, an attempt was made to determine the basis of this trend. Could individual differences factors other than those reflected in superior spatial visualization test scores account for it? Recall that the spatial groups did not differ in verbal fluency, the index of verbal ability most typically associated with sex differences and left-hemisphere functioning (see McGlone, 1980). Test scores were also available for the subjects tested here for a vocabulary (VOC) index of verbal ability (i.e., Advanced Vocabulary; Ekstrom et al., 1976) and for subjects' stated preferences for verbal (V) and imaginal (I) thinking (i.e., the Individual Differences Questionnarie; Paivio, 1971). In none of the studies reported here did the two ability groups (or, indeed, the four subject groups) differ in their IDQ-V (or IDQ-I) scores. High spatial-imagers did excel in VOC in the Picture Identification and Random Shapes studies, but correlations computed across all subjects, and for overall performance, revealed the absence of any significant relationship between VOC and picture identification, or 6- and 24-point shape recognition. (Interestingly, VOC correlated significantly and positively with 12-point recognition, the only level of complexity in which AV had a positive influence on performance.)

Perhaps more relevant here are the correlations computed between verbal scores (FLU, VOC, IDQ-V) and left *vs* right visual field performance *within* the spatial ability groups; that is, correlations pertinent to whether the ability groups "used" their verbal skills differentially in performing nonverbal tasks. These correlations suggested no clear reason for the RVF bias of high spatials. This is because any significant correlations obtained, which were pertinent to enhanced RVF performance, were not consistent across the nonverbal materials demonstrating this bias or across the sexes when, indeed, male and female high spatials did not differ in performance.

At the present time, the most plausible explanation for the RVF bias seems to be a "hard-wired" rather than a strategic one. That is, it is proposed here that the left hemisphere of high spatials processes spatial information as efficiently as the right. But we know that language-production systems are localized in the left hemisphere of right-handed individuals. Because all tasks described here required some form of verbal output, it seems reasonable to infer that the readier access of left-hemispheric encodings to the left-hemisphere language-production center resulted in the tendency to "favor" RVF presentation.

Unlike high spatials, low-spatial individuals are variable in their visual field performance across different types of nonverbal material. They tend to favor LVF presentation for pictures (see Figs. 1.3 and 1.1, center panel) and for simple random shapes (see Fig. 1.6). More complex random shapes and geometric forms, on the other hand, tend to yield a RVF superiority (see Figs. 1.6 and 1.1, right panels) although (unlike high spatials) the sexes may differ (see Fig. 1.7). The performance correspondence between simple random shapes and pictures may be explained by Vanderplas and Garvin's (1959) association-value norming study in which they report that "shapes of low complexity evoked . . . responses which were reflective of their resemblance to objects. Shapes of greater complexity seemed to evoke responses of greater variety of content, in the sense that they did not reflect clear resemblances of objects [p. 153]." The absence of a behavioral correspondence between simple shapes and geometric forms recognition may also be explained by Vanderplas and Garvin's report that although some of their simpler shapes strongly resembled geometric forms, these shapes often did not evoke content or even "yes" responses from their subjects.

This more complex pattern for low spatials has led to their designation as right-hemisphere dominant for spatial functions, albeit rather limited spatial functions. That is, low spatials do seem to be capable of right-hemispheric nonverbal processing when the stimuli resemble, or are referents of, simple real-world objects. But when stimuli are structurally complex, or perhaps more abstract symbolically, a left-hemispheric "linguistic" approach seems to become more adaptive in the face of poor spatial encoding skills (i.e., low spatial ability), particularly for females. The right-to left-hemisphere strategy change may be more evident in females than in males because of females' stronger left-hemispheric dominance for language. Correlational evidence mentioned earlier suggested that language bilateralized low-spatial males may also be linguistically processing highly complex shapes, albeit in the right hemisphere.

The results from a replication study of the simple (6-point) random shapes condition provide further insight into the type of encoding behavior engaged in by low spatials, particularly low-spatial males. The subjects in this replication study were the same as those in the Word Identification and Picture Matching studies. As before (see Study 4), high and low spatial-imagers differed significantly in performance—particularly RVF performance—although the Ability-Field interaction was not significant. Low-spatial males performed particularly poorly in this study, as they also tended to do in the earlier Shapes study for 6- and 12-point stimuli. But a postexperimental strategies questionnaire suggested a possible source of their difficulty. Although the majority of subjects in all four Imagery-Sex groups (5 or 6 out of 8) reported using an imagery strategy in performing the 6-point shapes matching task, low-spatial subjects—and particularly males—were more likely than high spatials to endorse as their primary strategy the statement "I held a visual image of *some part(s)* of the first shape in my 'mind's eye' and then matched it with the second shape," rather than "I held a *complete* visual image of the first shape. . . ." These data, although only suggestive at this point because of small sample sizes, do associate poor performance with an inability to hold a complete image in one's visual memory (see also Carpenter & Just, in press), *even* when it is relatively simple in structure. This inability seems to have less of a detrimental effect on LVF than RVF performance for low-spatial subjects.

Correspondence of the Proposed Framework to Other Abilities.   One implication of the proposed framework is that enhanced or above-average performance on a psychometrically-tested ability may not reflect superior functioning in the hemisphere typically associated with that ability. Instead, it may reflect bihemispheric involvement in the processes underlying that ability. Evidence in the literature relevant to other aptitudes or abilities, although sparse, nevertheless seems to concur with this speculation. These other abilities are musical aptitude and verbal ability.

Until recently, it has been assumed that music perception is predominantly mediated by the right hemisphere of the brain (see Bradshaw & Nettleton, 1981, for a review). Not only has this view been modified, with "an increasing emphasis upon bihemispheric mediation of musical functions" (Bradshaw & Nettleton, 1981, p. 53), but individual differences in musical experience and aptitude have qualified notions of any unihemispheric dominance for music perception. Most relevant here is a study by Gaede, Parsons, and Bertera (1978). These investigators found that musical aptitude and musical experience or training (see Bever & Chiarello, 1974) independently influence performance, but only musical *aptitude* predicts ear asymmetries on two music analysis tasks. Importantly, high aptitude individuals (regardless of gender) demonstrated *no* hemispheric (i.e., ear) differences on either a musical chord (simultaneous?) analysis test or a musical memory test that required sequential analysis. Low musical aptitude individuals, on the other hand, demonstrated right hemispheric superiority for the chord test and left hemispheric superiority for the memory sequence test. From these findings the authors conclude that musical aptitude is more critical than musical experience in determining hemispheric superiorities (cf. Bever & Chiarello, 1974) and that musical aptitude reflects "relatively fixed and enduring hemispheric processing perferences rather than potentially modifiable, educable hemispheric strategies" (p. 369).

The general pattern of these results is remarkably in accord with present speculations. So too are results reported in Hunt et al. (1975) with respect to verbal ability, if the data are re-interpreted within the present context. Relevant here is a study (by Poltrock, cited in Hunt et al., 1975) on judgments of temporal order. Subjects differing in verbal ability were presented pairs of speech and nonspeech sounds (i.e., ba, da, ga and buzz, hiss, tone, respectively) to the left and right ears, separated by an interval of 50 ms. They wrote down which sound, of the pair, was heard first. High verbals showed *no* ear advantage, regardless of stimulus type and regardless of the presumably sequential (i.e., left hemisphere) processing requirements of the task. Low verbals, on the other hand, showed "the sort of advantage that would be expected given the type of stimulus" (Hunt et al., 1975, p. 208); that is, a right ear (or left hemisphere) advantage for speech stimuli and a left ear (or right hemisphere) advantage for nonspeech stimuli. Together, these two instances provide convergent support for the notion that enhanced abilities may not be hemisphere specific but may reflect a general (i.e., "whole brain") processing attitude.

RELEVANCE OF THE PROPOSED FRAMEWORK TO GENERAL COGNITIVE FUNCTIONING

The purpose of this final section is to examine the relevance or utility of the proposed framework by addressing the following question: What difference does it make if individuals are characterized as lateralized for spatial or verbal functions, or both, or neither? This question can be answered in general terms first by arguing that if individual differences in hemispheric functioning are found to be associated with other behavioral differences among individuals, such as those involving higher levels of cognitive functioning, then valuable insights will have been gained into possible brain-behavior relationships. Can such associations be demonstrated here? My judgment is that they can; at least, the evidence is encouraging. It is evidence that will now be discussed.

A recent review of the literature on imagery ability and cognition (Ernest, 1977) concluded with a statement of need for closer examination of the relationship(s) among imagery ability, verbal processing, and sex differences. This conclusion was based, in part, on results reported in the learning and memory literature. A not-uncommon finding in this literature is the fact that (a) individual differences in spatial-imagery ability sometimes yield different effects for male subjects than for female subjects, and/or that (b) the sexes within a spatial-imagery group—*particularly* the high spatial group—do not always "behave" similarly. The organizing framework, or model, presented here provides one possible explanation for, or correlate of, these previously puzzling findings.

In one study (Ernest & Paivio, 1971a, Expt. 1), for example, subjects were required to free recall a mixed list of pictures and concrete nouns. A significant three-way interacion involving Ability, Sex, and Stimulus Type resulted. For males, high spatial-imagers excelled in both picture and (particularly) word recall. For females, high spatial-imagers also excelled in picture recall but *low* imagers excelled in word recall. This facility of low-imagery females in remembering unrelated strings of words has also been found in other studies involving the free recall paradigm (e.g., Stewart, 1965), as well as recognition memory (Stewart, 1965) and a modification of the Brown-Peterson short-term memory task (Anderson, 1973).

The results for pictures correspond to present (and past) findings that high spatial-imagery ability is typically associated with efficient picture processing. The "word" results, on the other hand, isolate as excelling those subject groups identified here as left-hemisphere dominant for language, namely, high-spatial males and low-spatial females.

The results of a recent investigation of recognition memory for pictures and concrete words can be interpreted similarly (Ernest, 1982b). Subjects in this study received homogeneous lists of 80 concrete words and 80 pictures. Following presentation of each list, a test list of 80 items was presented. It consisted of 40 "old" items as well as 40 distractor or "new" items. The subjects' task was to indicate whether each item in the test list was "old" or "new" and to rate the confidence of their judgments on a 4-point scale. Three scoring procedures were used—NC, representing the number correct (i.e., hits + correct rejections); a confidence-weighted score(CWS) whereby subjects' responses were weighted in accordance with the assigned confidence rating ("+" if correct, "−" if incorrect) and summed; and d', a measure of memory trace sensitivity.

Subjects had previously completed a large battery of imagery and verbal tests and questionnaires. Correlations were computed between these scores and the three recognition memory scores for pictures and words. Only correlations for the two spatial visualization tests used here to define spatial-imagery ability are presented in Table 1.2, and separately for males and females.

The significant correlations between the spatial tests and picture recognition memory for males and females is consistent with their superior picture processing skills as reported here and in previous studies (e.g., Ernest, 1979; Ernest & Paivio, 1971a). But the "word" results differ for the sexes. Recall that for males, high spatial ability is accompanied by left-hemisphere lateralization of language, perceptual trace persistence for words, and evidence for right-hemispheric processing of concrete words. Low spatial ability for males is associated with bilateralization of verbal functions and rapid trace decay for words. The significant correlations between spatial test performance and recognition memory for concrete words in Table 1.2 are interpretable in this light. For

TABLE 1.2
Pearson *r* Correlations between Spatial Visualization Tests and
Recognition Memory for Pictures and Concrete Words

	Males (n = 72)					
	Pictures			Concrete Words		
	NC	CWS	d'	NC	CWS	d'
Space Relations	.34**	.33**	.25*	.21	.17	.17
MPFB	.31**	.32**	.28*	.25*	.25*	.30*
	Females (n = 137)					
	Pictures			Concrete Words		
	NC	CWS	d'	NC	CWS	d'
Space Relations	.17*	.10	.20*	.06	.08	.03
MPFB	.23**	.20*	.20*	.03	.04	−.02

*p ≤ .05.
**p < .01.

females, however, low spatials have the "linguistic" qualities of high-spatial males, whereas high spatials have those of low-spatial males—although not as extremely so in either case. Zero to negative correlations may thus be expected and were, in fact, obtained.

The final reference to results from the cognitive literature concerns male-female performance differences within the *high* spatial-imagery ability group. Ability-Sex interactions found in two studies have assumed the general form illustrated in Fig. 1.9. One study was of paired-associates learning in which Stroop-type stimuli served as the stimulus terms (e.g., the word YELLOW printed in blue ink) and concrete nouns as responses (Ernest, 1968). Subjects were instructed to use as their *functional* stimulus either the word itself (ignoring color) or the color in which the word was painted. High-imagery females significantly surpassed high-imagery males whereas male and female low spatial-imagers did not differ. A second study investigated incidental learning (Ernest & Paivio, 1971a, Expt. 2). Subsequent to an orienting task in which briefly-exposed pictures, concrete words, or abstract words were to be identified, subjects were given an unexpected free recall task. Again, high-imagery females excelled. They recalled significantly more items than their male counterparts.

In neither of these studies were the Ability-Sex interactions qualified by the verbal/nonverbal character of the stimulus materials. That is, the interactions crossed the color/word functional stimulus conditions in the first study and the picture/concrete word/abstract word stimulus conditions in the second study. One

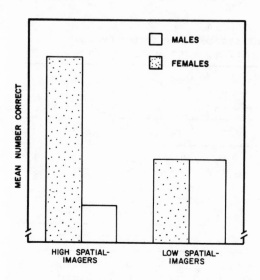

FIG. 1.9. General form of the interaction between spatial-imagery ability and sex differences in the cognitive literature.

possible explanation for the superior performance of high-imagery females emphasizes memory factors. Females typically excel in memory tasks regardless of the verbal/nonverbal nature of the material (e.g., Ernest, 1981b; Ernest & Paivio, 1971a, Expt. 1). Perhaps this advantage, combined with high spatial skills, particularly benefited high-imagery females. But this explanation is less than satisfactory for two reasons. First of all, females who are high in spatial-imagery ability sometimes excel in performance relative to all three subject groups (see Ernest & Paivio, 1971a, Expt. 2), *including low-spatial females*—in spite of the fact that high spatial ability does not seem to be associated with superior word memory in females (see Table 1.2). Secondly, a similar (significant) interaction occurred in an auditory recognition task that typically would be considered to fall outside the realm of "higher" cognitive functioning. In this study (see Ernest, 1979, Expt. 5), subjects received homogenous lists of environmental sounds, concrete words, and abstract words for identification. Each item was masked by white noise which decreased systematically in intensity over the 10 repetitions of an item. Male and female *high* spatial-imagers differed in performance; mean trials to recognition (across stimulus types) were significantly higher for males than for females. Low-imagery males and females did not differ.

Any explanation of the Ability-Sex interactions that could apply to all three instances of its occurrence would clearly be preferred. The framework of hemispheric functioning proposed here does not directly provide such an explanation but it nevertheless does allow some speculations that are open to further test.

Consider first the tasks themselves. All three involve distinct multiple stimulus elements or response requirements. In the first instance (i.e., Ernest, 1968), subjects had to attend to one component of a compound (Stroop) stimulus and ignore the other; in the second (i.e., Ernest & Paivio, 1971a, Expt. 2), subjects had to recall unexpectedly the names of stimuli they had just identified; and in the third study (i.e., Ernest, 1979, Expt. 5), the task (again) required that only one component (i.e., the signal) of a compound stimulus (i.e., signal + noise) be attended to. Further, and perhaps more important, in all three tasks the encoding strategy most conducive (one assumes) to good performance was evident either in the form of instructions to subjects (i.e., color *vs* word; Ernest, 1968), orienting task demands (i.e., written identification; Ernest & Paivio, 1971a, Expt. 2), or prior knowledge of stimulus mode (i.e., sounds *vs* words; Ernest, 1979, Expt. 5). Taken together, this intuitively-based task analysis suggests that superior performance on these tasks is associated with the ability to utilize/maintain an encoding strategy congruent with explicit task demands, particularly under circumstances of interference (as in the paired-associates learning and auditory recognition studies).

Consider now the subject groups most consistently implicated in performance differences—high-spatial females and high-spatial males. The only difference between these groups, according to the proposed framework, is in the lateralization of their verbal functions. Weak left hemispheric dominance (or bilateralization) for language, which characterizes high-spatial females, seems to be associated with a tendency *not* to process pictures verbally (when, in fact, it is not essential to performance) and *not* to spatially (i.e., right hemisphere) process concrete words. But these behavioral characteristics also describe low-spatial males—and high-spatial females on occasion surpass even them in performance (e.g., Ernest & Paivio, 1971a, Expt. 2).

It, therefore, seems more reasonable to infer that the important characteristic that distinguishes high-spatial females from high-spatial males—and indeed the other subject groups—is not bilateralization for language but bilateralization of *both* linguistic and spatial functions. Such bilateralization implies the existence of independent verbal and nonverbal or spatial processing systems that cross hemispheric boundaries. It also implies a relatively strict adherence to stimulus mode-processing mode congruence, a congruence which may be particularly adaptive under conditions of high interference. Although speculative at this stage, these notions are nevertheless testable using, for example, a concurrent task paradigm in which a noncentral or "unattended" task may, or may not, facilitiate processing of a central or "attended" task.

CONCLUDING REMARKS

Is high spatial-imagery ability associated with superior right hemispheric functioning? The evidence to date suggests not. It suggests that the nonverbal perceptual recognition superiority of high spatial-imagers is not right-hemisphere specific but seems to be associated with enhanced capabilities of the *left* hemisphere to process spatial information.

This conclusion emerged from the fact that, for high imagers, visual field differences are small and more stable in their direction across different types of nonverbal stimuli than for low imagers. Such evidence led to the suggestion that high spatial individuals may be "bilateralized" for spatial processing and to the further suggestion that enhanced abilities per se may reflect bihemispheric involvement in the processes underlying that ability.

Despite some support for these notions (e.g., Gaede et al., 1978; Hunt et al., 1975), they should be viewed as preliminary and speculative for several reasons. First, and in the context of spatial ability, visual field studies need to be completed using stimuli more strongly associated with right-hemispheric functioning—stimuli such as unfamiliar faces (e.g., Gilbert & Bakan, 1973), slanted lines (e.g., Kimura & Durnford, 1974), and localized dots (e.g., Kimura, 1969). Such studies would provide a strong test of the "bilateralization hypothesis" with respect to high spatial-imagers.

Second, "bilateralization" may only be apparent, reflecting other than real (i.e., neurological) "equipotentiality" of the left and right hemispheres for processing spatial information (see Bryden, 1979, 1980; Kinsbourne, 1970). Recall, for example, that the literature discussed at the beginning of this chapter pointed to a significant relationship between spatial ability and performance only when a spatial-imagery processing strategy is primed (e.g., Ernest, 1979) or identified as being used through mathematical modelling procedures (MacLeod et al., 1978; Mathews et al., 1980; Sternberg & Weil, 1980). Thus, "bilateralization" may reflect a general spatial processing attitude or strategy which preempts "hardwired" differences in the hemispheres. Although such a conclusion would be of interest in its own right, attempts to distinguish between these two alternatives are clearly required.

Third, "bilateralization" may be an artifact of high accuracy. Harshman and Krashen (1972, as cited in Marshall, Caplan, & Holmes, 1975), for instance, report that commonly-used measures of laterality (such as the laterality coefficient Right-minus-Left accuracy) are negatively correlated with total accuracy. That is, the degree of laterality declines as accuracy increases. It is not immediately apparent that such an explanation can account for the present results, however. This is because present speculations concerning the bilateralization (or lateralization) of spatial functions were based on more than statements of degree. They were based on evidence of direction and consistency in direction across different stimulus materials. Indeed, consistencies in direction (i.e., a RVF bias) occurred for high spatials regardless of the presence or absence of ability differences in overall accuracy. With respect to the lateralization, or bilateralization, of linguistic functions proposed here, the four subject groups did not differ in overall accuracy for word identification.

Nevertheless, such concerns need to be recognized when questions of degree of lateralization in different subject groups are asked. Bryden and Sprott (1981) have recently proposed a measure of lateralization which is not dependent on overall accuracy and which avoids the "undesirable statistical properties" of commonly-used laterality coefficients. Alternatively, others have determined task parameters (such as exposure duration) on an individual basis to ensure common and predetermined levels of accuracy across subjects and stimulus materials (e.g., Hannay, 1976; Hannay et al., 1976).

The proposed framework of hemispheric functioning, although speculative, has nevertheless proved to be useful. It queries the appropriateness of sex-related models of cerebral organization that do not consider individual differences in spatial ability. Clearly, these two factors will be confounded in most studies purporting to examine sex differences per se. It has yielded qualified support for Levy's (1974) view that language bilateralized individuals will have low spatial skills (see low-spatial males). But it also suggests that this will be true only if such individuals are right-hemispheric dominant for spatial processing (cf. high-spatial females). And finally, it has provided one possible explanation for recurrent and puzzling imagery-sex interactions in the cognitive literature.

ACKNOWLEDGMENT

*Preparation of this chapter, and the research reported in it, were supported by grants from the National Research Council of Canada (A0272) and Trent University's Research Committee (353201). The research assistance of Garth Coleman, Kristine McLaren, Jane Nixon, and Dawn Witherspoon is gratefully acknowledged. I am also grateful to Zenon Pylyshyn for the 12- and 24-point shapes and their lures, used in Study 4, as well as the algorithm for generating lures for the 6-point shapes. Special thanks are due Phil Bryden and John Yuille for their critical comments on an earlier draft of the paper.

REFERENCES

Allen, M. J., & Hogeland, R. Spatial problem-solving strategies as functions of sex. *Perceptual and Motor Skills*, 1978, *47*, 348-350.

Anderson, R. E. Individual differences in the use of imaginal processing. Unpublished doctoral dissertation, University of California (San Diego), 1973.

Annett, M. A classification of hand preference by association analysis. *British Journal of Psychology*, 1970, *61*, 303-321.

Barratt, P. E. Imagery and thinking. *Australian Journal of Psychology*, 1953, *5*, 154-164.

Bennett, G. K., Seashore, M. G., & Wesman, A. G. *Differential aptitude tests*. New York: The Psychological Corporation, 1947.

Bever, T. G., & Chiarello, R. G. Cerebral dominance in musicians and non-musicians. *Science*, 1974, *185*, 537-539.

Borod, J. C. & Goodglass, H. Lateralization of linguistic and melodic processing with age. *Neuropsychologia*, 1980, *18*, 79-83.

Bradshaw, J. L., & Nettleton, N. C. The nature of hemispheric specialization in man. *Behavioral and Brain Sciences*, 1981, *4*, 51-92.

Brooks, L. R. Spatial and verbal components of the act of recall. *Canadian Journal of Psychology*, 1968, *22*, 349-368.

Bryden, M. P. Evidence for sex-related differences in cerebral organization. In M. A. Wittig & A. C. Petersen (Eds.), *Sex-related differences in cognitive functioning: Developmental issues.* New York: Academic Press, 1979.

Bryden, M. P. Sex differences in brain organization: Different brains or different strategies? Open peer commentary in J. McGlone, 1980.

Bryden, M. P., & Rainey, C. A. Left-right differences in tachistoscopic recognition. *Journal of Experimental Psychology,* 1963, *66,* 568–571.

Bryden, M. P., & Sprott, D. A. Statistical determination of degree of laterality. *Neuropsychologia,* 1981, *19,* 571–581.

Carpenter, P. A., & Just, M. A. Sentence comprehension: A psycholinguistic processing model of verification. *Psychological Review,* 1975, *82,* 45–73.

Carpenter, P. A., & Just, M. A. Spatial ability: An information processing approach to psychometrics. In R. Wu & S. Chipman (Eds.), *Learning by eye,* in press.

Carroll, J. B. Psychometric tests as cognitive tasks: A new "structure of intellect." In L. Resnick (Ed.), *The nature of intelligence.* Hillsdale, N.J.: Lawrence Erlbaum Assoc., 1976.

Carroll, J. B. Psychometric approaches to the study of language abilities. In C. J. Fillmore, D. Kempler, & W. S-Y. Wang (Eds.), *Individual differences in language ability and language behavior.* New York: Academic Press, 1979.

Clark, H. Linguistic processes in deductive reasoning. *Psychological Review,* 1969, *76,* 387–403.

Clark, H., & Chase, W. On the process of comparing sentences against pictures. *Cognitive Psychology,* 1972, *3,* 472–517.

Cooper, L. A., & Regan, D. T. Attention, perception, and intelligence. In R. Sternberg (Ed.), *Handbook of intelligence.* New York: Cambridge University Press, in press.

Cronbach, L. J. The two disciplines of scientific psychology. *American Psychologist,* 1957, *12,* 671–684.

Cronbach, L. J. Beyond the two disciplines of scientific psychology. *American Psychologist,* 1975, *30,* 116–127.

Dee, H. L., & Fontenot, D. J. Cerebral dominance and lateral differences in perception and memory. *Neuropsychologia,* 1973, *11,* 167–173.

Ekstrom, R. B., French, J. W., Harman, H. H., & Dermen, D. *Manual for kit of factor-referenced cognitive tests.* Princeton, N.J.: Educational Testing Service, 1976.

Ellis, H. D., & Shepherd, J. W. Rocognition of abstract and concrete words presented in left and right visual fields. *Journal of Experimental Psychology,* 1974, *103,* 1035–1036.

Ernest, C. H. *Individual differences in imagery ability and compound stimulus effects in paired-associates learning.* Unpublished master's thesis, University of Western Ontario, 1968.

Ernest, C. H. *Spatial-imagery ability and the recognition of verbal and nonverbal stimuli.* Unpublished doctoral dissertation, University of Western Ontario, 1972.

Ernest, C. H. Imagery ability and cognition: A critical review. *Journal of Mental Imagery,* 1977, *1,* 181–216.

Ernest, C. H. Visual imagery ability and the recognition of verbal and nonverbal stimuli. *Acta Psychologica,* 1979, *43,* 253–269.

Ernest, C. H. Imagery ability and the identification of fragmented pictures and words. *Acta Psychologica,* 1980, *44,* 51–57.

Ernest, C. H. *Verbal codability, visual field, and spatial-imagery ability effects in picture recognition.* Manuscript in preparation, 1982. (a)

Ernest, C. H. *Imagery and verbal ability and recognition memory for pictures and words in males and females.* Manuscript in preparation, 1982. (b)

Ernest, C. H., & Paivio, A. Imagery and sex differences in incidental recall. *British Journal of Psychology,* 1971, *62,* 67–72. (a)

Ernest, C. H., & Paivio, A. Imagery and verbal associative latencies as a function of imagery ability. *Canadian Journal of Psychology,* 1971, *25,* 83–90. (b)

Fairweather, H. Sex differences in cognition. *Cognition,* 1976, *4,* 231–280.

Finke, R. A. Levels of equivalence in imagery and perception. *Psychological Review*, 1980, *87*, 113–132.

Fontenot, D. J. Visual field differences and nonverbal stimuli in man. *Journal of Comparative and Physiological Psychology*, 1973, *85*, 564–569.

Freedman, R. J., & Rovegno, L. Ocular dominance, cognitive strategy, and sex differences in spatial ability. *Perceptual and Motor Skills*, 1981, *52*, 651–654.

Gaede, S. E., Parsons, O. A., & Bertera, J. H. Hemispheric differences in music perception: Aptitude *vs* experience. *Neuropsychologia*, 1978, *16*, 369–373.

Garrick, C. Field dependence and hemispheric specialization. *Perceptual and Motor Skills*, 1978, *47*, 631–639.

Gilbert, C., & Bakan, P. Visual asymmetry in perception of faces. *Neuropsychologia*, 1973, *11*, 355–362.

Godden, D., & Baddeley, A. When does context influence recognition memory? *British Journal of Psychology*, 1980, *71*, 99–104.

Guilford, J. P. *The nature of human intelligence*. New York: McGraw-Hill, 1967.

Hannay, H. J. Real or imagined incomplete lateralization of function in females. *Perception and Psychophysics*, 1976, *19*, 349–352.

Hannay, H. J., Rogers, J. P., & Durant, R. F. Complexity as a determinant of visual field effects for random forms. *Acta Psychologica*, 1976, *40*, 29–34.

Hardyck, C., Tzeng, O. J. L., & Wang, W. S-Y. Cerebral lateralization of function and bilingual decision processes: Is thinking lateralized? *Brain and Language*, 1978, *5*, 56–71.

Harris, L. J. Sex differences in spatial ability: Possible environmental, genetic, and neurological factors. In M. Kinsbourne (Ed.), *Asymmetrical function of the brain*. New York: Cambridge University Press, 1978.

Harshman, R., & Krashen, S. An "unbiased" procedure for comparing degree of lateralization of dichotically presented stimuli. *UCLA, Working Papers in Phonetics*, 1972, *23*, 3–12.

Harshman, R., Remington, R, & Krashen, S. *Sex, language and the brain. Adult sex differences in lateralization*. Paper presented at the UCLA conference on human brain function, Los Angeles, 1974.

Hebb, D. O. Concerning imagery. *Psychological Review*, 1968, *75*, 466–477.

Hicks, R. E., & Kinsbourne, M. Human handedness. In M. Kinsbourne (Ed.), *The asymmetrical function of the brain*. New York: Cambridge University Press, 1978.

Hines, D. Recognition of verbs, abstract nouns and concrete nouns from the left and right visual half-fields. *Neuropsychologia*, 1976, *14*, 211–216.

Hunt, E. Intelligence as an information-processing concept. *British Journal of Psychology*, 1980, *71*, 449–474.

Hunt, E., Frost, N., & Lunneborg, C. Individual differences in cognition: A new approach to intelligence. In G. H. Bower (Ed.), *The psychology of learning and motivation*. New York: Academic Press, 1973.

Hunt, E., Lunneborg, C., & Lewis, J. What does it mean to be high verbal? *Cognitive Psychology*, 1975, *7*, 194–227.

Huttenlocher, J. Constructing spatial images: A strategy in reasoning. *Psychological Review*, 1968, *75*, 550–560.

Kail, R., Carter, P., & Pellegrino, J. The locus of sex differences in spatial ability. *Perception and Psychophysics*, 1979, *26*, 182–186.

Kimura, D. Cerebral dominance and perception of verbal stimuli. *Canadian Journal of Psychology*, 1961, *15*, 166–171.

Kimura, D. Left-right differences in the perception of melodies. *Quarterly Journal of Experimental Psychology*, 1964, *16*, 355–358.

Kimura, D. Spatial localization in the left and right visual fields. *Canadian Journal of Psychology*, 1969, *23*, 445–458.

Kimura, D., & Durnford, M. Normal studies on the function of the right hemisphere in vision. In

S. J. Dimond & J. G. Beaumont (Eds.), *Hemisphere function in the human brain*. New York: Wiley, 1974.

Kinsbourne, M. The cerebral basis of lateral asymmetries in attention. *Acta Psychologica*, 1970, *33*, 193–201.

Kinsbourne, M., & Hiscock, M. Does cerebral dominance develop? In S. J. Segalowitz & F. A. Gruber (Eds.), *Language development and neurological theory*. New York: Academic Press, 1977.

Kinsbourne, M., & Hiscock, M. Cerebral lateralization and cognitive development. *In Seventy-seventh Yearbook of the National Society for the Study of Education*. Chicago: University of Chicago Press, 1978.

Kučera, H., & Francis, W. N. *Computational analysis of present-day American English*. Providence, R.I.: Brown University Press, 1967.

Levy, J. Possible basis for the evolution of lateral specialization of the human brain. *Nature*, 1969, *224*, 614–615.

Levy, J. Psychobiological implications of bilateral asymmetry. In S. J. Dimond & J. G. Beaumont (Eds.), *Hemisphere function in the human brain*. New York: Wiley, 1974.

Ley, R. G., & Bryden, M. P. Right hemispheric involvement in imagery and affect. In M. E. Perecman (Ed.), *Cognitive processes in the right hemisphere*. New York: Academic Press, in press.

Likert, R., & Quasha, W. H. *Revised Minnesota paper form board test*. New York: The Psychological Corporation, 1941.

Macaulay, R. K. S. The myth of female superiority in language. *Journal of Child Language*, 1978, *5*, 353–363.

Maccoby, E. E., & Jacklin, C. N. *The psychology of sex differences*. Stanford, Calif.: Stanford University Press, 1974.

MacLeod, C. M., Hunt, E. B., & Mathews, N. N. Individual differences in the verification of sentence-picture relationships. *Journal of Verbal Learning and Verbal Behavior*, 1978, *17*, 493–508.

Marcel, A. J., & Patterson, K. Word recognition and production: Reciprocity in clinical and normal studies. In J. Requin (Ed.), *Attention and performance VII*. Hillsdale, N.J.: Lawrence Erlbaum Assoc., 1978.

Marks, D. F. Visual imagery differences in the recall of pictures. *British Journal of Psychology*, 1973, *64*, 17–24.

Marks, D. F. Mental imagery and consciousness: A theoretical review. In A. A. Sheikh (Ed.), *Imagery: Current theory, research and application*. New York: Wiley, in press.

Marshall, J. C., Caplan, D., & Holmes, J. M. The measure of laterality. *Neuropsychologia*, 1975, *13*, 315–321.

Mathews, N. N., Hunt, E. B., & MacLeod, C. M. Strategy choice and strategy training in sentence-picture verification. *Journal of Verbal Learning and Verbal Behavior*, 1980, *19*, 531–548.

McGee, M. G. Human spatial abilities: Psychometric studies and environmental, genetic, hormonal, and neurological influences. *Psychological Bulletin*, 1979, *86*, 889–918.

McGlone, J. Sex differences in human brain asymmetry: A critical survey. *Behavioral and Brain Sciences*, 1980, *3*, 215–263.

McGlone, J. Sexual variation in behaviour during spatial and verbal tasks. *Canadian Journal of Psychology*, 1981, *35*, 277–282.

Morton, J. Interaction of information in word recognition. *Psychological Review*, 1969, *76*, 165–178.

Morton, J., & Patterson, K. A new attempt at an interpretation, or, an attempt at a new interpretation. In M. Coltheart, K. E. Patterson, & J. C. Marshall (Eds.), *Deep dyslexia*. London: Routledge & Kegan Paul, 1980.

Moyer, R. S. Comparing objects in memory: Evidence suggesting an internal psychophysics. *Perception and Psychophysics*, 1973, *13*, 180–184.

Moyer, R. S., & Bayer, R. H. Mental comparison and the symbolic distance effect. *Cognitive Psychology*, 1976, *8*, 228–246.

Paivio, A. *Imagery and verbal processes.* New York: Holt, Rinehart, & Winston, 1971.

Paivio, A. Perceptual comparisons through the mind's eye. *Memory & Cognition*, 1975, *3*, 635–647.

Paivio, A. Dual coding: Theoretical issues and empirical evidence. In J. M. Scandura & C. J. Brainerd (Eds.), *Structural/process models of complex human behavior.* The Netherlands: Sijthoff & Noordhoff, 1978. (a)

Paivio, A. The relationship between verbal and perceptual codes. In E. C. Carterette & M. P. Friedman (Eds.), *Handbook of perception: Vol. IX: Perceptual processing.* New York: Academic Press, 1978. (b)

Paivio, A. Comparisons of mental clocks. *Journal of Experimental Psychology: Human Perception and Performance*, 1978, *4*, 61–71. (c)

Paivio, A. Imagery, language, and semantic memory. *International Journal of Psycholinguistics*, 1978, *5*, 31–47. (d)

Paivio, A. On weighing things in your mind. In P. W. Jusczyk & R. M. Klein (Eds.), *The nature of thought: Essays in honor of D. O. Hebb.* Hillsdale, N.J.: Lawrence Erlbaum Assoc., 1980.

Paivio, A., & Ernest, C. H. Imagery ability and visual perception of verbal and nonverbal stimuli. *Perception and Psychophysics*, 1971, *10*, 429–432.

Paterson, A., & Zangwill, O. L. Disorders of visual space perception associated with lesions of the right cerebral hemisphere. *Brain*, 1944, *67*, 331–358.

Penfield, W., & Roberts, L. *Speech and brain-mechanisms.* Princeton, N.J.: Princeton University Press, 1959.

Posner, M. I., Boies, S. J., Eichelman, W. H., & Taylor, R. L. Retention of visual and name codes of single letters. *Journal of Experimental Psychology Monograph*, 1969, *79*, 1–16.

Poulton, E. C. Range effects in experiments on people. *American Journal of Psychology*, 1975, *88*, 3–32.

Rosenfeld, J. B. *Information processing: Encoding and decoding.* Unpublished doctoral dissertation, Indiana University, 1967.

Schmuller, J. Stimulus repetition in studies of laterality. *Brain and Language*, 1980, *10*, 205–207.

Schmuller, J., & Goodman, R. Bilateral tachistoscopic perception, handedness, and laterality. *Brain and Language*, 1979, *8*, 81–91.

Segal, S. J., & Fusella, V. Influence of imaged pictures and sounds on detection of visual and auditory signals. *Journal of Experimental Psychology*, 1970, *83*, 458–464.

Sperry, R. W., & Gazzaniga, M. S. Language following surgical disconnection of the hemispheres. In C. H. Millikan & F. L. Darley (Eds.), *Brain mechanisms underlying speech and language.* New York: Grune & Stratton, 1967.

Stanovich, K. E., & West, R. F. Mechanisms of sentence context effects in reading: Automatic activation and conscious attention. *Memory & Cognition*, 1979, *7*, 77–85.

Sternberg, R. J., & Weil, E. M. An aptitude X strategy interaction in linear syllogistic reasoning. *Journal of Educational Psychology*, 1980, *72*, 226–239.

Stewart, J. C. *An experimental investigation of imagery.* Unpublished doctoral dissertation, University of Toronto, 1965.

Tapley, S. M., & Bryden, M. P. An investigation of sex differences in spatial ability: Mental rotation of three-dimensional objects. *Candian Journal of Psychology*, 1977, *31*, 122–130.

Thorndike, E. L., & Lorge, I. *The teacher's word book of 30,000 words.* New York: Bureau of Publications, Teachers College, 1944.

Underwood, B. J. Individual differences as a crucible in theory construction. *American Psychologist*, 1975, *30*, 128–134.

Vanderplas, J. M., & Garvin, E. A. The association value of random shapes. *Journal of Experimental Psychology*, 1959, *57*, 147–154.

Waber, D. P. Sex differences in cognition: A function of maturation rate? *Science*, 1976, *192*, 572–574.

Wickens, D. D. Encoding categories of words: An empirical approach to meaning. *Psychological Review*, 1970, *77*, 1–15.

Witelson, S. F. Sex and the single hemisphere: Specialization of the right hemisphere for spatial processing. *Science*, 1976, *193*, 425–427.

Young, A. W., & Ellis, A. W. Asymmetry of cerebral hemispheric function in normal and poor readers. *Psychological Bulletin*, 1981, *89*, 183–190.

Zoccolotti, P., & Oltman, P. K. Field dependence and lateralization of verbal and configurational processing. *Cortex*, 1978, *14*, 155–163.

Zurif, E. B., & Bryden, M. P. Familial handedness and left-right differences in auditory and visual perception. *Neuropsychologia*, 1969, *7*, 179–187.

2 What Does It Mean to be a High Imager?

Albert N. Katz
University of Western Ontario

Over 10 years ago Al Paivio (1969, 1971) revolutionized the study of cognitive psychology by approaching the study of mental imagery from an empirical perspective. The three operations he suggested involved manipulations of stimulus concreteness, mediational instructions, and individual differences. The first two of these variables have proven most informative regarding imagery processing and, indeed, examination of these variables have, to a large extent, defined the last 10 years of imagery research (for a review, see J. Richardson, 1980). Use of individual differences in imagery, however, has proven to be the poor cousin of these three procedures. Although the study of imagery abilities has a long and honest lineage which can be traced back to Galton (1880), the offspring of this labor has been, in general, quite disappointing. First, unlike manipulations based on the other two procedures, clear-cut and consistent relationships do not tend to emerge when variations in imagery level are used to predict task performance. A second disappointment is more general and is also found to some extent with the other two operational definitions of imagery. Even when relationships are observed, these relationships are, at best, only proxies for the criteria we are really seeking. If imagery is important as a symbolic system then the question we must ultimately be interested in is understanding how this symbolic system works to determine real-life decisions. How do differences in imagery level influence the vocations we choose to follow or the situations we see as being humorous or even the choice of the person we decide to marry? These are questions of "ecological validity": a second-generation of research that should follow the first generation of laboratory discovery and analysis. This second generation has not even been considered, at least with respect to imagery

39

level differences, partly, I believe, because of difficulties found at the first level of laboratory research.

A somewhat typical example of the difficulties with lab studies can be found with a recent study taken from my own laboratory. The experiment was a simple one and was based on the notion that most people claim that it is relatively easy to form an image to the object represented by a concrete noun. For instance, try to form an image to the word *dime*. Most people claim to do this relatively easily and when asked to "read-off" properties from this image they claim to do this quite easily as well. The most commonly reported image probably depicts an object that is round, shiny, silver and so on (see Katz, 1978b, 1981). For the past few years I have been interested in the nature of such "perceptual" properties associated with concrete nouns. For instance, consider the noun "cauliflower." "White" is invariably among the properties output when people are requested to consult their long-term memory for perceptual properties of the object represented by the noun. If, however, people are asked to rate items for typicality (cf., Rosch, 1975a) the white associated with cauliflowers is clearly rated as being an atypical or poor example of the concept "white." This distinction between production frequency and typicality ratings suggests that our knowledge of property information about objects is represented both in an imaginal, analog and in a nonimaginal, associative manner, with the former indexed by typicality and the latter by production norms. The methodological and theoretical concern, of course, is teasing apart these two components. Semantic verification (Katz, 1981), concept identification (Katz, 1978b) and metaphor judgment (Katz, submitted) tasks all have shown that the two variables can be independently manipulated.

These studies do not directly address the question of the *nature* of the information stored in one's long-term memory. A set of priming studies was conducted to examine this question based on the findings of Paivio and te Linde (1980) as well as others (e.g., Halff, Ortony & Anderson, 1976; Rosch, 1975b; Walker, 1975). These earlier findings showed that when people were presented with an adjective that described a perceptual property (such as color or shape) they would generate a representation of the prototype (best-example) of the perceptual category. Thus given the word "red," people appear to think about a central prototypic red (cf., Berlin & Kay, 1969). Recall also the point made earlier that the remembered properties associated with object names represent an analog relationship—at least when indexed by typicality ratings. If this is the case then one might expect that priming by a property adjective would facilitate responding to objects with "highly typical" properties and inhibit responding for objects with atypical properties (cf., Rosch, 1975b).

The experiment to examine this question was quite simple. People saw a pair of nouns (e.g., canary and daffodil) and were asked to push one lever if they believed the items shared a perceptual feature—such as color or shape—and another lever otherwise. The latency required to make the response was mea-

TABLE 2.1
Example of Stimuli Differing on
Typicality for Roundness with
Associated Production Frequency Values

Items	Normative Typicality Ratings[a]	Normative Production Frequency Values
Dime	1.6	12
Moon	2.0	3
Olive	3.5	6
Pot	5.0	33

[a]Scaling goes from 1 = best example (most typical) to 7 = poorest example (least typical).

sured. Naturally when participants responded in the affirmative they were then asked to tell the property on which they based their decision to confirm that they had indeed employed the normative property.

There were two manipulations of interest. First of all, the items had been chosen such that the critical property shared by the two nouns for the positive trials had been rated as being either a central, typical depiction of the perceptual concept or as a less central, poorer instance of the category (see Table 2.1). Thus, the nouns "moon" and "dime" are considered to be good prototypic examples of round objects whereas nouns like "pot" and "olive," while still considered to be round, are considered to be poor examples of round objects. Note also that the items were chosen to be roughly equivalent in production frequency across typicality levels, and hence any systematic difference could not be attributed to nonimaginal associative aspects.

The second manipulation was the imposition of a preceding prime. Two seconds before each noun pair was shown, participants heard either the word "Blank" or an informative, property descriptor such as the word "round." The prediction was based on the finding that people presented with a word like "round" generate a prototypic representation to this term. If the property found in the representation of nouns like "moon" and "dime" were also prototypic, one might expect the imposition of a prime to speed the time needed to decide that both nouns were round. On the other hand, if the property generated to nouns were nonprototypic, such as the roundness associated with olives and pots, one might expect the prime to actually slow the decision time, because the properties would not match the expectation set up by the prime. In short, an interaction of prime condition X typicality of property was predicted. The results are shown in Fig. 2.1. As can be seen the results are completely consistent with this position. Compared to the alert control word "Blank," the property prime either facilitated or inhibited performance depending on the typicality of the property associated to a pair of nouns.

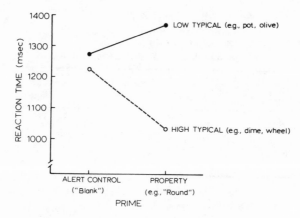

FIG. 2.1.   Reaction-time as a function of property typicality level and prime condition.

The point I emphasize is that we have here a task where imagery should be useful, and indeed where results consistent with analog, imaginal processing obtain. From a theoretical point of view one should be able to get convergent evidence for this position from the study of individual differences (Underwood, 1975). Consider again forming an image to a concrete noun. Presumably the more likely one is to use imagery, the more salient should be the constituent analog properties, like color and shape, that should be made available from a target word. Thus one might expect that the priming effect shown above would be more marked in high compared to low-imagery people. As a test of this hypothesis, all the participants also filled out the Individual Differences Questionnaire, or the IDQ, a measure of habitual imagery and verbal use constructed by Al Paivio (see Paivio, 1971, Ch. 14). The correlations between scores on this measure and corresponding reaction-times are shown in Table 2.2.

The interpretation of these data is also clear. There were no significant correlations. Apparently one's habitual use of imagery is not related to performance on a task in which, it seems, imagery should play the major mediating role.

It should be emphasized that the failure observed here is *not* unique. Although it is true that significant relationships between measures of individual differences in imaginal use are sometimes observed (see Ernest, 1977, for a review), there have been at least as many studies that fail to find a relationship (see J. Richardson, 1980, pp. 117–142). As Neisser (1970, p. 176) metaphorically put it, on reviewing this literature, "He who speaks loudest does not always have the most to say."

The question of this inconsistent literature is addressed for the rest of this chapter. Why do individual difference measures of imagery prove as unsuccessful as they do, and what might it mean when successful relationships are found? Basic problems in specifying the nature and specificity of the conditions under

TABLE 2.2
Correlations Between IDQ Imagery Level
and RTs as a Function of Prime
Condition and Typicality Level of
Properties

Prime Condition	Typicality Level	r
Blank	Hi	.08
	Low	−.06
Property	Hi	.15
Adjective	Low	.16

Note: Critical value of r required for significance at the .05 level is .432 (N = 20).

which the relationships should emerge are discussed. Finally, the nature of what is meant by individual differences in imagery is pursued.

SPECIFICATION OF TESTS AND TASKS

In studies of individual differences there are always at least two aspects that one has to consider: the *tests* that measure the individual differences and the performance *task* which is used to validate the test. With the case of imagery, two types of tests have been employed and the validating tasks have been those in which imagery has been assumed to play a major role. Typically the test and task are considered separately from one another. On one level this is not surprising because each is assessed independently. On another level, however, one should be aware that this separation encompasses what may be called the "trait" assumption. This assumption is that the imagery level measured by the test will be the same regardless of the image-evoking context. With respect to tasks, the assumption is that people will use imagery if the task demands it. There is no consideration of the possibility that people may modulate their level of imagery use as a function of the perceived nature of the validating task, and that this modulation may differ from person to person in lawful manners. This interactive possibility is discussed after tests and tasks are each examined, as is the tradition, separately.

Imagery Tests. The two types of tests can be classified as being either subjective, self-report or objective, behavioral in nature (see Table 2.3). In the former case, people are asked to introspect and report on aspects of their images, such as vividness (e.g., Sheehan, 1967a), manipulability (e.g., Gordon, 1949), or situations in which images would be used (e.g., Paivio, 1971, Ch. 14). In the latter case, people are shown stimulus objects and are asked to manipulate them

TABLE 2.3
Selected Individual Differences Tests of Imagery, with Characteristic
Item Descriptions

Subjective	Test Type	Objective

Subjective	Objective
QUESTIONNAIRE UPON MENTAL IMAGERY (Betts, 1909, Sheehan, 1967a) e.g., judge the vividness of your image to the sun sinking below horizon	FLAG TEST (Thurstone & Jeffrey, 1956) MINNESOTA PAPER FORM BOARD (Likert & Quasha, 1941) SPACE RELATIONS TEST (Bennett, Seashore & Wesman, 1947)
IMAGERY CONTROL (Gordon, 1949) e.g., can you see a car climb a steep hill INDIVIDUAL DIFFERENCES QUESTIONNAIRE (Paivio, 1971) e.g., when someone describes something I find that I create a picture of it in my mind as they talk—True or False	—test above are conceptually similar to mental rotation tasks, except accuracy and not RT is measured.

spatially in their mind and choose—from a set of alternatives—the object that would be in the correct orientation after manipulation. It is presumed that for people to perform these types of tasks, imagery processes mediate between stimulus presentation and one's ultimate choice.

One might expect that scores from these two types of tests would correlate highly with one another. They don't. The typical finding is that these two types of test load on factors quite orthogonal to one another (e.g., Di Vesta, Ingersoll & Sunshine, 1971; A. Richardson, 1977a). Moreover, there is suggestive neurological evidence (e.g., Basso, Bisiach & Luzzatti, 1980) that indicates that people who have localized damage to the left occipital lobe report loss of imagery, but at the same time show little in the way of deficits on performance tasks that test one's ability to use imagery. In contrast, spatial manipulation ability is impaired with right posterior damage, without report of a corresponding loss of phenomenal imagery (e.g., Ratcliff, 1979). This differentiation between the phenomenal experience of imagery and inferred behavioural indices of imagery use leads to obvious questions about the best type of test to use.

Whereas the objectivity of the behavioral test would make it seem the better of the two types, the self-report measures are preferred here. My reasons for this are both rational and empirical. Empirically, both types of tests have had about equal track records in predicting task performance (e.g., Ernest, 1977; A. Richardson, 1977a), and hence one is not preferable to the other for purely pragmatic reasons. Rationally, the subjective tests appear more directly linked to the construct of imagery than are the objective tests. Although self-report measures have an obvious link to examinations of the *phenomenon* of imagery (i.e., as a quasi-perceptual experience directly available only to the imager), the link from the use of spatial tests to the experience of imagery is not clear. It may seem that the flexible re-arrangement of objects in one's mind should be executed through the use of imagery. There is no principled reason, however, why spatial manipulations should only be performed in that way, if indeed ever in that mode. Pylyshyn (1979) has recently argued against using spatial manipulation as evidence of imaginal, analog processing and presented data in support of his arguments. Similarly Egan (1976) averred that spatial orientation tasks in particular represent "a form of concept verification in which examinees serially check the three spatial dimensions of a figure against their concept of what the figure should be [p. 24]." Clearly this need not follow an imaginal format. Alan Richardson (1977a), basing his comments on logic and data similar to that just reported, recently concluded that "self-report measures must necessarily serve as the initial criterion against which other more objective behavioural measures and physiological measures can be validated [p. 42]." The emphasis given here to self-report measures follows Richardson dictum.

Of course, if we are forced to depend on introspective reports we are also forced to face one of the oldest bugaboos of cognitive psychology. Just because people say they are using imagery, it doesn't necessarily follow that they are, in fact, doing so. People may not be *aware* of what really is driving their actions (see Nisbett & Wilson, 1977, for a recent exposition of this old argument). Even if people are aware, one can still argue that self-reports are especially subject to a host of response biases, and hence are suspect on those grounds. These are important concerns because they attack the validity of self-report data. Although we may never resolve the question of the functional necessity for imagery, the methodological concerns can be empirically considered. The evidence here is quite positive. First, most of the subjective tests have quite respectable reliabilities (White, Sheehan & Ashton, 1977). For example, the Betts' *Vividness of Imagery Scale* shows a test-retest reliability of .78 over a 7-month period (Sheehan, 1967b). Moreover, most subjective tests have been shown to be reasonably free of such common response biases as social desirability, familiarity with internal events, and differences in the criteria employed in reporting on one's image. Paivio's IDQ has been shown to be especially good in this respect (A. Richardson, 1977a). Finally, there are some studies that do show predictive validity (e.g., see White et al., 1977). In short, the signs that subjective imagery tests will ultimately prove to be particularly good predictors of imagery-mediated performance are most encouraging.

Despite these positive indicants, the suspicion must continue that one reason why measures of individual differences in imagery so often fail to predict cognitive task performance is due to inadequate measures of the individual differences. For the most part tests which purport to measure imagery abilities fail to meet the exacting levels now found in the mental test construction literature. Jackson (1970), for instance, has outlined a sequential strategy for test construction involving consideration of both the theoretical nature of the construct being measured and the use of sophisticated techniques to ensure item homogeneity, content saturation, control of response biases and so on. Despite the long history of imagery test usage, the construction of imagery tests are, in contrast to the procedures described by Jackson, still in the horse-and-buggy stage. A caveat is clearly warranted. Until more sophisticated imagery tests are constructed, the researcher who uses them should keep in mind that the construct validity of these tests have not yet been established.

Validating tasks. Conceptual difficulties do not end with the tests employed to measure imagery. Even if there were tests that perfectly measured an individual's imagery level, one would need to question the opposite end of the predictive relationship, i.e., the tasks used to validate these tests.

It is very possible that a failure to find a relationship is due to a poor comprehension of the validating tasks. What is needed is a clear analysis of the component processes which make up such tasks (cf., Sternberg, 1979) before one can use them to validate individual difference measures. Componential analysis has not yet been done for most presumed imagery tasks. Nonetheless, the evidence is mounting that so-called imagery tasks need not be performed *only* in an imagistic mode. Pylyshyn (1979) and Egan (1976) have been cited already in this context with respect to spatial manipulation tasks. In addition, the mental scanning experiments of Kosslyn (1975) have been criticized by Richman, Mitchell and Reznick (1979) on the grounds that the performance data of scanning can be caused by implicit or tacit knowledge of the distance-time relationship, Time = Distance/Speed. Thus, they claim that nonanalog, nonimagistic processes can be just as legitimate an explanation as an imagery explanation. Pylyshyn (1981) has elaborated this concern and concludes that, at least with the "imagery" tasks he reviews, a "tacit knowledge account is more plausible [p. 16]" an explanation for the data than is recourse to imaginal manipulation. Among his reasons for reaching this conclusion is his position that imagery tasks tend to be cognitively penetrable, i.e., altered by events *rationally* connected with the meaning of inputs. Thus, Pylyshyn claims, the data is explicable by recourse to symbolic representations such as beliefs and goals and not to the structural properties of the image per se.

Pylyshyn's arguments are most persuasive with respect to tasks in which performance data is assumed to be due solely to the structure of the image media. However, they do not directly apply to the question of whether imagery processing can be said to exist as an independent form of representation with special processing consequences in general, nor to the question of whether there are individual differences on this form. Pylyshyn's analysis does suggest another reasonable possibility, however. This possibility is that tacit knowledge and task constraints work interactively, and this interactive effect leads to individual differences in imagery use. That is, one's beliefs guide a person to the processing mode he or she believes best meets the (perceived) demands of the task. The focus then is not on ability *per se* but on the internal conditions that predispose a person to bring these abilities to bear.

Interactive Effects. Certain tasks can be solved imaginally, but can also be solved with nonimaginal processes as well. If everyone tried to use imagery only in solving such a task, and people differed in the amount of imagery available for use, then one should expect a positive relationship between one's imagery level and success in performing the task. However, if only some people decide to use imagery, while others decide to solve the task non-imaginally, no such relationship should occur. Perhaps it is this mixture of strategies that has prevented test-task relationships from reaching significance.

Recent data suggest that this possibility is not as unlikely as it might seem. MacLeod, Hunt and Mathews (1978) examined the time needed to comprehend statements such as "plus not above star" and decide whether the statements match a pictorial representation. Consistent with the interaction of task X subject discussed above, they found that people reliably solved the problem in either one of two ways: i.e., according to an analytic constituent comparison model proposed by Carpenter and Just (1975), or by generating a visual image to the statement and comparing the image to the picture. That is, only some people solved the task imaginally, although it is doubtless the case that even those who employed the nonimaginal strategy would have been shown to possess imaginal abilities on standard tests. Cooper (1976) in a direct test of spatial manipulation tasks also isolated two types of respondents. Type I people appeared to solve the task by making a holistic comparison of the rotated figure to the probe stimulus whereas Type II people appear to make analytic point-by-point comparisons. Again a seemingly imaginal task can be solved either in an image-like fashion or by nonimaginal means. These results certainly are consistent with the view that for any given task more than one processing mode can achieve the desired goal.

The argument promoted here is that the use of imagery in a given task that can be solved either imagistically or nonimagistically reflects a choice a person has made. At the simplest level the choice must mean the person believes that there is more to be gained than lost by using imagery. At a more subtle level the position demands that a specific set of individual difference variables must be seriously examined: differences in sensitivity about knowing when imagery will be useful; biases in preferring imagery to other processes, and, one's view of imagery per se. For instance, if one believes that imagery usage reflects compulsive or nonrealistic thinking then one might decide not to use imagery in a task one perceives as logical and goal-oriented. These differences will be elaborated in the next section. The point to be emphasized here is that tasks do not demand use of a given process, and when imagery is used it is because the individual has somehow decided on its appropriateness.

The question, of course, is how and why some people decide to use imagery whereas others do not. The individual difference variables discussed in the previous paragraph are an initial attempt to address these questions. My feeling is that these variables will ultimately have to be examined within the context of the complete personality. Work in my laboratory suggests that an individual's personality might not only play a mediating role in one's choice of using imagery, but also in the manner in which the imaginal processes are expressed. The research was concerned with finding "styles" relevant to creative performance from tests of creativity. One hundred participants took a battery of tests over a 6-hour period. The creativity tests were based on different theoretical rationales, were both verbal and nonverbal in nature, and, in total, generated 10 distinct scores. These scores were then subjected to a Modal Profile technique developed by Skinner (1977). In brief the technique involves a Q-type factor analysis that allows for the identification of reliable subject-clusters, i.e., the identification of groups of people who show the same pattern of strengths and weaknesses in their creativity test scores. Over 90% of my sample was unambiguously classified to one of four patterns (see Table 2.4).

The scores shown in Table 2.4 are based on a mean = 50 and a standard deviation = 10. Scores at least ±1 standard deviation are underlined to emphasize their interpretive importance. These differences are interpreted as reflecting differences in the style of processing information. For the purposes of this

TABLE 2.4
Modal Profiles for Creativity Measures

Processes	Creativity Processing Profiles (Types)			
	I	II	III	IV
Torrance Verbal				
Fluency ($\bar{x}$ = 68.4, SD = 24.2)	43	54	44	46
Flexibility ($\bar{x}$ = 33.4, SD = 9.6)	42	51	46	44
Originality ($\bar{x}$ = 64.6, SD = 37.2)	43	*61*	54	48
Torrance Figural				
Fluency ($\bar{x}$ = 18.0, SD = 12.4)	*66*	43	46	53
Flexibility ($\bar{x}$ = 13.4, SD = 4.4)	*62*	41	48	51
Originality ($\bar{x}$ = 25.7, SD = 11.7)	*60*	47	43	45
Elaboration ($\bar{x}$ = 103.1, SD = 46.6)	57	*74*	48	51
Barron-Welsh RA Scale (x = 26.7, SD = 12.8)	49	43	*73*	*35*
Remote Associate Test (x = 10.3, SD = 5.4)	*34*	39	37	50
Verbal Closure (x = 68.5, SD = 17.2)	45	47	*62*	*76*

paper only Styles I and IV are elaborated. This selection is based on the finding that these two styles (but not the others) consisted of people who scored very high on the imagery scale of the IDQ. That is, there is one group of high imagery people who show inverse abilities on figural divergent thinking tasks and in finding remote associates (Type I) and a second group who exhibited the abilities needed to isolate words from a background set of nonsense letters and showed a preference for simple pictures (Type IV). These two styles are exact parallels to the "initiator" and "esthetic" types isolated by Gough and Woodworth (1960) in their analysis of creative scientists. Thus we seem to have clearly delineated stylistic types, both of whom habitually choose to employ imagery in everyday situations. Work both in my lab and by Gough and Woodworth (1960) indicate that these two stylistic types also show quite different personality characteristics: the initiator is an ambitious, reflective, intellectually-driven person whereas the esthetic person tends to be impatient, skeptical, and rebellious. In short, although both types are "high" imagers, this imagery advantage is expressed through different personalities, and presumably corresponding differences in goals, expectations, and motives. It is clear that these personality differences can easily be accommodated with the stylistic differences reported above. That is, intellectually driven, Type I people might well use their imagery abilities in elaborative ways, thus producing the high figural divergent thinking scores. On the other hand suspicious, skeptical, Type IV people might use that same ability to pick apart the world, to look for hidden messages and hence show the high closure scores that they did.

The point of these data is that imagery test scores should not be assumed to have the same effect across all people; the nature of the task and the personality of the individual combine to indicate when and how imagery processes will be employed. It may well be that the failure to find the predictive relationships sought between imagery tests and tasks are, in part, due to our failures to consider imagery abilities in these interactive manners.

Tests and Tasks: Conclusion.   Tests of imagery ability are, for the most part, psychometrically primitive, and the processes underlying the tasks employed to validate these tests poorly understood. These difficulties have had the effect of focusing attention on either the test or the task, and not on the interactive effects of the two. An interactive perspective, which focuses on both partners equally, suggests two conclusions. First, tasks that one intuitively believes should engage imagery processes may not do so for all people. The question becomes: why does a person opt to use or not to use imagery in a given task? The second conclusion answers this question. Level of imagery use is related to the conjoint influence of personality characteristics and perceived goals of task. In short, imagery "ability" should be viewed not as a static trait brought to bear willy-nilly but rather as the processing result of the chronicle created by the interaction of a person's stable personality characteristics with the problem-space suggested to the person while engaging the task-at-hand. In the next part of this paper some of the ways that interactive effects can lead to reliable individual differences in imagery employment are discussed.

WHAT DOES IT MEAN TO BE A HIGH IMAGER?

So far the discussion has centered around why tests that measure individual differences in imagery are such inconsistent predictors of performance. I would now like to turn the question around slightly. When we do find predictability, what does this tell us about the *nature* of individual imagery levels? Knowing, for instance, that the Betts' *Questionnaire Upon Mental Imagery* predicts mental rotation tells us very little unless we have a clear idea of what goes into getting a high score on the test. To date, imagery has most typically been viewed as an ability (or set of abilities) distributed unequally in the population. The assumption is that with asymptotic performance, individual differences in imagery are due to differences in capacity. For example, people might differ in the vividness with which they can call up an image, or the rate at which it can be mentally manipulated, or the latency with which it fades from memory. Because we are talking about asympototic performance, by definition, individual differences cannot be overcome by psychological manipulations such as instructions or training procedures, although manipulations that directly influence capacity, such as drugs, might prove effective. The evidence for abilities is basically inferential since we only measure performance and from this data assume underlying capacities. Nonetheless belief in the reality of abilities is endemic in psychological lore. This belief remains even though evidence for a capacity source for imagery (or any other) differences is defined in a negative way. Factors other than asymptotic performance can be a source of differences. When all other sources can be discounted, we are left with a capacity source. The state of the art is such that one cannot either directly manipulate capacity or dismiss other potential sources.

The earlier discussion on interactive effects highlight additional reasons for concerns in attributing imagery differences to "ability" differences. Although not necessary to the concept the term "ability" nonetheless connotes that a given psychological function will express itself in all relevant situations. Thus "intelligent" people will act in an intelligent manner and "paranoidal" people will act suspicious and hostile in almost all situations. Presumably imaginal people will, in like manner, be generally powered by imagery processes. As I have tried to point out earlier in this chapter, such an approach ignores the fact that the same so-called ability will be expressed quite differently by people of different personalities and may or may not be called upon in different situations. What is needed is not a measure of asymptotic performance (which one is never sure has been obtained) but rather an understanding of the interactive chronicle of person and task. Four such interactive sources for individual imagery differences were briefly mentioned earlier. They will now be discussed in more detail.

Imagery as a Difference in Proficiency

Proficiency refers to the adeptness with which a person employs his or her imaginal processes. In short imaginal processing can be viewed as a skill, learned like any other skill. Thus, for example, two people might both have the same native capacity but might differ in the proficiency with which this ability is used. I think this, in part, is what Paivio meant when he wrote that variations in imagery "may be regarded as symbolic habits resulting from *different patterns of experience*" (Paivio, 1971, p. 477—italics mine). This position is interactionist in as much as imagery differences are seen as representing differences occurring at only one time. Presumably if two people tested at time zero were measured again at time n any initial differences may have disappeared or become exaggerated due to differences in the life histories and characters of the people living these differences. Unlike the capacity view, one obvious implication of this position is that long-term psychological manipulations, such as extensive practice with use of imagery, might reduce or even eliminate individual differences. There are, to my knowledge, no such long-term studies.

Viewing imagery as a skill (or set of skills) has one very pragmatic consequence. One can envision the theoretical characteristics of an image and seek performance tasks which tap these various skills. Some such tests are already available (e.g., see Burnham & Clark, 1955). Naturally, the caveat given with the earlier discussions of spatial manipulation tests and of validating tasks remains: to use a performance test as a measure of a specific imagery-based skill one has to show the appropriate convergent and discriminant validity, i.e., the imagery task should correlate more highly with other imagery based tasks than with tasks that are purportedly mediated by nonimaginal processes.

Imagery Differences from a Meta-Cognitive Viewpoint

The discussion above viewed individual differences as due to a set of skills developed through a life-time of interactions with one's environment. From an interactionist point of view one can argue: (a) that having a skill is, by itself, insufficient and, (b) the interactions can predispose one to favour certain skills over other "equally-strong" skills. The first of these two positions will be argued in this section and the second in the following section.

With respect to the position that skills, by themselves, are insufficient explanation of individual differences consider the effects of instructional manipulations on the differences observed in imagery levels. As mentioned in the previous section *long-term* training procedures would be expected to reduce or eliminate the differences between high and low imagers. Short-term manipulations, such as telling people to use imagery mediation in a given task, might not have that effect since it seems unreasonable to expect long-term habits to be over-ruled by such a transient manipulation. Two studies in which such instructions were given will be discussed as especially pertinent. The first was a recently completed doctoral study by Mike Vallis of the University of Western Ontario. His interest was in determining whether one can use imagery tests to predict the efficacy of therapeutic interventions (based on imagery techniques) that are aimed to over-come phobic fears. His sample of rat phobics answered a battery of both subjec-tive and objective imagery tests and were then given either a therapeutic interven-tion based on imagery (e.g., covert modeling) or one based on verbal media-tion (e.g., self-instructions). Both therapies were equally effective in eliminating the phobia. Of interest to the present discussion was the relationship of imagery test score to performance in handling the phobic object (the measure of effi-cacy). For people given the imagery-based therapy, the higher the score on the subjective tests of imagery level the more effective was the therapy. That is, high imagers benefitted more from an imagery-based therapy than did low ima-gers. With the verbal therapy, the complete opposite result obtained, i.e., high imagers did more poorly than low imagers. The failure of the objective measures to show analogous results confirm again the divergence of the two types of so-called imagery tests. However, the main result I would like to emphasize here is that imagery skill *by itself* was not effective; only when the person knew when and how to use the skill were behavioural effects observed.

The second exemplary case employed a more traditional lab task. Ashton, McFarland, Walsh and White (1978) investigated a chronometric analysis of a rotation task employed by Cooper and Shepard (1975). People were instructed either to image the stimuli or were given no such instructions. Betts' (1909) vividness scores were obtained for each person. Under both instructional sets the typical rotation effect obtained, i.e., there was a linear relationship between the number of degrees an object had to be mentally rotated and the speed with which the task was performed. Of more immediate interest was the relationship of this effect to the measure of individual differences. To quote, "individual imagery ability of the respondent was shown to be an important variable if use of imagery was suggested to the subject by the experimenter. When no such suggestion was made, then imagery ability lost its importance—*people with good/vivid imagery do not, apparently, employ this skill in the present paradigm unless specifically instructed to do so*" (Ashton et al., 1978, p. 260—italics mine). These data taken in conjunction with Vallis' suggests, at least in some cases, that individual differences in imagery will not emerge unless people first realize that imagery processing is called for. The implication would be that people differ in their sensitivity or knowledge about when to use their imagery skills. Instructions help people to employ these skills only when they are otherwise insensitive to the fact that imagery is needed. One must also assume that only when everyone is using imagery mediational processes will differences in skill come into play. From this perspective the instructional effects observed by Ashton et al. (1978) would arise because the instructions cause everyone in their sample to engage in the appropriate activity, and people differ in their skill in using this activity.

The novel emphasis here is that a source of individual differences in imagery level can be attributed to a meta-cognitive system that samples the environment and monitors the strategies a person should use for maximal effectiveness. The analogy here is with meta-memory literature (see Flavell & Wellman, 1977). This literature ascribes differences in memory ability to differences in knowing that a strategy, such as rehearsal, helps in retaining items in memory, and, moreover, is particularly necessary under certain conditions (such as with supraspan lists). The argument is that a similar executive processor is present here as well, i.e., one might characterize high imagers as those who are more sensitive to the tasks that can be solved by imagistic means. Following the arguments made earlier, monitoring and execution functions are seen as being quite separate from one another. For performance on imagery tasks to show facilitation, one's monitoring sensitivity must be matched with the appropriate executive skills. Knowing what one should do without the resources to actually execute this knowledge should not lead to performance benefits. This position leads to a clear prediction: instructions to use imagery should facilitate the performance only of those people low in meta-cognitive monitoring but high in executive skills. In any event the meta-cognitive abilities necessary to monitoring the task environments and deciding that use of imagery is appropriate might systematically differ from person to person, somewhat independent of proficiency.

I couldn't find research directly on image monitoring differences in the literature, although there is some developmental work on related questions now underway at Project Zero, at Harvard University (for example, see Silverstein, Winner, Cadogan & Gardner, 1980). As a first step in examining possible monitoring differences in adults, I had participants rate the likelihood they would use imaginal and verbal associative strategies in solving a set of 44 different tasks. The tasks themselves were of two types. Based on several factor-analytic studies, the tasks were those which have been shown to load unambiguously on either imagery or nonimagery factors. The studies consulted were: Di Vesta et al. (1971), Paivio (1968), and Rubin (1980). In each case the tasks employed here as imagery tasks were those which appreciably loaded on the imagery factor isolated in each of those studies, while the nonimagery tasks were randomly selected from the other isolated factors. I should emphasize these tasks were chosen *a priori* to best represent imagery or nonimagery involvement. The subjects were not actually asked to perform the tasks. Instead I took the instructions from the procedure sections of each of the tasks involved and asked people to rate how—given these instructions—they *believed* they would do the task. Imagery and verbal strategies were described and people asked to rate the likelihood with which they would use these two strategies along 7-point scales. Note that the participants were never actually asked to do the task, but rather had to

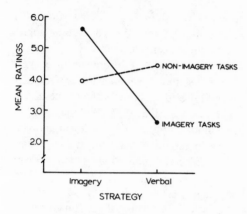

Fig. 2.2.   Mean ratings of degree to which people believe they would employ imaginal and non-imaginal, verbal strategies for tasks chosen a priori as imaginal or non-imaginal.

monitor what they thought they should do. The assumption is that the ratings should reflect their monitoring sensitivity. Each of the 102 people who made these estimates also took the IDQ. For the present purposes, the design can be considered as a $2 \times 2 \times 2$ factorial in which the factors are IDQ-imagery level (either high or low as determined by a median split), Strategy Likelihood Ratings (on both the verbal and imagery scales) and Type of task (imaginal or nonimaginal). The critical findings are the interactions of these variables. First of all the interaction of Task $\times$ Likelihood of strategy use reached significance $F(100) = 498.3$, $p < .0001$. As can be seen in Fig. 2.2, people generally claimed they would likely use imagery strategies to a greater extent with the imaginal tasks and verbal associative strategies with the nonimagery tasks. This is consistent, of course, with the notion that people are generally sensitive to the fact that imagery and verbal processes are differentially useful with the two types of task. Second, individual imagery level interacted with monitoring ratings. As can be seen in Fig. 2.3, high imagers were more likely to claim they would use imagery,

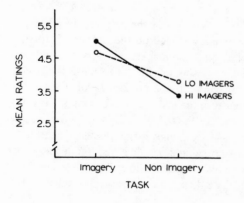

FIG. 2.3.   Mean ratings of imaginal and non-imaginal believed use for high and low imagers.

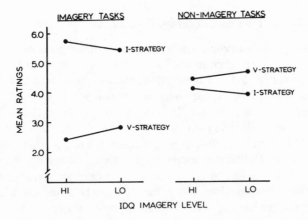

FIG. 2.4.   Mean ratings as a function of task type, strategy type and imagery level.

whereas low imagers were more likely to claim they would use verbal strategies in solving the tasks, $F(1,100) = 5.64$, $p = .02$. It is as if high imagers have a tendency to prefer imagery strategies, and low imagers verbal strategies, regardless of task type.

What about the critical triple interaction of task type × imagery level × preferred strategy? If a monitoring explanation is correct, one might expect that, for tasks involving imagery use, high imagers would be specifically likely to choose imagery as the preferred strategy whereas for low imagers, this preference shouldn't be as large. With nonimagery tasks the complete reversal might be expected so that verbal strategies would now be particularly preferred by the low imagery participants. The interactive pattern was exactly in the direction predicted (see Fig. 2.4). Unfortunately, it failed to reach significance. This is, however, only preliminary data. More pure imagery and nonimagery tasks, and a sample size larger than the one employed here are needed. Nonetheless the data are most encouraging and augur well for the continued use of rating tasks as a means of assessing imagery monitoring differences. One can derive an obvious scale to measure an individual's image monitoring sensitivity (IMS) from the rating data. This score is the subtractive difference in the average image rating given to image and nonimage tasks. That is, $IMS = I_i - I_{ni}$, where I = average imagery rating, i = image tasks and ni = nonimage tasks. The more sensitive a person is to the fact that certain tasks are more efficiently handled imagistically whereas others benefit from nonimaginal processing the greater will be the IMS score. *A priori* assessment of IMS and image skill level should permit the factorial examination of these two presumed sources of individual differences in imageability, and of the theorized interactive effects of these variables under different instructional conditions discussed above.

Imagery Differences as Encoding Preference

It has been argued that people might differ in their imaginal skills and in their sensitivity in knowing when to use these skills. A third interactionist position related somewhat to both of these positions can also be conceptualized. The argument is that due to one's learning history one acquires a preference to use imagery, regardless of task-type. Thus in line with arguments advanced earlier one can dissociate skill from preference. Learning histories may be such that two people might be equally skillful at using imagery but might differ in their predisposition to do so. Unlike the monitoring argument, the argument made here is that the "natural" failure to employ one's skill (and, conversely, the positive effects obtained by providing instructions to image) is due not to a failure to adequately monitor the task but rather to a predisposition or *bias* to first use imagery regardless of signs regarding the appropriateness of that symbolic system for a given task. The analogy in this case would be with the concept of cognitive styles, such as, for instance, the neuropsychological construct of "hemisphericity" (i.e., that habitual employment of processes from one of the cerebral hemispheres in problem-solving—see Katz, 1978b).

I believe Paivio's view of individual differences as due to differences in symbolic habit can be ascribed partly to the notion of styles or preferences. The importance of stylistic differences has a long history in the study of imagery differences. Angell (1910) and Betts (1909) both suggested that people differed in preferred imagery mode, with mode referring to imagery from different sensory sources (e.g., preference differences for auditory vs. visual imagery). More recently, Anne Roe (1951) found that research scientists in different subject fields used different types of imagery. Biologists, for example, reported use of visual imagery while psychologists used verbal imagery. Even more recently, this distinction between visual and verbal modes of thought was captured in Paivio's IDQ and A. Richardon's (1977b) *Verbalizer-Visualizer Questionnaire.*

To my knowledge there is only one study (J. Richardson, 1978) that has attempted to measure preference within a sensory mode in recent years. To quote from that study: "In studying individual differences in memory coding, I would suggest that the crucial question is not how well a subject employs a given mode of symbolic representation, but which is his preferred mode of representation. We should therefore not be interested in the ability to construct and manipulate mental images, but in the preference for mental imagery as a mnemonic code." Richardson explicitly sought to examine coding preference by measuring the accuracy with which a person can judge whether an item had earlier been presented as a picture or word. If a person had a preference for using imagery then both pictures and concrete words should be encoded in the same format, whereas people who did not have such a preference would be more likely to encode the items in different formats. Presumably the more one preferred the use of imagery, the less able he or she should be able to differentiate an item's presentation mode since both types of items would have been represented imaginally. Richardson found consistent recall differences which could be predicted by this preference measure.

The rating data discussed in the last section also provided data consistent with a preference position. Recall that high imagery people were more likely to prefer image strategies regardless of type of task. Conversely low imagery people preferred verbal strategies. (Stewart, 1965, Experiment II found analogous findings when imagery level was defined by spatial manipulation tests). In a manner analogous to that performed for image monitoring sensitivity an individual preference for imagery (PI) scale can be derived from the ratings: $PI = I-V$. That is, regardless of type of task, the average image rating minus the average verbal rating would give a measure of the degree to which a person preferred image strategies. Naturally such a scale permits one to conduct the factorial type of studies for disentangling preference from skills analogous to those suggested earlier for monitoring sensitivity. One especially tantalizing area for research using this scale is in incidental learning paradigms since that is one of the few verbal learning tasks in which a fairly consistent relationship has been observed between an individual's imagery level and memory performance, particularly when the participants are required to rate or otherwise operate upon the stimuli at input (see Ernest, 1977). Because people are not expecting subsequent recall in these tasks it seems likely that their encoding of these items would reflect automatic, preferred modes of thinking relatively free of the controlled, outcome-driven strategies one would find with intentional learning. If this is due to high imagers having a greater preference for imagery use, and such use having positive mnemonic consequences, then one should be able to orthogonally vary the preference index, intentionality of instructions, and skill level. The predictions of such a study would be clear: superior incidental recall should occur only in those people who *prefer* to use imagery (high PI) and at the same time have the requisite imagery skill needed for the task at hand.

Imagery Differences as a Manifestation of Self-Presentational Tendencies

The three previous interactive sources all viewed high-low imagery differences as due to the way people handled potentially imagistic conditions. The perspective was fundamentally problem-solving in nature, i.e., given a situation people were presumed to act as if they made a decision about the most appropriate way to handle the situation. High imagers are presumably those people with the imagery skills and/or monitoring sensitivity and/or preferential tendencies that favoured imagistic contexts. The interactive source to be discussed now also involves the way that people handle potential imagery contexts. Unlike the problem-solving sources, however, the emphasis will be on the interpretation a person wishes to put on the context, and the perceived consequence that this interpretation has on how the person views (and wishes to project) him or herself. Thus it is argued that imagery may be seen as being more or less central to the self-concept of a person. People, for instance, might see themselves as very imaginative but not logical. This view may be either central or peripheral to one's self-concept and may be valued either positively or negatively. People may wish to project themselves as either being high or low imagers. To the extent those various concepts are central and positive to self-concept, this projection of self would, naturally, be reflected on scores obtained on self-report measures of imagery level.

The present position is that this influence on self-report measures should not be viewed as a generalized social desirability bias (e.g., see Ashton & White, 1975), but rather as a sign of the values that a person wishes to say are important about himself. That is, self-reports can be just as informative as hair styles, clothes, professed sexual orientation, etc., as a statement of self. This perspective was forcefully expounded by Goffman (1959) and has been studied more recently by social psychologists under the heading of impression management. In this more recent exposition people are viewed as attempting to manipulate the impression that other people have of them. To my knowledge there are no direct tests of the possibility that imagery processes play a role in a person's self-concept. What is obviously needed are experiments in the tradition of Rogers, Kuiper and Kirker (1977) and of Hampton (1981). In the former case people rated terms as relevant or not relevant to self, whereas in the latter people produced traits they believed defined abstract concepts. As applied to the present concern, Hampton's technique would be modified such that the abstract concept might be something like "internal processing characteristics that describe me." In either case the data should be able to differentiate people for whom imagery processes are central from those for whom it is not. The prediction is that for people for whom image processing is more central, higher scores on self-report imagery measures, like the IDQ or Betts, should obtain. If this result did occur, systematic examination of people differing in self-concept imagery centrality would tell us much about how (image) processing, environmental contexts and self-concept interact to produce ecologically-valid patterns of responding.

Naturally all this will remain speculative until the requisite experiments are performed. As stated above, direct evidence for the proposition is not yet available although the existence of imagery self-concept effects is completely predictable from an interactionist position. Although direct evidence is not available some indirect evidence is indicated from my laboratory which augurs well for the eventual validation of the concept.

The evidence comes from some work I have recently completed on reports about creativity. The study was correlational in nature. A set of six scores were obtained on 46 people. Three of these scores were based on performance tests of creativity. There was a score based on verbal creativity tests, figural tests and

TABLE 2.5
Correlations Between Creativity Factor Scores, IDQ Scales, and
Domino's (1970) Creativity Scale

	2	3	4	5	6
1. Verbal creativity factor (I)	−.135	−.130	.028	−.109	.065
2. Figural creativity factor (II)	*	.094	.084	.229*	.070
3. Aesthetic creativity factor (III)		*	−.031	−.036	−.081
4. IDQ: Verbal			*	.358**	.370***
5. IDQ: Imagery				*	−.009
6. Domino Score					*

*p = .07.
**p = .009.
***p = .007.

aesthetic preference test. In addition there were three self-report measures obtained. Two of these are familiar by now. These are the Imagery and the Verbal scores from the IDQ. The last measure was the Domino (1970) scale, a measure taken from the Adjective Check List. This measure represents the 59 adjectives that reliably differentiate people who wish to represent themselves as being creative from people who don't represent themselves that way. The correlation matrix for these measures is shown in Table 2.5. One can see that the self-report measures don't correlate significantly with performance measures, although there is a marginal positive relationship observed between IDQ imagery scores and performance on figural tests of creativity. Of immediate interest are the relationships between Domino scores and the two IDQ scales. Whereas there was a positive relationship for the verbal scale there was virtually no association with the imagery scale. It seems that professed speech, but not imagery habits, predict the adjectives a person is willing to choose as descriptive of himself as a creative person. From an impression-management perspective this suggests that the implicit theory of creativity captured by the Domino scale is related to self-report statements typically associated with language skills. The relationship found with speech may not be too surprising since speech styles have been shown to influence person perception, and that artistic-literary creators tend to speak in special ways, such as via prominent use of compounds and hedges (see Newcombe & Arnkoff, 1979). In any event the data indicate a relationship between habitual symbolic usuage and a measure of a person's presentational image. This success augurs well for the possibility that imagery scores as well may be related to some persona that a person wishes to show the world. Such relationships when they do emerge, as I am sure they will in the next few years, will tell us not only about the internal processing employed by a person but also about the social psychological conditions that permit the person to announce their employment.

CONCLUSION

The interactionist model for individual differences adopted here recognizes the complexity of both the environment and of the individual. The environment is seen as something akin to an intellectual landscape with many routes available from Point A to Point B. Some, but certainly not all of these routes, are imaginal. The individual is seen as an information-processor who is in constant accommodation with this environment. From the individual's perspective, the driving motivation is in making the most sense of this environment with the least cost. The type of questions driving the individual are: given that I have to get to Point B, will process X do the job most efficiently? What are the consequences of adopting process X to my self-concept or to the way other people see me? This accommodation is seen as an ongoing interchange between person and environment such that the answers given to the questions above will change as a function of success in employing process X in environment Y.

The interactionist model can be contrasted to the fundamentally static model assumed by trait or ability theorists. Whereas the traditional model assumes that a measure of individual differences reflects asymptotic performance, the interactionist model assumes that the so-called ability alters with changing environmental consequences. Whereas the traditional model assumes that the ability is brought forth willy-nilly, the interactionist model recognizes that the use of the so-called ability is the result of a monitoring of the environment and evaluation of its usefulness at the time. Finally, whereas the traditional view holds that performance is more or less directly related to the strength of one's ability, the interactionist position holds that performance depends on an interaction of distinctive factors. The level of skill, the sensitivity of monitoring, the preferential orientation adopted and the nature of one self-concept were specific factors suggested here as partners in this interaction.

The implication of the interactionist position is that these factors can be examined both individually and conjointly. Also, in the best tradition of Al Paivio, I believe that there are clear testable consequences of adopting this position. The skill of a person can be directly operationalized by performance on relevant behavioural tasks. Measurements for both image monitoring sensitivity and for imagery processing preference are suggested in this chapter. Finally, while a direct operationalization of imagery self-concept has not yet been achieved, the direction pioneered by Rogers et al. (1977) clearly points the way. Assessment of each of these factors would permit their factorial manipulation, as well as the factorial effects observed with mediational instructions or intentionality of instruction. Some of the predictions of this position have already been discussed: for instance, interactive effects of mediation instructions, skill and monitoring sensitivity would be expected such that instructions to image should only benefit high skill-low monitoring people. Other specific predictions can be found in the paper proper and others can be directly deduced from the theoretical position.

What then does it mean to be a high imager? I would argue that people might be high imagers because of a host of interactive factors, with these factors somewhat separable from one another. It is completely possible that two people might be seen as high imagers for different reasons. For instance, under environmental conditions in which skill differences are of minimal importance, imagery level might be determined more by monitoring sensitivity differences or by differences in self-concept. In any event the conditions under which the different factors become more or less important should be empirically determinable.

In conclusion, it is necessary again to stress that our ultimate goal is to understand real-life decision-making, and not just the artificial proxies studied in our laboratories. An interactive approach seems ideal for this pursuit because the emphasis is on seeing how a person accommodates with his or her environment, and on the sources necessary to make this accommodation. My hope is that ten years from now, when we gather next to honour Al Paivio for yet another decade of academic excellence, the empirical questions regarding the validation of the interactive sources and the specification of when each source assumes prominence will have long been answered, and replaced by questions regarding their place in more ecologically valid situations.

ACKNOWLEDGMENT

Preparation of this manuscript, and of my experiments reported within, were supported by NSERC grant A7040 and SSHRC grant 410-78-0487.

REFERENCES

Angell, J. Methods for the determination of mental imagery. *Psychological Monographs,* 1910, *13,* 61–107.

Ashton, R., McFarland, K., Walsh, F., & White, K. Imagery ability and the identification of hands: A chronometric analysis. *Acta Psychologica,* 1978, *42,* 253–262.

Ashton, R., & White, K. The effects of instructions on subjects' imagery questionnaire scores. *Social Behavior and Personality,* 1975, *3,* 41–43.

Basso, A., Bisiach, E., & Luzzatti, C. Loss of mental imagery: A case study. *Neuropsychologia,* 1980, *18,* 435–442.

Bennett, G., Seashore, M., & Wesman, A. *Differential Aptitude Tests.* New York: Psychological Corp., 1947.

Berlin, B., & Kay, P. *Basic color terms: Their universality and evolution.* Los Angeles: University of California Press, 1969.

Betts, G. *The distribution and functions of mental imagery.* New York: Teachers College, 1909.

Burnham, R., & Clark, J. A test of hue memory. *Journal of Applied Psychology,* 1955, *39,* 164–172.

Carpenter, P., & Just, M. Sentence comprehension: A psycholinguistic processing model of verification. *Psychological Review*, 1975, *82*, 45–73.

Cooper, L. Individual differences in visual comparison processes. *Perception and Psychophysics*, 1976, *19*, 433–444.

Cooper, L., & Shepard, R. Mental transformations in the identification of left and right hands. *Journal of Experimental Psychology: Human Perception and Performance*, 1975, *1*, 48–56.

Di Vesta, F., Ingersoll, G., & Sunshine, P. A factor analysis of imagery tests. *Journal of Verbal Learning and Verbal Behavior*, 1971, *10*, 471–479.

Domino, G. Identification of potentially creative persons from the Adjective Check List. *Journal of Consulting and Clinical Psychology*, 1970, 35, 48–51.

Egan, D. Accuracy and latency scores as measures of spatial information processing. *U.S. Naval Aerospace Medical Research Laboratory*, 1976, Technical Report 122Y, 1–27.

Ernest, C. Imagery ability and cognition: A critical review. *Journal of Mental Imagery*, 1977, *2*, 181–216.

Flavell, J., & Wellman, H. Metamemory. In R. Kail and J. Hagen (Eds.), *Perspectives on the Development of Memory and Cognition*. Hillsdale, N.J.: Lawrence Erlbaum Associates, 1977.

Galton, F. Statistics of mental imagery. *Mind*, 1880, *5*, 301–318.

Goffman, E. *The presentation of self in everyday life*. Garden City, N.Y.: Doubleday, 1959.

Gordon, R. An investigation into some of the factors that favour the formation of stereotyped images. *British Journal of Psychology*, 1949, *40*, 156–167.

Gough, H., & Woodworth, D. Stylistic variations among professional research scientists. *Journal of Psychology*, 1960, *49*, 87–93.

Halff, H., Ortony, A., & Anderson, R. A context-sensitive representation of word meanings. *Memory and Cognition*, 1976, *4*, 378–383.

Hampton, J. An investigation of the nature of abstract concept. *Memory and Cognition*, 1981, *9*, 149–156.

Jackson, D. N. A sequential system for personality scale development. In C. D. Spielberger (Ed.), *Current topics in clinical and community psychology*, Vol. 2. New York: Academic Press, 1970.

Katz, A. Creativity and the right cerebral hemisphere: Towards a physiologically based theory of creativity. *Journal of Creative Behavior*, 1978, *12*, 253–264. (a)

Katz, A. Differences in the saliency of sensory features elicited by words. *Canadian Journal of Psychology*, 1978, *32*, 156–179. (b)

Katz, A. Knowing about the sensory properties of objects. *Quarterly Journal of Experimental Psychology*, 1981, *33A*, 39–49.

Katz, A. Metaphoric relationships: The role of feature saliency. Submitted for publication.

Kosslyn, S. The information represented in visual images. *Cognitive Psychology*, 1975, *7*, 341–370.

Likert, R., & Quasha, W. *Revised Minnesota Paper Form Board Test*. New York: Psychological Corp., 1941.

MacLeod, C., Hunt, E., & Mathews, N. Individual differences in the verification of sentence-picture relationships. *Journal of Verbal Learning and Verbal Behavior*, 1978, *17*, 493–507.

Neisser, U. Visual imagery as process and as experience. In J. S. Antrobus (Ed.), *Cognition and affect*. Boston: Little, Brown, and Co., 1970.

Newcombe, N., & Arnkoff, D. Effects of speech style and sex of speaker on person perception. *Journal of Personality and Social Psychology*, 1979, *37*, 1293–1303.

Nisbett, R., & Wilson, T. Telling more than we can know: Verbal reports on mental processes. *Psychological Review*, 1977, *84*, 231–259.

Paivio, A. A factor-analytic study of word attributes and verbal learning. *Journal of Verbal Learning and Verbal Behavior*, 1968, *7*, 41–49.

Paivio, A. Mental imagery in associative learning and memory. *Psychological Review*, 1969, *76*, 241–263.

Paivio, A. *Imagery and verbal processes.* New York: Holt, Rinehart and Winston, 1971.

Paivio, A., & te Linde, J. Symbolic comparisons of objects on color attributes. *Journal of Experimental Psychology: Human Perception and Performance,* 1980, *6*, 652–661.

Pylyshyn, Z. The rate of "mental rotation" of images: A test of a holistic analogue hypothesis. *Memory and Cognition,* 1979, *7*, 19–28.

Pylyshyn, Z. The imagery debate: Analogue media versus tacit knowledge. *Psychological Review,* 1981, *88,* 16 16–45.

Ratcliff, G. Spatial thought, mental rotation and right cerebral hemisphere. *Neuropsychologia,* 1979, *17,* 49–54.

Richardson, A. The meaning and measurement of mental imagery. *British Journal of Psychology,* 1977, *68,* 29–43. (a)

Richardson, A. Verbalizer-visualizer: A cognitive style dimension. *Journal of Mental Imagery,* 1977, *1,* 109–126. (b)

Richardson, J. T. E. Mental imagery and memory: Coding ability or coding preference? *Journal of Mental Imagery,* 1978, *2,* 101–115.

Richardson, J. T. E. *Mental Imagery and Human Memory.* New York: St. Martin's Press, 1980.

Richman, C., Mitchell, D., & Reznick, J. Mental travel: Some reservations. *Journal of Experimental Psychology: Human Perception and Performance,* 1979, *5,* 13–18.

Roe, A. A study of imagery in research scientists. *Journal of Personality,* 1951, *19,* 459–470.

Rogers, T., Kuiper, N., & Kirker, W. Self-reference and the encoding of personal information. *Journal of Personality and Social Psychology,* 1977, *35,* 677–688.

Rosch, E. Cognitive representations of semantic categories. *Journal of Experimental Psychology: General,* 1975, *104,* 192–233. (a)

Rosch, E. The nature of mental codes for color categories. *Journal of Experimental Psychology: Human Perception and Performance,* 1975, *1,* 303–322. (b)

Rubin, D. 51 properties of 125 words: A unit analysis of verbal behavior. *Journal of Verbal Learning and Verbal Behavior,* 1980, *19,* 736–755.

Sheehan, P. W. A shortened form of Betts' Questionnaire upon mental imagery. *Journal of Clinical Psychology,* 1967, *23,* 386–389. (a)

Sheehan, P. W. Reliability of a short test of iamgery. *Perceptual and Motor Skills,* 1967, *25,* 744. (b)

Silverstein, L., Winner, E., Cadogan, P., & Gardner, H. Fantasy's source: Children's awareness of imagination. *Harvard Project Zero,* August 1980.

Skinner, H. "The eyes that fix you": A model for classification research. *Candian Psychological Review,* 1977, *18,* 142–151.

Sternberg, R. The nature of mental abilities. *American Psychologist,* 1979, *34,* 214–230.

Stewart, J. *An experimental investigation of imagery.* Unpublished doctoral dissertation, University of Toronto, 1965.

Thurstone, L., & Jeffrey, T. *Flags: A test of space thinking.* Chicago: Industrial Relations Center, 1956.

Underwood, B. J. Individual differences as a crucible in theory construction. *American Psychologist,* 1975, *30,* 128–134.

Walker, J. Real-world variability, reasonableness judgments, and memory representations for concepts. *Journal of Verbal Learning and Verbal Behavior,* 1975, *14,* 241–252.

White, K., Sheehan, P., & Ashton, R. Imagery assessment: A survey of self-report measures. *Journal of Mental Imagery,* 1977, *1,* 145–169.

3 Picture Memory

Stephen Madigan
University of Southern California

PICTURE MEMORY

In 1894 Kirkpatrick reported the results of an experimental study of memory for spoken words, printed words, and real objects. Using what would be much later called an RTT procedure, Kirkpatrick presented lists of ten items, followed by an immmediate free recall test and a second test some 72 hours later. There were 329 subjects, male and female students from elementary school through university. Although some details of his experimental design and procedure would not get by a contemporary editor or reviewer (e.g., failure to counterbalance materials and test orders) the results were striking and impressive, as Fig. 3.1 indicates. There was the by-now familiar superiority in recall of objects over words in immediate recall, and a positively huge difference after the 72-hour retention interval. If the antiquity of this study makes the reader uneasy, the results of a replication of Kirkpatrick's experiment by Calkins (1898) are reassuring: Using a sample of 50 college women, Calkins reproduced all of Kirkpatrick's effects, including the apparent interaction of modality and retention interval, with recall of words declining by 50% or more over the retention interval, and recall of objects dropping by less than 20%.

These early studies of item concreteness effects serve to define the significance of picture memory and object memory experiments. It is basically that human memory is extremely sensitive to the symbolic modality of presentation of event information. In any terms, the effects of symbolic modality (verbal *versus* pictorial) are large, reliable and general ones, and as such ought to influence the development of theories of cognition and memory and demand satisfactory accounting for by any such theories.

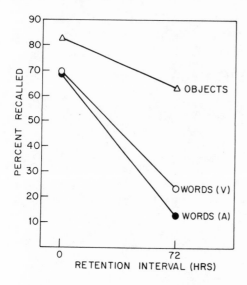

FIG. 3.1. Immediate and delayed recall of auditory (A) and visual (V) words and objects. Data from Kirkpatrick, 1894.

Whereas the impact of pictorial representation on memory was well documented as much as 80 years ago, there was little systematic study of the effect over the next 50 years. Although this neglect can be understood in terms of the fate of cognitive theory in general over that period it is still surprising that the systematic study of human learning that did occur made so little of the importance of symbolic stimulus modality. Human learning theory developed into an almost exclusively *verbal* learning theory: McGeoch (1942) dealt at length with the characteristics of material that influenced learning, but made no mention of picture-word or object-word differences. Scattered studies of picture effects (e.g., Bousfield, Esterson, & Whitmarsh, 1957), demonstrating relatively powerful effects, appeared to have little impact.

The systematic study and appreciation of the importance of picture memory effects dates from the mid 60s, particularly in conjunction with the treatment of picture effects in Paivio's (1971) integrative treatment of imagery in learning and memory. As well as providing an enduring theoretical framework for understanding picture effects (dual-code theory), that work itself contains a thorough review of picture-memory research, and is referred to throughout this chapter.

The purpose of this chapter is to examine the major empirical generalizations that have come out of research on the encoding and retention of pictorial information, and to evaluate a number of attempts to explain picture memory effects. No thorough literature review will be attempted; one already out-of date bibliography includes almost 700 entries (Standing, Bond, Hall, & Weller, 1972). Instead, an attempt will be made to update the review provided by Paivio (1971), with an emphasis on those studies that have proven significant for theoretical development. This will be followed by a consideration of four approaches to the explanation of picture memory effects.

MEMORY AND THE PICTURE EFFECT

The first section of this chapter reviews the empirical basis of the "picture effect"—the effect of pictorial and object representations, as compared to verbal ones, on a variety of measures of learning and memory. This review is largely concerned with documenting the scope and reliability of the picture effect. Explanations of the picture effect, particularly those based on studies of controlled encoding effects, will be covered in a later section.

Memory Tasks and Picture Effects

In one way, it is easy to characterize the picture effect in standard memory test procedures, because so many studies essentially show what Kirkpatrick and Calkins reported: substantial improvement of performance with pictorial representations of to-be-remembered material. Kirkpatrick's and Calkins's results have been replicated many times. In general, free recall is ordered along the concreteness continuum, increasing through abstract words to concrete words to pictures to real objects (Paivio, 1971; Bevan & Steger, 1971). Serial position analyses indicate that the recency effect is roughly similar for word and picture lists, with the total recall difference based on picture superiority in the secondary memory portion of the curve (Madigan, McCabe, & Itatani, 1972).

Picture effects in associative (paired-associate) learning have been extensively analyzed, the original studies seeking similarities between picture effects and item concreteness (C) and abstractness (A) effects (Paivio, 1971; Paivio & Yarmey, 1966). The speed of acquisition of paired-associate lists with words is regularly ordered in terms of concreteness and stimulus-response function: C-C, C-A, A-C, and A-A in decreasing order of ease of learning. The parallel comparison of words and pictures does not duplicate this ordering: Although pictures have a clearly facilitating effect when used as stimuli or cue items (Postman, 1978), so that P-W pairs are learned much faster then W-W pairs, there may actually be a slight negative effect of pictures used as response items, so that P-P pairs may not be equal to P-W pairs, and W-P pairs may be inferior to W-W pairs (or at least not show a usual picture effect). Paivio (1971) suggests that this may be due to the decoding or transformation demands of tests that use a pictorial event but demand a verbal response.

Recognition tests have provided some of the best-known and most striking evidence for the sensitivity of memory to symbolic modality of presentation. Several experiments have demonstrated very high recognition accuracy rates for pictures, as compared to words, when the amount of material presented is very large (Nickerson, 1965; Shepard, 1967; Standing, 1973; Standing, Conezio, & Haber, 1970). Standing's study is probably the most striking in this respect: subjects viewed from 10 to 10,000 complex pictures, and, following a 48 hour retention interval, were tested with subsets of presented pictures. Estimates of amount stored were generally power functions of amount presented, with exponents near unity. This result led Standing (1973) and Postman (1978) to conclude that capacity for this kind of recognition may be essentially unlimited. (An important fact about picture superiority in recognition, to be discussed in some detail later, is that picture presentation produces better recognition than word presentation even when the test format of material is verbal.)

The robustness of the picture effect on recognition memory is evident in the results of an unpublished study of mine that included three experimental operations intended to depress picture recognition accuracy. In this experiment, under intentional learning conditions, subjects were first exposed to a sequence of 90 presentations consisting of the kinds of stimulus events illustrated in Fig. 3.2. In one condition subjects saw slides and at the same time heard the common label for the object depicted in the slide. In another condition subjects saw slides but heard the name of a different object. In a third condition subjects heard a name only, with no object shown. All three kinds of presentations occurred in a mixed

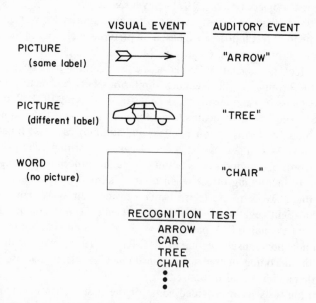

FIG. 3.2. Examples of visual and auditory events in the picture-word experiment. (See text for details).

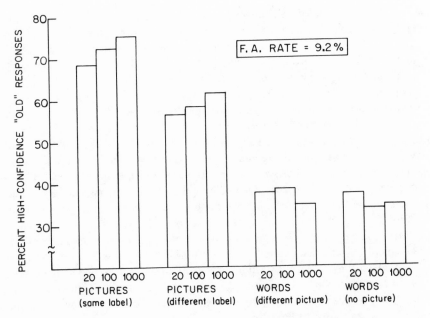

FIG. 3.3.   Recognition performance as a function of imput modality, labeling, and exposure items.

sequence. In addition, picture duration was varied. With an inter-stimulus interval of 4 sec pictures were displayed for 20, 100, or 1000 msec, followed by a low-luminance post-exposure field. The yes–no recognition test that followed was entirely verbal: only names of objects (old and new) were presented. Accordingly, picture recognition could be expected to suffer with (a) very brief exposures; (b) incorrect labeling and possibly interference with any covert labeling (Smith & Magee, 1980) and (c) absence of picture cues in the test.

Fig. 3.3 shows the results in terms of the percent of high-confidence "old" responses in the recognition test. Picture recognition was adversely affected by incorrect labeling, and by reduced display time. But it is also clear that picture superiority was still substantial even under the worst combination of conditions. The results interestingly show that the effect of picture display time was remarkably small: a 20 msec exposure was all that was needed to produce a large picture effect. Under the conditions of this experiment some postexposure processing of pictures is possible and highly likely (Weaver, 1974), and a rapid sequence of 20 msec exposures with very short ISIs would produce relatively low levels of recognition (Intraub, 1980). Presumably the storage of information about picture details would also suffer with very brief exposures; but it is still interesting that the pictorial facilitation of recognition can occur with viewing times that do not permit a single directed eye movement. The naturalistic viewing of complex scenes may involve patterns of eye movements and rests correlated with the information content of different regions of a picture (Loftus, 1972) but the establishment of "scanpaths" (Noton & Stark, 1971) does not seem necessary for subsequent picture recognition.

Although item recall and item recognition both display large facilitative effects of pictorial representations, the two kinds of test procedures do not appear to respond in the same way to the variation of some dimensions of picture complexity or detail. Although Paivio, Rogers and Smythe (1968) failed to find any better recall of colored line drawings as compared to black-and-white versions, such an effect has been reported a number of times. Bousfield et al. (1957) found free recall of words accompanied by colored line drawings of their object referents to be better than recall of black and white versions, which were in turn recalled better than the verbal labels of the objects. Madigan and Lawrence (1980) compared free recall of words (object names), black and white outline drawings of objects, and colored slides of the objects (from which the drawings were prepared) in an RTTT procedure. The colored slides were photos of objects in natural settings, and included color and a great deal of background detail. There was a substantial picture effect as well as a detail/color effect over all three recall trials, as shown in Fig. 3.4.

Such results for unaided (free) recall stand in curious contrast to the results of similar manipulations in recognition experiments, where picture detail or complexity appears to have little or no effect on recognition accuracy. Such an

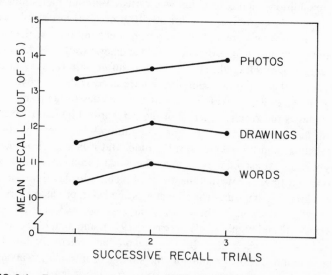

FIG. 3.4.   Free recall over three test trials for photos, drawings, and words. From Madigan and Lawrence, 1980. Reprinted by permission.

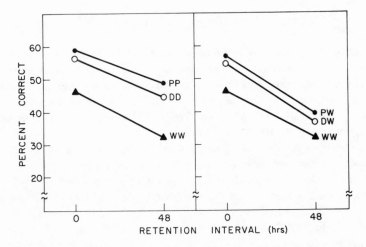

FIG. 3.5. Immediate and delayed recognition for photos, drawings and words, with same and different study and test formats.

outcome was first reported by Nelson, Metzler and Reed (1974). They used photographs of complex natural scenes, "embellished" and "unembellished" line drawings of the scenes, and verbal descriptions of the scenes, with a yes-no recognition test for different groups of subjects at zero and 72-hour retention intervals. Recognition of verbal descriptions was much poorer than picture recognition at both intervals, but there was no effect of picture detail or complexity.

We have recently replicated essentially the same outcome in a study (to be discussed later in a different context) that used the same kinds of materials as the Madigan and Lawrence experiment (colored and detailed object photos, line drawings, object names). Figure 3.5 shows that at zero and 48-hour retention intervals, item recognition was (as usual) much better for pictures than for words, but picture complexity had very little effect in the immediate test: the difference between photos and drawings is not significant. All of these effects were obtained when test format was the same as study format (left panel) or when all items were tested as words (right panel). This study also avoided possible ceiling effects in the immediate test that may have been present in the Nelson et al. (1974) study.

Thus it appears that picture detail or complexity can be added to the list of variables that has differential effects on recall and recognition (Tulving, 1976). The conclusion, however, cannot be extended to include a separable dimension of pictures, "vividness": as Standing (1973) has shown, pictures that are presumably equally complex and detailed but differ in the unusualness of their content appear to vary in recognition, with the more vivid or unusual depictions producing better recognition.

STORAGE OF SPECIFIC PICTURE INFORMATION

Although many studies of picture memory have focused on the effects of pictorial representation on recall and recognition tasks that most often require verbal responding, another concern of picture memory research has been the question of the storage of specific picture information. It is clear that there is more to picture processing and recall than just the facilitation of item recall and recognition: the presentation of a sequence of pictures also produces the encoding of information about dimensions and features of pictured items. This issue can be broadened to include the storage and representation of features of the visual environment in general, rather than dealing only with static viewing of symbolic representations.

Some of the most interesting data available for this problem have come out of studies utilizing incidental memory tests for picture detail and characteristics. For example, Loftus (1977) found that memory for the color of an object (a book) appearing in a sequence of slides depicting a complex event was quite accurate, with color recognition displaying a symmetrical generalization or confusion gradient around the true hue value. Information about spatial orientation also appears to be a routinely encoded dimension of pictured objects and scenes. Standing et al. (1970) tested recognition memory for pictures of complex natural scenes with a forced-choice procedure, one version of which required the usual kind of discrimination (between a previously presented picture and a new distractor picture). A second test procedure required a discrimination between an old slide and a left-right reversed (mirror-image) version. Although this discrimination was much more difficult than the standard one, accuracy was surprisingly good, considering the number of pictures that had been presented, the incidental nature of the test, and the inherent difficulty of the discrimination. With the orientation-discrimination test, for example, mediation of recognition through prior verbal labeling is not possible, and recognition through detection of isolated picture details would be generally ineffective as well. Bartlett, Till and Levy (1980) have reported similar levels of picture recognition when the test requires discrimination of left-right reversals.

The storage of specific picture information and its accessibility was examined in a more direct fashion by Madigan and Hamovitch (1976), using procedures similar to Cooper and Shepard's (1973) tests of image generation. Subjects saw a series of three slides depicting complex natural scenes. Each slide was given a simple name during presentation (e.g., "railroad," "farm," "rifle"). A test slide presented one of the three slides, in its original form, or in a left-right reversed version, and subjects had to classify it as same or different. On half the trials (the noncued trials) the test slide was preceded only by a ready signal. On the other half, the *name* of the upcoming test slide was presented, 4 sec before test onset. The point of this operation was to determine the extent to which subjects could use the verbal cue to access information about picture orientation, and to create a kind of imaginal template to facilitate responding to the test

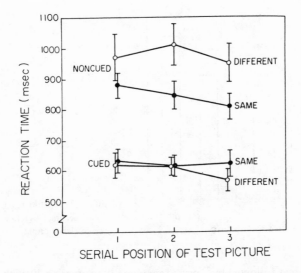

FIG. 3.6.   Reaction time to classify test pictures as same or reversed version of presented pictures with and without advance identity information. From Madigan and Hamovitch, 1976. Reprinted by permission.

stimulus. Fig. 3.6 shows the effects of this form of cuing on reaction times: a very large reduction in mean reaction time compared to noncued tests; a reduction in the variability of RT's; and the reversal or at least elimination of the same-different RT difference found in noncued tests. The same general outcome could probably be obtained with procedures requiring the storage of and access to other dimension of pictorial stimuli, such as color and size. Evidence for the encoding and persistence of information about dimensions would take the form of increased speed (and possibly increased accuracy) of test judgments.

Other, perhaps simpler methods point to the same conclusion. In an unpublished study subjects were shown a series of 40 line drawings, naming each one at presentation. With a 5-sec inter-stimulus interval, pictures were exposed for .5

TABLE 3.1
Percent High-Confidence Hits and Correct
Rejections

	Exposure Duration			
	.5 sec		4.0 sec	
	Noncued	Cued	Noncued	Cued
Hits	36	44	45	53
Correct Rejections	27	34	36	52

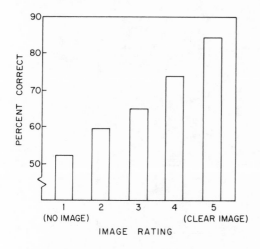

FIG. 3.7. Picture reversal discrimination accuracy as a function of prior image clarity rating.

or 4 sec. This was followed by a period in which the names of 20 of the pictures were presented, ånd subjects were asked to rate the "clarity" of the images evoked by the names. The final stage of the experiment was a postcued recognition task for all 40 pictures, requiring classification of test pictures as same or different (reversed). In this study there was an effect of the prior image-generation on accuracy (see Table 3.1) and there was also an interesting relationship between rated image clarity and subsequent probability correct for individual subject-items. Fig. 3.7 shows the probability correct as a function of prior image-clarity rating, and the results could hardly be more regular.

The possibility of rehearsal of pictures has been investigated in a number of ways. It now seems clear that postexposure processing of complex pictures is possible and highly effective (Tversky & Sherman, 1975; Weaver, 1974). Watkins and Graefe (1981), using procedures similar to the "image clarity" experiment, found clear evidence for retrieval of picture information from long-term memory. Although they declined to specify exactly what this rehearsal might consist of, it is difficult to characterize it in terms other than access to specific pciture information, particularly in a situation such as the image-clarity experiment, where access to and rehearsal of only the name or verbal label of the picture would not have much if any influence on the later recognition test that required responding on the basis of specific picture characteristics.

EXPLAINING PICTURE EFFECTS

The extensive empirical data base produced by studies of picture effects poses an important theoretical problem. There is in the first place the problem of explaining why variation of symbolic modality of presentation has large and reliable effects across any number of tasks, with pictorial representations facilitating recall, recognition, and associative learning. The second explanatory problem comes out of the evidence for the encoding, representation, and accessibility of specific picture information, with the attendant problem of specifying a storage format to represent such information.

Four explanatory approaches will be considered: (a) explanation of picture-word differences in terms of complexity and discriminability; (b) in terms of levels, depths or effortfulness of processing; (c) in terms of dual-code theory and its variants; and (d) in terms of abstract-propositional theory. These cannot all be regarded as directly competing hypotheses, nor do they all offer explanation at the same level. At the same time they all present analyses of at least some picture effects that allow comparisons and evaluation.

Complexity and Discriminability

At various times it has been suggested that picture-word differences may reflect only the greater discriminability of pictures as compared to words. Certainly in most simple experimental comparisons of words and pictures there are no attempts made to equate the two kinds of material in terms of surface physical characteristics. Because picture recognition accuracy can be made arbitrarily high or low by variation of target-distractor similarity (Goldstein & Chance, 1970), and can in fact be predicted from the similarity of *verbal* descriptions of the pictures (Wyant, Banks, Berger, & Wright, 1972), differences in the relative discriminability of sets of words and pictures might be the source of the picture effect in recognition: "Indeed, until performance on sets of equally complex and discriminable pictorial and linguistic forms is compared, little can be said concerning the superiority of picture recognition" (Anderson, 1976, p. 379). Anderson and Paulson (1978) adopt a similar approach to the explanation of picture superiority when pictures and words have both been processed in meaningful ways, ascribing the picture superiority to the greater discriminability of pictures in the recognition phase.

Without denying either the potent effects of similarity and the hard-to-avoid confounding of discriminability and symbolic modality, it can be argued that the discriminability hypothesis cannot account for much if any of the picture effect. In the first place, attempts to equate words and pictures for differences in discriminability may not radically alter the picture effect. Wells (1972) tested short-term retention of simple forms or their verbal descriptions, with attempts to control and equate size, color and spatial distribution. From two experiments it was concluded that "minimizing non-essential differences between pictorial and verbal stimuli does not necessarily result in both types of stimuli being remembered equally well [p. 251]."

A second problem with the discriminability hypothesis is that is appears to suggest that variation of the physical or surface characteristics of material should improve recall or recognition *in general*. However, there appear to be no studies of free recall or recognition that show that varying the physical characteristics of a set of words within a list has a large facilitating effect on recall or recognition of the list as a whole. Such variation is generally effective only for isolated items, as in the Zeigarnik effect.

Attempts to explain the picture effect in recognition in terms of partial recognition or "distinctive feature" detection really come apart in the light of numerous demonstrations that item recognition is greatly improved by picture representations even when the pictures do not appear at all in the recognition test. These are studies that compare the effect of input or study formats (words or pictures) by using a common test format (words only). Experiments by Borges, Stepnowsky and Holt (1977), Jenkins, Neale, and Deno (1967), Paivio (1976), Scarborough, Gerard, and Cortese (1979), and Snodgrass and McClure (1975) include such a comparison. The general finding is that while changing an item's format from picture (at study) to word (at test) may slightly reduce recognition accuracy, compared to a picture-picture condition, a substantial picture effect is still obtained, with picture-word material much better recognized than word-word material.

Figure 3.8 shows the results of a recent study of ours that demonstrates the essentials of this effect. (These data are redrawn from Fig. 3.5.) In this experiment, subjects first saw a set of 88 photos, or line drawings, or words (object names), followed by an immediate recognition test for half of the material and a 48-hour delayed test for the other half. Different groups of subjects saw pictures at both study and test (P-P and D-D conditions), or pictures at study and then verbal labels at test (P-W and D-W conditions). Figure 3.8 shows that the basic picture effect was hardly influenced at all by this change of format, at least in the immediate test. Picture presentation greatly improves recognition even when the pictures are not presented in the test.

This finding is an interesting one for several reasons. First, as Paivio (1976) has noted, it suggests that the picture effect in recognition is largely an input (or study or encoding) effect. It also argues strongly against explanations of picture superiority in recognition in terms of recognition of isolated picture details at the time of testing. The outcome also appears to be a case of (cued) recall exceeding recognition, to the extent that subjects in the P-W and D-W conditions had to essentially perform a cued-recall test in a way that P-P or W-W subjects did not (Scarborough et al., 1979).

Perhaps this general finding is really not at all that unusual: It is already well known that picture presentation improves free recall where pictorial cues are not presented in the test phase at all. Figure 3.8 also suggests that at longer retention intervals there may well be a sizeable decrement in recognition accuracy with change of format from study to test. But one basic conclusion from the effect remains: The picture effect on recognition is not dependent on attention to details or partial recognition at the time of a recognition test.

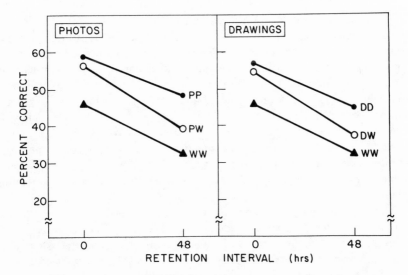

FIG. 3.8.   Recognition of photos (P), drawings (D), and words (W) in immediate and delayed tests.

Encoding Levels and Stages

A second approach to the explanation of picture effects revolves around possible picture-word differences in the initial encoding of verbal and pictorial material. Although the original levels-of-processing concept (Craik & Lockhart, 1972) has fallen on hard times in a number of respects, (Nelson, Walling & McEvoy, 1979), the general approach it espoused remains influential, especially in terms of its impact in directing attention to the need for and importance of control of encoding processes. Although the picture superiority effect in recall and recognition is so reliably obtained with intentional learning procedures and some kinds of incidental learning procedures, major exceptions to it occur in studies that control or impose certain kinds of processing requirements.

One of the first-reported of these actually followed from a prediction from dual-code theory: Imaginal encoding of concrete words should produce picture-like effects in recall. Paivio and Csapo (1973) found just this effect: recall of concrete words was equal to recall of picture names when subjects were required to generate an image for each word at presentation. However, a number of other kinds of orienting tasks appear capable of producing the same general outcome. Paivio (1975) found that directing subjects to imagine the words or to rate the pleasantness of the words yielded equivalent recall.

Durso and Johnson (1980) conducted a large-scale comparison of word and picture recall and recognition under a variety of orienting and processing requirements. There were three major categories of tasks, as classified by Durso and Johnson: *verbal* tasks, requiring naming and specification of the last letter of the item's name; *imaginal* tasks, involving image generation and ratings of the difficulty of drawing the item; and *referential* tasks, requiring judgments about characteristics of the real-world referents of words and pictures such as size, animacy, and function. The key result was that the usual picture superiority effect was obtained only with the verbal tasks. With referential tasks Durso and Johnson report that there were essentially no picture-word differences; and with imaginal tasks there was a significant *reversal* with words displaying better recognition. This general pattern of results was obtained in a second experiment that used free recall instead of recognition testing, although pictures produced slightly but consistently better performances under all three classes of orienting tasks.

Durso and Johnson (1980) conclude that the occurrence of a picture effect or of a picture-word difference depends on the processing strategies or responses subjects make to pictures and words, and in particular on whether or not the processing involves access to or activation of information about the real-world referents of items as opposed to processing directed at the item per se, as in simple word-naming or processing a picture *qua* picture.

At least some parts of this conclusion can be accepted as a valid empirical generalization, especially given earlier studies that demonstrated some of the same outcomes. To move beyond this to an explanation of the picture effect requires some additional considerations. One of these comes out of a series of studies by Smith and Magee (1980). They had subjects pronounce the name of words and pictures, or categorize words and pictures. Consistent with earlier results (Potter & Faulconer, 1975), they found that words were pronounced faster than they were categorized and pictures were categorized faster that their labels were pronounced. They also found that item recognition in a final test depended on stimulus format (word or picture) and also on the initial processing task. With a naming task, pictures enjoyed a very large advantage in recognition, compared to words, but with a prior categorization task picture-word differences were either very small or even slightly reversed. When subjects were required to generate category names, as opposed to making a dichotomous category judgment, a picture superiority effect was obtained but it was a relatively small one, again compared to picture-word differences following a naming task. The reduction or elimination of picture superiority following categorization is consistent with the other demonstrations of the effects of forced semantic processing that have been cited.

The idea that pictures more readily or regularly access semantic codes than do words is the core of Durso and Johnson's proposed interpretation of picture effects. As they point out, it is also a component of the sensory-semantic model developed by Nelson and his colleagues (Nelson, 1979; Nelson, Reed, & McEvoy, 1977). This model assumes that both pictures and words access a common meaning code, but that pictures do this more directly than do words. In particular, words must progress through a stage of access to phonemic information prior to activation of their semantic codes. Pictures access phonemic information about their verbal labels *after* semantic access. (These assumptions are clearly consistent with much of Smith and Magee's (1980) naming and categorization data.)

Another assumption of the Nelson model is that the *sensory* code of words and pictures differ, with the differences directly reflecting the differences that typically exist in the surface or measureable physical characteristics of words and pictures: Pictures are more discriminable and more distinctive than words. This assumption has received some strong experimental support. Nelson, Reed, and Walling (1976) used pictures as stimulus items in a paired associate task with independent variation of both the conceptual and schematic similarity of the stimulus set. High schematic similarity was instituted by presentation of a set of pictures of objects of similar shape (e.g., knife, baseball bat, nail) with relatively low conceptual similarity. Nelson et al. (1976) predicted that high schematic similarity should greatly weaken the picture effect, and this was precisely what they found: Pictures were no better as cues than words at a relatively slow rate of presentation, and were actually less efficient cues at a faster rate of presentation. As Nelson (1979) observes, the picture effect is tied to the visual features of pictures, as compared to those of words, and in particular to their greater discriminability. Note however that this is not a simple discriminability hypothesis because it makes the prior assumption that information about visual features is regularly and effectively encoded, retained, and retrieved. If pictures (or nonverbal features of stimuli in general) and words shared a completely common and abstract storage format then there would be no reason to expect that visual similarity would have any differential effects for words and pictures.

Dual-Code Theory

Dual-code theory is the most explicit and detailed treatment of a general idea that has found much less formal expression elsewhere, as in Koestler's (1969) description of memory as consisting of two separate systems, "abstract and picture strip." The distinction between the presentation code and the conceptual code of events (Rabinowitz, Mandler, & Barsalou, 1979) parallels dual-code theory (and also Nelson's sensory-semantic model) in its postulation of two kinds or levels of encoded information. The independence of retention of name and picture information (Bahrick & Boucher, 1968) and the lack of effect of verbal elaboration on retention of specific picture information (Rafnel & Klatzky, 1978) are findings supportive of the general dual code concept.

Because dual-code theory is discussed elsewhere in this book, and because its ramifications extend far beyond picture memory studies, what will be considered here are only those aspects of the theory that bear on explanation of picture effects. The core of dual-code theory is described as follows by Paivio and Lambert (1981):

> Dual code theory . . . is based on the assumption that memory and cognition are served by two separate symbolic systems, one specialized for dealing with verbal information and the other for nonverbal information. The two systems are presumed to be interconnected but capable of functioning independently. Interconnectedness means that representations in one system can activate those in the other, so that for example, pictures can be named and images can occur to words. Independence implies, among other things, that nonverbal (imaginal) and verbal memory codes, aroused directly by pictures and words or indirectly by imagery and verbal encoding tasks, should have additive effects on recall [p. 532-533].

For present purposes, another assumption of dual code theory is also important: that imaginal codes are less efficient than verbal ones in dealing with temporal and sequential information, but more efficient in dealing with spatial information.

Dual-code theory was first developed to account for imagery effects in verbal learning studies (Paivio, 1971). Because picture effects fit so well into the abstract-concrete dimension, logically and empirically, dual-code theory was extended rather naturally to explain them in the same fashion: pictures, like concrete words, may be represented by imaginal as well as by verbal codes. Paivio (1975) and Paivio and Csapo (1973) have provided some compelling evidence for the reality of dual-coding effects involving pictures: Presentation of a pictorial representation of an item and presentation of a verbal representation of the same concept have independent and additive effects on recall, unlike picture-picture or word-word representations.

Another instance of a word-picture difference that is not solely a quantitative difference in performance level was reported by D'Agostino, O'Neil and Paivio (1977) in a comparison of levels of processing effects with abstract words, concrete words, and pictures. Three orienting tasks were used that presumably differed in depth of processing required. Although the usual levels of processing effects were obtained for concrete words, they were not for abstract words and pictures. Specifically, abstract word recall did not differ for phonemic and semantic processing; and picture recall was not different for phonemic and semantic processing. (Recall for all three kinds of materials was poorest for the structural task, but still best for pictures.) If all three kinds of materials were in fact processed to the same depth, all three should have shown the same pattern of orienting task effects; the fact that they did not indicates that processes other than level of encoding have to be invoked to account for the results. D'Agostino et al. (1977) suggest, for example, that the equality of recall of pictures following phonemic and semantic processing could be interpreted in terms of dual coding that results from phonemic processing, offsetting the influence of a nonsemantic encoding.

However, the explanation of picture effects in terms of a code-redundancy mechanism has never been entirely successful or satisfactory. The first problem is that it has sometimes seemed necessary to postulate an inherent superiority of imaginal or pictorial codes. There may well be separate verbal and imaginal codes, and they may summate in recall or performance, but they do not contribute equally to the process. The superiority of imaginal or pictorial codes may reside in distinctiveness and discriminability (Paivio, 1975; Paivio & Csapo, 1973), a suggestion that has become a central feature of Nelson's sensory-semantic model. As Paivio (1971) noted, explaining picture effects by postulating an inherent superiority of picture codes is circular and theoretically empty. However, a study such as that by Nelson et al. (1977) testing a discriminability or distinctiveness interpretation seems to be a step towards a genuine explanation along these lines.

Another difficulty with applying dual code theory (or at least a code-redundancy version of it) to picture effects is the possibility that picture presentation does not routinely or automatically result in the generation or activation of a corresponding verbal code (Nelson, 1979). The kinds of pictorial representations typically used in experiments in this area may be readily and quickly named, if subjects are required to do so, but it does not appear to be an obligatory part of encoding. In addition suppression of the name code or at least interference with its generation does not greatly reduce picture superiority, as attested to by the results shown in Fig. 3.3.

Another issue in the evaluation of dual code theory has to do with picture effects in serial recall. Memory tasks requiring the processing of order information have sometimes shown one of the rare cases of a negative effect of pictorial representation. At rates of presentation too great to allow easy implicit labeling, pictures are inferior to words in immediate recall (Paivio & Csapo, 1971). Paivio (1971) describes similar results of other kinds of tests of retention of order information (discrimination of recency, serial reconstruction). This finding has influenced the development of dual-code theory, leading to the assumption that imaginal codes do not easily represent sequential-temporal information.

This generalization appears to rest on somewhat shaky grounds, however. As Paivio (1971) noted, there were a number of inconsistencies in the literature at the time this hypothesis was formulated (i.e., cases of picture superiority in sequential memory tests). Since that time, there have been reports that do little to clarify the issue. Schiano & Watkins (1981) compared memory spans for word and picture lists and found only small and nonsignificant picture-word differences (but also the usual large ones when a free-recall task was used). However, using a partial report (probe) test Dhawan and Pellegrino (1977) found much better sequential recall for pictures than for words over the first half of 14-item lists.

Why a partial-report (probe) procedure should show a picture effect whereas a whole-report (forward serial recall) procedure does not is not at all clear, and generalizations about picture effects and serial order memory should be made cautiously until this is resolved. The entire problem may be a difficult one to deal with however because of the difficulty of separating item information and order information contributions. Given that pictures exhibit greater levels of item information than words, and assuming that ordered recall is dependent on item information (in a logical sense), then comparisons of levels of serial recall or order information for words and pictures are biased in favor of pictures. (Dual code theory might in fact take this to suggest that those studies finding a slight picture decrement in serial recall are actually underestimating the extent of word superiority.)

A different approach to the general possibility that verbal and pictorial codes may be differentially suited to the representation of different domains of information was reported by Anderson (1976) in a comparison of the retention of spatial and temporal attributes of presentation of arrays of words and pictures. Instead of considering the absolute levels of accuracy obtained with words and pictures, Anderson instead examined the relative levels of accuracy within each stimulus class when the memory tests required the processing of temporal or spatial information. Although Anderson found consistent picture superiority in terms of overall performance levels the more important result was that there was an interaction of symbolic modality (picture, word) with type of test (spatial, temporal): Spatial information was better processed than temporal for pictures, but temporal information was processed better that spatial information for words. As Anderson notes, this is consistent with the general "spirit" of this particular assumption of dual code theory. Snodgrass, Burns, and Pirone (1978) report results pointing to the same general conclusion. Although studies using standard serial learning or recall procedures have not consistently shown a picture-induced decrements in performance the contrast of spatial and temporal processing with words and pictures does support the dual-code characterization of the specialization of verbal and nonverbal systems.

In sum, dual code theory has had a number of successes in dealing with picture effects, but has encountered some difficulties as well, especially when picture effects are interpreted solely in terms of code redundancy. It should be pointed out at the same time that dual code theory also accounts for concreteness effects with verbal material and no other rival explanation of these effects has been particularly successful. (See Paivio, Ch. 14, this volume.)

Picture Memory and Propositional Theories

Explanations of picture memory effects in terms of imaginal codes (and probably in terms of sensory codes as well) have been subjected to the same kinds of criticisms leveled at imagery theory in general by theorists advocating models of memory representation in terms of abstract propositional forms (Anderson & Bower, 1973; Pylyshyn, 1973). Largely on logical grounds, this approach rejects any models of representation closely tied to perceptual concepts or states, starting with crude notions involving the "storage of pictures" but also rejecting more sophisticated distinctions between verbal and nonverbal modes of storage or representation. Representations of experience or knowledge is instead described in terms of an abstract set of relations and states called propositions.

One thrust of this viewpoint in connection with picture memory research has been to document and demonstrate the limitations of any idea of a literal picture memory, and to point instead to the involvement of abstractive and interpretive processes in picture memory. Thus, a series of line drawings will be poorly remembered if a subject is unable to interpret the drawings in a meaningful way, whereas memory for the same drawings, presented in the same way will be much better if a conceptual interpretation or labeling is provided (Bower, Karlin, & Dueck, 1975).

Neither dual-code theory nor sensory-semantic theory is seriously discommoded by demonstrations of elaborative encoding effects (conceptual or verbal elaboration of to-be-remembered pictures) because neither theory is really a "naive image" theory that posits a raw kind of picture or image storage. The main issue raised by a comparison of these theories with abstract-propositional ones has to do with the question of the need for postulating two different representational modes. As Anderson (1976), Anderson and Paulson (1978), and Ternes and Yuille (1972) describe the issue, the evaluation of the dual-code hypothesis revolves around finding evidence for qualitative as opposed to purely quantitative differences: do pictorial and verbal memory processes obey different laws, as Anderson and Paulson put it. In general, propositional theorists approach the main body of picture-effect data in terms of differential levels of processing, or discriminability, or more generally in terms of picture-word differences that do not require assumptions or conclusions about different representational formats. A related approach is to attempt to demonstrate that similarity effects, interference effects, and retention characteristics may not differ for words and pictures except in quantitative ways. Anderson and Paulson (1978) adopted this approach in a study of recognition of faces that were presented in pictoral form or in the form of a set of verbal descriptions. They demonstrated that both formats of presentation were affected in much the same way by a similarity or confusability variable (the number features shared by different pictures or descriptions in a set). This effect was regarded as being essentially the same as effects produced in studies of memory for sentences (the fan effect), and consistent with abstract-propositional theory.

At this point in time, the evaluation of a propositional account of picture memory effects is difficult because the development of that theory has taken place mainly in the context of studies utilizing sentence and textual material— material that may be more easily described or represented in the network-node format widely used by this theoretical approach. As Stopher and Kirsner (1981) note, the Anderson and Paulson study is one of the few direct tests of propositional theory as an account of picture effects. That the adequacy of propositional theory in this regard is still an open question is indicated by Stopher and Kirsner's studies that paralled Anderson and Paulson's in a number of important respects. These studies involved the presentation of information about the relationship between two objects ("the clock is on the television") with this information presented in verbal or in pictorial form. As in the studies of the fan effect a major variable was the number of different relationships in which an item occurred in the set presented to a subject. Following a learning phase subjects were required to classify events (verbal statements or pictorial representations) as true (describing a previously learned relationship) or false (describing a relationship not previously presented). In two studies Stopher and Kirsner replicated the fan effect for verbal material (longer RTs for tests that involved items that shared features) but found no such effect (and in fact found reversals of the RT difference) for pictorial material. Their conclusions were that "the two experiments lend no support to the view that information about sentences and words depends on common representational and retrieval systems [p. 39]."

Stopher and Kirsner's experiments certainly indicate that the application of at least some versions of propositional theories to picture memory effects is unsuccessful and that modifications of the theories definitely seem required to account for modality effects. At the same time, it is not clear how Stopher and Kirsner's results follow directly from dual-code theories either. They are certainly consistent with the conclusion that picture and word processing and memory may be qualitatively different, but this is more of an empirical generalization than a theoretical account. The problem for both dual-code and propositional theories is to account for such effects with something more than *ad hoc* attribution of specific properties to the representation of words and pictures.

PROBLEMS AND PROSPECTS

Picture memory research, viewed as a whole, documents the potency of pictorial representation in establishing memorial and cognitive structures, and presents a very large set of empirical relationships that have to be satisfactorily accounted for theoretically. Of the theoretical accounts that have been presented, those that involve the assumption of different representational formats for nonverbal and verbal material seem most strongly supported to date. Such accounts differ in how strong a dividing line is drawn between the two formats, but deciding among them is difficult at this point. What seems certain to continue as a major theoretical concept is the idea of an imaginal storage or representation (or the closely related idea of strong and effective sensory representation), and a separate verbal-conceptual one.

This chapter closes with a consideration of some additional unresolved problems and questions for picture memory research. One arises out of current understanding and interpretation of levels of processing effects on pictures. It is clear that the most direct and effective way of eliminating the picture-word difference in recall and recognition is to require semantic processing of concrete words; this will produce performance levels comparable to those obtained with pictures that are processed the same way. Some demonstrations of this effect have been interpreted as squarely supporting dual-code theory, as in Paivio and Csapo's experiments with imaging to words. But the same effects can be produced by a task requiring rating of pleasantness (Paivio, 1975) or semantic appropriateness (D'Agostino et al., 1977). Such effects may be interpreted in terms of uncontrolled dual coding (i.e., image generation during the semantic processing), but a depth interpretation may be possible as well, particularly if verbal and pictorial materials involve different rates or sequences of access to their permanent codes. Accordingly, it would be of interest to determine the effects on recall of concrete words (or pictures) of an orienting task that involved a semantic or relatively "deep" level of processing but that at the same time did not allow activation of a sensory or pictorial code.

Another problem area for picture memory research concerns what might be called the "grain" of picture memory or visual memory in general. As Shepard (1967) pointed out, we routinely store information about the visual environment, and (at least introspectively) this information is visual in some sense. Shepard's example of counting the number of windows in a room from memory can be multiplied endlessly, so that we can state, if asked, what color the brand name Kellog's is printed in on a box of cereal, or whether Harry Truman wore glasses, or which way the *Mona Lisa* figure is turned.

These questions (and their answers) may not be examples of the really critical stuff of mental life, but they do illustrate the operation and utility of a memorial and cognitive system with an amazing capacity.

The problem of the grain and capacity of picture memory or visual memory is raised by the sort of counter-example reported by Nickerson and Adams (1979), in which they found that memory for the physical details of a very commonly encountered object (a penny) was very poor. Although spectacular "failures" of visual memory such as these have sometimes led to the conclusion that memory is really abstractive in nature, demonstrations of the actual preservation of specific information cannot be disregarded. The real problem is to identify those encoding dimensions and conditions that do or do not give rise to lasting information about scenes, events, and objects. Studies of the separable dimensions of pictorial displays (Mandler & Parker, 1976; Pezdeck & Evans, 1979) that are well or poorly retained (object presence and location; orientation; etc.) are examples of this kind of work.

Finally, there might also be a broadening of picture-memory research to include the encoding and preservation of information about the visual environment that is not "pictorial" in the usual sense. Rothhopf's (1971) demonstration of incidental memory for locational and spatial information in a text is a case in point. The extent and in particular the functional significance of this kind of information is poorly understood. A similar observation can be made about reports of the retention of information such as the type face or case of printed words (Kirsner, 1973). The idea that such information is not stored (or decays very rapidly) seems incorrect.

When Von Neuman (1958) dealt with the problem of estimating the capacity of the human central nervous system, his estimates appear to have been greatly influenced by what he saw as the very high rate of processing of visual information. His estimates were extremely high ones, certainly relative to the computing machines of that time. The visual-analyzing and recognition capacity of the brain are far from being realized in modern devices, and one stumbling block (in addition to problems of matching human receptor capacities) is simply the amount of memory required to store the information needed to reproduce visual inputs. Presumably much less memory would be required to have a machine perform Standing's 10,000-picture yes–no recognition task (because only certain features might have to be stored), but even this may be beyond any practical machine memory at this point in time. Clearly, an understanding of picture memory and the means by which we acquire and maintain information about the visual environment is an experimental, theoretical, and technological challenge.

REFERENCES

Anderson, R. E. Short-term retention of the where and when of pictures and words. *Journal of Experimental Psychology: General*, 1976, *105*, 378–402.

Anderson, J. R., & Bower, G. H. *Human associative memory*. Washington, D.C.: Winston, 1973.

Anderson, J. R., & Paulson, R. Interference in memory for pictorial information. *Cognitive Psychology*, 1978, *10*, 178–202.

Bahrick, H. P., & Boucher, P. Retention of visual and verbal codes of the same stimuli. *Journal of Experimental Psychology*, 1968 *78*, 417–422.

Bartlett, J. C., Till, R. E., & Levy, J. C. Retrieval characteristics of complex pictures: Effects of verbal encoding. *Journal of Verbal Learning and Verbal Behavior*, 1980, *4*, 430–449.

Bevan, W., & Steger, J. Free recall and abstractness of stimuli. *Science*, 1971, *172*, 597–599.

Borges, M. A., Stepnowsky, M. A., & Holt, L. H. Recall and recognition of words and pictures by adults and children. *Bulletin of the Psychonomic Society*, 1977, *9*, 113–114.

Bousfield, W. A., Esterson, J., & Whitmarsh, G. A. The effects of concomitant colored and uncolored pictorial representations on the learning of stimulus words. *Journal of Applied Psychology*, 1957, *41*, 165–168.

Bower, G. H., Karlin, M. B., & Dueck, A. Comprehension and memory for pictures. *Memory & Cognition*, 1975, *3*, 216–220.

Calkins, M. W. Short studies in memory and association from the Wellesley College laboratory. *Psychological Review*, 1898, *5*, 451–462.

Cooper, L. A., & Shepard, R. N. Chronometric studies of the rotation of mental imagaes. In W. G. Chase (Ed.), *Visual information processing*. New York: Academic Press, 1973.

Craik, F. I. M., & Lockhart, R. S. Levels of processing: A framework for memory research. *Journal of Verbal Learning and Verbal Behavior*, 1972, *11*, 671-684.

D'Agostino, P. R., O'Neill, B. J., & Paivio, A. Memory for pictures and words as a function of level of processing: Depth or dual coding? *Memory & Cognition*, 1977, *5*, 252-256.

Dhawan, M., & Pellegrino, J. W. Acoustic and semantic interference effects in words and pictures. *Memory & Cognition*, 1977, *5*, 340-346.

Durso, F. T., & Johnson, M. K. The effects of orienting tasks on recognition, recall, and modality confusion of pictures and words. *Journal of Verbal Learning and Verbal Behavior*, 1980, *19*, 416-429.

Goldstein, A. G., & Chance, J. E. Visual recognition memory for complex configurations. *Perception and Psychophysics*, 1970, *9*, 237-241.

Intraub, H. Presentation rate and the representation of briefly glimpsed pictures in memory. *Journal of Experimental Psychology: Human Learning and Memory*, 1980, *6*, 1-12.

Jenkins, J., Neale, D., & Deno, S. Differential memory for picture and word stimuli. *Journal of Educational Psychology*, 1967, *58*, 303-307.

Kirkpatrick, E. A. An experimental study of memory. *Psychological Review*, 1894, *1*, 602-609.

Kirsner, D. An analysis of the visual component in recognition memory for verbal stimuli. *Memory & Cognition*, 1973, *1*, 449-453.

Koestler, A. Abstract and picture strip. In G. A. Talland & N. C. Waugh (Eds.), *The pathology of memory*. New York: Academic Press, 1969.

Kunen, S., Green, D., & Waterman, D. Spread of encoding effects within the nonverbal domain. *Journal of Experimental Psychology: Human Learning and Memory*, 1979, *5*, 574-584.

Loftus, E. F. Shifting human color memory. *Memory & Cognition*, 1977, *5*, 696-699.

Loftus, G. R. Eye fixations and recognition memory. *Cognitive Psychology*, 1972, *3*, 525-551.

McGeoch, J. A. *The psychology of human learning*. New York: Longmans, Green, 1942.

Madigan, S., & Hamovitch, M. Image generation in picture recognition. *Candian Journal of Psychology*, 1976, *30*, 55-62.

Madigan, S., & Lawrence, V. Factors affecting item recovery and reminiscence in free recall. *American Journal of Psychology*, 1980, *93*, 489-504.

Madigan, S., McCabe, L., & Itatani, E. Immediate and delayed recall of words and pictures. *Canadian Journal of Psychology*, 1972, *26*, 407-414.

Mandler, J. M., & Parker, R. E. Memory for descriptive and spatial information in complex pictures. *Journal of Experimental Psychology: Human Learning and Memory*, 1976, *2*, 38-48.

Nelson, D. L. Remembering pictures and words: Appearance, significance, and name. In L. S. Cermak & F. I. M. Craik (Eds.), *Levels of processing in human memory*. Hillsdale, N.J.: Lawrence Erlbaum Assoc., 1979.

Nelson, D. L., Reed,U. S., & McEvoy, C. L. Learning to order pictures and words: A model of sensory and semantic encoding. *Journal of Experimental Psychology: Human Learning and Memory*, 1977, *3*, 485-497.

Nelson, D. L., Reed, U.S., & Walling, J. R. Picture superiority effect. *Journal of Experimental Psychology: Human Learning and and Memory*, 1976, *2*, 523-528.

Nelson, D. L., Walling, J. R., & McEvoy, C. L. Doubts about depth. *Journal of Experimental Psychology: Human Learning and Memory*, 1979, *4*, 24-44.

Nelson, T. O., Metzler, J., & Reed, D. Role of details in the long-term recognition of pictures and verbal descriptions. *Journal of Experimental Psychology*, 1974, *102*, 184-186.

Nickerson, R. S. Short-term memory for complex meaningful visual configurations: A demonstration of capacity. *Canadian Journal of Psychology*, 1965, *19*, 155-160.

Nickerson, R. S., & Adams, M. J. Long-term memory for a common object. *Cognitive Psychology*, 1979, *11*, 287-307.

Noton, D., & Stark, L. Scan paths in eye movements during pattern perception. *Science*, 1971, *171*, 308–311.

Paivio, A. *Imagery and verbal processes*. New York: Holt, Rinehart, & Winston, 1971.

Paivio, A. Coding distinctions and repetition effects in memory. In G. H. Bower (Ed.), *The psychology of learning and motivation*. Vol. 9. New York: Academic Press, 1975.

Paivio, A. Imagery in recall and recognition. In J. Brown (Ed.), *Recall and recognition*. New York: John Wiley, 1976.

Paivio, A., & Csapo, K. Short-term sequential memory for words and pictures. *Psychonomic Science*, 1971, *24*, 50–51.

Paivio, A., & Csapo, K. Picture superiority in free recall: Imagery or dual coding? *Cognitive Psychology*, 1973, *5*, 176–206.

Paivio, A., & Lambert, W. Dual coding and bilingual memory. *Journal of Verbal Learning and Verbal Behavior*, 1981, *20*, 532–539.

Paivio, A., & Yarmey, A. D. Pictures *versus* words as stimuli and responses in paired-associates learning. *Psychonomic Science*, 1966, *5*, 235–236.

Paivio, A., Rogers, T. B., & Smythe, P. C. Why are pictures easier to recall than words? *Psychonomic Science*, 1968, *11*, 137–138.

Pellegrino, J. W., Siegel, A. W., & Dhawan, M. Differential distraction effects in short-term and long-term retention of pictures and words. *Journal of Experimental Psychology: Human Learning and Memory*, 1976, *2*, 541–547.

Pezdek, K., & Evans, G. W. Visual and verbal memory for objects and their spatial locations. *Journal of Experimental Psychology: Human Learning and Memory*, 1979, *5*, 360–373.

Postman, L. Verbal learning and memory. *Annual Review of Psychology*, 1975, *26*, 291–335.

Postman, L. Picture-word differences in the acquisition and retention of paired associates. *Journal of Experimental Psychology: Human Learning and Memory*, 1978, *4*, 146–157.

Potter, M. C., & Faulconer, B. A. Time to understand pictures and words. *Nature*, 1975, *253*, 437–438.

Pylyshyn, Z. W. What the mind's eye tells the mind's brain: A critique of mental imagery. *Psychological Bulletin*, 1973, *80*, 1–24.

Rabinowitz, J. C., Mandler, G., & Barsalou, L. W. Generation-recognition as an auxilary retrieval strategy. *Journal of Verbal Learning and Verbal Behavior*, 1979, *18*, 57–72.

Rafnel, K. J., & Klatzky, R. L. Meaningful interpretation effects on codes of nonsense pictures. *Journal of Experimental Psychology: Human Learning and Memory*, 1978, *4*, 631–646.

Rothhopf, E. Incidental memory for location of information in text. *Journal of Verbal Learning and Verbal Behavior*, 1971, *10*, 608–613.

Scarborough, D. L., Gerard, L., & Cortese, C. Accessing lexical memory: The transfer of word repetition effects across task and modality. *Memory & Cognition*, 1979, *7*, 3–12.

Schiano, D. J., & Watkins, M. J. Speech-like coding of pictures in short-term memory. *Memory & Cognition*, 181, *9*, 110–114.

Shepard, R. N. Recognition memory for words, sentences, and pictures. *Journal of Verbal Learning and Verbal Behavior*, 1967, *6*, 156–163.

Smith, M. C., & Magee, L. E. Tracing the time course of picture-word processing. *Journal of Experimental Psychology: General*. 1980, *109*, 373–392.

Snodgrass, J. G., Burns, P. M., & Pirone, G. V. Pictures and words in time and space: In search of the elusive interaction. *Journal of Experimental Psychology*, 1978, *107*, 206–230.

Snodgrass, J. G., & McClure, P. Storage and retrieval properties of dual codes for pictures and words in recognition memory. *Journal of Experimental Psychology: Human Learning and Memory*, 1975, *1*, 521–529.

Standing, L. Learning 10,000 pictures. *Quarterly Journal of Experimental Psychology*, 1973, *25*, 207–222.

Standing, L., Bond, B., Hall, J., & Weller, J. A bibliography of picture-memory studies. *Psychonomic Science*, 1972, *29*, 406–416.

Standing, L., Conezio, J., & Haber, R. Perception and memory for pictures: Single-trial learning of 2500 visual stimuli. *Psychonomic Science,* 1970, *19,* 73–74.

Stopher, K., & Kirsner, K. Long-term memory for pictures and sentences. *Memory & Cognition, 1981, 9,* 34–40.

Ternes, W., & Yuille, J. C. Words and pictures in an STM task. *Journal of Experimental Psychology,* 1972, *96,* 78–86.

Tulving, E. Ecphoric processes in recall and recognition. In J. Brown (Ed.), *Recall and recognition.* New York: Wiley, 1976.

Tversky, B., & Sherman, T. Picture memory improves with longer on time and off time. *Journal of Experimental Psychology,* 1975, *104,* 114–118.

Von Neuman, J. *The computer and the brain.* New Haven: Yale University Press, 1958.

Watkins, M. J., & Graefe, T. M. Delayed rehearsal of pictures. *Journal of Verbal Learning and Verbal Behavior,* 1981, *20,* 532–539.

Weaver, G. E. Effects of postimulus study time on recognition of pictures. *Journal of Experimental Psychology,* 1974, *103,* 799–801.

Wells, J. E. Encoding and memory for verbal and pictorial stimuli. *Quarterly Journal of Experimental Psychology,* 1972, *24,* 242–252.

Wyant, S., Banks, W. P., Berger, D., & Wright, P. W. Verbal and pictorial similariy in recognition of pictures. *Perception and Psychophysics,* 1972, *12,* 151–153.

4 Imagery Instructions and the Organization of Memory

Ian Begg
McMaster University

The intent of this chapter is to raise several questions about the memorial consequences of imagery instructions. The main point is that imagery instructions affect the manner in which material is mentally organized. That is, the instructions directly influence encoding operations, and thereby determine the traces that reside in the memory system. Because any organization of traces is more useful for some retrieval demands than others, imagery instructions will benefit memory performance in some circumstances more than others. It is even the case, as I shall demonstrate shortly, that imagery instructions can hurt memory performance. The message is, therefore, not that imagery *helps* memory, but rather that imagery *influences* the memory system.

Let me dwell for a moment on this latter point. We have all observed the rise of imagery from being mentalistic baggage to being a reluctantly accepted factor in memory. In some cases, unfortunately, imagery has become a mindless catch-all. The message being sent by Allan Paivio and other serious researchers was that imagery is an important memory process that demands the attention of memory theories. The message being received was all too often "see how imagery helps memory." The late Wayne Bartz once asked me, in jest, whether anyone had yet done an experiment to see whether imagery works in the bathroom. We can see the same type of failure to understand in the memory literature. That literature contains studies in which some imaginal manipulation had no effect on memory performance, with conclusions that the findings pose difficulties for some magical entity called "imagery theory."

Let us ritually purge ourselves of the ridiculous notion that imagery helps memory. Imagery is an encoding process that has important consequences for the memory system. The challenge for imagery theories is to describe the manner in which imagery affects the memory system, and to tell us how those effects map into measures of memory performance. Quite simply, we need an encoding theory on the one hand, and a retrieval theory on the other. Although the two theories are separate, it is necessarily the case that performance will reflect an interaction between the two. A given retrieval demand can be accomplished more readily with some arrangements of memory information than others, and a given memory arrangement is more useful for some retrieval demands than others. Consequently, a good encoding theory tells us the ranges of retrieval demands for which its structures are useful, and a good retrieval theory tells us how the information to be retrieved should be structured for efficient use. Later on, I shall present an encoding theory and a retrieval theory that address imagery as a memory process. First, however, let us review a concrete metaphor in order to illustrate some key concepts and principles.

A Useful Metaphor

My favorite conceptual peg from which to approach memory systems is the telephone book, not because I think human memory is like such a book, but rather because the book is such a familiar and clear case of information storage, and use of the book is such an obvious example of information retrieval. Let us bask for a moment in the rare luxury of having a visible memory system, rather than the hypothetical and inferential system possessed by humans, and consider the book from the perspective of memory-theoretic terms. First, consider the informational structure of the book's memory system. The basic structural unit, or trace, has three constituent members, a name, an address, and a telephone number. The members are *horizontally* organized within their own trace. The consequence of this horizontal organization is that once the trace is accessed by any means, each member of the trace is available for use. In other words, the major value of horizontal organization of members into traces is only evident after the trace has been located. Although there are many different ways the traces in a telephone book could be organized, the must general structure is to array the traces serially, with the names in alphabetical order. That is, there is a *vertical* organization from trace to trace. Note that this vertical organization by names does not mean that the associated addresses are ordered nonrandomly, nor that the numbers are ordered in any systematic way. In short, factors that determine vertical organization of traces have absolutely nothing to do with factors that determine horizontal organization of members within those traces.

Second, let us consider the use of a directory, again in memory-theoretic terms. The typical use is that we have a name and wish to know its number. This use has two distinct stages. First, the trace must be located. Second, the unknown member of the located trace must be accessed. In short, we have here an act of cued recall. In locating a typed name that corresponds to a mental name cue, the retrieval strategy is a successively narrowing, serial, self-terminating search. Thus we begin with the correct directory, locate the municipality within that directory, flip through for the right general location, locate the page, find the name, and check initials and address if necessary. The location process might be difficult if there is a long directory, or if we are unsure of the municipality within the book, or if the name is a common one, but, regardless of the events during contact, once the correct trace has been found the number is right there waiting. That is, the second stage, trace use, cannot be enjoined without successful completion of the first stage, trace contact. Thus use is completely dependent on contact. However, in another sense the stages are independent, because the factors that determine the ease of locating the trace are completely unrelated to what else the trace contains beyond the member corresponding to the cue.

Let us now pull together some of the storage and retrieval principles that characterize a telephone book. I shall, of course, stress the ones that I believe are most important for the purpose at hand and will, in later sections, specify their pertinence more precisely. There are several properties that pertain to *trace organization*. The entire system can be described as having some number of traces, each of which has three members, and further, the traces are organized with respect to each other. The system could be organized in other ways either by changing the number of members in each trace, or by changing the basis of trace-to-trace organization. Trace organization thus refers to the number of traces in the system, and their size—the number of members in each trace—as well as to the higher-order organization from trace to trace. The metaphor also makes it apparent that, at least in principle, organization from trace to trace is unrelated to and independent of organization from member to member within traces, and further that trace-to-trace organization on the basis of some members does not imply the existence of trace-to-trace organization on the basis of other trace members.

The metaphor also illustrates some important principles of information retrieval. Most important, retrieval entails two successive stages, namely trace contact and trace use. Trace use is entirely dependent on trace contact, since the trace cannot be used unless it is contacted. However, other than that particular sequential dependency, trace contact and use are independent concepts. Trace contact depends on factors that are unrelated to the factors that provide organization among members within the traces. Further, the utility of a target trace does not affect the ease or likelihood that a cue will contact that trace, nor does the ease of access in any way tell us whether the contacted trace contains members other than the one contacted by the cue.

From the metaphor, we thus discover that a memory system for retaining single members contains some number of traces, each contining some number of members. Independent of the number of traces and their size, traces can be organized with respect to each other. Retrieval of the retained members requires that appropriate traces be contacted, and that the contacted traces provide information about other members. Contact depends on the number of traces, their trace-to-trace organization, and the adequacy of cue information to discriminate among traces on the basis of matching the cue to some retained member. In turn, trace use depends on the presence of other members of the contacted trace, beyond the member contacted by the cue. Let us now abandon the telephone book as a metaphor, but let us bear in mind the principles of information storage and retrieval in the ensuing discussion.

Imagery Instructions

To begin with, the contrast of interest is between two types of imagery instructions. One condition, known as joint, relational, or interactive imagery, has subjects instructed to image members interacting together. For instance, form an image in which the referents for *railroad* and *mother* are interacting in some way. The other condition, separate imagery, has subjects form a separate image for each member. Thus look left and image a *railroad,* then look right and image a *mother.* If proper care is taken, these conditions differ in one and only one way, namely that the relational condition has two members in each trace, but the separate condition has one member in each trace. At least at the time of study, the two do not differ in the number of *members* encoded, nor in the trace-to-trace organization.

In terms of encoding, relational imagery results in the formation of fewer but larger traces than does separate imagery. However, the two conditions require retention of the same number of members—the list words. The consequence of this organization for retrieval is that joint imagery will excell in tasks in which *member-to-member organization* within traces is crucial, that the two will be equivalent in tasks that depend on the *number of members* retained, and that separate conditions will excell in tasks that depend on the *number of traces* retained. At this point, three tasks—cued recall, item recognition, and free recall—are reviewed briefly. The point of the review is to indicate that the basic principles of information storage and retrieval are reasonably well demonstrated in the tasks, and to suggest factors that might perturb the operation of the principles. These factors will then be addressed further by several experiments that are presented in moderate detail.

Cued Recall

Cued recall is an experimental procedure in which one member of a studied pair (or larger set) is presented as a cue for the subject to recall the other member of the pair, called the associate of that cue. Just as a telephone number cannot be retrieved with the name cue unless the number is actually encoded with the name, so a to-be-remembered item cannot be recalled with a list cue unless the cue and its associate were jointly encoded during study (cf., Tulving & Thomson, 1973). Consequently, interactive imagery should lead to much better cued-recall performance than separate imagery. Gordon Bower (1970) first demonstrated a recall advantage for relational imagery, whether or not recall is conditionalized on cue recognition.

Since Bower's (1970) demonstration, the advantage for relational imagery in cued recall has been obtained by other researchers with adults (e.g., Begg, 1973, 1978) and children (e.g., Begg & Anderson, 1976; Begg & Young, 1977; Dempster & Rohwer, 1974), and has been generalized to a variety of other contexts. For example, the advantage obtains, and is large, even if the cued-recall test is a surprise test after three prior free-recall tests (.64 vs. .19; Begg, 1978, Experiment 2). Likewise, the advantage obtains if the cued-recall test follows a recognition test, and only items correctly recognized are scored in recall (.66 vs. .11; Begg, 1978, Experiment 1). The point is that we are dealing with a large and robust effect.

Although the effect is large and robust, cued recall does measure the outcome of both trace contact and trace use. The reviewed studies do show that the effect in recall can be obtained with contact controlled, but there is still the possibility that the size of the advantage may be attenuated because of factors influencing contact. For example, Winograd and Lynn (1979) have argued that, in many studies, separate imagery conditions require the subjects to reuse the same mental context for each studied item, while relational conditions suggest different contexts. In one experiment, they showed that a standard relational condition markedly exceeded a separate condition with a shared context (.61 vs. .10), but that a separate condition with a unique context for each pair showed an improved level of performance (.45). In a second experiment, subjects in both the relational and separate conditions were presented with unique or shared contexts. With a shared context, the advantage for interaction was large (.51 vs. .10), but, with unique contexts for both, the advantage was tiny (.64 vs. .60). For now, the point is that there are indeed ways to attenuate the advantage for interaction in cued recall. This point, and Winograd's and Lynn's arguments, will be considered again later, following a discussion of item recognition.

Item Recognition

Item recognition is perhaps the simplest memory test of all. Following study, subjects are asked to indicate whether test items were or were not present in the study list. In theoretical terms, recognition succeeds if the test item contacts the trace in which the same nominal item was encoded during study. The principles discussed earlier lead us to expect that contact depends on the number of *members* retained, not the number of traces, or whether or not the retained member has other members in its trace. The same assumption on the independence of item information and relational information has been made and supported by several investigators in different areas of memory research (e.g., Einstein & Hunt, 1980; Humphreys, 1978).

The question here is whether members encoded jointly or separately are differentially recognizable. In general, the two are not associated with differences in recognition (Begg, 1978, Experiment 1; Bower, 1970; Dempster &

Rohwer, 1974). That is, the mere fact of joint as opposed to separate encoding is not sufficient to produce differences in recognition. However, joint and separate encoding may differ in ways other than that mere fact, and some of these ways may influence recognition. Let us briefly consider ways in which joint storage could help and hinder recognition for individual items.

At first blush, the general expectation is, for most people, that interaction will help recognition. I think the reason for this expectation is the implicit notion that the memory system can only retain a certain amount of information, and, since interaction reduces the number of traces to be retained, it should be less likely to exceed that limit. Let me make a few comments about this implicit notion. In the first place, it is not clear that storing *railroad–mother* as one image does reduce the number of bits of information necessary to distinguish the members from other members in the list, as opposed to two images. It may well be the case that imaging *white* and *horse* together reduces storage requirements, because horses have some color anyway (Begg, 1972). It may also be the case that concrete items require less capacity to retain than abstract items (Begg, 1973) because they are more distinct from each other to begin with (Begg, Upfold, & Wilton, 1978). However, such concerns do not apply to joint images of two unrelated, arbitrarily paired referents. In the second place, even if there is a limit to memory, and even if that limit does pertain to the number of traces, most memory experiments only require retention of a few items, rarely more than 100, so that there is a good possibility that the limit is not reached. And finally, there is simply no evidence that joint imagery ever exceeds separate imagery in recognition memory for the words included in those images.

Once the first blush has faded, the most likely possibility seems to be quite the opposite, namely that interaction will hurt recognition—not because of the fact of interaction, but rather because making unrelated referents interact may perturb those referents enough to reduce their recognizability. After all, imaging a *mother* interacting with a *railroad* may require a sufficient liberalization of motherhood so that the resultant image would not allow access by *mother* presented alone. Indeed, Baker and Santa (1977a, b) have found reduced recognition for items processed intergratively. For that matter, Begg (1979, Experiment 3) has also found reduced recognition for jointly processed items rather than separately processed items. More recently, McGee (1980) has replicated those results, and has argued that it is the general case that interaction reduces item recognition. However, McGee is wrong. The fact of interaction is not sufficient to reduce recognition, nor is it easy to demonstrate reduced recognition, as we shall see shortly, following a brief discussion of free recall.

Free Recall

Free recall is a procedure in which people simply report, in any order, the items just studied. People are not, however, as free as they could be, because they tend to recall related items together. The recall protocol can be scored in terms of the number of studied sets represented in recall by at least one item, and the average number of items recalled for each of those sets; the product of these two numbers is, of course, the total number of words recalled. Based on the principles we have been considering, the number of chunks in recall should be related to the number of traces in memory, and the length of those chunks should be related to the size of the traces. Simply put, items remembered as a few large traces should appear in a few long chunks, whereas items remembered as many small traces should appear as many short chunks (cf., Martin, Fleming, Hennrikus & Erickson, 1977). Thus interaction should exceed separation in measures of the organization of recall, but should fall short of separation in measures of the number of chunks recalled. Since total recall is the product of the two, we should not expect any systematic difference between the two conditions.

Although, as was true with recognition, the first hasty expectation is for interaction to exceed separation in total recall, generally the two do not differ (Begg, 1973, 1978; Hasher, Riebman & Wren, 1976; Janssen, 1976). Further, with analyses as described in the preceding paragraph, interaction does exceed separation in member-to-member organization within remembered sets, and separation does exceed interaction in the number of sets present in recall (Begg, 1978). Once more, the basic principles seem to be quite sound.

One of the experiments reported by Begg (1978, Experiment 4) merits closer attention. The basic procedure for the experiment was that subjects imaged sets of three nouns either by forming a single image for each triplet, or by forming a single image for each word. In a standard condition, interaction exceeded separation in the organization of recall, separation exceeded interaction in the number of triplets for which at least one member was recalled, and the two did not differ reliably in the total number of words recalled. In a second condition, subjects learned a mnemonic that provided a trace-to-trace organization. Specifically, imaging the members of one triplet was done at the numeral 1 on a clock, the next triplet at the numeral 2, and so on. The effect of this mnemonic was to equate the interactive and separate conditions in the number of sets recalled, just as the cued-recall procedure does, thereby enabling the larger interactive units to produce higher levels of recall.

A further consequence of the mnemonic was to reduce the difference between interaction and separate conditions in the organization of recall. Why should this be so? In a standard condition, separately imaged members have no organizational sharing, whereas interactively imaged members are organized with regard to each other. In the mnemonic condition, however, the separately imaged items are indirectly associated with each other since each is specifically associated with the same context—the numeral. This is precisely the possibility raised and investigated by Winograd and Lynn (1979). Separately imaged items may show associative recall without being associated with each other, but rather if each is associated with some other information such as context. Consequently, it should be possible to attenuate the difference between conditions in cued recall. However, we should bear in mind that such attenuation does not mean that interaction doesn't "work" in the experiment; after all, no one has yet said that interactive processing is the only way for items to become associated.

Some Further Investigations

The preceding sections present a clear case and good evidence for the view that imagery is an encoding process that effectively determines the organization of the memory system following study, and accordingly tells where imagery will help, hurt, or be irrelevant to measures of memory performance. However, the book isn't closed yet, since much is unknown, and since some questions raised in the preceding sections await good answers. The point of the experiments to be described is as much to illustrate the lines those answers might require as it is to answer the questions. Let us therefore proceed to a number of experiments concerning recall and recognition. Various issues will be raised in the course of presentation.

Experiment 1: Additivity

The first experiment to be reported is described in more detail elsewhere (Begg, 1979, Experiment 3). However, enough detail will be described for present purposes, and some features of the data not included in the earlier report will be outlined. The basic procedure was to have subjects study pairs of concrete nouns, followed by a yes-no recognition test for single words from the pairs, followed in turn by a cued-recall test. For half the pairs, the recognition target was the same item that was used as the cue in recall, and for the other half, the target was the to-be-recalled member of the pair. The concern is thus with recognition as a measure of trace contact, and recall as a measure of trace use; only the unconditional recall data will be addressed here, since conditionalized data told the same story.

The members of each pair appeared on a television monitor side by side for 10 sec during which the subjects processed the items separately or interactively. In phase 1 of study, 52 pairs were presented. Subjects either produced a separate verbal associate for each word, or a single associate to link each pair. In phase 2, there were again 52 pairs; 26 were new, and 26 were pairs studied in phase 1. In this phase, subjects either formed a separate image for each word, or an interactive image for each pair. In sum, there were thus pairs studied once separately, pairs studied once interactively, pairs studied twice by two different separate processing tasks, pairs studied twice by two different interactive tasks, and pairs studied twice, once separately and once interactively.

The question of interest is whether two study occasions contribute independently to memory. The basic rationale is outlined in detail by Paivio (1975). Suppose a particular study method is effective enough that half the items in a list are remembered. If a second study with the same method occurred, what would happen? At one extreme, suppose the method had already worked on all the items for which it was appropriate; in this case, further study would be useless, and performance would remain at .50. Another possibility is independent contribution. That is, if half the items were learned on one occasion, then half the remainder should be learned on a second occasion. In other words, .75 should be remembered. Thus there are two benchmarks in interpreting performance.

What does it mean if performance after two study trials is no better than performance after one? Basically, the meaning is that the second study is useless. Not surprisingly, this outcome is rare—trials do have effects. However, the range between no improvement and independent contribution shows declining degrees of uselessness. At independence, the procedure used in study is just as effective for items not learned on the first trial as it was on the first trial for items learned on that trial. To the extent that the second study trial is redundant with the first, we should expect performance to fall short of independence, declining to the level of once-studied items as redundancy increases.

An interesting question concerns cases in which twice-studied items show greater levels of performance than one would expect from independence. What this means is that items not learned on the first occasion were nonetheless affected on that occasion, effectively preparing them so that the second study is particularly effective. This cannot occur unless the second study is accomplished by referring to the results of the first. Simply put, if performance exceeds independence, we have *prima facie* evidence of trace interaction in memory. Performance cannot exceed independence if each study simply lays down an independent trace—the traces must, rather, have some cross talk.

Let us now consider the results of the experiment. First, the patterns of observed results will be discussed, then the questions of independence will be raised. The results appear in Fig. 4.1. The left-hand panel of the figure shows recognition hit rates and cued-recall proportions for items studied once, averaged over the verbal and imaginal procedures. Note that joint processing reduced item recognition but increased recall relative to separate processing. Thus there is indeed evidence that joint processing can reduce the individual identity of single items, although, as we saw earlier, joint processing is not sufficient for such reduction; this question will be addressed in later experiments. The point for now is that joint processing enhances cued recall even in cases in which recognition, hence access with the joint traces, is reduced.

The three right-hand panels show performance for twice-studied items, compared to the level of performance that would obtain if the two study occasions contributed independently to retention. First, note the recognition performance. Recognition is best with two separate studies, worst with two joint studies, and just about in the middle for items studied once separately and once jointly. Quite clearly, recognition for twice-studied items is better than for once-studied items. Equally clearly, recognition is about at the level expected by independence.

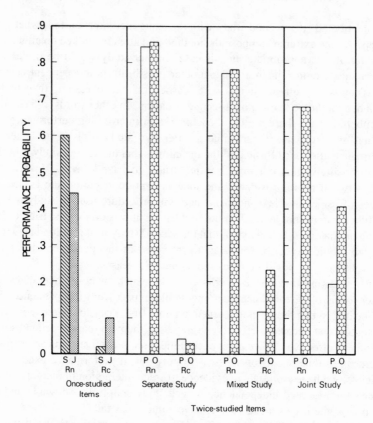

FIG. 4.1.   Cured recall (Rc) and recognition (Rn) of items studied separately (S) or jointly (J) on a single study trial, compared to memory for items studied twice by either procedure or once by each. For twice-studied items, performance observed (O) is compared to the level predicted (P) by assuming independent contributions of the two study trials. (Calculated from Begg, 1979, p. 121).

Apparently, then, studying items a second time either separately or jointly is just as effective for learning items missed after one study occasion as either procedure is for learning in the first place. There is no indication that the first study occasion in any way prepares the items for the second. Thus, with regard to recognition, we have evidence that joint processing can reduce an item's individuality, and that whatever aspects of processing render an item recognizeable seem to do so independently over study occasions. Thus one separate study makes about .60 of the items recognizeable, and a second separate study makes about .60 of the remainder recognizeable; one joint study makes about .44 of the items recognizeable, and a second joint study adds .44 of the remainder.

The picture is quite different with cued recall. Recall was best for pairs studied twice jointly, worst for pairs studied twice separately, and about in the middle for pairs studied once by each procedure. Twice-studied items were far above once-studied items for the pairs studied jointly on either one or two trials, but items studied twice separately are very close to the floor on all measures. There is no evidence that adding a second separate study improves performance at all, let alone improving it beyond independence. However, if either study trial was joint, two study occasions show performance well in excess of independence. Apparently, any of the meaningful processes considered in this study prepare items so that a second processing occasion has fertile ground to work with. There is indeed strong evidence for trace interaction in memory from occasion to occasion.

In sum, what do we know now, and what else remains to be learned? It certainly appears that whatever factors are responsible for trace contact are independent of the factors that bind members into a single trace. Joint processing does not mean that items will lose their individual identity, but there are at least some cases in which such loss occurs (Baker & Santa, 1977a, b; McGee, 1980). It is not yet clear under what conditions such a detrimental effect on recognition will occur. On the other hand, joint processing does enhance cued recall even if it hurts recognition in the same task; this is indeed a robust effect.

It also appears that trace contact, as assessed by recognition, accrues over study occasions independently; the effectiveness of a second study trial is no more or less for already studied items that were unlearned than for new items. However, trace utility, as indexed by the association between items, is especially enhanced if at least one study occasion is directed at ways the items can interact with each other. Again, trace contact is subject to influences, trace utility is subject to influences, and neither set of influences is causally related to the other. The whole question of independent, additive contributions of different processing tasks is a fertile area for investigation, the surface of which has barely been scratched.

Experiment 2: Degrees of Togetherness

The second experiment to be described, like the first, asks whether the factors that influence trace contact are independent of the factors that influence the utility of contacted traces. Additionally, however, the question is raised regarding whether interaction and separation are two distinct categories with nothing in between. The work of Winograd and Lynn (1979) and of Begg (1978, Experiment 4) shows that separately imaged items can show associative performance at improved levels if each of the separately imaged items is associated with some common mediator, even if they aren't directly associated with each other. However, those investigations did not assess recognition for individual items.

The present experiment was a simple one, with three groups of subjects who studied 60 pairs of concrete nouns, presented for 5 sec for each word of the pair on videotape. One group of subjects imaged each pair jointly, imagining a picture frame above the monitor. Another group performed the usual separation procedure, imaging the first member of the pair, that appeared alone on the left side of the screen, in a frame to the left of the monitor, then imaging the second member to the right of the monitor. The third group was a mix. The subjects imaged both pair members in a single image above the monitor, as in the joint procedure, but kept the objects in the image separate from each other, as in the separation procedure.

Following study, there was a recognition test then a recall test. For half the pairs, the member tested in recognition was later presented as the recall cue, and for the other half, the recognition target was the item that was to be recalled in the

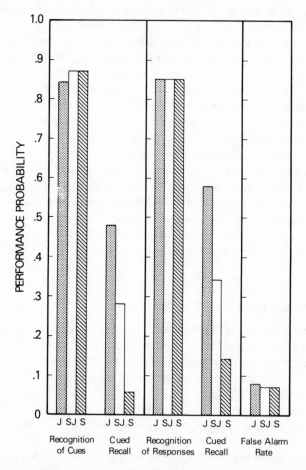

FIG. 4.2.   Measures of recall and recognition for pairs studied by joint imagery (J), separate imagery (S), or a combination (SJ).

second task. Thus the procedure was simple. So were the results, as shown in Fig. 4.2. In recognition, it made absolutely no difference which pair member was tested, nor which study procedure was used. Here, then, is another case in which the processing tasks produce equivalent recognition performance.

In marked contrast, look at the recall probabilities. Two things are evident. First, recall was somewhat better for pairs if the to-be-remembered item was presented earlier as a recognition target than if the cue was the target, $F(1,51) = 16.3$. This finding was also present in the previous experiment (see Begg, 1979), so apparently the recognition test does afford another study occasion for to-be-recalled items (see also Broadbent & Broadbent, 1977). However, and more importantly, the three different study procedures differed markedly from each other, $F(2,51) = 33.7$. Thus, having a common image as context for the items, even if they do not interact in that image, provides enough mediating information for one member to contact the other in many more cases than with separate images, but not in as many cases as with interactive representation.

Once again, we can see strong influences on recall by factors that have no bearing on recognition. Recognition itself, however, may enhance later recall because it does give one more opportunity to study the item in question. Interaction and separation are not always qualitatively different encoding events, because the separation procedure yields better recall if the separately imaged items share an imaginal context than if they do not, but even having a shared context does not bring recall up to the level of joint imagery.

Thus the experiment gives answers. However, it also raises a question. Why does interaction sometimes hurt recognition and sometimes have no effect? Although the later experiments will also address this question, let me anticipate by saying I don't have a good answer, although I do know some possible factors that aren't answers. For example, in the experiment just considered, and in Begg (1978, Experiment 1) the pair members were presented successively, and there was no difference in recognition. In the first experiment, the pair members were presented simultaneously, and there was a difference in recognition. This appeared to be a good lead, but, as the next experiment will show, it turned out to be a red herring.

Experiment 3: Interaction Again

As just suggested, one reason for this experiment was to compare simultaneous and successive processing to see whether that difference had any bearing on whether interactive and separate processing affect recognition differently. Just to simplify matters for later, the variable was ineffective in recognition, with a .80 hit rate for each condition, and without qualifying other effects; however, in recall, simultaneously processed items were indeed better recalled, .23 vs. .13, $F(1,108) = 18.5$. Thus all we have is another factor that influences associative recall but not recognition of individual members. With that matter out of the way, let us consider the experiment as if the variable was not included in the first place.

Subjects studied 60 concrete pairs (and 20 fillers) for a total of 10 sec for each pair, followed by a recognition test for the cue members of half the pairs and the response members for the other half, followed in turn by a cued-recall test for all 60 pairs. Again to simplify matters, let me point out that once again recognition testing of the response produced better recall than did recognition testing of the cue, $F(1,108) = 16.1$, although the difference was larger in joint than separate conditions, $F(1,108) = 4.85$, and although the cues were slightly better recognized than the responses in the first place [.82 vs. .78; $F(1,108) = 15.4$].

More importantly, there were six different processing conditions, representing a cross of separate and joint processing with rote, verbal, or imaginal study. In the rote condition, subjects simply repeated the A and B terms for each pair separately (AAA... BBB...) or jointly (AB AB...) for the study interval. In the verbal condition, subjects either generated a separate verbal associate for each pair member, or a single linking associate for the pair. In the imaginal condition, subjects either formed a separate image for each pair member, or they formed a single interactive image for each pair.

The results are presented in Fig. 4.3. Let us consider each of several effects in turn. First, false alarms appear in the right-hand panel. Clearly, rote processing has a much higher false-alarm rate than the meaningful conditions, $F(2,108) = 17.5$; no other differences were even close to being reliable, so recognition can be considered on the basis of hit rates, which will underestimate the difference in recognition between the rote and meaningful conditions.

Second, consider recognition hits. Rote processing is lower than the two meaningful conditions, which are quite close to each other, $F(2,108) = 28.1$. Additionally, joint processing, on the average, reduced recognition, $F(1,108) = 28.1$; in absolute terms, the reduction because of joint processing was only present in the meaningful conditions—the interaction was not reliable, but if it were, a difference of .05 between means would be significant. In any event, whether or not the reduction in recognition of jointly processed items only applies to meaningful processing, we do have another case in which joint processing makes items less recognizeable when tested as single items than does separate processing. It isn't a big effect, but it is real and does occur with enough regularity to be considered as a factor in retention.

Finally, consider recall. Here there is a whopping effect of joint processing exceeding separate processing, $F(1,108) = 91.0$, and a solid instructional effect, $F(2,108) = 18.4$, as well as an interaction between the two, $F(2,108) = 12.8$; the interaction shows that the different processing tasks were not very different for the separation conditions. Whether the small difference reflects only a floor effect, because the conditions were truly abysmal, or increased likelihood of cue contact, since the means are ordered the same way in each

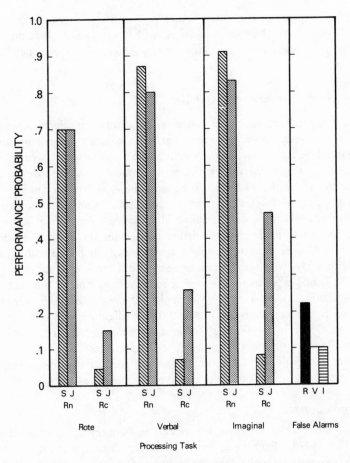

FIG. 4.3. Recall (Rc) and recognition (Rn) after separate (S) or joint (J) study, for several processing tasks.

task, is impossible to tell. However, the clear increase from rote to verbal to imaginal joint processing cannot merely reflect differential ease of access. Joint processing, even if it is rote, helps cued recall. Joint processing is, therefore, not the exclusive province of imagery instructions, although it appears to find a particularly welcome home there.

Again, there are answers and questions. One answer that keeps cropping up is that factors that make items more recognizable are separable from factors that make items more cohesively bonded into traces. And, yes, that one will crop up again later. One question that keeps cropping up is why joint processing sometimes reduces item recognition, and sometimes does not. Note that the logical possibility that interaction could help recognition becomes less and less tenable. But, still, my desire for closure makes me want to know why interaction can hurt or not hurt apparently at random; something is different between the classes of events—but what? The next experiment will take a final look at the question. Frankly, the answer is not that important in a theoretical sense, but I'd like to know.

Experiment 4: Invisible Butterflies

The next experiment was rather complex, but can be considered in small packages. The basic purpose was, once again, to contrast recognition and recall following different instructions. As before, the recall tests followed the recognition tests. However, the recognition testing procedure was expanded to allow measurement of different facets of recognition, so that recall can be compared across a variety of different intervening recognition events. Additionally, all the pairs in this experiment were meaningful adjective-noun pairs of several types. The purpose was to determine whether advantages for interactive imagery in recall would be lessened if the items were meaningfully paired in the first place, or, alternatively, whether separate imagery could break up a sensible organization. The actual experiment consisted of remembering a single long list (64 pairs and 24 filler pairs), presented on videotape at the rate of one pair every five sec, followed by a recognition test (7 to 10 min in duration) and a common cued-recall test (7 min in duration); 20 subjects served in each cell of a 3 (recognition test) × 3 (instructions; rote repetition, separate imagery, joint imagery) design. However, the results will be reported separately for each of three classes of pairs, namely different sense, invisible, and synonym-antonym pairs.

Different Senses

The nouns for this set of pairs were chosen from the nouns selected by Begg and Clark (1975). Each noun has at least two distinct meanings that can be stressed by pairing it with different adjectives. For example, *mathematical function* and *social function* are different senses, except perhaps for friendly statisticians. Forty such pairs were initially selected, half to be memory items, and half to be recognition distractors and, of course, half the subjects saw each sense of each noun. The pairs were studied either by a standard rote control procedure, a standard separate imagery procedure, or a standard joint imagery procedure. Following study, there was one of three recognition tests, then a recall test in which each of the 20 studied adjectives appeared as a cue for recall of the associated noun. It is important to note that the recall test was identical for all groups, although they differed in the initial study task, and the opportunity for additional study afforded by the recognition test. Let us now consider the different recognition tests in more detail.

In each recognition test, the 20 studied nouns all appeared as recognition targets, but in different ways. First, the 20 nouns appeared along with the 20 nouns from the distractor pairs, in a standard *item recognition* test. In a second condition, the *pair recognition* test, the 20 studied pairs appeared along with the

20 distractor pairs. In each case, subjects simply indicated whether each target—pair or word—was old or new. In the third condition, 10 of the studied pairs appeared along with the nouns from the other 10 pairs, each appearing with the adjective from the alternate sense. Subjects classified each pair as being identical to a studied pair, or as being in a different sense; this manipulation defines the *identical vs. alternate senses* condition. Note that the 20 studied nouns all appeared in recognition, and were all requested targets in recall.

Why were the different recognition tests used? Recall from earlier McGee's (1980) finding that separately imaged items exceed jointly imaged items in recall, a finding that is not exceptionally general. McGee also measured recognition for pairs against new pairs and against repaired items, and found an advantage in these tasks for joint imagery. The present conditions allow a further examination of such effects and, in addition, allow several interesting contrasts in recall.

The results for the different recognition conditions and subsequent recall appear in Fig. 4.4. First, consider recognition, expressed as the difference be-

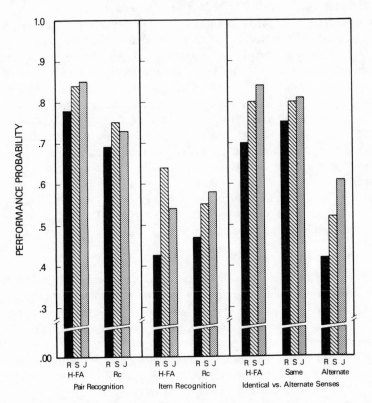

FIG. 4.4.   Recall (Rc) and recognition (H-FA) following rote repetition (R), separate imagery (S), or joint imagery (J). Each panel considers a different recognition test, and recall following that test.

tween hits and false alarms. The recognition results are the leftmost set of columns in each of the three panels of the figure. The rote groups do have the worst recognition generally, and arithmetically at least, the joint conditions slightly exceed the separate conditions in the two pair tasks, while separation enjoys an advantage in item recognition, as reported by McGee (1980). However, the magnitudes of the differences are not impressive.

Recall as well shows some interesting patterns. Again, recall is lowest in the rote conditions. Joint imagery did not exceed separate imagery by nearly as much as is found in typical experiments with unrelated pairs. Indeed, if the pairs appeared intact during the recognition test, the two types of imagery are indistinguishable both in the pair recognition test, in which the pairs were discriminated from new pairs, and in the recall of pairs appearing intact in the identical vs. alternate sense test. The intact pairs discriminated from pairs with adjectives stressing the alternate sense were remembered better than the pairs discriminated from new items, $t(119) = 5.74$, showing an effect of the intervening test.

The effect of the intervening test also appears in that both preceding groups were reliably better recalled than the pairs whose nouns had appeared alone or with new adjectives in the recognition test. More interestingly, however, there is a healthy instructional effect in the latter case. That is, even if the nouns appeared with new adjectives, the old adjectives differed in their effectiveness as cues depending on instructions. The instructional effect is less in the condition in which items appeared alone in recognition, presumably because of the reduced opportunity for study of the target nouns in the joint condition, in which the nouns were not well recognized.

In general then, the different-sense pairs show us that the difference between joint and separate imaging in cued recall can be much attenuated, and even removed, if the materials are meaningful pairs, and if the pairs appear for a recognition test prior to recall. If the nouns appear alone or with new adjectives, there is still some evidence of the usual advantage, although of much smaller magnitude than in the studies reviewed earlier. The following sections will go further in examining the same concerns.

Invisible Pairs

Another set of items in each list consisted of concrete nouns paired with "invisible" or "visible" adjectives. Adjectives denoting substantiality (e.g., colorful, distinct, radiant, specific) or insubstantiality (e.g., invisible, transparent, vague, obscure) were selected from Roget's Thesaurus. Ten pairs of each sort appeared in the study list, with another ten selected to serve as distractors in recognition. The basic experiment will be reviewed, then results averaged over the two sorts of pairs will be presented, followed by a detailed discussion of invisibility and the questions it raises for imagery theories. As in the preceding section, there were three recognition tests. First, the item test had the 20 studied nouns along with 20 new nouns, and the pair test had the 20 studied pairs along with 20 new pairs, half of which were "invisible." Subjects classified each test item as new or old. In the third condition the recognition test was more complex, containing three types of test items. First, there were intact pairs (50% of the test items); second, there were repairs consisting of studied nouns and studied adjectives from different pairs of the same sort (25%); third, there were pairs consisting of a studied noun and a new adjective of the same sort. Subjects classified the test items into one of the three categories (identical, repaired, or new adjective). As before, recall followed recognition.

First, consider the results averaged over the two sorts of pairs, as presented in Fig. 4.5. As in the previous section, recognition results were in expected directions, but the differences were not of impressive magnitude. Thus rote study yielded the poorest recognition performance. Joint imagery arithmetically exceeded separate imagery in pair recognition against new pairs, as well as pair recognition against pairs with new adjectives or repaired adjectives. There were differences in recall over instructions and over the types of recognition test. Following pair recognition, recall was better than after item recognition, but jointly imaged items exceeded separately imaged items by less than 10%, show-

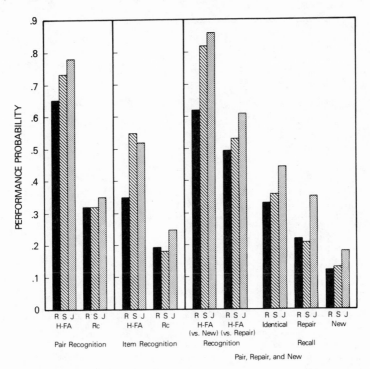

FIG. 4.5.   Recall (Rc) and recognition (H-FA) after rote (R), separate (S), or foint (J) study. Each panel presents results of a different recognition test, and of recall following that test.

ing once more that the instructional differences are markedly attenuated if used with meaningful pairs. In the more complex recognition task, joint imagery enjoyed a greater advantage in recall, but still less than usual. Additionally, intact test items were recalled better than items that had been repaired in recognition, which were in turn better than pairs whose nouns had appeared with new adjectives in recognition.

Finally, let us consider invisibility. Of all cases in which joint imagery ought to hurt recognition, perhaps the most fascinating was suggested by Luria (1968), whose mnemonist "forgot" an egg by picturing it against a white background. Several interesting experiments immediately suggest themselves around this general line. For example, it would be interesting to contrast recognition of "*black cat*" and "*egg*" pictured as "black cat in a coalbin" and "egg in snow" as opposed to "egg in a coalbin" and "black cat in snow." Similarly, some items lose individuality in collections, as in the case of a *pebble* (on the beach), or a *pianist* (in an orchestra). Would these items be well recognized in each other's natural habitat? Another example might be to "hide" an item inside another, as

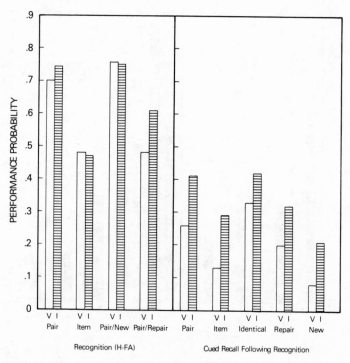

FIG. 4.6. Recognition and recall in several tasks for pairs with "invisible" (I) and "visible" (V) adjectives. See text for explanation.

in imaging *lung-body* as opposed to *nose-face;* the former is hidden, the latter manifest. As a final example, image a mother at a disco; the image might well be an identifiable person, but would she be a mother?

The present case is of the same variety as the preceding examples, but was chosen because it bears on another interesting question raised by Anderson and Hidde (1971). Anderson and Hidde asked whether the beneficial effects of imagery were due to (a) the process of generating an image, or (b) the image itself. At least on the surface, an invisible butterfly is a case in which the imagery process is engaged, but in which the resultant image, if it is indeed possible to form, would necessarily be beyond the scope of the mind's eye. In order to play with this question, I chose adjectives like invisible (and dim, murky, etc.) as well as adjectives like visible (and crisp, overt, etc.) from Roget's Thesaurus, and paired them with concrete nouns. Surely this manipulation should succeed in making the nouns less recognizable in the "invisible" pairs than the "visible" pairs. Recall should be interesting too.

The results are presented in Fig. 4.6. Quite obviously, invisibility did not reduce item recognition, or any other measure of recognition. Indeed, if there is any effect, it is that invisibility helped recognition of pairs vs. repaired items. And look at recall! Invisibility produced recall at about twice the level of visibility. I shall interpret these results as being more comfortable with the notion that the process of imaging, rather than the image itself, underlies the enhanced bonding of members into unitary memory traces.

Synonyms and Antonyms

The final pairs in this experiment were pairs for which a synonym and antonym contrast could be made. For example, *dirty shirt* has *filthy shirt* and *clean shirt* as contrasts. The study list contained 24 such pairs, with distractors for recognition selected as well. Following study, there was either an item recognition test for list nouns vs. new nouns, a pair recognition test for list pairs vs. new pairs, or a more complex test. In this latter test, half the recognition targets were intact pairs, one quarter were the synonym pairs of studied items, and the remainder were the antonym pairs of other studied items. Subjects classed each test item as identical, synonymous, or antonymous, then completed a cued-recall test as usual.

By and large, we should not anticipate any surprises by this time, but it will be interesting to compare instructions in recognition of items against synonyms. Joint imagery ought to hurt this discrimination as well as item discrimination. The results are presented in Fig. 4.7. In recognition, the two types of imagery were, as before, comparable in the recognition of pairs as opposed to both new pairs and antonyms. Separate imagery again was arithmetically beyond joint imagery in both item recognition and discrimination between pairs and synonyms, but the differences were again modest in magnitude. Joint imagery

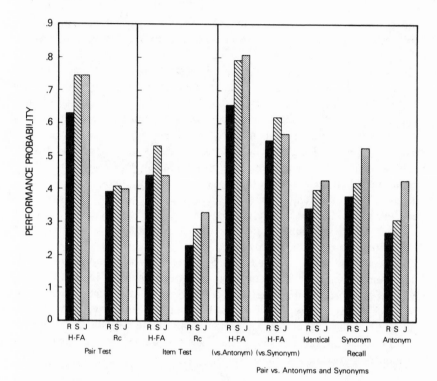

FIG. 4.7.   Recall (Rc) and recognition (Rn) for pairs studied by rote (R), separate imagery (S), or joint imagery (J). Each panel refers to performance on and after a different recognition test.

again showed an advantage over separate imagery in recall, but only of any substance in recall of pairs that did not apear in recognition although the nouns appeared with synonymous or antonymous adjectives. Even in those cases, however, the difference is a mere shadow of the big differences in the first three experiments.

Some Conclusions

This was a complex experiment, but there are a few simple conclusions. With meaningful pairs as stimuli, the effects of imagery instructions on recall are of much smaller magnitude than with unrelated pairs of nouns. Across the experiment, the largest advantages for joint imagery are in cases in which the recall cue (the adjective) did not appear in the intervening recognition test. In recognition, there were small differences between instructions such that joint imagery was slightly better for measures of pair recognition, with separation being slightly better for item recognition and for discrimination between items and their synonyms.

General Discussion

To this point we have shared several ideas and quite a lot of data. Each presented experiment shares some themes with the others, and each adds its own bit of novelty to an increasingly complex picture of what imagery does, and the consequences for memory of what imagery has done. I shall now selectively pull together some of the threads just considered.

There is little room to doubt the proposition that subjects asked to image items process items quite differently than subjects asked to process those items in other ways, nor the proposition that different sorts of imagery instructions produce differently organized memory systems. However, imagery instructions are less influential with meaningful pairs than with arbitrarily paired items. Perhaps it is the case that imagery is a good process for putting things together if no obvious connection suggests itself, but is redundant if the connection is already compelling.

Although we cannot doubt that imagery does something important in the memory system, this fact alone does not tell us the memorial consequences of what was done. Imagery is perhaps the most powerful process for binding items together—a truly remarkable glue, as it were. But binding is only binding. Every coin in my pocket has a head and a tail bound together too, but that fact won't help me find a quarter. Likewise, bound memory items are in general no easier to find than singletons and are, in enough cases to warrant further study, somewhat harder to locate.

Images, coins, and telephone books converge on the conclusion that encoding factors and retrieval processes that bear on the location of memory traces have nothing to do with the factors that bind items into traces or the processes that enable us to retrieve additional information beyond the minimum required for location. Because contact and use are independent in this sense, but dependent in the sense that contact is a necessary stage prior to use, the clever experimenter can provide evidence of independence or dependency as the need arises.

Our same clever experimenter can also provide evidence that any encoding process is beneficial, harmful, or irrelevant to memory performance by taking advantage of the fact that encoding and retrieval are interdependent. Any encoding format is more appropriate for some needs than others, and any need is served more effectively by some formats than others.

Upon exposure to the notion that experiments can show almost any effect we wish, students often throw up their hands in dismay. But soon they realize the notion is a challenge for the future rather than an epitaph for our careers. It is no longer satisfactory for researchers to assemble a list of mnemonic recipes—imagery helps memory; organization helps memory; distinctiveness helps memory; drunkenness hurts memory. Rather, the science of memory has begun. We know enough to assemble theoretical accounts in which we say what it is that our encoding tasks do to the memory system. We know enough to assemble theoretical accounts in which we say what it is that our retrieval tasks need. These accounts may still be wrong, but that is unimportant. Knowing how and why they are wrong is the important thing for helping direct our future efforts.

Out of the conglomeration of results presented here there are three questions that I find particularly fascinating. The first concerns trace interaction from study occasion to study occasion. If it is true that associative recall benefits from a second study even more than the independent sum of the two occasions, then we all ought to be happy to hear the same talk twice, at least if we do any interactive processing on one of the occasions. The second question concerns recognition. I find it maddening that interaction only hurts recognition sometimes; it makes sense that it would hurt and it makes sense that it would not, but it makes no sense to flip-flop between the two outcomes for reasons that escape me. And finally, why does invisibility enhance cued recall?

ACKNOWLEDGMENT

Preparation of this article and all the experiments were supported by NSERC grant A8122. All the work described was conducted by Carolyn Hopkins, whose assistance over the last few years has been of excellent quality and unbelievable quantity.

REFERENCES

Anderson, R. C., & Hidde, J. L. Imagery and sentence learning. *Journal of Educational Psychology*, 1971, *62*, 526–530.
Baker, L., & Santa, J. L. Context, integration and retrieval. *Memory and Cognition*, 1977, *5*, 308–314. (a)
Baker, L., & Santa, J. L. Semantic integration and context. *Memory and Cognition*, 1977, *5*, 151–154. (b)
Begg, I. Recall of meaningful phrases. *Journal of Verbal Learning and Verbal Behavior*, 1972, *11*, 431–439.
Begg, I. Imagery and integration in the recall of words. *Canadian Journal of Psychology*, 1973, *27*, 159–167.
Begg, I. Imagery and organization in memory: Instructional effects. *Memory and Cognition*, 1978, *6*, 174–183.
Begg, I. Trace loss and the recognition failure of unrecalled words. *Memory and Cognition*, 1979, *7*, 113–123.
Begg, I., & Anderson, M. C. Imagery and associative memory in children. *Journal of Experimental Child Psychology*, 1976, *21*, 480–489.
Begg, I., & Clark, J. M. Contextual imagery in meaning and memory. *Memory and Cognition* 1975, *3*, 117–122.
Begg, I., & Young, B. J. An organizational analysis of the form-class effect. *Journal of Experimental Child Psychology*, 1977, *22*, 503–519.
Begg, I., Upfold, D., & Wilton, T.D. Imagery in verbal communication. *Journal of Mental Imagery*, 1978, *2*, 165–186.

Bower, G. H. Imagery as a relational organizer in associative learning. *Journal of Verbal Learning and Verbal Behavior*, 1970, *9*, 529-533.

Broadbent, D. E., & Broadbent, M. Effects of recognition in subsequent recall: Comments. *Journal of Experimental Psychology: General*, 1977, *106*, 330-335.

Dempster, R. N., & Rohwer, W. D. Component analysis of the elaborative encoding effect in children's learning. *Journal of Experimental Psychology*, 1974, *103*, 400-408.

Einstein, G. O., & Hunt, R. R. Levels of processing and organization: Additive effects of individual-item and relational processing. *Journal of Experimental Psychology: Human Learning and Memory*, 1980, *6*, 588-598.

Hasher, L., Riebman, B., & Wren, F. Imagery and the retention of free-recall learning. *Journal of Experimental Psychology: Human Learning and Memory*, 1976, *2*, 172-181.

Humphreys, M. S. Item and relational information: A case for context independent retrieval. *Journal of Verbal Learning and Verbal Behavior*, 1978, *17*, 175-187.

Janssen, W. *On the nature of the visual image.* Soesterberg, The Netherlands: Institute for Perception TNO, 1976.

Luria, A. R. *The mind of a mnemonist.* L. Soltaroff (Trans.). New York: Basic Books, 1968.

Martin, E., Fleming, F. G., Hennrikus, D. J., & Erickson, E. A. Studies of the length-difficulty relation in serial memorization. *Journal of Verbal Learning and Verbal Behavior*, 1977, *16*, 535-548.

McGee, R. Imagery and recognition memory: The effects of relational organization. *Memory and Cognition*, 1980, *8*, 394-399.

Paivio, A. Coding distinctions and repetition effects in memory. In G. H. Bower (Ed.), *The psychology of learning and motivation*, (Vol 9). New York: Academic Press, 1975.

Tulving, E., & Thomson, D. M. Encoding specificity and retrieval processes in episodic memory. *Psychological Review*, 1973, *80*, 352-373.

Winograd, E., & Lynn, D. S. Role of contextual imagery in associative recall. *Memory and Cognition*, 1979, *7*, 29-34.

5 Pictures and Words in Semantic Decisions

John te Linde
University of Calgary

One paradigm of semantic memory research requires people to make timed judgments about two concepts presented either as outline drawings or as printed words. Given the concepts *chimpanzee* and *mouse,* for example, people are asked; which is larger in real life? (e.g., Paivio, 1975); which is more intelligent? (e.g., Banks & Flora, 1977); are the concepts members of the same semantic category? (e.g., Pellegrino, Rosinski, Chiesi & Siegal, 1977). In such semantic decision tasks, so named because they draw on our conceptual knowledge about the objects, pictures have typically produced faster response latencies than words. In this chapter I first, briefly outline accounts of this result both from common coding and dual coding approaches to the representation of meaning in memory. Second, I will present the results of experiments where pictures and words were used in decisions about object color, associative relatedness and size. The findings allow some choices to be made among the various accounts of picture-word latency differences in semantic decisions.

Common Code Approaches

Within the common code approaches to memory representation several accounts for the picture advantage in semantic decisions have been proposed. Before examining these accounts it is important to emphasize that in the common code view pictures and words are assumed to access semantic information in a single conceptual system that is neither word-like nor picture-like (Potter, 1979). Our understanding of the concept *apple,* for example, involves information stored in memory as a set of amodal abstract propositions bearing no resemblance to the verbal label, picture symbol, or actual object that may have activated the con-

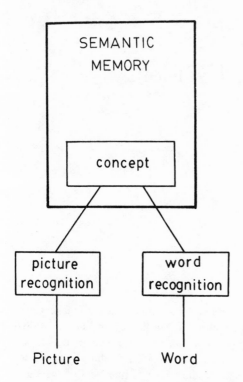

FIG. 5.1.   Schematic representation of a common coding model showing picture and word access to a single conceptual store.

cept. In a typical common code model, such as shown in Fig. 5.1, the process leading to our understanding of a visually presented word or picture is in two stages. For a word the first stage involves recognition of the verbal label. This process may include locating the label in a "lexical dictionary" perhaps organized in terms of phonetic or orthographic features. Morton's (1969) logogen model of word recognition would be one way to describe word recognition here. However word recognition is accomplished, the second step in understanding the word involves accessing the conceptual system where the concept's meanings and associations are found. Similarly, pictures are understood by first recognizing their visual pattern, which again may include locating the picture in a "dictionary of appearances" (Potter, 1979), and then accessing the same semantic code or meaning features in the conceptual system that corresponding words contact. Thus, differences in the recognition process aside, pictures and words are equivalent in that they converge on a single concept. The concept can be seen as a node in a processing network (e.g., Anderson & Bower, 1974) or as a file containing relevant features (e.g., Smith, Shoben & Rips, 1974). In either case, the important point is that the same node or file in the conceptual system makes semantic information equally available about a pictured or named concept.

I shall now outline two common coding accounts for the picture advantage. These accounts attribute the advantage to time differences in the encoding of pictures and words prior to semantic access.

Greater picture distinctiveness.   In this account, pictures and words both require analogous processing before semantic access (e.g., the parsing of visual features during recognition), but pictures require less time than words for these events. One reason for speedier picture encoding, advanced by Friedman and Bourne (1976), is that pictures are more distinctive (i.e., they share fewer common perceptual features amongst themselves) than words. It is as if pictures, in order to be identified, need be discriminated from a smaller set of possible alternatives than words. Once identified, however, the same semantic information is equally available to pictures and words. Friedman and Bourne support their account of the picture advantage with the example of the increase in reaction time obtained when the probe stimulus in a memory search task, such as Sternberg's (1969), is visually degraded, because the only encoding operation required for successful performance is the identification of the stimulus.

Acoustic-phonemic coding of words.   A second common coding account for faster picture decision times is that words go through an extra acoustic or phonemic processing stage before semantic processing. No such stage is involved in encoding pictures and so they take less time to access the common conceptual system. Pellegrino et al. (1977) have argued for this view of the picture advantage. As evidence, Rosinski, Pellegrino, and Siegel (1977) showed that the picture advantage in decisions about category membership decreased from first to fifth graders. They suggested that the increased verbal experience of fifth graders allowed for faster acoustic-phonemic coding of the words and hence improved verbal access to the single conceptual system. Evidence for the acoustic coding of words was also taken from the results of a probe memory experiment by Dhawan and Pellegrino (1977). Dhawan and Pellegrino found that memory for words showed semantic interference for items near the beginning of a list and acoustic interference for items near the end of a list. This suggested that the more recent verbal items go through an acoustic processing stage before semantic processing. In contrast, memory for pictures showed semantic interference and a low level of acoustic interference in all list positions, which suggested that pictures receive relatively direct and immediate semantic processing and little acoustic processing.

The Dual Code Approach

In contrast to common coding models the dual coding approach postualtes that language and knowledge of the world are represented in functionally distinct verbal and nonverbal memory systems. The verbal system is specialized for

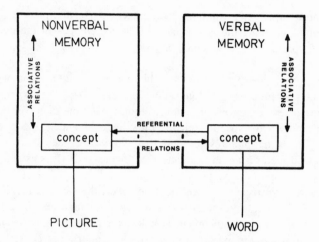

FIG 5.2. Schematic representation of the dual coding model showing picture and word access to the nonverbal and verbal symbolic systems.

dealing with linguistic information and structures. Perceptual information, such as the sizes and shapes of objects, is stored in the nonverbal or image processing system. Among other things, the two systems are independently accessed by their relevant stimuli. The imagery system is activated more directly by perceptual objects or pictures than by linguistic units and structures, with the converse being true for the verbal system. At a referential level the two systems are partially interconnected so that the word *apple*, for example, can arouse a stored image and a picture of an apple can be named. But this translation from one system to another takes time; an assumption that has implications for reaction time in semantic decision tasks. According to dual coding, picture-word latency differences in semantic decisions are a function of which system, verbal or nonverbal, the information needed to make a response is stored. When the required conceptual information is stored nonverbally pictures produce faster decision latencies because words must first be translated into their nonverbal representations. Conversely, a latency advantage for words is predicted when the required conceptual information is stored in the verbal system. A simple representation of the dual code approach is given in Fig. 5.2.

Conclusions From Past Research

Paivio (1975) obtained data in support of dual coding by showing, among other things, that decisions about object size, which are presumably mediated within the nonverbal system, were faster with pictures than with words. Other investigators, however, have demonstrated picture advantages for semantic decisions along abstract dimensions. For example, Banks and Flora (1977) found that pictures were faster than words in decisions about animal intelligence (but see Paivio & Marschark, 1980, for qualifications of this result). Pellegrino et al. (1977) showed a picture advantage in decisions about category membership. Common coding models have argued that such results cannot be explained by a dual coding approach. They say that abstract information, not easily represented in images, should be stored in the verbal system of the dual code model, but that this results in the unsupported prediction of a word advantage. Dual coding has responded to the argument by claiming that abstract information may indeed be represented in the nonverbal system. Paivio (1978) has himself demonstrated picture advantages in semantic decisions along such abstract dimensions as pleasantness and monetary value. He argued that such abstract attributes are properties of things rather than words and are accordingly represented and processed within the nonverbal system (see Paivio, 1978, 1979, for a more detailed discussion of this point).

In sum, picture advantages have been found in a number of semantic decision experiments along a variety of dimensions. Both the common code and dual code models have proposed conflicting accounts for why pictures produce faster decision latencies than words. The common code view says that pictures somehow possess a faster access than words to a common conceptual system. The dual code view sees picture-word latency differences as stemming from a time-consuming translation from one symbolic code to another and that semantic information required in the decision tasks to date is typically stored nonverbally.

Semantic Decisions Along Color, Associative Relatedness, and Size Dimensions

I shall now consider several experimental results that may help to clarify some of the controversy about the source of picture-word latency differences in semantic decisions. A clear prediction from the two common coding accounts for the picture advantage is that pictures should always be faster than words in semantic decision tasks. Paivio and te Linde (1980), however, have shown that pictures are not faster than words in decisions about object brightness and color. Participants in one experiment were asked to indicate which of a pair of named or pictured objects was lighter in real life. For example, which is lighter, an apple or a tomato? The pairs varied in their brightness ratios according to normative ratings so that sometimes the choice was easy and sometimes more difficult in varying degree. The results, summarized in the top portion of Table 5.1, showed an interaction so that when the choice was easy pictures and words did not differ in decision time, but when the choice was harder words were faster than picutres. In another experiment subjects were required to select one of two hues that was closer to the typical color of a pictured or named object. For example, which is closer to the usual color of a basketball, red or green? Difficulty of the decision was again varied according to a subtractive distance measure computed from the

TABLE 5.1

Mean Brightness Decision Time (Sec) for Picture and Word Pairs as
a Function of Scaled Brightness Ratio and Mean Hue Decision Time
for Pictures and Words as a Function of Scaled Subtractive Distance

		Brightness Ratios				
		1.30	1.47	1.77	2.13	3.46
Brightness Decisions	Pictures	2.098	1.507	1.410	1.406	1.201
	Words	1.545	1.337	1.304	1.236	1.205
		Subtractive Distances				
		0–3	4–7	8–11	12–16	
Hue Decisions	Pictures	1.848	1.798	1.539	1.420	
	Words	1.807	1.705	1.568	1.480	

distances between the items on the hue circle. The results, given in the bottom portion of Table 5.1, again showed that pictures and words did not differ in the time to make the choice. The principal importance of these results is that they contradict the common coding prediction of a picture advantage. Both common coding accounts above attribute picture-word effects to processing differences for the stimuli before semantic access. As such, they do not allow that decisions along particular dimensions, in this case brightness and hue, can decrease or eliminate the picture advantage. But the dual coding model, which holds that picture-word latency differences are a function of where the information being judged is stored, also did not predict the results. Concrete perceptual information, such as object brightness and color, should be stored in the nonverbal symbolic system and therefore yield faster picture response times. Dual coding was able to accomodate the discrepancy by considering the results of certain neuropsychological studies. These studies (see De Renzi, Faglioni, Scotti & Spinnler, 1972; De Renzi & Spinnler, 1967) conducted with aphasic patients, implicated verbal mechanisms in the processing of long-term memory information about object color, even when such subjects were tested on nonverbal tasks. Therefore, the absence of a picture advantage in brightness and hue decisions may be due to the representation of some color information in the verbal system to which words have more immediate access.

The failure to obtain a picture advantage in brightness and hue decisions calls into question the general common coding assumption of faster semantic access for pictures. Several experiments that I conducted (te Linde, in press) were designed to test in a more explicit manner the common coding as well as the dual-coding approaches to picture-word latency differences in semantic decisions. Following are the principal results of two of these studies.

Both experiments compared pictures and words in decisions about object size and associative relatedness. The two common coding approaches above predict that pictures should maintain a constant response time advantage over words across different decision tasks. This is a logical prediction because in both approaches, picture-word latency differences are assumed to occur prior to the access of any semantic information. The dual coding approach, however, allows for the possibility of a response time interaction for pictures and words in size and association decisions. Size decisions should produce a clear picture advantage because such information is assumed to be represented nonverbally. But information about the associative relatedness of concepts may be stored in both the verbal and nonverbal systems. The dual representation of associative relationships is especially likely for concrete concepts because both language and perceptual experience can play a role in forming and maintaining such links. Consider, for example, that the association between *hammer* and *nail* can be developed by encountering these concepts together in both linguistic and perceptual contexts. The ensuing simultaneous representation of such connections in both the verbal and nonverbal systems would allow that association decisions about pictured and named concepts can be made equally fast, because either system can mediate the response.

The first study operationalized size and association decisions as follows. For size decisions pairs of concepts that were very similar or very different in real life size, according to normative ratings (e.g., thimble-acorn, key-dress), were presented tachistoscopically to subjects who answered the question: Are the two items on the screen in front of you generally the same size in real life? Subjects responded either "yes" or "no" by pushing an appropriate button. Association decisions were operationalized in a similar fashion. Pairs of associated and nonassociated concepts (e.g., mouse-cheese, car-tomato), selected from norms published in Postman and Keppel (1970), were presented to subjects who answered the question: Are the two items on the screen in front of you associates of each other? The time to make both types of decisions for picture-picture (P-P), picture-word (P-W), and word-word (W-W) pairs was recorded. For both size and association decisions the common coding approaches predict that response times should be fastest for P-P pairs, intermediate for P-W pairs, and slowest for W-W pairs. Furthermore, the magnitude of the latency differences between these three pair types should remain relatively constant across the two kinds of decisions. Dual coding, on the other hand, predicts that the above response time ordering for the three pair types should occur only in size decisions. Association decisions, according to the model, should yield equivalent latencies for P-P and W-W pairs, for the reasons given earlier. In addition, it was expected that

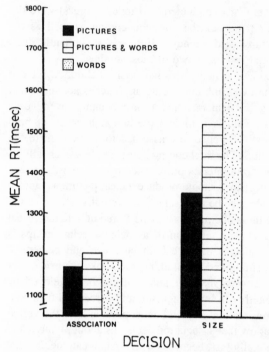

FIG. 5.3.   Mean response times for picture-picture, picture-word, and word-word pairs in size and association decisions.

comparatively slower decision latencies for P-W pairs might occur here because for such pairs one of the items should require translation to a symbolic code common with the other (either verbal or nonverbal) before a decision can be made.

The results of this experiment are given in Fig. 5.3. As can be seen the predicted response time ordering of the three pair types from the common coding and dual coding approaches was obtained for size decisions. Picture-picture pairs were significantly faster than picture-word pairs which, in turn, were faster than word-word pairs. For association decisions the three stimulus conditions yielded no significant response time differences. Overall, the interaction of stimulus material (P-P, P-W, W-W) by type of decision (size and association) was statistically significant.

The principal feature of these results is that picture-word effects depended on the type of decision. Such an interaction is clearly not predicted by common coding models that account for typically obtained picture advantages in terms of a constant advantage in semantic access. For such models to be correct, the P-P < P-W < W-W latency ordering obtained for size decisions should also have occurred in association decisions. The pattern of results suggests instead that conceptual information can be distinguished in terms of its relative availability to pictures and words. The data therefore support the dual coding approach that makes this kind of distinction for verbally and nonverbally represented information. Thus, size decisions, which make use of nonverbally stored information, yield faster response times for pictured concepts. The absence of an overall picture or word advantage in association decisions is consistent with the dual coding interpretation that associations between concrete concepts may be simultaneously represented in both symbolic systems.

One feature of the data in Fig. 5.3 is not consistent with what might be predicted from dual coding. For association decisions it was expected that P–W latencies might be slower than those for P–P and W–W pairs. The reasoning behind this prediction was that since referential connections but not associative connections are assumed to exist between the two symbolic systems of the dual code model (see Fig. 5.2), one of the items in a P–W pair would have to be translated into a symbolic code common with the other before associative relatedness could be determined. There was a small trend for longer P–W latencies but this difference is less than what might be predicted for code translation time from the size decisions in Fig. 5.3. Perhaps then, associative connections do exist between symbolic systems so that the representation of *hammer* in the verbal system, for example, is directly linked to the representation of *nail* in the nonverbal system. This modification would explain the equivalent P–P, P–W, and W–W association decision times because translation to a common symbolic code would not be required for P–W pairs in order to determine whether the items were associated. An unpublished experiment by Allan Paivio and myself examined a perhaps oversimplified prediction from such a modified model. If the two systems are connected at associative as well as referential levels then deciding whether a pictured concept and a different named concept are associatively related should take no more time than deciding whether a picture and a word represent the same concept. The results of the study showed that, in fact, such association decisions do take longer to complete than identity decisions. This result suggests that associative connections may not exist between the symbolic systems, or if they do, they take longer to evaluate than referential connections. We are presently conducting further research on this question.

Consistent with the data in Fig. 5.3, another study comparing pictures and words in size and association decisions showed that picture advantages are dependent on the kind of conceptual information being judged. Subjects in this study were shown either two pictures or two words in succession and had to decide whether the items were both large, both small, or whether the two items were strong or weak associates of each other. The responses "large" and "small" thus represent size decisions and the responses "strong" and "weak" represent decisions about associative relatedness. From normative data the four responses were mutually exclusive so that only one response was correct for any given pair. For example, the pair *cow-butter* represent weak associates but are neither both large nor both small objects. Decision times for subject's spoken responses were measured and the results are given in Fig. 5.4 for pictures and

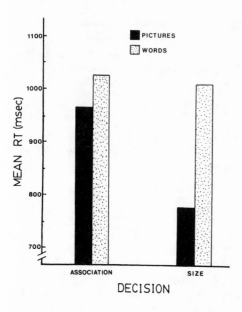

FIG. 5.4. Mean response times for picture pairs and word pairs in size and association decisions.

words in size and association decisions. As in the earlier experiment the results again showed a response time interaction such that pictures were significantly faster than words only for size decisions. The trend towards a picture advantage in association decisions was statistically unreliable ($p > .25$). The results are thus consistent with the principal conclusion of the previous experiment. This conclusion is that picture-word effects in semantic decisions are not the sole result of faster picture access to a single conceptual system but are dependent on the kind of information required for a response.

The data in Fig. 5.4 are important not only because they replicate the interaction of the earlier experiment but also because they rule out an alternative common coding account of the data. This alternative might claim that association decisions do not produce clear picture advantages because, for words, such decisions do not require semantic access. Instead word association decisions might be made from information stored in a nonsemantic lexical dictionary, perhaps of the sort proposed by Collins and Loftus (1975) to accompany their spreading-activation model of semantic memory. The Collins and Loftus lexicon contains the names of the concept nodes in the conceptual network but is organized according to phonemic and orthographic similarity. The organizational structure of this lexical dictionary could be expanded to include links between frequently co-occuring graphemic strings such as table-chair or tree-leaf. Consequently words need only be processed to this graphemic level for association information to be retrieved. But a feature of the data in Fig. 5.4 does not support this interpretation. For the particular kinds of judgments made in this experiment, size and association decisions made from word stimuli produce equivalent response latencies. If words, as is claimed by one of the common coding approaches, are first processed at a phonetic (and perhaps graphemic) level before semantic processing, then size decisions, which require semantic access, should always be slower than association decisions. This was clearly not the case in the present experiment. Thus it is logical to assume that, for both pictures and words, size and association decisions are made from information stored in semantic memory. Therefore we are left with the inability of common coding approaches to account for the decision time interactions.

It is readily apparent from the studies reviewed here that picture-word latency differences in semantic decisions are dependent on the kind of conceptual information involved. Thus, the common coding view that pictures and words differ only in access time to the same conceptual information is incorrect and needs to be revised. One modified way to view picture and word processing within a common coding framework is to assume that all conceptual information is stored in one system but that pictures and words initially access different features of a concept's meaning. This modification contradicts a traditional belief in the abstractness or amodality of conceptual representation (see Pylyshyn, 1973) since conceptual information is now distinguished in terms of its relative availability to pictures and words. Nonetheless, the change could account for the finding that certain semantic decisions, like those along color and associative relatedness dimensions, produce no clear picture advantages whereas decisions along other dimensions, such as size, show the effect. And, indeed, the revision has been accepted by certain common code adherents such as Durso and Johnson (1979) and Kieras (1978). Durso and Johnson suggest that words initially activate a larger and more generic set of information than pictures which access more situation-specific aspects of meaning. There is no clear specification of what may constitute the more generic information a word activates but Durso and Johnson compare their distinction for pictures and words to earlier distinctions between core and peripheral aspects of meaning (Miller & Johnson-Laird, 1976; Smith et al., 1974). In this comparison, words activate meaning components closest to the core concept whereas pictures access peripheral meaning components further in semantic distance from the core.

Kieras (1978) also distinguishes the representation of verbal and pictorial information at a conceptual level. He argues that all conceptual knowledge can be expressed in the same *format* of propositions or as a network of concepts interconnected by relations. But the representation of verbal and pictorial concepts can differ in both form and content. With regard to form, word meanings and picture meanings may differ in the particular configuration of relations that each possesses in the conceptual network. Specifically, Kieras suggested that pictorially generated representations possess a larger number of interconnections in the network than verbally generated representations. With regard to content, Kieras proposed that the representation of ordinary scenes may involve the specification of visual and spatial properties only defined in perceptual terms, whereas verbal semantic representation can use components that are abstract and hence have no perceivable referents.

Note that Kieras' form distinction for word and picture meanings seems to contradict the distinction of Durso and Johnson where words, in order to at first activate a larger and more generic set of semantic information, would presumably possess a greater number of conceptual relations than pictures. More importantly, note that Kieras' content distinction for verbal and pictorial representation very closely resembles earlier distinctions made from the dual coding approach (Paivio, 1971/1979). Considered at this level, Kieras' position simply becomes a formal restatement of the dual coding approach and so offers nothing new to our understanding about the conceptual representation of pictured and named concepts. Nor does it say more than dual coding about what kinds of conceptual information are more readily available to the two kinds of stimulus material.

This chapter began by considering common code and dual code approaches to picture-word latency differences in semantic decisions. The results of several studies suggest that such latency differences are dependent on the kind of semantic information required in the decision. The data thus support approaches that distinguish conceptual information in terms of its relative availability to pictures and words. The dual coding model makes this distinction for verbally and nonverbally represented information. Modified common coding approaches that permit pictures and words to initially access different conceptual information are either vague about the precise nature of this differentially accessed information or converge on dual coding notions.

ACKNOWLEDGMENT

Portions of the research reported here were supported by a postdoctoral fellowship and a grant (A0087 to Allan Paivio) from the Natural Sciences and Engineering Research Council of Canada.

REFERENCES

Anderson, J. R., & Bower, G. H. *Human associative memory.* Washington, D.C.: Hemisphere Publishing Corporation, 1974.

Banks, W. P., & Flora, J. Semantic and perceptual processes in symbolic comparisons. *Journal of Experimental Psychology: Human Perception and Performance,* 1977, *3,* 278–290.

Collins, A. M., & Loftus, E. F. A spreading-activation theory of semantic processing. *Psychological Review,* 1975, *82,* 407–428.

De Renzi, E., Faglioni, P., Scotti, G., & Spinnler, H. Impairment in associating colour to form, concomitant with aphasia. *Brain,* 1972, *95,* 298–304.

De Renzi, E., & Spinnler, H. Impaired performance on color tasks in patients with hemispheric damage. *Cortex,* 1967, *3,* 194–217.

Dhawan, M., & Pellegrino, J. W. Acoustic and semantic interference effects in words and pictures. *Memory & Cognition,* 1977, *5,* 340-346.

Durso, F. T., & Johnson, M. K. Facilitation in naming and categorizing repeated pictures and words. *Journal of Experimental Psychology: Human Learning and Memory,* 1979, *5,* 449-459.

Friedman, A., & Bourne, L. E. Jr. Encoding the levels of information in pictures and words. *Journal of Experimental Psychology: General,* 1976, *105,* 169-190.

Kieras, D. Beyond pictures and words: Alternative information processing models for imagery effects in verbal memory. *Psychological Bulletin,* 1978, *85,* 532-554.

Miller, G. A., & Johnson-Laird, P. N. *Language and Perception.* Cambridge, Mass.: The Belknap Press of Harvard University Press, 1976.

Morton, J. Interaction of information in word recognition. *Psychological Review,* 1969, *76,* 165-178.

Paivio, A. *Imagery and verbal Processes.* New York: Holt, Rinehart, & Winston, 1971. (reprinted by Lawrence Erlbaum Assoc., 1979)

Paivio, A. Perceptual comparisons through the mind's eye. *Memory & Cognition,* 1975, *3,* 635-647.

Paivio, A. Mental comparisons involving abstract attributes. *Memory & Cognition,* 1978, *6,* 199-208.

Paivio, A. On weighing things in your mind. In R. W. Klein & P. W. Jusczyk (Eds.), *The nature of thought.* Hillsdale, N.J.: Lawrence Erlbaum Assoc., 1979.

Paivio, A., & Marschark, M. Comparative judgments of animal intelligence and pleasantness. *Memory & Cognition,* 1980, *8,* 39-48.

Paivio, A., & te Linde, D. J. Symbolic comparisons of objects on color attributes. *Journal of Experimental Psychology: Human Perception and Performance,* 1980, *6,* 652-661.

Pellegrino, J. W., Rosinski, R. R., Chiesi, H. L., & Siegal, A. Picture-word differences in decision latency: An analysis of single and dual memory models. *Memory & Cognition,* 1977, *5,* 383-396.

Postman, L., & Keppel, G. *Norms of word association.* New York: Academic Press, 1970.

Potter, M. C. Mundane symbolism: The relations among objects, names, and ideas. In N. R. Smith & M. B. Franklin (Eds.), *Symbolic functioning in childhood.* Hillsdale, N.J.: Lawrence Erlbaum Assoc., 1979.

Pylyshyn, Z. W. What the mind's eye tells the mind's brain: A critique of mental imagery. *Psychological Bulletin,* 1973, *80,* 1-24.

Rosinski, R. R., Pellegrino, J. W., & Siegal, A. W. Developmental changes in the semantic processing of pictures and words. *Journal of Experimental Child Psychology,* 1977, *23,* 282-291.

Smith, E. E., Shoben, E. J., & Rips, L. J. Structure and process in semantic memory: A featural model for semantic decisions. *Psychological Reivew,* 1974, *81,* 214-241.

Sternberg, S. Memory scanning: Mental processes revealed by reaction-time experiments. *American Scientist,* 1969, *57,* 421-457.

te Linde, D. J. *Picture-word differences in decision latency: A test of common coding assumptions. Journal of Experimental Psychology: Learning, Memory, and cognition,* in press.

6

Comprehension Effects in Comparative Judgments

Alain Desrochers
William M. Petrusic
Carleton University

The ease of comprehending a question depends to a large degree on how it is formulated. Consider the following example: Is Allan healthier than average? This simple question actually involves a number of sub-problems, in addition to encoding the given information. For instance, who is Allan? Are the authors assuming that you should know which Allan they are referring to? What do they mean by average health? The readers must fill in all this information before they can attempt to answer the question. The answer will, of course, be "correct" insofar as the problem-solvers made the same inferences as the writers about Allan's identity and the meaning of average health.

The general focus of this chapter deals with the relation between reading comprehension and the decisional process in symbolic comparisons. The emphasis on reading comes from the fact that, in this task, graphic displays constitute the primary source of information to solve the problems. Between the presentation of the printed stimuli and the ultimate decision, a variety of psychological events are assumed to occur. As is apparent below, the characterization of these events varies with the particular theoretical model under consideration.

This chapter is divided into four sections. First, we briefly discuss the concept of verbal comprehension. Second, we present a general framework for the description and evaluation of various models of comparative judgments. In the last two sections, we present the preliminary results of two experiments designed to examine the effects of specific linguistic variables on symbolic comparisons. One experiment involves instructions and stimuli from two different languages (i.e., English and French). In the other, French-speaking participants are asked to make judgments with positive and negative comparative forms (e.g., plus grand "more large" and moins grand "less large").

THE CONCEPT OF VERBAL COMPREHENSION

The simplest way of defining the term "comprehension" may be as the process by which the meaning of a symbolic event is apprehended. This definition implies that the "meaning" to be apprehended can be specified precisely. Although this may seem to be a fairly simple task, philosophers, linguists, and psychologists have struggled with the analysis of meaning for decades. In recent years it has become apparent that word meanings do not always lend themselves easily to criterial-feature descriptions (Rosch, 1978). It is now more common to consider word meanings as inherently vague and flexible. That is, the word standing by itself is frequently insufficient to convey semantically unambiguous information. The meaning of a word may vary a great deal depending on the context in which it occurs (Anderson & Ortony, 1975; Caramazza & Grober, 1976; McCloskey & Glucksberg, 1978). Thus, the meaning of words may not always be self-determined or self-contained, rather it is often context-sensitive.

An implication of this context-sensitivity of word meanings is that the process of apprehension must involve the "pooling" of information from various sources to disambiguate a statement. In addition to whatever is extracted from the word itself, information may be derived from the situational context or from implicit inferences from long-term knowledge. How this information is actually brought into the comprehension process is not clear yet, but a tentative framework was proposed by Miller and Johnson-Laird (1976). They suggested that a word is represented in memory as a set of decision procedures that specify its pragmatic and semantic usage and as a set of relations between its meanings and the meanings of other words. These decision procedures include linguistic operations as well as perceptual and functional characteristics of objects, actions, and events. Although there is no general consensus on the ultimate form of cognitive representation, it undoubtedly plays a central role in language comprehension. Conceptualizing the notion of representation in terms of procedures, operations, or skills may indeed be a very useful approach to the study of verbal comprehension.

The early factor-analytic research showed that language comprehension is a multidimensional ability. The exact number and nature of these dimensions, however, is still in dispute. Davis (1968) claimed that comprehension is best characterized by eight independent skills. Carroll (1972) later pointed out that the amount of unique variance in the tests of these skills justifies the inference of only five distinct skills: remembering word meanings, following the structure of a passage, finding answers to questions asked explicitly or in paraphrase, drawing inferences from the content, and recognizing a writer's purpose, attitude, tone, and mood. Even these five skills are very highly correlated in high-school populations. Still other investigators find that literal and inferential reading skills are empirically undistinguishable (e.g., Spearritt, Spalding, & Johnston, 1977). Reading comprehension ability is also substantially correlated with intelligence tests, even nonverbal intellectual skills such as figure analogies (Carroll, 1972). After considering these findings, one may wonder if reading comprehension can actually be decomposed into distinct and independent skills. In the factor-analytic approach it is generally assumed that the presence of a distinct skill is not a *sine qua non* condition for another distinct skill to be observable. This assumption is not so important for interactive information processing systems. If the process of comprehending actually involved the application of skills in an interactive fashion, then one would not be surprised to find that the so-called independent skills are highly correlated.

An example of such an interactive model of reading comprehension was proposed by Kintsch and van Dijk (1978) for text processing. Although the problem of text processing is far more complex than that of comparative judgments, Kintsch and van Dijk's (1978) model shares several components with the specific models to be described later. These components are stages of processing, a working-memory system, and provisions for implicit inferences and related reasoning processes.

We may now try to extend our definition of the term "comprehension" a little further. We first assume that comprehension is a goal-oriented problem-solving activity. The general goal is to determine what is said or what is asked. However, the specific demands of a comprehension problem may not always be explicit. In pursuing a particular goal, as vaguely defined as it may be, the reader may have to pool and organize information from various sources, such as the conceptual representation of the given words in long-term memory, the given context, and the outcomes of implicit inferences and other reasoning processes. The goal is reached when the reader can make an overt or covert response relative to the particular comprehension problem at hand. In many cases, no prejudgment needs to be made on the accuracy of the solution; accuracy is often defined in relation to another problem-solver's solution.

STAGES OF PROCESSING IN COMPARATIVE JUDGMENTS

The notion of stage is virtually inherent to all current theories of information processing. The first prototypical model of reading proposed in this tradition involved serial nonoverlapping stages through which a visual display undergoes various transformations (e.g. Gough, 1972; Mackworth, 1972). The restrictive assumptions of an invariant sequence of stages and bottom-up processing soon were relaxed, however, to accommodate new empirical findings suggesting that long-term memory plays an important role at the early stages of language processing. For instance, higher-order knowledge of letter clusters and words appear to facilitate the perception of individual letters of a string (Allport, 1979; LaBerge, 1977; McClelland & Rumelhart, 1981). Furthermore, contextual information strongly influences word recognition (Becker, 1980; Fowler, Wolford, Slade, & Tassinary, 1981; Marcel, 1980).

As in the literature on reading processes, the notion of stages determines the form of several models of comparative judgments. Current models appear to involve five broad stages of processing: (a) information extraction from visual displays, (b) implicit inferences, (c) storage of information in working memory, (d) choice decision, and (e) response selection. Depending on the particular model, these processes may occur in a serial, iterative or parallel fashion, and the characterization of each stage may vary in explicitness and detail. Before describing some current approaches to comparative judgements, we briefly discuss two components common to most models, namely, the information extraction or encoding process and the concept of working memory.

Information Extraction From Visual Displays

The factors that influence the ease of information extraction from visual displays, in a symbolic comparison task, may be of various sorts. Some of these factors are general, such as alterations of the physical properties of the displays (e.g., degradation of print, unusual orientation of word letters). Another such variable is the reader's fluency in the language in which the printed words are presented. These difficulty factors have received very little attention in the context of comparative judgments, primarily because researchers have been interested in other substantive issues. Preliminary results pertaining to the effects of the reader's language fluency, however, will be presented in a later section of this chapter.

Other difficulty factors are specific either to the stimuli or the comparatives. These include the symbolic class of the stimuli (e.g., linguistic, pictorial, or numeric), and the form of the comparatives. We shall return to the word-picture effects on comparative judgments in the section on the dual-coding model. The particular aspect of the comparative that received most attention is its "lexical markedness." This concept was extended by linguists (e.g., Bierwisch, 1967) to describe the semantic criteria that define the antonimity of bipolar adjectives and comparatives. This notion was then introduced in psychology to explain aspects of human performance in tasks of deductive reasoning (Clark, 1969; Huttenlocher & Higgins, 1971) and sentence comprehension (Carpenter, 1974; Clark, 1970). More recently, it was shown that the time needed to make a symbolic comparison was longer when the comparative was marked (e.g., smaller) than when it was unmarked (Banks & Flora, 1977; Hinrich, Yurko, & Hu, 1981; Holyoak & Mah, 1981; Marschark, 1981; Marschark & Paivio, 1979).

Another aspect of the comparative is whether it is positive (e.g. more intelligent, more stupid) or negative (e.g., less intelligent, less stupid). Virtually all studies of comparative judgments have involved only the positive forms. Interesting questions arise when we contrast positive and negative forms, however. For instance, is "less intelligent" interpreted the same way as "more stupid"? We return to this general problem in the fourth section of the chapter.

The Concept of Working Memory

The notion of a working memory system derives primarily from the work of Atkinson and Shiffrin (1968). The heuristic value of this concept is apparent in the interpretation of human performance in several cognitive tasks, such as prose comprehension (Baddeley & Hitch, 1974; Kintsch & van Dijk, 1978), probability judgments (Brainerd, 1981), and mental arithmetic (Hitch, 1978; Svenson & Hedenborg, 1980). In a model of comparative judgments, a working-memory system may fulfill two important functions. The first one is the temporary retention of information drawn from long-term knowledge while a decision is being made. Regarding this function, specific assumptions can be made about its capacity, its persistence, the kind of information that can be stored in it, and how this information is to be organized. A second function of working memory is to store the cumulative results of intermediate steps of information processing. This component of the working-memory system may take the form of a stochastic counter (Pike, 1968) or an accumulator (Vickers, 1979). This mechanism keeps track of the work done in solving the problem and determines the final decision. Regardless of its ultimate form, the notion of working memory plays a central role in most models of comparative judgments.

We now examine the storage and process components of four current models of comparative judgements and how they account for the main temporal characteristics of choice judgments.

The Semantic-Coding Model

One of the more explicit models is Banks' (1977) semantic coding model. A fundamental postulate of this approach is that knowledge is represented in long-term memory as precoded attribute information rather than quantitative attribute information or sensory isomorphs. An immediate implication of this postulate is that physical objects are not represented internally by analog values along a continuous dimension, rather they are represented by category labels.

The model assumes three broad stages of processing: (1) encoding of the printed information, (2) choice decision, and (3) response selection. These stages take place in an interactive fashion and contribute additively to the global decision time. The encoding stage involves two processes. First, discrete or categorical codes are generated by drawing information from semantic memory. These codes remain in a temporary and limited-space data base, that is, a working memory. Although it is not clear how these codes are retrieved from long-term knowledge, they are assumed to include: (a) general information about the absolute position of the stimuli along a particular attribute (e.g., large vs. small), and (b) specific information about their relative position on the attribute. For example, two small numbers, such as 3 and 4, may be coded as "small" and "small +," respectively. This code generation process may occasionally produce identical codes for the two stimuli. At this point, a decision is made as to whether the codes are discriminable. This code discrimination process accounts for the distance effect because the closer the two stimuli on the relevant attribute the more likely they are to be assigned the exact same code and, thereby, to be recoded until discrimination is possible. How this information is recoded in working memory is not specified. Banks (1977) points out, however, that the subprocesses responsible for this operation may vary a great deal from one experimental situation to another.

Once the discriminability of the codes has been established they are matched against the instruction code. This matching subprocess of the choice stage accounts for the semantic congruity effect in the following way: if the codes for absolute information do not match the instruction (e.g., which is larger, given two codes "small" and "small +"), they must be translated into the proper format (e.g., "small" and "small +" into "large +" and "large," respectively). Thus, the congruity or "cross-over" effect, as it was dubbed by Audley and Wallis (1964), who were among the first to investigate this problem, amounts essentially to a variation in translation time.[1] The mechanism by which this operation is performed remains to be specified. Finally, response selection follows from the appropriate transformation of the codes and the output of the code that is consistent with the instruction.

In summary, Banks characterizes working memory as a very limited-capacity data base. The discrete codes retrieved from semantic memory and stored in this data base specify the overall absolute and relative position of two stimuli along a conceptual attribute. The generation of these codes is interactive insofar as they are to be checked repeatedly for discriminability during the encoding stage and

---

[1]The semantic coding model is indistinguishable from the probabilistic translation model developed by Wallis and Audley (1964) for psychophysical comparisons. This model admits a graded semantic incongruity effect because coding (categorization) is probabilistic and, hence, the probability that translation is required approaches one as the stimuli become more extreme on the attribute, while it is required on only approximately one half of the trials for intermediate stimuli. Such models can be rejected when a fully graded incongruity effect is obtained in the absence of probabilistic coding of intermediate stimuli as Jamieson and Petrusic (1975) found.

for matching with the instruction during the choice decision stage. The discriminability check accounts for the distance effect while the matching subprocess accounts for the congruity effect.

The Dual-Coding Model

Paivio's (1971, 1978b, 1979) dual-coding model contrasts in various ways with Banks' semantic coding. First, it postulates that long-term knowledge involves two distinct substrates or systems, one for pictorial (and perceptual) information and the other for linguistic information. Each system is responsible for encoding, storing, and retrieving a particular type of information. The "imagery" system is specialized for processing pictorial information, and generating and analyzing mental images. The verbal system is concerned with the perceptual processing and production of language. The representational units in the verbal system are the functional units of language, which Morton (1969) referred to as "logogens." These two systems are assumed to be interconnected, so a pictorial stimulus can directly activate the image system and, indirectly, its corresponding logogen in the verbal system. In contrast, a word stimulus can directly activate a logogen in the verbal system and, indirectly, an image in the other system.

Information stored in the imagery system is assumed to be represented in an analog fashion. That is, the representation of physical objects has the same sensory properties as the actual objects. More specifically, Paivio (1978b) states that "the functional representations in the image system are assumed to be perceptual isomorphs or analogs, in the sense that they 'contain' modality-specific information concerning the perceptual attributes of things. Thus perceptual distinctions along such continuous dimensions as size, color, and shape are presumably represented in a fine-grained form in long-term perceptual memory [p. 529]."

Dual coding was never introduced explicitly as a stage model but recent additions to it allows us to discuss it in such terms. The model involves (at least implicitly) three broad stages of processing: (1) encoding of graphic displays and access to their internal representation, (2) choice decision, and (3) response selection. These stages occur in a sequential fashion and contribute additively to the total decision times. A unique feature of this model is that it accounts for the variability of access time due to the type of presented stimuli and particular instruction given. A typical and recurrent finding is that comparison times are shorter with pictures than words as stimuli when people are required to compare their referents on dimensions such as physical size, weight, pleasantness, monetary value, intelligence, and angularity (Paivio, 1975, 1978a, 1978a, 1979; Paivio & Desrochers, 1980b; Paivio & Marschark, 1980). In the model, attributes such as the ones just listed pertain to our "knowledge of things" rather than our "knowledge of words." Therefore, when word stimuli are presented their perceptual representation is accessed in the image system via the verbal system.

When pictorial stimuli are shown, however, the imaginal representation is accessed more directly, accounting for the shorter access time. In agreement with this view, Paivio (1975; 1978c) also found that the forementioned pictorial advantage over word stimuli is reversed for comparative judgements of word pronounceability and frequency of occurence in the language. Thus, picture-word effects are accounted for in terms of the relation between the composition of long-term knowledge and the particular demands of the comparison task.

A recent addition to the encoding process has been referred to as the "expectancy hypothesis" (Marschark, 1981; Marschark, Ch. 11, this volume; Marschark & Paivio, 1979). In this context, expectancy refers to a mechanism by which readers prepare for a particular range of stimuli when the presentation of the comparative precedes that of the two stimulus items. For instance, if the instruction *larger* is presented first, the reader *expects* to be shown large stimuli. The mechanism underlying the notion of expectancy has not yet been specified in detail, but it appears to pertain to some implicit inferences in the reading process (Marschark, Ch. 11, this volume). The semantic congruity effect in comparative judgments is interpreted in terms of this hypothetical mechanism. A simple and testable prediction follows from this hypothesis: No congruity effect should be observed when the comparative is presented after the stimuli, because no expectancy should be set up by the instruction. Experimental results reported by Marschark and Paivio (1979) confirm this prediction, whereas others reported by Banks and Flora (1977) and Holyoak and Mah (1981) disconfirm it. The issue is still in dispute.

It is apparent that the dual-coding model makes no explicit provisions for a temporary storage system. We will suppose that the presented information on any given trial, in a symbolic comparison task, is retained in some way in either or both the image and the verbal systems, while the decision is being made. Paivio (1975) suggests that the use of a small set of stimuli, instead of a large set, results in a different "build up of associative connections among the stimuli," but no further specification is provided. Once the internal representations are accessed, the actual comparison process is assumed to proceed in the same way as for perceptual comparisons, whatever the process may be. The mechanism by which the response is selected also remains unspecified.

In summary, the dual-coding model postulates different forms of representation for pictorial and linguistic information. This feature of the model accounts for interactions between the stimulus medium and the particular attribute in the symbolic comparison, although a recent study reporting the absence of a medium effect in comparisons of object color and brightness (Paivio & te Linde, 1980) departs somewhat from the expected pattern of results. A mechanism, referred to as "expectancy" is put forward to explain the semantic congruity effect. The comparison and response selection stages are not specified in detail. In this regard, it is fair to say that dual coding is still more a model of memory representation than a full-blown model of comparative judgements. However, it makes provisions for some unique memorial processes that are not explicit in other decision models.

The Scan Plus Comparison Model

Moyer and his collaborators (Moyer & Bayer, 1976; Moyer & Dumais, 1978, proposed the "scan plus comparison" model, which also assumes that the internal representation of stimuli preserves analog information. The similarity with dual coding, however, does not extend much beyond this point. Moyer (1976, 1978) and his collaborators do not commit themselves to any particular forms of internal representation, such as images. All they assume is that "the relations among stored representations of objects correspond to the relations among the actual objects [p. 236]."

The scan plus comparison model involves four broad stages of processing: (1) encoding of the printed stimuli and search for their internal representation, (2) retrieval from long-term memory of values corresponding to the position of the stimuli on a particular continuous dimension and storage of these values in working memory, (3) choice decision, and (4) response selection. Each of these stages contributes additively to the global decision time. Somewhat like dual coding, this model attempts to account for the variability in the time required to access the internal representation of the stimuli. This is apparent in the first stage of processing. For example, once the stimulus "shoe" is located in semantic memory, it should take less time to locate "sock" than "monkey." This prediction is indeed confirmed by numerous studies of semantic memory (e.g., Holyoak, Dumais, & Moyer, 1979).

Readers subsequently retrieve, for each stimulus term, an absolute value that corresponds to its location on the dimension. These two values are then deposited in working memory and "ordered according to magnitude." The capacity of this data base is not necessarily restricted to two elements. When a small set of stimuli is used in the task, all magnitudes may be stored in working memory as an array of increasing absolute values. The congruity effect is assumed to occur because the comparative determines which end of the array of values the search will start at. The closer the target values are to the starting point of the search, the quicker they are found. Thus, if the size of two stimuli is small, relative to the experimental set, the search will be terminated sooner with the instruction "smaller" than with the instruction "larger."

Additional provisions are necessary for experimental tasks involving sets of stimuli that exceed the capacity of working memory. Moyer and Dumais (1978) first assume that lexical entries in long-term memory are at least roughly ordered in magnitude along various continuous dimensions. When the instruction is presented, the reader immediately accesses an associate in long-term memory. For example, if the instruction is "smaller," the internal representation of a small object (e.g., ant or blueberry) may be activated and this internal location serves as the starting point of the search for the representation of the stimuli. Therefore, if the starting point corresponds to a small object, less time will be needed to localize other small objects than large objects. Once the stimulus values are found they are stored in working memory and used for the actual comparison.

The decision rule for the comparison is taken from a random walk model proposed by Buckley and Gillman (1974). According to this rule, the decision-maker computes the difference between the two absolute values and adds the result to a counter. Since the values in working memory are ordered in magnitude, the difference may be positive or negative, causing the counter to increase or decrease in value. When the counter exceeds a preset positive or negative criterion (or boundary), a decision is made. The selection of the overt response is determined by the sign of the counter value. If after adding the difference between the two values to the counter neither criteria have been exceeded, the respondent is assumed to compute the difference again, add it to the counter, and compare the new counter value to the criteria. This routine is repeated until a criterion has been reached or exceeded. This iterative process accounts for the distance effect. The more similar the stimulus values are, the smaller their computed difference is. Consequently, whenever the difference or counter step size is small, more iterations are necessary to reach a boundary. The main stages of the scan plus comparison model may be summarized in the following way:

$$RT = K + I (Ea + Sa + Eb + Sb + Cab)$$

where K is the minimum amount of time needed to respond, I the number of iterations necessary to reach a boundary, Ea the time to encode stimulus A, Sa the time to retrieve the representation of stimulus A, Eb the encoding latency for stimulus B, Sb the retrieval latency for stimulus B, and Cab the time necessary to compute the difference between the two absolute values.

Thus, both the dual coding and scanning plus comparison models make some explicit provisions for variability in memory search time. The exact characterization of the process, however, varies with the assumed memory structures in each model. In Moyer's model, the semantic congruity effect is explicitly attributed to variation in search time; the comparative form determines the starting point of memory search.

The distance effect, in turn, is localized at the choice decision stage, and it is presumed to reflect the variable number of information sampling covert trials necessary for an overt response to be made. The rate of evidence accumulation in favor of one response or another is assumed to vary with the distance between the stimuli on the attribute. Although Moyer and Dumais (1978) adopt the random walk decision model of Buckley and Gillman (1974), it should be pointed out that a variety of models elaborated in psychophysical (e.g., Link & Heath, 1975;

Vickers, 1979) and preferential choice research (e.g., Petrusic & Jamieson, 1978) are equally plausible. In fact, it is not clear whether this simple form of the random walk model is appropriate when the stimuli are rarely confused, as is typically the case in symbolic comparison tasks.

The Reference Point Model

The fourth class of models to be discussed in this section is referred to as "reference point" models. All models of this class assume that the representation of information in memory is analog rather than discrete or categorical and that the comparison of two stimuli is based on the difference between each item relative to an ideal or reference point. The notion of ideal point derives directly from Coombs' (1950) unfolding theory of preferential choice. Variations in the current versions of the model include different assumptions about the properties of the representation of the stimuli in long-term memory. Marks (1972), for instance, assumes that a stimulus is represented in memory by a set of values and the variance of these values is proportional to the distance of the stimulus from the reference point on the same dimension. Holyoak (1978) and Jamieson and Petrusic (1975), in contrast, make no assumption about the variance of the stimulus representations.

Jamieson and Petrusic's (1975) version, called the discrepancy ratio model, explicitly extends Greenberg's (1963) ratio model for Coombs' (1950) unfolding theory to stimulus comparisons. In a comparative judgment task, the presentation of a particular instruction is assumed to activate an ideal or reference point, I, in memory and the presentation of a pair of stimuli, x and y, activates the internal representations, X and Y, on the relevant continuum. Subjects compare the two stimuli by computing the subjective distance between each stimulus and the reference point, yielding the two difference values, $d(X, I)$ and $d(Y, I)$. The decision rule is based on the ratio of the two distances relative to a criterion, C. Judgment time is assumed to be a monotone decreasing function of the distance of the discrepancy ratio from the criterion. The semantic congruity effect follows naturally from the algebra of the model; and, in the case where the criterion is unbiased ($C=1$), the congruity effect is fully graded and symmetrical about the bisector of the two reference points suggested by the bipolar comparatives (e.g., Larger/Smaller). The model elegantly accounts for both the full "cross-over" effect and the funnel effect by simply varying the criterion bias parameter. Unlike Marks' (1972) early version of the reference point model, the discrepancy ratio model assumes that the form of the stimulus representation is independent of the form of the comparative.

Holyoak (1978) proposed an extension of the discrepancy ratio model by explicitly assuming the form of the function that relates the distance of the ratio from the criterion, in the unbiased case, and by specifying four broad stages of processing for the usual symbolic comparison task. These stages are : (1) encoding the printed words, (2) assessing the distance from each stimulus to the reference point, (3) comparing two derived distances, and (4) selecting the response. During the first stage, values corresponding to the magnitude of the stimuli on a given dimension are retrieved from long-term memory. A third value suggested by the instruction and representing the reference point is also retrieved from memory. We will suppose that these three values are temporarily held in working memory while the decision rule is applied.

The second stage involves the computation of $d(X, I)$ and $d(Y, I)$. In the third stage, subjects compare the two derived distances by computing the ratio $d(X, I)/d(Y,I)$. A value proportional to the quantity $\log d(X,I) - \log d(Y,I)$ is then added to a counter, according to a random walk process.[2] Evidence in favor of one response or the other is accumulated in the counter by re-computing the distances and the ratio. Thus, the process captured by Stages 2 and 3 is iterative and the number of necessary iterations depends on the positive and negative boundaries of the walk and the distance between the stimuli. Finally, response selection is determined by the sign of the accumulated value when a boundary is reached.

LINGUISTIC CODING EFFECTS IN COMPARATIVE JUDGMENTS

An issue that has aroused a great deal of interest among cognitive scientists is the composition of the bilingual's lexical memory (for reviews, see McCormack, 1977; Paivio & Begg, 1981; Paivio & Desrochers, 1980; Reynolds & Flagg, 1977; Taylor, 1976). Just how are two languages organized in someone's memory? Admittedly, this is a very difficult question to answer. Many attempts have been made to infer this lexical organization pattern from performance on recall and speeded decision tasks. The comparative judgment task offers a novel situation for probing the composition of bilinguals' lexical memory.

This experimental task allows a great deal of flexibility. For instance, we can vary factorially the language of the comparative (SMALLER, PLUS PETIT, LARGER, PLUS GROS), the language of the first stimulus, and the language of the second stimulus. This within-list manipulation permits us to examine the effects of activating the respondents' two languages simultaneously or only one of their languages.

Early studies involving bilingual participants indicated that the pattern of decision latencies typically reflects the relative level of fluency in each language. Macnamara (1967b), for example, reported that language fluency affects picture-word verification latencies. Bilinguals with a greater mastery of English

---

[2]Holyoak's (1978) use of the simple random walk model is equally subject to the criticisms made earlier concerning Moyer and Dumais' (1978) use of this model.

than French took longer to indicate whether the word stimulus denoted the object represented in the picture when the word was in the weaker language. In a subsequent experiment, Macnamara (1967b) presented unbalanced bilinguals with short sentences (e.g., A hen has a wing; A hen has a door). The participants were asked to decide as quickly as possible whether each statement was true or false. Decision times were substantially longer when the sentences were presented in the respondent's weaker language.

These and other similar findings (d'Anglejan, Gagnon, Hafez, Tucker, & Winsberg, 1979; Costermans & Galland, 1980; Dornic, 1979, 1980; Mägiste, 1979) strongly suggested that the overall comparative judgement latencies would also vary as a function of the participant's relative fluency in the two languages. To help interpret this expected contrast, we included in the experiment balanced or nearly balanced French-English bilinguals and English unilinguals with minimal knowledge of French. We compared the performance of these two types of participants in order to determine the influence of general knowledge of the two languages, independent of the familiarity with the particular stimuli used in the experimental task, on comparative judgments. If, indeed familiarity with the small set of stimuli is the only factor influencing overall performance on this task, the effect of language would be expected to be very weak after a very large number of trials. If, in contrast, performance remains partly dependent upon the general level of fluency in each language, one would expect decision times to vary in each language, regardless of the extent of familiarity with the particular stimuli used in the experiment.

A special feature of this experiment is that only four university students were involved, although a very large number of observations were obtained from each. Two of the participants were very fluent in both English and French; the other two were functionally English unilingual, although they had received some exposure to French in high-school. Fluency was measured with two 7-point rating scales, one for each language. Both bilinguals rated their knowledge of each language by giving the maximum scores, whereas unilinguals provided the maximum score for English and the minimum score for French. This measure, admittedly crude, has been shown to be very highly correlated with various paper-and-pencil fluency tests (Macnamara, 1967a).

The materials included six English animal names and their French translation (see Table 6.1). Two other animal names and their translation (i.e., FLEA, PUCE, WHALE, and BALEINE) were also shown occasionally to minimize the effect of end point strategies. The animal names were selected on the basis of two criteria: (a) their translation equivalents had to be noncognates, and (b) the stimuli in the set were pairwise supraliminally different. The four comparative instructions were LARGER, SMALLER, and their respective French translation PLUS GROS and PLUS PETIT.

The four participants were given a list of the experimental and practice animal names as well as the two comparatives in the two languages prior to the experiment. The two unilingual participants were required to overlearn the French

TABLE 6.1
English Stimuli and their
French Translation Equivalent

Stimulus Language	
English	French
BEE	ABEILLE
MOUSE	SOURIS
RABBIT	LAPIN
SWAN	CYGNE
LAMB	AGNEAU
HORSE	CHEVAL

translations at home and return to the laboratory a week later. At the beginning of the first laboratory session, both bilinguals and unilinguals were tested for recall in writing of all the verbal items. Disregarding minor spelling errors, recall was found to be perfect, when either the English or French names were used as retrieval cues for the recall of the translation equivalents.

The experiment involved 10 sessions of 524 trials each. These 524 trials included: (1) 24 practice trials at the beginning of the session, (2) 480 experimental trials with all pairs of animal names in all linguistic and order combinations presented with each of the four instructions, and (3) 20 trials with the end point items interspersed throughout the experimental set. Each trial consisted of the following sequence of events: (a) a 2-sec delay, (b) simultaneous presentation of an instruction and a pair of animal names in a horizontal row near the center of a video monitor, and (c) the words remained on the screen until the subject pressed a key to indicate her response. No feedback was given for accuracy or speed. A short break was scheduled after each block of 100 trials. The presentation order was random and the random order was different on each session and for every participant. The words were displayed on an Electrohome video monitor and a DataGen Nova 1220 computer controlled the timing, sequencing, and presentation of the trials. The computer also recorded the responses and the reaction times.

We first present the global effects of the linguistic composition of the materials on each participant's decision times. An analysis of variance was conducted on the raw reaction times, after eliminating outliers above 3500 msec (i.e., .79% of a total of 17,280 observations). The observations from the initial laboratory session, which was viewed as warm up, were also discarded. The descriptive statistics are reported in Tables 6.2 and 6.3. The results of the analysis performed on DY's latencies revealed only a significant effect of lexical marking, $F(1, 4295) = 17.44$, $p < .001$ and this was also the only significant effect observed in ML's latencies, $F(1, 4256) = 5.46$, $p < .02$. Thus, in both cases, presentation of the marked comparative, relative to the unmarked one, resulted in longer decision times, regardless of the language of the instruction.

TABLE 6.2
Median Judgment Time, Mean Judgment Time, Standard Deviation,
and Number of Observations For each Linguistic Coding Condition
With the Bilingual Subjects: DY and ML

Subject	Language of the Stimuli	Language of the Instruction				
		French		English		
		Larger	Smaller	Larger	Smaller	
DY	French-French	1177	1192	1198	1229	1222
		1279	1343	1302	1341	1316
		371	457	368	408	
		270	270	269	269	
	English-English	1222	1295	1197	1343	1263
		1307	1351	1302	1402	1341
		424	466	401	421	
		269	269	270	269	
	French-English	1174	1217	1205	1274	1233
		1294	1303	1319	1388	1326
		448	429	441	450	
		269	270	270	270	
	English-French	1288	1278	1240	1274	1290
		1353	1369	1317	1411	1393
		406	462	364	482	
		270	270	269	268	
		1226	1259	1235	1302	
		1308	1342	1310	1386	
ML	French-French	1158	1183	1184	1199	1195
		1294	1292	1284	1363	1308
		467	448	442	502	
		269	269	268	265	
	English-English	1197	1173	1191	1257	1191
		1321	1328	1309	1385	1333
		516	499	487	557	
		270	266	267	266	
	French-English	1152	1231	1188	1272	1209
		1305	1376	1318	1360	1339
		549	543	492	486	
		265	264	270	265	
	English-French	1207	1181	1213	1242	1204
		1331	1298	1306	1369	1323
		480	484	423	522	
		267	268	268	267	
		1173	1188	1195	1245	
		1312	1324	1304	1369	

TABLE 6.3
Median Judgment Time, Mean Judgment Time, Standard Deviation,
and Number of Observations For each Linguistic Coding Condition
With the Unilingual Subjects: DD and KA

Subject	Language of the Stimuli	Language of the Instruction				
		French		English		
		Larger	Smaller	Larger	Smaller	
DD	French-French	1407	1369	1318	1402	1376
		1499	1504	1413	1522	1485
		447	505	429	474	
		267	267	266	265	
	English-English	1376	1405	1272	1363	1339
		1441	1508	1370	1431	1438
		458	508	494	455	
		269	268	268	265	
	French-English	1385	1408	1284	1325	1334
		1417	1463	1395	1410	1421
		396	424	444	418	
		269	268	266	268	
	English-French	1361	1380	1269	1361	1340
		1461	1485	1364	1459	1442
		439	496	443	456	
		269	265	267	268	
		1373	1378	1285	1366	
		1455	1490	1386	1456	
KA	French-French	1188	1120	1052	1132	1112
		1170	1240	1157	1191	1190
		365	414	370	374	
		267	268	268	268	
	English-English	1111	1135	1065	1076	1090
		1174	1226	1120	1142	1166
		363	425	364	413	
		270	267	268	269	
	French-English	1093	1122	1049	1073	1088
		1188	1184	1151	1122	1161
		391	396	404	342	
		270	265	267	267	
	English-French	1073	1154	1049	1096	1096
		1189	1224	1139	1156	1177
		325	416	379	367	
		270	267	268	266	
		1095	1139	1060	1097	
		1181	1218	1142	1152	

The same analyses were computed on the latencies collected from unilingual participants. Three statistically significant main effects were found in DD's latencies and no interaction effects approached significance. First, the French instructions resulted in longer latencies than did the English, $F(1, 4259) = 13.70$, $p < .001$. Second, latencies were longer when the comparative was marked than when it was unmarked, regardless of the language of the instruction, $F(1, 4259) = 14.17$, $p < .001$. Finally, decision times were substantially longer when both animal names were presented in the weaker language rather than any other linguistic combination, $F(3, 4259) = 3.75$, $p < .01$.

The analysis of KA's latencies revealed only two statistically significant main effects. The decision times were longer when the instruction was presented in the weaker language than in the dominant one, $F(1,4269) = 19.35$, $p < .001$. The presentation of the marked comparatives, relative to the unmarked, resulted in slower decision, $F(1,4269)=4.42$, $p < .03$. The performance of KA was not significantly affected by the linguistic code of the stimuli.

Three aspects of these results are of particular interest. First, the lexical markedness of the comparative does appear to influence the performance of all four subjects. The interesting feature of the present pattern of results is that the lexical marking effect is observed in both languages, even with the unilingual subjects. There is even some suggestion in the data that the magnitude of lexical marking is enhanced in one's weaker language, although this effect is not statistically significant.

The second and somewhat surprising finding is that the trials in which the stimuli appeared in different languages did not significantly increase the difficulty of the judgement task. By presenting the comparative and the stimuli in a horonzital row, we attempted to build into the experiment a variable number of language switches. Such inter-language transitions have sometimes been shown to inflate comprehension latencies. Macnamara and Kushnir (1971, Experiment 2), for example, presented bilingual readers with same-language and mixed-language sentences in the context of a sentence-verification task. The mixed-language sentences included one, two, or three language switches (e.g., Tous les chickens sont grey). The global verification times increased with the number of language switches in the sentences.

Macnamara and Kushnir's (1971) finding, however, contrasts with those of other studies in which the linguistic composition of the stimuli had no effect on judgment times. Caramazza and Brones (1980), for instance, required Spanish-English bilinguals to decide as quickly as possible whether the referent of a noun belonged in a particular category. On each trial, a category-name and an instance-name appeared on the screen. These names were either from the same language or from different languages. Although the usual typicality and semantic distance effects were observed, the language manipulation had no reliable effect on decision times. A critical difference between these two studies may involve the extent of syntactic relations between verbal units. For reasons not entirely clear to us, language-switch effects are typically absent in comprehension tasks involving syntactically unrelated stimuli (e.g., Caramazza & Brones, 1980; Dalrymple-Alford & Aamiry, 1967). Although we expected the comparative judgment task to resemble that used by Macnamara and Kushnir (1971, Experiment 2), our results are more similar to those reported by Caramazza and Brones (1980).

Finally, the only factor that consistently differentiated between bilinguals and unilinguals was the language of the comparative. Except for the increased overall latency due to presenting unilingual DD with the two animal names in his weaker language, the language of the stimuli had no reliable effect on the subjects' overall performance. The discrepancy between the effects of the language of the comparative and that of the stimuli can hardly be explained in terms of familiarity, since all the verbal items were learned to a strict criterion before the experiment began. Furthermore, each comparative was presented five times more frequently than any one of the experimental stimuli.

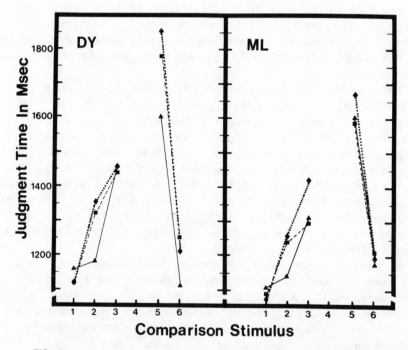

FIG. 6.1.   Median judgment times for the stimuli compared with stimulus 4 (swan, in the ordering bee, mouse, rabbit, swan, lamb, horse) for the French-French (triangles; n = 72), English-English (diamonds; n = 72), and the mixed language (squares; n = 144) stimulus pairs. The plot in the left panel is for bilingual subject DY and in the right panel for bilingual subject ML.

A simple explanation suggested by Paivio's dual-coding model is that the cognitive representations of the two types of words are fundamentally different. Animal names would be coded in the verbal system as logogens. Their physical referents, however, would be represented in the image system, and imagens are, by definition, language-free representations. Any influence of the language of the stimuli on performance would have to be interpreted as encoding effects because, for the comparison, the critical information is to be found in the image system. The comparative, in contrast, refers to an abstract relation. Thus, it would likely be represented only in the verbal system. Any influence of the language of the comparative on performance would be attributed to the difficulty of encoding the item and of manipulating the extracted information within the verbal system.

Turning now to some aspects of the microstructure of the data, it can be seen in Figs. 6.1 and 6.2 that all four subjects exhibit a very similar pattern of distance effects. Judgment latencies monotonically decrease as the distance between the pairs increases. This pattern is found in all language conditions, although DD and DY present substantial language-condition differences for the stimuli adjacent to Stimulus 4 (i.e., only for relatively difficult decisions). For subject DD, this

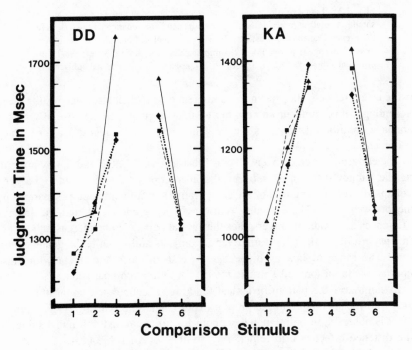

FIG. 6.2.   Median judgment times as in Fig. 6.1. The plot in the left panel is for unilingual subject DD and in the right panel for unilingual subject KA.

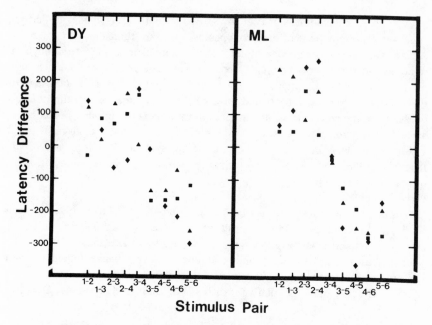

FIG. 6.3.   Latency difference (time to select the larger animal—time to select the smaller animal) in msec for the adjacent pairs and pairs separated by two steps for the French-French (triangles; n = 36), English-English (diamonds; n = 36), and mixed language (squares; n = 72) stimulus pairs. The plot in the left panel is for bilingual subject DY and the plot in the right panel is for bilingual subject ML.

discrepancy reflects the enhanced comprehension difficulty that results from presenting both stimuli in French, his weaker language. In the case of DY, the language-condition differences for the stimulus pair 4-5 suggest greater fluency in French.

The congruity or cross-over effect is illustrated in Fig. 6.3 and 6.4 by presenting the latency differences between the instructions "Smaller" and "Larger" (collapsed over the language of the comparative) for all animal pairs separated by one or two steps. These figures show a finely graded plot and the latency differences are gradually reversed as the animal pairs become increasingly large. This pattern of results is uniform over all subjects and stimulus-language conditions. The range of latency differences is also in close agreement with those reported by Jamieson and Petrusic (1975) for animal comparisons.

In summary, the pattern of lexical marking, distance, and congruity effects are by no means unique to the present experiment. The typical lexical marking effect is observed in both languages, both for bilingual and unilingual subjects. The distance effect is also remarkably similar for all subjects in all stimulus-language conditions. These findings indicate that, once the experimental materials have become familiar to the subjects, it becomes very difficult to dif-

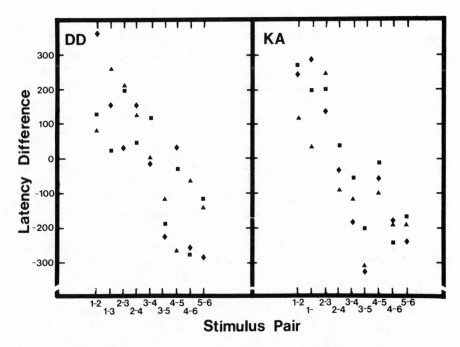

FIG. 6.4. Latency difference as in Fig. 6.3. The plot on the left panel is for unilingual subject DD and in the right panel for unilingual subject KA.

ferentiate unilinguals from bilinguals from their performance in the various stimulus-language conditions. The only consistent contrast available in the present data is provided by the effect of the instruction language. Unilinguals typically experience more difficulty in processing the instruction when it is shown in their weaker language, while no such differential difficulty is observed with bilinguals.

POSITIVE AND NEGATIVE INSTRUCTIONS IN COMPARATIVE JUDGMENTS

The distinction between positive and negative comparatives is particularly evident in the Romance languages, such as French. In these languages, comparative forms are typically expressed in two words, namely an adverb (more/less) indicating the sign and an adjective (e.g., large/small) specifying the attribute. The interpretation of these various comparative forms raises both empirical and theoretical questions. On the empirical side, one may wonder whether the usual distance, congruity, and lexical marking effects are observed when negative comparatives are used in the experimental task.

Segui and Bertoncini (1978) reported a series of picture-sentence verification experiments in which French-speaking subjects were shown a picture of two ribbons of different colors and a comparative sentence (e.g., The red ribbon is less long than the blue ribbon). The sign and markedness of the comparative were varied factorially in the experimental sentences and the task was to indicate as quickly as possible whether the sentence described the relation present in the picture. The verification latencies revealed that negative comparatives were uniformly much more difficult to comprehend than positive comparatives. Furthermore, there was an interaction between the sign and the markedness of the comparative; the sign variable had a larger effect on the marked than on the unmarked comparative. These global effects are insufficient, however, to determine how the different comparative instructions are interpreted by the reader; they provide no information about the interaction between the comparative form and the ordinal position of the stimuli on a scale. As a first step toward the clarification of these points, we now present the preliminary results of a comparative judgment experiment with digits and the four forms of the French comparative.

Two native speakers of French participated in this experiment. The materials included all pairwise combinations of the digits 1 through 9, and the four forms of the French comparative for magnitude: PLUS GRAND "larger", PLUS PETIT "smaller," MOINS GRAND "less large," and MOINS PETIT "less small." The experiment involved eight sessions of 600 trials each. These 600 trials included: (a) 24 practice trials at the beginning of the session, and (b) 576 experimental trials with all 72 pairwise combinations (36 pairs in each of two presentation orders) of the 9 digits presented twice with each of the four instructions. The procedural details concerning the presentation of the trials and the collection of the responses are identical to the animal size comparison experiment reported previously.

The global effects of the two variables of the comparative generally replicated the findings reported by Segui and Bertoncini (1978). The relevant descriptive statistics are presented in Table 6.4. The analysis of variance computed on BE's raw latencies revealed three statistically significant effects. First, the negative comparatives were found to result in longer latencies than positive ones, $F(1, 4026) = 4.37$, $p < .001$. More time was also needed to make a decision with the marked than with the unmarked comparatives, $F(1, 4026) = 4.16$, $p < .001$. These two main effects were qualified by a significant interaction, $F(1, 4026) = 5.09$, $p < .001$, indicating that the lexical marking effect was observed only with the negative comparatives.

The reaction times collected from the second subject ML revealed an identical pattern. Decisions were slower with negative than positive comparatives, $F(1, 4011) = 9.70$, $p < .001$. Marked comparatives resulted in longer latencies than unmarked ones, $F(1, 4011) = 8.48$, $p < .001$. These main effects were also qualified by a significant interaction, $F(1, 4011) = 3.25$, $p < .006$, reflecting a larger effect of lexical marking with negative than with positive comparatives.

TABLE 6.4
Median Judgment Time, Mean Judgment Time, Standard Deviation, and Number of Observations for each Form of the French Comparative

Subject	Adjective	Sign of the Comparative		
		More	Less	
BE	Large	688	765	721
		715	804	760
		138	217	
		1007	1008	
	Small	678	828	744
		712	900	806
		161	286	
		1008	1007	
		686	792	
		714	852	
ML	Large	817	986	892
		885	1074	980
		294	389	
		1008	1003	
	Small	838	1059	930
		905	1156	1030
		294	417	
		1005	999	
		826	1020	
		895	1115	

Inspection of Table 6.4 clearly shows that the magnitude of the sign effect is considerably larger than that of the lexical marking effect. Furthermore, the magnitude of the lexical marking effect is also inflated as the difficulty of the decision process is increased by presenting a negative comparative.

The global effects discussed above are also clearly evident upon closer examination of the data. Figure 6.5 illustrates the usual distance effects for both subjects. It also shows that, for ML, judgments with negative comparatives were uniformly longer than with positive comparatives. The same configuration is observed for subject BE, except for a single violation in the pattern. Importantly, both subjects exhibited faster responding to the unmarked form of the negative comparative than to its marked form. Figure 6.5 also reveals interesting individual differences in the use of positive comparatives. The full congruity effect is

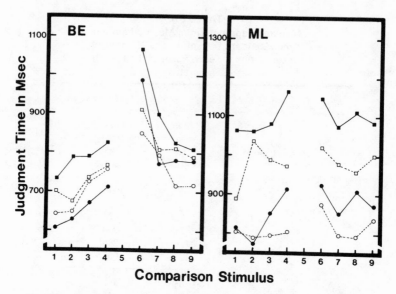

Fig. 6.5. Median judgment times for the digits compared with digit "5" for the instructions "plus petit" (closed circles), "plus grand" (open circles), "moins petit" (closed squares), and "moins grand" (open squares), n = 28 for each condition. The plot in the left panel is for subject BE and for subject ML in the right panel.

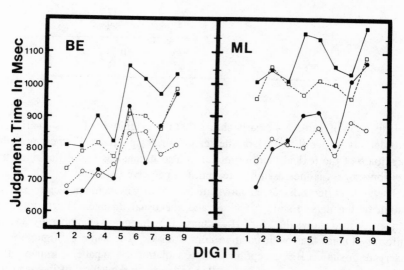

FIG. 6.6. Median judgment times as in Fig. 6.5. The plot in the left panel is for subject BE and for subject ML in the right panel. Points are plotted at the midpoints of successive adjacent pairs.

evident for subject BE, whereas subject ML generally responded faster with the unmarked form of the comparative.

The effects of the four instructions on judgment latencies are shown for the adjacent digit pairs in Fig. 6.6. With the positive comparatives, the congruity effect is observed for both subjects, while neither this effect nor its reverse is evident with the negative comparatives. In almost every case, judgments with negative comparatives were uniformly faster for the unmarked than the marked form. This finding provides no support for the notion that negative comparatives are translated into their linguistically equivalent positive forms before the decisional process. A number of alternative models of the sequencing of comparison and translation are currently being tested.

SUMMARY

This chapter is concerned with the relation between reading comprehension and the decision process in symbolic comparisons. The characterization of this decisional process was discussed in the context of four classes of models of comparative judgments. These models were presented and compared within a general stages-of-processing framework.

The preliminary results from two experiments were reported. In the first, French-English bilinguals and English unilingual subjects compared the remembered physical size of various animals. The language code of the stimuli and that of the comparative forms were factorially varied. These linguistic variations did not significantly influence the overall performance of the bilinguals. The only linguistic variable that consistently affected both unilingual subjects' judgmental latencies was the language of the instruction; decision times were longer when the instruction was presented in French than when it was presented in English. Substantial and fully graded semantic incongruity effects were found to be independent of the linguistic manipulations for each of the four subjects. Upon examining specific comparison pairs, the findings suggest distance effects are amplified with increasing decision difficulty for unilinguals when the stimuli appear in their weaker language, whereas the linguistic coding manipulation has a weaker effect on the distance–judgment time configuration for bilinguals.

French-speaking subjects were required to compare the magnitude of pairs of digits in the second experiment. The sign (positive/negative) and the lexical marking of the comparative were factorially varied to obtain four forms of the French comparative. Judgment times were generally much longer with the negative comparatives than with the positives. This effect was particularly enhanced when the comparative was marked. Orderly distance effects were observed with all four comparative forms, whereas the congruity effect was apparent only with positive comparatives. Although this latter pattern of results remains to be explained, it clearly indicates that negative comparatives are not translated into their linguistically positive form prior to the comparison process.

ACKNOWLEDGMENT

This research was supported by a Quebec Ministry of Education postdoctoral fellowship awarded to Desrochers. The work, conducted at the Department of Psychology, Carleton University, Ottawa, Ontario, was also supported by a National Science and Engineering Research Council grant (A8628) awarded to Petrusic.

REFERENCES

Allport, A. Word recognition in reading. In P. A. Kolers, M. E. Wrolstad, & H. Bouma (Eds.), *Processing of visible language*, Vol. 1. New York: Plenum Press, 1979.

Anderson, R. C., & Ortony, A. On putting apples into bottles—A problem of polysemy. *Cognitive Psychology*, 1975, 7, 167-180.

d'Anglejan, A., Gagnon, N., Hafez, M., Tucker, G. R., & Winsberg, S. Solving problems in deductive reasoning: Three experimental studies of adult second language learners. *Working Papers on Bilingualism*, 1979, 17, 1-23.

Atkinson, R. C., & Shiffrin, R. M. Human memory: A proposed system and its control processes. In K. W. Spence & J. T. Spence (Eds.), *Advances in the psychology of learning and motivation research and theory*. Vol. II. New York: Academic Press, 1968.

Audley, R. J., & Wallis, C. P. Response instructions and the speed of relative judgments. I. Some experiments on brightness discrimination. *British Journal of Psychology*, 1964, 55, 59-73.

Baddeley, A. D., & Hitch, G. Working memory. In G. H. Bower (Ed.), *The psychology of learning and motivation*. New York: Academic Press, 1974.

Banks, W. P. Encoding and processing of symbolic information in comparative judgements. In G. H. Bower (Ed.), *The psychology of learning and motivation*, Vol. 11. New York: Academic Press, 1977.

Banks, W. P., & Flora, J. Semantic and perceptual process in symbolic comparisons. *Journal of Experimental Psychology: Human Perception and Performance*, 1977, 3, 278-290.

Becker, C. A. Semantic context effects in visual word recognition: An analysis of semantic strategies. *Memory and Cognition*, 1980, 8, 493-512.

Bierwisch, M. Some semantic universals of German adjectives. *Foundations of Language*, 1967, 3, 1-36.

Brainerd, C. J. Working memory and the developmental analysis of probability judgment. *Psychological Review*, 1981, 88, 463-502.

Buckley, P., & Gillman, C. Comparisons of digits and dot patterns. *Journal of Experimental Psychology*, 1974, 103, 1131-1136.

Caramazza, A., & Brones, I. Semantic classification by bilinguals. *Canadian Journal of Psychology*, 1980, 34, 77-81.

Caramazza, A., & Grober, E. Polysemy and the structure of the subjective lexicon. In C. Rameh (Ed.), *Georgetown University round table on languages and linguistics*. Washington, D.C.: Georgetown University Press, 1976.

Carpenter, P. A. On the comprehension, storage, and retrieval of comparative sentences. *Journal of Verbal Learning and Verbal Behavior*, 1974, 13, 401-411.

Carroll, J. B. Defining language comprehension: Some speculations. In J. B. Carroll & R. O. Freedle (Eds.), *Language comprehension and the acquisition of knowledge*. Washington, D.C.: Winston, 1972.

Clark, H. H. Linguistic processes in deductive reasoning. *Psychological Review*, 1969, 76, 387-404.

Clark, H. H. Comprehending comparatives. In G. B. Flores d'Arcais & W. J. M. Leveit (Eds.), *Advances in Psycholinguistics*. Amsterdam: North-Holland, 1970.

Coombs, C. H. Psychological scaling without a unit of measurement. *Psychological Review*, 1950, *57*, 145-158.

Costermans, J., & Galland, J. Sur l'accessibilité du lexique chez les bilingues. *Revue Canadienne de Psychologie*, 1980, *34*, 381-387.

Dalrymple-Alford, E., & Aamiry, A. Speed of responding to mixed language signals. *Psychonomic Science*, 1967, *9*, 535-536.

Davis, F. B. Research in comprehension and reading. *Reading Research Quarterly*, 1968, *3*, 499-545.

Dornic, S. Information processing in bilinguals: Some selected issues. *Psychological Research*, 1979, *40*, 329-348.

Dornic, S. Information processing and language dominance. *International Review of Applied Psychology*, 1980, *29*, 119-140.

Fowler, C. A., Wolford, G., Slade, R., & Tassinary, L. Lexical access with and without awareness. *Journal of Experimental Psychology: General*, 1981, *7*, 341-362.

Gough, P. B. One second of reading. In J. F. Kavanagh & I. G. Mattingly (Eds.), *Language by ear and by eye*. Cambridge, Mass.: MIT Press, 1972.

Greenberg, M. G. J-Scale models for preference behavior. *Psychometrika*, 1963, *28*, 265-271.

Hinrich, J. V., Yurko, D. S., & Hu, J. M. Two-digit number comparison: Use of place information. *Journal of Experimental Psychology: Human Perception and Performance*, 1981, *7*, 890-901.

Hitch, G. J. The role of short-term working memory in mental arithmetic. *Cognitive Psychology*, 1978, *10*, 302-323.

Holyoak, K. Comparative judgments with numerical reference points. *Cognitive Psychology*, 1978, *10*, 203-243.

Holyoak, K. J., Dumais, S. T., & Moyer, R. S. Semantic association effects in a mental comparison task. *Memory and Cognition*, 1979, *7*, 303-313.

Holyoak, K. J., & Mah, W. Semantic congruity in symbolic comparisons: Evidence against an expectancy hypothesis. *Memory and Cognition*, 1981, *9*, 197-204.

Huttenlocher, J., & Higgins, E. T. Adjectives, comparatives, and syllogisms. *Psychological Review*, 1971, *78*, 487-504.

Jamieson, D. G., & Petrusic, W. M. Relational judgments with remembered stimuli. *Perception and Psychophysics*, 1975, *18*, 373-378.

Kintsch, W., & van Dijk, T. A. Toward a model of text comprehension and production. *Psychological Review*, 1978, *85*, 363-394.

LaBerge, D. The perception of units in beginning reading. In L. B. Resnick & P. A. Weaver (Eds.), *Theory and practice of beginning reading instruction*. Hillsdale, N.J.: Lawrence Erlbaum Assoc., 1977.

Link, S. W., & Heath, R. A. A sequential theory of psychophysical discrimination. *Psychometrika*, 1975, *40*, 77-111.

Mackworth, J. F. Some models of the reading process: Learners and skilled readers. *Reading Research Quarterly*, 1972, *7*, 701-733.

Macnamara, J. The bilingual's linguistic performance—A psychological overview. *Journal of Social Issues*, 1967, *23*, 58-77. (a)

Macnamara, J. The effects of instruction in a weaker language. *Journal of Social Issues*, 1967, *23*, 121-135. (b)

Macnamara, J., & Kushnir, S. L. Linguistic independence of bilinguals: The input switch. *Journal of Verbal Learning and Verbal Behavior*, 1971, *10*, 480-487.

Mägiste, E. The competing language systems of the multilingual: A developmental study. *Journal of Verbal Learning and Verbal Behavior*, 1979, *18*, 79-89.

Marcel, A. Explaining selective effects of prior context on perception: The need to distinguish conscious and preconscious processes in word recognition. In R. Nickerson (Ed.), *Attention and Performance VIII*. Hillsdale, N.J.: Lawrence Erlbaum Assoc., 1980.

Marks, D. F. Relative judgment: A phenomenom and a theory. *Perception and Psychophysics*, 1972, *11*, 156–160.

Marschark, M. *Comparative magnitude judgments with digits and other number stimuli*. Unpublished manuscript, Department of Psychology, University of North Carolina at Greensboro, 1981.

Marschark, M., & Paivio, A. Semantic congruity and lexical marking in symbolic comparisons: An expectancy hypothesis. *Memory and Cognition*, 1979, *7*, 175–184.

McClelland, J. L., & Rumelhart, D. E. An interactive activation model of context effects in letter perception: Part I. An account of basic findings. *Psychological Review*, 1981, *88*, 375–407.

McCormack, P. D. Bilingual linguistic memory: The independence-interdependence issue revisited. In P. A. Hornby (Ed.), *Bilingualism: Psychological, social, and educational implications*. New York: Academic Press, 1977.

McCloskey, M. E., & Glucksberg, S. Natural categories: Well-defined or fuzzy sets? *Memory and Cognition*, 1978, *6*, 462–472.

Miller, G. A., & Johnson-Laird, P. N. *Language and perception*. Cambridge: Harvard University Press, 1976.

Morton, J. Interaction of information in word recognition. *Psychological Review*, 1969, *76*, 165–178.

Moyer, R. S., & Bayer, R. H. Mental comparison and the symbolic distance effect. *Cognitive Psychology*, 1976, *8*, 228–246.

Moyer, R. S., & Dumais, S. T. Mental comparison. In G. H. Bower (Ed.), *The psychology of learning and motivation* (Vol. 12). New York: Academic Press, 1978.

Paivio, A. *Imagery and verbal processes*. New York: Holt, Rinehart, and Winston, 1971.

Paivio, A. Perceptual comparisons through the mind's eye. *Memory and Cognition*, 1975, *3*, 635–647.

Paivio, A. The relationship between verbal and perceptual codes. In E. C. Carterette & M. P. Friedman (Eds.), *Handbook of perception. Vol. 9: Perceptual processing*. New York: Academic Press, 1977.

Paivio, A. Comparisons of mental clocks. *Journal of Experimental Psychology: Human Perception and Performance*, 1978, *4*, 61–71. (a)

Paivio, A. Dual coding: Theoretical issues and empirical evidence. In J. M. Scandura & C. J. Brainerd (Eds.), *Structural/process models of complex human behavior*. Alphen aan den Rijn, the Netherlands: Sijthoff and Noordhoff, 1978. (b)

Paivio, A. Imagery, language and semantic memory. *International Journal of Psycholinguistics*, 1978, *5*, 27–43. (c)

Paivio, A. Mental comparisons involving abstract attributes. *Memory and Cognition*, 1978, *6*, 199–208. (d)

Paivio, A. On weighing things in your mind. In P. W. Jusezyk & R. W. Klein (Eds.), *The nature of thought*. Hillsdale, N.J.: Lawrence Erlbaum Assoc., 1979.

Paivio, A., & Begg, I. *The psychology of language*. Scarborough: Prentice-Hall, 1981.

Paivio, A., & Desrochers, A. A dual-coding approach to bilingual memory. *Canadian Journal of Psychology*, 1980, *34*, 388–399. (a)

Paivio, A., & Desrochers, A. *Symbolic comparisons of object weight*. Unpublished data, Department of Psychology, University of Western Ontario, 1980. (b)

Paivio, A., & Marschark, M. Comparative judgments of animal intelligence and pleasantness. *Memory and Cognition*, 1980, *8*, 39–48.

Paivio, A., & te Linde, J. Symbolic comparisons of objects on color attributes. *Journal of Experimental Psychology: Human Perception and Performance*, 1980, *6*, 652–661.

Petrusic, W. M., & Jamieson, D. C. Relation between probability of preferential choice and time to choose changes with practice. *Journal of Experimental Psychology: Human Perception and Performance*, 1978, *4*, 471–482.

Pike, A. R. Latency and relative frequency of response in psychophysical discrimination. *British Journal of Mathematical and Statistical Psychology*, 1968, *21*, 161–182.

Reynolds, A. G., & Flagg, P. W. *Cognitive Psychology*. Cambridge, Mass.: Winthrop, 1977.

Rosch, E. Principles of categorization. In E. Rosch & B. B. Lloyd (Eds.), *Cognition and categorization*. Hillsdale, N.J.: Larence Erlbaum Assoc., 1978.

Segui, J, & Bertoncini, J. La vérification des phrases comparatives. *Année Psychologique*, 1978, *78*, 129–144.

Spearritt, D., Spalding, D., & Johnston, M. *Measuring reading comprehension in the upper primary school*. Canberra: Australian Government Publications Service, 1977.

Svenson, O., & Hedenborg, M. L. Strategies for solving simple subtractions as reflected by children's verbal reports. *Scandinavian Journal of Educational Research*, 1980, *24*, 157–172.

Taylor, I. *Introduction to psycholinguistics*. New York: Holt, Rinehart and Winston, 1976.

Vickers, D. *Decision processes in visual perception*. New York: Academic Press, 1979.

Wallis, C. P., & Audley, R. J. Response instructions and the speed of relative judgments. II. Pitch discrimination. *British Journal of Psychology*, 1964, *55*, 133–142.

7 Properties of Mental Color Codes

Paul R. D'Agostino
Gettysburg College

Rosch (1973, 1977) has argued persuasively that color categories as well as other natural categories are not logical bounded entities in which all instances that possess a small set of critical features have equal status as category members. Rather, she maintains that color categories are internally structured into a prototype or best example with nonprototype members ordered from good to poor in terms of their similarity to the prototype. In 1975 Rosch published a series of experiments (Rosch, 1975a) designed to determine whether this prototype structure is reflected in the mental representation of color categories. She explored the structure of mental color codes using a priming paradigm in which subjects judged whether pairs of color chips were physically identical. On priming trials subjects were given the name of the appropriate color category prior to the presentation of the test pair. She reasoned that a prime can only facilitate a judgment when it activates a mental code which contains information needed to make the match. If the mental code generated to the category name corresponds to the prototype of the category, then judgments involving good members of the category (those similar to the prototype) should be facilitated more than judgments which involve poor examples of a category. In fact, it was found that for *same* judgments, responses to good pairs were facilitated and responses to poor pairs inhibited when the prime was presented prior to the test pair. A replication of this basic finding is presented in Fig. 7.1. These effects were eliminated when the prime was presented simultaneously with the test pair. Thus, Rosch concluded that in response to the category name subjects generated a representation of the category prototype that contained more information in common with good than with poor members of the category. Because the prime was only effective

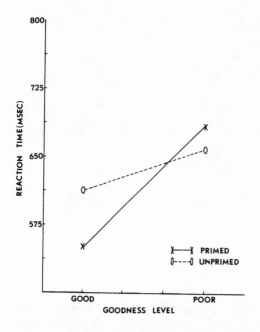

FIG. 7.1. Mean reaction time for same judgments as a function of priming condition and goodness level.

when presented prior to the test pair, she argued that information contained in the category prototype facilitated the encoding of good members of the category rather than a later decision process.

Rosch (1975b, 1977) also made some inferences about the nature (format) of mental color codes. Posner's work (Posner, 1969) and her own research on semantic categories (Rosch, 1975b) demonstrated that given physical-identity instruction, stimuli are processed at a physical level and not at the level of meaning. Therefore she reasoned that in order for a prime to facilitate the perceptual/encoding process with such instructions, the cognitive representation generated to the prime must contain information appropriate to the physical level of analysis. That is, the representation must be in the form of a concrete visual code (image) which contains at least some of the information available when color stimuli are perceived. The following experiments were designed to further explore the structure and the properties of mental color codes.

The first study (Neumann & D'Agostino, 1981) was concerned with the specificity of mental color codes. The plan of this study was to use the Rosch procedure to examine priming effects across a broad range of goodness levels when the prime was either an actual prototype color chip or the name of the color category. If the conceptual representation generated to the color name is in the form of a precise concrete visual code then it should contain much the same information as the physical code produced when the best example of a color category is perceived. Therefore, the priming effects should be similar under the two conditions. However, if the conceptual code is less specific than the physical code, then priming effects under the name condition should extend over a greater number of goodness levels than for the chip condition.

In this study judgments were made under physical-identity instructions at four goodness levels. Under the chip condition on primed trials the appropriate prototype color chip was presented prior to the test pair. Under the name conditions on primed trials the category name preceded the presentation of the test pair. In order to control for modality effects the name of the color category was presented visually under the visual-name condition. Because Rosch used an auditory prime, an auditory-name condition was included for comparison.

All subjects received *same* and *different* pairs at four levels of goodness from each of eight color categories. Each of these 64 pairs were tested under the primed and unprimed conditions for a total of 128 judgments. Independent groups of 16 subjects were tested under the chip condition, the visual-name condition and the auditory-name condition.

The stimuli consisted of color chips from *The Munsell Book of Color: Glossy Finish Collection* (Munsell Color Company, 1966). Test pairs were mounted on 7.6 cm × 12.7 cm white cards separated by 1.27 cm. Prototype chips and category names used as primes were mounted/typed in the center of the cards.

The eight categories consisted of those proposed as universal by Berlin and Kay (1969) and used by Rosch (1975a) in her research. The categories were red, yellow, green, blue, orange, brown pink, and purple. The prototype color chips that served as primes were also those used by Rosch. For each color category a pool of color chips was formed consisting of the prototype chip, a poor example chip from the saturation set used by Rosch (1975a) in her Experiment 3 and all chips falling between these two extremes. Within a color category pool, the chips varied primarily in terms of saturation with brightness differences restricted to no more than two Munsell units. In each category, the poor example chip used by Rosch was assigned to Goodness Level 4. A group of three judges examined each category pool and selected the chip most similar to the prototype and assigned this chip to Goodness Level 1. The judges selected two other chips from each pool and assigned them to Levels 2 and 3 such that the distance between successive levels was roughly equivalent. To minimize gross differences among color categories, chips assigned to the various levels were displayed on a master board during the selection process. The color chips selected for each color category are identified by Munsell notation in Table 7.1.

A stimulus set consisted of an identical pair of chips at each goodness level for every color category for a total of 32 *same* pairs. There was a corresponding number of *different* pairs formed by randomly pairing each chip with a same-level chip from a different color category. Each of these 64 test pairs was presented under the primed and unprimed conditions. Two random orders of the stimulus deck were prepared and used equally often under the name and chip conditions.

TABLE 7.1
Color Stimuli for All Categories

Category	Prototype	Goodness Level			
		1	*2*	*3*	*4*
Red	5R 4/14	5R 4/12	5R 3/10	5R 3/8	5R 3/6
Yellow	2.5Y 8/16	2.5Y 8/12	2.5Y 7/10	2.5Y 6/8	2.5Y 6/4
Green	2.5G 5/12	2.5G 5/10	2.5G 4/8	2.5G 3/8	2.5G 3/4
Blue	2.5PB 4/10	2.5PB 4/8	2.5PB 3/8	2.5PB 2/8	2.5PB 2/4
Pink	5R 8/6	5R 8/4	5R 7/4	5R 6/4	5R 6/2
Orange	2.5YR 6/16	2.5YR 6/14	2.5YR 5/14	2.5YR 5/10	2.5YR 5/8
Brown	5YR 3/6	5YR 3/4	5YR 2/4	5YR 3/2	5YR 2/2
Purple	5P 3/10	5P 3/8	5P 2/8	5P 2/6	5P 2/4

Test pairs were presented in a Gerbrands two-field tachistoscope. Subjects were instructed to press the *same* switch if members of the test pair were physically identical and the *different* switch if members of the test pair were from different color categories. Subjects were told to respond as quickly as possible without error. On primed trials subjects under the chip condition were shown the appropriate prototype chip for 2 sec prior to the test pair. Subjects were instructed to name the color of the prototype chip when it was presented. Under the visual-name condition subjects were shown the name of the color category for 2 sec prior to the test pair and were required to read the name aloud. Under the auditory-name condition, the experimenter said the category name 2 sec prior to the presentation of the test pair and subjects were required to repeat the category name. On unprimed trials all subjects saw a blank card and said the word "blank." Primed and unprimed trials were alternated as in the procedure used by Rosch.

Subjects received a brief practice session that consisted of repeated presentations of four *same* and four *different* pairs similar to the test pairs. During this practice subjects were given feedback on the correctness of their responses as well as their reaction time.

The mean reaction time for correct *same* and *different* judgments under each experimental condition is shown in Fig. 7.2. The question of primary interest was whether for *same* judgments the relationship between priming and goodness level changed as the nature of the prime (chip vs. name) was manipulated. Preliminary analyses were carried out to determine whether the modality of the name prime (visual vs. auditory) was of any importance. These analyses revealed that for both *same* and *different* responses the main effects of goodness level, priming and color category were significant. However neither the modality effect nor any interaction with modality approached significance. Therefore, in the main analysis only the two visual prime conditions (chip vs. visual-name) were included. A four-

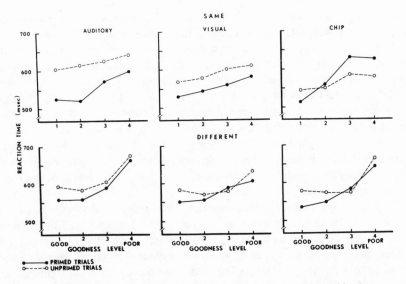

FIG. 7.2.   Mean reaction time as a function of experimental condition.

way analysis of variance (Priming × Goodness Level × Color Category × Prime Type) was carried out separately on *same* and *different* judgments, with the significance level set at $p < .05$.

For *same* responses, the critical Priming × Goodness Level × Prime Type interaction was significant, $F(3,90) = 2.79$. As can be seen in Fig. 7.1, priming facilitated *same* responses at all goodness levels under the visual-name condition but under the chip condition priming facilitated Level 1 responses but inhibited responses at Goodness Levels 3 and 4. Simple interaction effects were significant only under the chip condition, $F(3,45) = 5.60$.

For *different* responses there was a main effect of goodness level, $F(3,90) = 44.96$, and priming, $F(1.30) = 8.08$, but neither the Priming × Goodness Level nor the Priming × Goodness Level × Prime Type interactions were significant.

The overall error rate was 5.5%. Error rates in the chip, visual-name and auditory-name conditions were 6.1%, 5.1% and 5.4% respectively.

In summary, the important finding was that for *same* responses the prototype chip facilitated responses to good pairs (Level 1) and inhibited responses to poor pairs (Levels 3 and 4) whereas the category name facilitated responses at all goodness levels.

This experiment was designed to determine if the conceptual representation generated to the category name is as specific and precise as the physical code produced by the best example of the color category. The plan was to measure priming effects across various goodness levels when the prime was either a prototype color chip or the name of a color category. It was assumed that a prime could facilitate the encoding of a test pair only if the representation produced to the prime contained at least some of the information available when color stimuli are perceived (Rosch, 1975a). If the conceptual representation generated to the color name was in the form of a precise visual code comparable to the physical code produced to the prototype chip, then priming effects should have been similar under the two conditions. Clearly, this was not the case. Under the chip condition, the prime facilitated performance only when the test pair was highly similar to the prototype chip. Under the name conditions, the prime facilitated performance at all goodness levels. Given the logic of the present experiment, these data suggest that mental color codes contain less specific physical information than does the physical code produced when the best example of the color category is perceived.

Despite the fact that the procedure used in the present study was very similar to Rosch (1975a) and that the poor test pairs (Level 4) consisted of the poor example chips used by Rosch in her Experiment 3, we did not replicate her finding that priming with a category name facilitated responses to only good members of a category. There is little reason to question the reliability of her results or doubt her conclusion that mental color codes are internally structured. At the same time, the present finding was produced under both visual and auditory-name conditions as well as in a preliminary study that used a different set of color chips.

It may be possible to account for these data within the Rosch framework if it is assumed that the internal structure of a color category is not entirely fixed but can be modified by context and task demands. Rosch (1975a) has demonstrated that with extensive practice over a 2-week period the structure of a color category can be modified such that priming effects are found with both good and poor members of a category. Without extensive practice, it may be difficult to modify category structure if exposed to only the extremes of category membership in a task where the prototype structure is appropriate on 50% of the priming trials. In the present study good members of the category (Level 1) were presented on only 25% of the priming trials and therefore the effectiveness of an unmodified structure may have been less than in the Rosch studies. In addition, exposure to a broad range of goodness levels may have permitted progressive modification of category structure which may be difficult to achieve when exposure is restricted to just good and poor examples of a category. This explanation suggests that there may be considerable plasticity associated with the internal structure of color categories. The next study (D'Agostino, in press) was designed to further examine this property of mental color codes.

If the structure of mental color codes is at least partially dependent on context then it should be possible to modify this structure simply by varying the order in which test pairs at the various goodness levels are presented. Exposure to all test pairs involving moderate goodness levels (Levels 2 and 3) prior to the presentation of the more extreme test pairs (Levels 1 and 4) should facilitate code modification and extend priming effects to the poor example test pairs. If subjects are initially exposed only to the extremes of category membership (Levels 1 and 4) then little code modifications should occur and priming effects should be restricted to good example test pairs as Rosch (1975b) reported. The effects of test pair order should be limited to the name prime condition because under the chip condition priming effects are presumably mediated by the physical codes produced when the best example chip is perceived.

The stimulus materials and general procedure were similar to that previously described. Thus, all subjects received *same* and *different* pairs at four levels of goodness from each of eight color categories. Each of these 64 pairs was tested under the primed and unprimed conditions for a total of 128 judgments. However, under the 1 and 4 first condition subjects were presented with all 64 test pairs involving Levels 1 and 4 prior to the presentation of test pairs involving Levels 2 or 3. Under the 2 and 3 first condition subjects were presented with all 64 test pairs involving Levels 2 and 3 prior to the presentation of any test pair involving Levels 1 or 4. Independent groups of 16 subjects were tested under each test pair order condition. In one experiment all subjects were tested under an auditory-name condition whereas in another experiment all subjects were tested

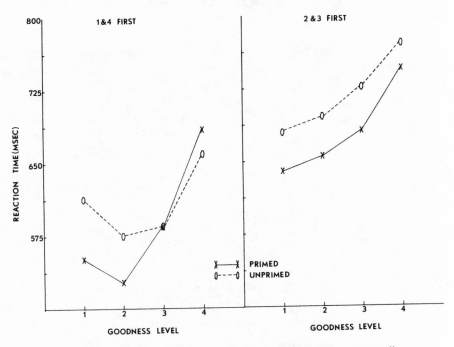

FIG. 7.3.   Mean reaction time for same judgments under the name prime condition.

under a chip prime condition. To facilitate communication these two studies will be described as a single experiment.

Error rates for all conditions ranged from 1 to 3%. The mean reaction time for correct *same* judgments under the name prime condition is shown in Fig. 7.3. It can be seen that under the 2 and 3 first condition priming facilitated performance at all goodness levels whereas for the 1 and 4 first condition facilitation was limited to goodness Levels 1 and 2. Although the Priming × Goodness Level × Test Order interaction was only marginal, $F(3,90) = 2.39$, $p<.08$, additional planned analyses indicated that the Priming × Goodness Level interaction was significant only under the 1 and 4 first condition, $F(3,45) = 6.87$.

Reaction time for correct *same* judgments under the chip condition is shown in Fig. 7.4. Analyses revealed a significant Priming × Goodness Level interaction, $F(3,90) = 8.58$, which did not vary with test pair order. Under both order conditions, priming facilitated performance for good examples of a color category (Levels 1 and 2) and inhibited performance for poor examples (Level 4).

These data support the hypothesis that the nature of the mental representation generated to a category name can be readily modified by context. Whereas intitial exposure to the extremes of category membership produced priming effects for *same* judgments which are restricted to good examples of the color category, initial exposure to moderate goodness levels extended priming effects to all goodness levels.

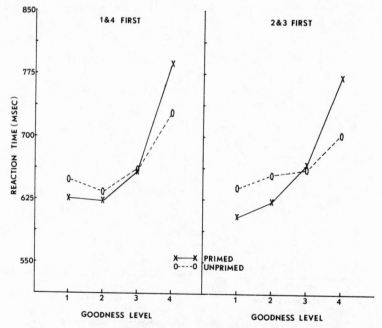

FIG. 7.4.   Mean reaction time for same judgments under the chip condition.

This apparent plasticity can be understood by thinking of mental color codes in terms of knowledge structures or schemata (e.g., Rumelhart & Ortony, 1977). In the absence of contextual information, the values assigned to the variables of a color schema may be determined by variable constraints which are part of the schema. These constraints are probably biased toward prototypical values as Rosch (1975a) suggests. However, in a particular context the values assigned to these variables may be determined at least in part by the properties of the particular exemplars which are presented. The process of assigning values to variables in a particular context may be similar to the process of prototype abstraction with artificial categories. Strauss (1979) has recently reported that when adults observed exemplars with feature values that were not widely separated, the prototype representation was formed by averaging the feature values of the exemplars. Feature averaging did not occur when the feature values of the exemplars were widely separated. Similarly, when subjects are exposed to color chips from a broad range of goodness levels, the values assigned to the variables of a color schema may be based on the average of the values of the exemplars. Prototype values may also be included in this average. However, when initial exposure is limited to the extremes of category membership (i.e., values are widely separated) feature averaging may not occur and values may be assigned to variables according to the variable constraints specified by the schema. As noted earlier these constraints are probably biased toward prototypical values. Viewed in this way, the plasticity of mental color codes becomes associated with the instantiation of a color schema. The internal organization of the schema remains relatively fixed (Rosch, 1975a).

Finally, the above analysis implies that the precision or specificity of mental color codes should also vary with context. In the present studies priming effects were obtained under certain conditions at all goodness levels. These data suggest that the mental representation generated to the category name was not very precise but contained information appropriate to the perception of virtually all category members. On the other hand, priming effects under the 1 and 4 first condition were restricted to good examples of the color category under both the name and chip conditions. In this instance, it appears that the mental representation generated to the category name contained information nearly as precise and specific as the physical code available when the best example was perceived. Thus, it does seem that the specificity of mental color codes is at least partially determined by context.

REFERENCES

Berlin, B., & Kay, P. *Basic color terms: Their universality and evolution.* Berkeley: University of California Press, 1969.

D'Agostino, P. R. Plasticity of mental color codes. *American Journal of Psychology,* in press.

Munsell Color Company. *The Munsell book of color: Glossy finish collection.* Baltimore, Md.: Munsell Color Company, 1966.

Neumann, K. M., & D'Agostino, P. R. Specificity of mental color codes. *American Journal of Psychology,* 1981, *94,* 451–459.

Posner, M. I. Abstraction and the process of recognition. In G. H. Bower & J. T. Spence (Eds.), *The psychology of learning and motivation* (Vol. 3). New York: Academic Press, 1969.

Rosch, E. On the internal structure of perceptual and semantic categories. In T. E. Moore (Ed.), *Cognitive development and the acquisition of language.* New York: Academic Press, 1973.

Rosch, E. Cognitive representations of semantic categories. *Journal of Experimental Psychology: General,* 1975, *104,* 192–233. (a)

Rosch, E. The nature of mental codes for color categories. *Journal of Experimental Psychology: Human Perception and Performance,* 1975, *1,* 303–322. (b)

Rosch, E. Human categorization. In N. Warren (Ed.), *Advances in cross-cultural psychology* (Vol. 1). London: Academic Press, 1977.

Rumelhart, D. E., & Ortony, A. The representation of knowledge in memory. In R. C. Anderson, R. J. Spiro, & W. E. Montague (Eds.), *Schooling and the acquisition of knowledge.* Hillsdale, N.J.: Lawrence Erlbaum Assoc., 1977.

Strauss, M. S. Abstraction of prototypical information by adults and 10-month-old infants. *Journal of Experimental Psychology: Human Learning and Memory,* 1979, *5,* 618–632.

8

Schemas and Images In Self-Recognition

A. Daniel Yarmey
University of Guelph

Who would have thought that in the 1980s someone who was trained in the traditional area of experimental psychology would be addressing this audience on something as soft-minded as the "self." Times, interests, and people change. But do they really change? The "geritol set" of Allan Paivio's former students can remember, I am sure, attending meetings of the Canadian Psychological Association and the Psychonomic Society in the 60s and receiving polite but restrained interest from fellow researchers when they learned we were studying mental imagery. As we know, mental imagery was a legitimate memory phenomena to the early Greek philosophers and continued to be studied and practiced up to the present century. However, after Watson's (1913) attack on mentalism and memory images, academic psychology lost interest in this concept. It wasn't until the 1960s that theorists, such as Hebb (1968), Holt (1964), Mowrer (1960), and Paivio (1969), of course, to mention only a few, showed an interest in a revival of imagery.

Not surprisingly, with the rise of logical positivism and operationalism, similar pressures were put onto the concept of self. When academic psychology broke away from the discipline of philosophy in the late 19th and early 20th centuries, the study of the self was of concern to psycholoanalysts and to other schools of psychotherapy. By the 1940s academic psychologists, such as Allport (1943) and Sherif (1947), began to show renewed interest in the roles and functions of ego-involvements. But it is only in the last ten years or so that social and cognitive psychologists have recognized the importance of self-awareness, self-reflection, self-perception, and other attributes of the concept of self for the study of behavior.

More recently, Hazel Markus (1980) has hypothesized how the self-concept is related to thought and memory. The first section of this chapter presents an overview of studies that have focused on memory for information related to one's self. In the second section, an attempt is made to show how self-referencing in memory can have its theoretical base in a dual-coding approach to memory. I intend to argue that self-recognition may be understood both theoretically and empirically in terms of verbal and nonverbal imagery. Although the nature of the representational units of the self-concept in thought and memory could be understood in terms of a propositional model (Anderson, 1978), this issue is beyond the scope of this paper.

The Self-Concept and Social Information Processing

The most central of all psychological experiences has to be the sense of self. Knowledge about our personal identity and our place in the physical world and in the social environment with all of their respective diversities of information, impinge on and are reflected by our sense of self. Information overload forces us to be selective in attentional and memorial processes. One of the stimuli that we are very selective about is information about ourselves. The well-known *cocktail party effect*, whereby people attending to one conversation will hear their names being mentioned, but hear nothing else coming from the opposite side of the room (see Moray, 1959), is an example of selective self-attention. Markus (1980) suggests that "in general, when thinking about the social world, the self is quite likely to be distinctive and of particular interest to us [p. 103]." In order to fully understand thought and memory it is important to evaluate an individual's frame of reference, or cognitive structures, which organize, modify, and integrate information, especially in relation to information pertaining to the self, and to significant others.

A review of how schemas develop in either the Piagetian or Bruner sense is beyond the scope of this paper. Similarly, no attention will be given here to the development of self-schemas. Of interest, however, is the content of self-schemas. Most of the research in this field has focused on traits or verbal propositions. Thus, people describe themselves in such traitlike terms as "I am honest," "I am athletic," "I am friendly," and so on. These traits have an important role in memory. According to Cantor and Mischel (1979), trait terms function as prototypes or summaries that organize a large amount of conceptually similar information. In one study, subjects were given information about a hypothetical person which suggested that she was introverted (e.g., "Jane is shy"). Later, when tested for their recognition memory for the original statements, subjects falsely identified statements that were conceptually related to the prototype of the concept of introvert.

Markus (1977) has shown in her own research that people have self-schemas only about aspects of behavior that are important to them. Those individuals, for example, who have a self-schema about independence, as opposed to those who think of themselves as dependent, behave differently on a variety of cognitive tasks. The former make faster decisions about themselves and respond more frequently to information that describes them as being "assertive" and "individualistic," because it is consistent with their self-schema.

Memory for information about the self. Evidence that memory for decisions related to one's self is superior to memory for other types of information, including judgments about strangers, has been found by Rogers and his colleagues (e.g., Kuiper & Rogers, 1979; Rogers, 1977; Rogers, Kuiper & Kirker, 1977) and by Bower and Gilligan (1979). Apparently, recall of self-reference traits as opposed to information about others is superior because self-referencing information is highly organized in a well differentiated memory structure. Markus (1980) speculates that one of the factors that promotes memory for self-descriptive materials is their vividness, concreteness and salience. All of these characteristics, of course, fit Paivio's (1971) dual coding theory of memory which is specialized for processing both linguistic information and nonverbal imagery information.

Although the self-concept has been empirically and theoretically defined in terms of verbal descriptions, Markus (1980) states that a self-schema could include images and representations that cannot be described in words. John Mueller has attempted to test the hypothesis that self-reference for pictorial materials, specifically human faces of strangers, also yields superior retention. However, compared to the research on verbal memory, the self-reference effect using facial stimuli has failed to show a superiority. In one study, Mueller, Bailis and Goldstein (1979) manipulated self-reference by asking subjects to make either abstract decisions or physical feature decisions about facial stimuli. Four types of study decisions were made: abstract-self ("Does this person look more intelligent than you?"), abstract-nonself ("Does this person look intelligent?"), physical-self ("Does this person weigh more than you?"), physical-nonself ("Does this person weight more than 150 lbs?"). Results showed that depth of processing (abstract over physical feature) produced the usual memory superiority in face recognition (Bower & Karlin, 1974), but there was no evidence for a self-reference memory superiority. The failure to find a benefit due to self-reference in facial recognition has been replicated by Meuller and his colleagues in four additional investigations (Bailis & Mueller, in press; Courtois & Mueller, 1979; Mueller, Courtois & Bailis, 1981; Mueller, Nicodemus & Ross, 1981).

A reasonable question to ask is why does self-referencing show a positive effect on verbal memory but not on facial memory? Mueller et al. (1981) offer the following explanations:

1. Since face memory is generally good perhaps a ceiling effect operates which restricts any gains of self-referencing. Their own data, however, rule out this explanation.

2. Verbal memory has been tested by recall whereas facial memory has been examined by recognition. Perhaps, a recall-recognition difference accounts for the failure to find the effect with faces.

3. The types of decisions made for faces have been somewhat different than those for trait descriptions. This discrepancy may be part of the problem but Mueller and his colleagues feel that a more fundamental problem exists.

4. Following Lord (1980), Mueller et al. (1981) suggest a distinction between the self-schema as a verbal list of attributes and the self-image. Unlike verbal attributes, they suggest that the self-image is a poor mnemonic aid. However, they accept Lord's (1980) assumption that an individual compares a facial photograph of a stranger with his or her own self-image schema (without proof, I may add, that there is such a thing as a facial self-image).

Lord (1980) theorizes that self-schema represents propositional, verbal or semantically encoded knowledge about the self. He hypothesizes that visual encoding comprises two sorts of memory images, self-images and other-images. "Self-images are mental representations of scenes in which the self is involved, other images are mental representations of scenes in which other people are involved [p. 259]." Lord states that self-images are perceptually nonsalient and nonattended, in contrast to other-images, which may be salient and dynamic. These differences probably account for the failure to find superior retention for facial self-referent comparisons (see also Jones & Nisbett, 1971). The above theorizing of visual encoding is easily accommodated in Paivio's dual-coding model. However, a detailed description of self-images and other-images and their probable connections to the verbal memory system remains to be explored, and is beyond the goals of this paper.

Earlier, I mentioned that Mueller and Lord, among others, assume that people can generate self-facial images (an assumption that I also hold), but that few data are available to support this belief. I know that investigators interested in personality and clinical problems have studied such phenomena as body image and phantom limb phenomena for over 40 years (see Shontz, 1969), but these are not the kind of images and memory data I refer to. My own research for the last two or three years has been directed to filling this gap. Let me briefly describe two of these studies and mention as well one "not so serious" study for your amusement.

Study one.   The major purpose of this investigation was to study the difference between males and females in their identification and recognition memory for different photograph poses of their own face. Goffman (1959) proposed that people have a sense of self-image that represents the "real me," as well as an image of themselves that changes as they move from one social situation to another. Assuming that subjects can identify a facial photograph of themselves that approximates or represents their "real self," a question of theoretical importance is whether they can identify this photograph later in a recognition test when it is presented among similar self-photographs? If the self functions like a prototype in information processing, recognition of a photograph representing the real self should be relatively accurate.

Goffman (1959) also proposed that people have social images of themselves that are usually temporary and changeable and are not necessarily congruent with body images. Three body images or, more specifically, facial expressions that people often project are sociability, intelligence, and trustworthiness. One issue, however, is how salient and memorable these images are to the individual?

Subjects were photographed with a Polaroid camera as they projected each of the above three facial expressions. After deciding which face of 10 best represented each characteristic, and judging which photograph best represented their "real self," a recognition memory test of poses was given. Half of each sex were tested under intentional learning conditions and the remainder were tested under incidental learning conditions (for further details, see Yarmey 1979b).

Results failed to reveal any response biases for either sex in their verbal identification of poses. Females were reliably superior to males in recognition memory of their most sociable face and in recognition of their real self. No significant differences between the sexes were found for recognition of the most trustworthy pose or most intelligent pose. These findings indicate that females are not generally superior to males in facial recognition, but instead, are superior only on specific processing demands. No reliable differences were found between intentional and incidental learning.

Looking for the moment only at decisions involving the real self, differences were found between males and females in the selection of which pose category best fitted their "real me" image. Women predominantly chose their real self from the sociable projections (75%) and seldomly selected from intelligent (15%) or trustworthy projections (10%). Males also made more of their real self selections from the sociable poses (45%), but, in contrast to females, also selected relatively frequently from trustworthy poses (35%).

In view of the importance of self for both males and females, it is interesting to speculate about the superiority of females over males in memory for self-images. One hypothesis is that women gaze more frequently at their mirror reflections and overlearn self-images more so than do males. Another hypothesis states that women are in a "more vulnerable social position, in the past at least, [which] has made them more sensitive to, and more conscious of, signs of *genuine* feeling and affection" (Liggett, 1974, p. 244)). The notion of female's vulnerability is interesting because of its evolutionary significance in primates. Research by Lawick-Goodall (1971) indicates that monkeys communicate their submissiveness by displaying smiles or grins. On the human level, Deux (1976) has used this evidence to support an hypothesis of female submissiveness. She suggests that women are more likely to display wide grins and to show their teeth while smiling whereas men more frequently smile without exposing their teeth. An analysis of the photographs in the present study showed that females smiled more frequently than males, and displayed their teeth reliably more often when smiling. These results suggest among other things that females probably have a self facial-schema that differs from males. Study two attempted to test this hypothesis in a more rigorous fashion.

Study two.   In order for someone to look at a photograph of herself or himself and judge that the snapshot is a "good" picture, that it captures her or his "real" personality, suggests the existence of some sort of body image-schema or prototype. Most of us, for example, have verbal and/or image-schemas of the prototypic female Hollywood movie star, the absent minded professor, and the archetypal British butler. These prototypes are well-structured, stable memory representations. How permanent, however, are self-image schemas? Orbach, Traub and Olson (1966) suggest that people do not have a constant, internalized schema of their physical appearance but, instead, have a wide range of body images, each of which is an acceptable representation of themselves. Orbach et al., make this claim from the following evidence. They found that subjects given the task of manipulating a distorting mirror until their reflection appeared normal complained that they had forgotten precisely what they looked like, and accepted a wide range of mirror reflections as perfectly good representations of their bodies. Nevertheless, to conclude on the basis of these findings and the methodology employed that self-images are unstable may be premature.

In the present study a set of photographs was taken of each subject and self-rated on a 9-point scale in terms of the degree to which the photographs resembled their imaginal prototype of "real-self." One week later subjects returned to the laboratory for a recognition memory test. Self-image prototypes were investigated through an analysis of false alarms. Following the argument of Rogers, Rogers and Kuiper (1979), a false alarms effect is present if there is an increase in false positives (saying that an item was in a study list when it was not) as a function of similarity of an item to the prototype. Consequently, if subjects are given half of their own photographs as study items (OLD), and the remainder as foils (NEW) on the recognition test, evidence of a false alarms effect would be shown if there is an increase in false alarms to NEW items as a function of the similarity of each photograph to the self-image schema. The self-photographs were divided into four levels of self-reference ranging from "not like the real me," to "very much like the real me." The study items (OLD) and the foils (NEW) had an equal number of photographs from each of the four self-reference categories (see Yarmey & Johnson, in press, for further details).

The results showed a reliable increase in false alarms on the NEW photographs from the lowest to the second closest category of the "real-me prototype." Except for the highest level of self-reference, photographs used as foils that were most similar to the prototype were most difficult to recognize. We argue that these results indicate that when someone looks at their own photograph and states "that doesn't look like me," this judgement is based in part on an imaginal self-schema.

Because subjects recognized both NEW and OLD photographs at the highest level of self-reference they had to do more than merely compare these stimuli with internal representations of the original photographs. Subjects must have had a *specific* memory for both of these types of items which overcame their tendency to compare the photographs to the visual prototype. High recognition for both NEW and OLD photographs of high self-reference is probably related to the personal significance or extreme meaningfulness of these self-photographs.

In the "real world," retention of visual details over relatively long periods of time often is important. This information probably is stored in long-term memory as a cognitive prototype. The fact that subjects rated their self-photographs one week prior to the recognition memory test suggests that the imaginal self-schema must be relatively reliable in order to obtain the results found in this experiment. However, theorists such as Markus (1980) state that schemas are modified by experience and should not be conceptualized as final, complete products. Without further research it is impossible to estimate the duration of the imaginal self-schema over a period longer than one week.

Results also were consistent with study one. Females were reliably superior to males in self-recognition and, even more interesting, males and females differed reliably in nonverbal behaviors reflecting differences in their image of real-self. Females smiled more than males, were more open in their smiles, and had a greater tendency to show teeth than did males. Furthermore, these behaviors intensified with increasing approximation to their real-self schema. In addition, females displayed heightened relaxation in posture as they approached their real-self, whereas males showed additional tenseness as they approached the category representing their real-self schema.

To rule out the possibility that the false alarms effect was a function of chance, or that the distractor faces for some odd reason were unusually difficult to remember the more similar they were to the real-self schema, a follow-up study was conducted. Exactly the same experimental design of study two was followed with the exception that 16 male and 16 female subjects studied photographs of faces of subjects of their own sex from the previous study, rather than photographs of their own faces. Presumably, strangers do not know the self-facial schema of others apart from guessing, consequently, the false alarms effect should not be present. The results supported the prediction. Females, once again, were superior to males, and subjects learned target faces reliably better than foils, but there was no significant false alarms effect for the foils as found in study two. Following the recognition test, we asked subjects to take a phenomenological perspective and try to imagine that they were the person photographed. They were asked to sort the 40 photographs into the four categories ranging from "unlike real me" to "real me" as that person would. The sortings of photographs compared to the actual sortings done originally by the photographed person proved to be unsystematic or random. This suggests that self-facial schemas are private and stable imaginal representations that mediate the behavior of the significant individual and not others.

It may be concluded that studies one and two establish the robustness of research in cognition and personality by showing that the nonverbal imagery system includes self-images. This evidence combined with the findings of other researchers (Lord, 1980; Markus, 1977; Rogers et al., 1977; Rogers et al., 1979) strongly supports the hypothesis that the self-schema includes verbal propositions, self-images, and other-image representations.

Study three. The final study I wish to report on is the one mentioned earlier as being "not so serious." This investigation can be considered a follow-up of the nonverbal facial expressions reported in study two. Some of you may not know of the recent death of one of psychology's great journals, *The Worm Runner's Digest.* In its last issue, two of my colleagues at the Univeristy of Guelph, Davis and Simmons (1979), reported an investigation in which their judges were unable to differentiate among facial expressions of rats. When rats were induced to produce 12 separate and distinct mood states such as: tiredness, ecstacy, confusion, fury, and so on, judges could not discriminate one facial expression from another. Now, this may not seem to be a major problem, but these findings attack the foundations of Darwin's (1872) classical work in psychology, published in *The Expression of the Emotions in Man and the Animals.* Several hypotheses can be offered as to why Davis and Simmons failed to find differential facial expressions in rats. One hypothesis is that all of their subjects came from a visible minority, such as an Asiatic strain, and, as all occidentals know, "All Orientals look alike." Because all of the judges were white, there may have been a cross-race effect similar to what happens in the psychology of eyewitness testimony (see Yarmey, 1979a). Another possibility is that Davis and Simmons were insensitive and did not really know their subjects. It seems that they failed to take into account their subject's personality attributes and self-concepts.

The present investigation attempted to correct this failure. Ten rats came from the University of Guelph colony of animals used by Davis and Simmons, and 10 came from the local psychiatric center. All subjects were given a battery of personality tests designed to reveal information about their self-concept: the RAT (Rat Apperception Test); the Draw-a-Rat Test; the Ratachack Ink Blot Test; and the Rat-FACS Test (Rat Facial Affect Coding System). After weeks of training, the rats were induced to produce 12 separate and distinct mood states. An artist, who was not aware of their personality scores, drew their facial photographs as they emoted (see Yarmey, in press, for further details).

The analysis of personality scores revealed that all of the rats selected from the University of Guelph colony were internalizers, whereas the rats selected from

INTERNALIZERS

tiredness   ecstasy   confusion   fury

EXTERNALIZERS

tiredness   ecstasy   confusion   fury

FIG. 8.1   Examples of facial expressions of rats classified as internalizers and externalizers. (Yarmey, in press. Reprinted by permission of the *Journal of Irreproducible Results*).

the psychiatric hospital were all mixed up. However, some of these rats were externalizers. If you look at Fig. 8.1 it is apparent that internalizers show very little signs of facial emotionality. However, externalizers display many different facial expressions.

These results support the observations, conclusions and generalization of Darwin (1872). The next step for researchers is to show how the self-schema, imagery and verbal processes operate in the rat. On the other hand, there are enough problems for us to study on memory, imagery and the self-schema in humans that we can leave the work on the noble rat to other more qualified investigators, such as Davis and Simmons.

REFERENCES

Allport, G. W. The ego in contemporary psychology. *Psychological Review*, 1943, *50*, 451–478.
Anderson, J. R. Arguments concerning representation for mental imagery. *Psychological Review*, 1978, *85*, 249–277.
Bailis, K. L., & Mueller, J. H. Anxiety, feedback, and self-reference in face recognition. *Motivation and Emotion*, in press.

Bower, G. H., & Gilligan, S. G. Remembering information related to one's self. *Journal of Research in Personality*, 1979, *13*, 420-432.

Bower, G. H., & Karlin, M. B. Depth of processing pictures of faces and recognition memory. *Journal of Experimental Psychology*, 1974, *103*, 751-757.

Cantor, N., & Mischel, W. Prototypicality and personality: Effects on free recall and personality impressions. *Journal of Research in Personality*, 1979, *13*, 187-205.

Courtois, M. R., & Mueller, J. H. Processing multiple physical features in facial recognition. *Bulletin of the Psychonomic Society*, 1979, *14*, 74-76.

Darwin, C. *The expression of the emotions in man and the animals.* London: John Murray, 1872.

Davis, H., & Simmons, S. An analysis of facial expression in the rat. *The Worm Runner's Digest*, 1979, *21*, 81-82.

Deux, K. *The behavior of women and men.* Monterey, California: Brooks/Cole, 1976.

Goffman, E. *The presentation of self in everyday life.* Garden City, New York: Doubleday, 1959.

Hebb, D. O. Concerning imagery. *Psychological Review*, 1968, *75*, 466-477.

Holt, .R .R. Imagery: The return of the ostracized. *American Psychologist*, 1964, *19*, 254-264.

Jones, E. E., & Nisbett, R. E. *The actor and the observer: Divergent perceptions of the causes of behavior.* Morristown, N.J.: General Learning Press, 1971.

Kuiper, N. A., & Rogers, T. B. The encoding of personal information: Self-other differences. *Journal of Personality and Social Psychology*, 1979, *37*, 499-514.

Lawick-Goodall, J. V. *In the shadow of man.* Boston: Houghton-Mifflin, 1971.

Liggett, J. *The human face.* London: Constable, 1974.

Lord, C. G. Schemas and images as memory aids: Two modes of processing social information. *Journal of Personality and Social Psychology*, 1980, *38*, 257-269.

Markus, H. Self-schemata and processing information about the self. *Journal of Personality and Social Psychology*, 1977, *35*, 63-78.

Markus, H. The self in thought and memory. In D. M. Wegner & R. R. Vallacher (Eds.), *The self in social psychology.* New York: Oxford University Press, 1980.

Moray, N. Attention in dichotic listening: Affective cues and the influence of instructions. *Quarterly Journal of Experimental Psychology*, 1959, *11*, 56-60.

Mowrer, O. H. *Learning theory and the symbolic processes.* New York: Wiley, 1960.

Mueller, J. H., Bailis, K. L., & Goldstein, A. G. Depth of processing and anxiety in facial recognition. *British Journal of Psychology*, 1979, *70*, 511-515.

Mueller, J. H., Courtois, M. R., & Bailis, K. L. Self-reference in facial recognition. *Bulletin of the Psychonomic Society*, 1981, *17*, 85-88.

Mueller, J. H., Nicodemus, D. R., & Ross, M. J. Self-awareness in facial recognition. *Bulletin of the Psychonomic Society*, 1981, *18*, 145-147.

Orbach, J., Traub, A., & Olson, R. Psychophysical studies of body image: II. Normative data on the adjustable body-distorting mirror. *Archives of General Psychiatry*, 1966, *14*, 41-47.

Paivio, A. Mental imagery in associative learning and memory. *Psychological Review*, 1969, *76*, 241-263.

Paivio, A. *Imagery and verbal processes.* New York: Holt, Rinehart, & Winston, 1971 (Reprinted by Lawrence Erlbaum Associates, Hillsdale, N.J., 1979).

Rogers, T. B. Self-reference in memory: Recognition of personality items. *Journal of Research in Personality*, 1977, *11*, 295-305.

Rogers, T. B., Kuiper, N. A., & Kirker, W. S. Self-reference and the encoding of personal informations. *Journal of Personality and Social Psychology*, 1977, *35*, 677-688.

Rogers, T. B., Rogers, P. J., & Kuiper, N. A. Evidence for the self as a cognitive prototype: The "false alarms effect." *Personality and Social Psychology Bulletin*, 1979, *5*, 53-56.

Sherif, M. *The psychology of ego-involvements.* New York: Wiley, 1947.

Shontz, F. C. *Perceptual and cognitive aspects of body experience.* New York: Academic Press, 1969.

Watson, J. B. Psychology as the behaviorist views it. *Psychological Review*, 1913, *20*, 158-177.

Yarmey, A. D. *The psychology of eyewitness testimony*. New York: Free Press, 1979. (a)

Yarmey, A. D. Through the looking glass: Sex differences in memory for self-facial poses. *Journal of Research in Personality*, 1979 *13*, 450-459. (b)

Yarmey, A. D. Emotion in the rat face. *Journal of Irreproducible Results*, in press.

Yarmey, A. D., & Johnson, J. Evidence for the self as an imaginal prototype. *Journal of Research in Personality*, in press.

9 Paivio's Dual-Coding Model of Meaning Revisited

Fraser Bleasdale
Trent University

The primary focus of this chapter concerns the nature of semantic representation and its relation to memory. Looking back over my graduate-student years, it is clear that the seeds of my curiosity concerning semantic representation and memory were long ago germinated and well cultivated by coffee-punctuated discussions with Allan Paivio, in whose honor this symposium was held. I remember on one occasion walking down the halls of Middlesex College with Allan when he mentioned that he had been exploring the notion of meaning as imagery. My response was neither as opportune nor thoughtful as it might have been, and I remember the resultant look of surprise on Allan's face.

But anecdotes aside, the nature of semantic representation, and its relationship to imaginal and linguistic processes is a challenging issue. This chapter addresses the issue in three main sections. The first section reviews some alternative possibilities concerning the nature of semantic representation in memory. Section two presents experimental evidence from two naming latency studies which is consistent with Paivio's dual-coding theory that semantic representation is functionally distinguished by verbal and imaginal components. In the third section it is suggested, both in light of the experimental evidence presented in this chapter, and in light of a review of the literature, that a dual verbal input feature be added to Paivio's concept of the representational level of meaning. Finally, a tentative model is proposed to integrate some of the ideas discussed throughout the chapter.

THE NATURE OF SEMANTIC REPRESENTATION

It would appear logical, not only from a phylogenetic but also from an ontogenetic perspective, to assume that linguistic ability is preceeded by the acquisition of nonverbal, perceptually-based information. A child gains knowledge of the world, and learns the meaning of things, long before he or she understands language or is able to speak. If knowledge and meaning are acquired before language, then epistemological and semantic information initially must be, and subsequently may remain, essentially nonverbal.

Jean Piaget (1936, cited by Ginsburg & Opper, 1969), for example, has written piquantly in favor of a perceptual base to memory. According to Piaget, knowledge structures, or schemata, start to be formed almost from birth, when the infant actively manipulates, touches, and interacts with the environment. As the infant manipulates objects, sensory-motor schemata are developed and changed to accommodate new information. Over a period of time, schemata become internalized in the form of thought. It is not until later that the child may be able to express verbally the knowledge that he has gained as a result of interacting with the world. According to Piaget, then, knowledge structures are basically formed from the coordinated remnants of sensory and motor signals that have been generated as the child has interacted with the world.

Paivio (1971) incorporated Piaget's view, suggesting that linguistic competence and performance are based on a substrate of imagery. Imagery includes not only static representations of objects, but also dynamic representations of action sequences and relationships between objects and events. With time, linguistic labels and descriptions become associated with imagery representations. However, Paivio (1971) conjectures that although language develops from an initial imaginal base, and although language and imagery remain interlocked, linguistic representation eventually develops a partly autonomous structure of its own, such that ''verbal behavior and verbal understanding are possible at a relatively autonomous intraverbal level, i.e., free of dependence not only upon a concrete situational context but to some extent from imagery as well [p.438].''

The concept of independent verbal and imaginal semantic representation is at the heart of Paivio's tri-level, dual-coding model of meaning (Paivio, 1971; Paivio & Begg, 1981; see Fig. 9.1). According to the model, meaning is viewed as inherent to three types of processes, namely representational, referential and associative processes. After verbal and nonverbal stimuli (e.g., words and pictures) have received an initial, relatively peripheral, sensory analysis, they are usually recognized by a logogen and an imagen respectively. Logogens and imagens are basically feature recognizers that accrue information concerning the features of incoming verbal and nonverbal stimuli. When the features of a stimulus sufficiently match those of a logogen or imagen, the threshold for the logogen or imagen will have been reached, allowing access to further semantic, phonemic and/or pictorial information.

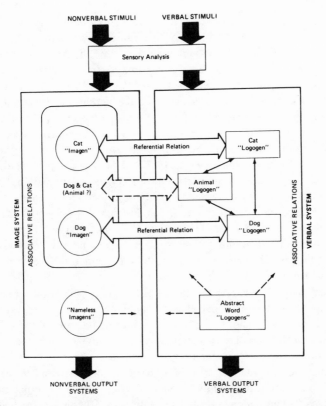

FIG. 9.1. Schematization of Paivio's model of representational, referential, and associative levels of meaning (after Paivio and Begg, 1981, Reprinted by permission).

After representational codes have become available, both verbal and nonverbal representations may be referentially processed. That is, words (especially concrete ones) may be imaged, and pictures (or line drawings, or objects) may be named. At the third level of meaning, associative relations may form intraverbally among logogens, and intraimaginally among imagens. Two key aspects of the model for the present discussion are, first, that meaning arises intrinsically as a property of tri-level processing in both the verbal and imaginal systems and, second, that words, whether high or low imagery, are initially processed by a single verbal system. The latter point will become relevant in later discussions of experimental data.

Philip Seymour (1973, 1976) also has addressed the question of the nature of semantic memory. His model for what he calls symbolic, lexical, and pictorial memory has more boxes, and, therefore, seems more complex than Paivio's model. Nonetheless, the two models overlap to a considerable degree. Seymour (1976) points out that in his model pictorial memory (including the pictorial register and semantic memory store) corresponds to what Paivio calls the imagery system. Likewise, lexical memory (including the phonemic register) corresponds to what Paivio labels the verbal system. Aside from the greater detail in Seymour's model, the two models differ primarily in their interpretation of the nature of semantic representation. Whereas Paivio maintains that meaning is inherent in, and tied to, the processing of the verbal and imaginal systems, Seymour (1976) argues that the semantic store is an abstract, propositional store common to either verbal or pictorial input, but with a closer affinity to perceptual (nonverbal) information. He maintains that the semantic store is "for description of properties of the perceptual world [p.77]." Semantic representation would involve encoding perceptual properties of objects and their spatial relations. As support for his view, Seymour relies heavily on research by Eleanor Rosch who has shown comparable category priming and typicality of category membership effects with pictures and words. The argument is that the typicality and priming effects were mediated by input from a common perceptually oriented semantic register, to the lexical system in the case of words, and to the pictorial system in the case of pictures.

To recapitulate, Paivio and Seymour differ on two main points conerning the nature of semantic memory. First, Paivio contends that semantic representation is not amodal, nor ahistorical, in the sense that meaning arises only as information is processed in the verbal and imaginal systems. Seymour, on the other hand maintains that semantic representation is independent of either verbal or pictorial origins, and is conceptualized best in an abstract, propositional form. Second, while Paivio attributes potentially autonomous functioning to verbal and imaginal processes, Seymour contends that semantic representation, though abstract in form, is perceptually, and nonverbally predisposed.

Sperber, McCauley, Ragain and Weil (1979) reported a series of naming latency studies designed to evaluate the nature of semantic representation. Naming latency tasks typically involve presenting pairs of words and measuring the time it takes to name the seond item of the pair. If the first and second item of a pair conceptually relate (violin-flute), rhyme (eight-gate), or are identical (house-house), then naming latency for second items of these pairs will decrease as compared to unrelated pairs (tree-virtue; e.g., Meyer, Schvaneveldt, & Ruddy, 1975). The decrease in latency for related as compared to unrelated pairs is called a "priming effect" and, accordingly, the first item of each pair is called a "prime," and the second item is called a "target."

Theoretically, the priming effect may be due to the prime word incrementing the feature count of the target word's logogen prior to the presentation of the target word. The frequency count for a given target word logogen would be incremented when the visual, phonemic, or semantic features of the prime word overlap with those of the target word. Presumably similar processes would apply to imagens or iconogens. By this account, both Seymour and Paivio's model would lead to the prediction that picture pairs should show a priming effect, just as word pairs do, because both models postulate logogen and imagen/iconogen systems. Likewise both models would predict significant priming effects for the mixed picture-word/word-picture pairs. Seymour's model suggests that feature descriptions from the semantic register, whether arising from the pictorial or lexical system, should be fed back to the logogen system via the common semantic data store, so that either related words or pictures ought to act as primes for other words or pictures. Paivio's model also would predict priming for mixed pairs. Whereas Seymour's model suggests feedback to the logogen system from a common, propositional semantic store, Paivio's view might be that feedback to the logogen system is from a common, imaginal semantic store. Feedback from a common, imaginal semantic store would be possible since, according to the dual-coding model, both pictures and high imagery words have ready access to imaginal semantic information.

Sperber et al. (1979) presented subjects with pairs of pictures, pairs of words, and mixed picture-word/word-picture pairs. The task was simply to name the target word or label the target picture for each pair. The results showed that when the prime and target items of each pair were from the same semantic category (e.g., trumpet-guitar), there were significant priming effects for all pair types with effects being greatest for picture-picture pairs, and lower but equal for word-word and picture-word/word-picture pairs. As argued earlier, the significant priming effects for all pair-types are consistent with both Seymour and Paivio's model. Also greater priming effects for picture-picture pairs might be expected if semantic representation is basically perceptual. However, with perceptually-biased semantic representation, it might also be expected that word-picture or picture-word, mixed pairs would show stronger priming effects than word-word pairs because partial pictorial information (either as a prime or target item) should be more compatible with a perceptually-biased semantic system than no pictorial information. In keeping with the foregoing reasoning, Sperber et al. (1979) concluded that the lack of priming differences for word-word as compared to mixed pairs is evidence against the notion of a perceptually oriented semantic system. The superiority of picture-picture priming effects was interpreted as being due to overlap in visual features common to pictorial representations of conceptually related prime and target pictures.

The lack of evidence for a perceptually-oriented semantic system was interpreted by Sperber et al. (1979) as a failure to confirm Paivio's (1978) "more extreme view, in that he assumes that all semantic information is represented in a nonverbal (imaginal) representational system [p.342]." Sperber et al.'s interpretation of Paivio's view extends beyond Paivio's position that semantic representation is initially perceptual-motor, to suggest that all semantic representation is strictly nonverbal/imaginal. This interpretation of Paivio's view does not allow the possibility of nonperceptual, verbally based semantic representation that is autonomous to, or at least less closely identified with, concrete experience of the real world as compared to the other more perceptual, nonverbal information.

Moreover, a major problem with Sperber et al.'s study, as with many other studies, is that they employed pictures and words—concrete, high imagery words, that is—to draw conclusions about semantic representation. A simple dual-coding position would maintain that concrete words are imageable and, therefore, like pictures have ready access to a common imagery system. Consequently, concrete words and pictures may not constitute the appropriate stimuli with which to test between dual coding and common, propositional coding models, nor between models that postulate autonomous dual coding as compared to perceptual (imaginal) semantic representation.

A better test of the nature of semantic representation would involve the use of high- and low-imagery words rather than high-imagery words and pictures. Following Paivio's dual-coding model, it would be expected that concrete, high-imagery words are readily processed as imaginal/visual memory representations, whereas abstract, low-imagery words are processed primarily as verbal/phonemic representations. The studies that are reported in the following section used a naming latency task with high- and low-imagery words as stimuli. If there is autonomous verbal and imaginal semantic representation as Paivio's model suggests, priming effects would be expected for conceptually related high-high imagery pairs and low-low imagery pairs. If processing for low-imagery words is verbal/phonemic, whereas processing for high-imagery words is primarily imaginal/visual, then mixed high-low and low-high imagery pairs should not show priming effects. On the other hand if, as Seymour's model maintains, semantic representation is abstract, propositional, and common to both lexical and pictorial memory, then mixed high-low and low-high imagery pairs should show priming effects because both high and low imagery primes should prime high, and low imagery target words via the intermediary common, propositional semantic store. Finally, if semantic representation is perceptually, nonverbally biased, then priming effects involving the associated pairs should be larger for items that are more readily converted to a perceptually related, imaginal representation. According to Paivio's model, concrete high-imagery words are more readily imaged than abstract, low-imagery words and, therefore, high-high imagery pairs should show greater priming effects than low-low imagery pairs.

NAMING LATENCY EXPERIMENTS

Experimental sequencing and data collection for the two studies reported here was controlled by an Apple II computer, and consisted of two phases. Phase I involved a naming latency task, and phase II was an incidental memory test for the prime items seen in phase I. In Experiment 1, subjects were shown pairs of words on the computer video display and required to read the prime word covertly and to name the target item aloud as quickly and accurately as possible. For both Experiments 1 and 2, twenty subjects served in phase I, then in phase II

TABLE 9.1
High (H) and Low (L) Imagery Examples of Words from Experiments
I and II

Unrelated			Related		
Prime	Target		Associated	Rhymed	Identical
H	H	yacht-eye (37)[a]	keg-beer (12)	bloom-room (12)	arrow-arrow (24)
L	H	comfort-cell (37)	deal-cards (12)	soul-mole (12)	
L	L	honour-wait (37)	truth-false (12)	oral-moral (12)	interest-interest (24)
H	L	ship-oxygen (37)	dummy-stupid (12)	cry-try (12)	

[a]( ) = number of trials per condition.

one half of the subjects (N = 10) were given a surprise cued-recall test, and the other half were given a surprise recognition test. For purposes of this discussion, however, only the naming latency and cued-recall data are discussed.

For the cued-recall test, subjects were shown the target word from each pair of words in the same trial sequence in which they had been presented in phase I, and asked to type in the prime word that had preceeded the target word.

Two hundred and ninety-two word pairs were selected such that, for half of the pairs, the prime and target were related and, for the remainder, unrelated. If the prime and target were related, they could be either associated, rhymed, or identical. In addition, the 292 pairs were selected such that the prime and target were either high-or low-imagery words. Primes and targets were matched for number of syllables, and rhyme and associative strength as indexed by the number of times the rhyme or associative word was given as a response. Familiarity ratings for prime and target items showed no systematic differences. Table 9.1 gives examples of the word-pairs that were used in the experiments.

Experiment 1.

Figure 9.2 shows the priming effect in msec (i.e., the difference between each related condition and its unrelated control) for high-and low-imagery prime and target word pairs that were associated, rhymed or identical. Looking first at the associated condition, significant priming effects occurred only for homogeneous pairs, that is, high-high and low-low imagery pairs, and not for mixed pairs (Newman Keuls C.D. for high-high=14.6; for low-low=16.9, p's < .05). Based on the assumption that high-imagery words may be processed mainly in an imagery system, whereas, low-imagery words are processed mainly in a verbal system, these results suggest that associations between prime and target words facilitate naming latency only if both prime and target items are processed primarily within either the imagery or verbal system. These results are not supportive of a common representational model such as Seymour's. A common

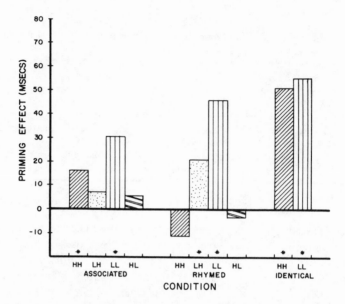

FIG. 9.2.   Priming effects in milliseconds for associated, rhymed, and identical word pairs with high and low imagery primes and targets. (* designates significant priming effect, all *p*'s at least .05; Experiment I.)

representational model would maintain that because both abstract and concrete items are processed to a common propositional, semantic level, there should be priming within mixed high-low and low-high imagery word pairs, just as there is for homogeneous low-low and high-high imagery word pairs. Thus, the failure to find priming effects for mixed pairs fails to confirm predictions based on a common, propositional model of semantic representation.

The priming effect for associated high-high imagery pairs was not significantly greater than that for low-low imagery pairs (Newman Keuls C.D.=19.7, $p > .05$) as would be expected if semantic representation is biased toward perceptual/imaginal processing and if concrete, high-imagery words are more readily encoded in perceptual/imaginal form. Rather, the lack of difference between high-high and low-low imagery priming effects is consistent with Paivio's contention that although semantic representation is initially perceptual/imaginal, nonetheless, linguistic semantic representation gains a degree of autonomy from the perceptual/imaginal representational system from which it emanated. Moreover, the nonsignificantly different priming effects for the associated low-low as compared to the associated high-high imagery pairs suggests not only that semantic representation need not be perceptually biased but, furthermore, that processing in the verbal system is no less efficient in terms of priming effects than processing in the imagery/perceptual system.

Admittedly, drawing conclusions based on nonsignificant differences is usually risky. In this case, however, the practice is comparatively safe because not only are the priming effects for the high-high imagery pairs not significantly greater than for low-low imagery pairs but, in fact, the trend is opposite that predicted from the assumption of a perceptually/imaginally prejudiced semantic system.

Priming effects for associated pairs of words may be assumed to result from overlapping semantic features shared by prime and target words. Priming effects for rhymed and identical pairs are usually assumed to result from overlapping phonemic and visual features. Hence, priming effects for rhymed and identical pairs probably do not reflect the nature of semantic representation in the same way as for associated pairs. Identical word pairs, for example, showed greater priming effects than associated pairs, as might be expected if priming occurs as a result of the overlap of more peripheral sensory or visual features early in the processing sequence. Likewise, the pattern of results for the rhymed pairs was not like that for associated word pairs. For the rhymed condition, significant priming effects occurred only for pairs with low imagery prime words, that is, for the low-high and the low-low imagery pairs (Newman Keuls C.D. for low-high=16.3; for low-low=18.3, p's < .05). Given that priming effects for rhymed pairs rely on common phonemic features of prime and target words, the rhymed condition results suggest that the presentation of a concrete, high-imagery prime item does not increment the frequency count of phonemic features that overlap with those of the following target word. Perhaps phonological encoding is not as immediate or salient for high imagery as compared to low imagery words. This possibility and its implications are discussed in more detail later.

Following the phase I naming latency task, subjects were given an incidental cued-recall test for the prime items, with the target items of each pair as the cue. For both the associated and rhymed conditions, recall was significantly greater if the prime words were high imagery rather than low (i.e., high-high and high-low recall > low-low and low-high; Newman Keuls C.D. for associated pairs=1.53; for rhymed pairs = 2.04, p's < .05; see Fig. 9.3). This would be expected if the priming effects observed in phase I were due to imaginal representation of high-imagery prime words, since imaginal representation should facilitate cued recall. Recall for the high-high and low-low imagery, identical conditions were not significantly different from each other (Newman Keuls C.D. = 1.53, p > .05), but recall for both conditions was significantly lower than for high-high and high-low pairs in the rhymed and associated conditions (all p's < .05). The latter findings would be expected if the naming and encoding of identical pairs was based largely on less central, graphemic/visual feature analysis that reduced the emphasis on imaginal encoding of high-high imagery items.

Summary of Experiment 1.   Experiment 1 showed that, for a naming latency task, associative priming effects occurred only for homogeneous word-pairs (high-high and low-low imagery). On the assumption that high-imagery words were processed primarily as images, whereas, low-imagery words were pro-

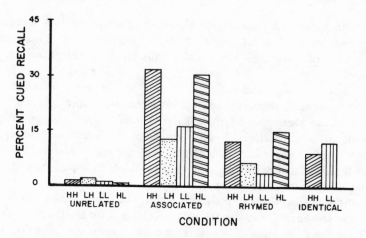

FIG. 9.3.   Percent cued recall for unrelated, associated, rhymed, and identical
word pairs with high and low imagery primes and targets (Experiment I).

cessed verbally, the associative priming result indicated that associative priming
occurs within either the imaginal or the verbal processing system, not between
the two systems. The latter interpretation is consistent with Paivio's model which
maintains that semantic representation arises from the tri-level processing of
relatively autonomously functioning verbal and imagery systems. On the other
hand, the aforementioned results were not consistent with common coding
theories of semantic representation. Because priming effects were not significantly different for the high-high and low-low associated pairs, the data were
interpreted as lending no support to the notion that semantic processing favors
perceptual/imaginal representation.

Priming in the rhymed condition occurred only for pairs with low-imagery
prime words. It was suggested that perhaps phonological encoding was more
primary for low-imagery than high-imagery words. Finally, results of the incidental cued recall test showed better recall for those conditions in which imagery
had been hypothesized to influence the preceeding naming latency task. Specifically, recall was best for the high-high and high-low imagery pairs in the associated and rhymed conditions. As would be expected if identical pairs were
processed at a more peripheral level, reducing the need for imaginal processing
of high-imagery items, recall for high-high and low-low imagery pairs was not
significantly different.

Experiment 2.

Much of the theorizing thus far has been based on Paivio's dual-coding model,
and on the assumption that concrete, high-imagery items may be processed
mainly in the imaginal system, whereas, abstract, low-imagery items are pro-

cessed primarily in the verbal system. If the latter reasoning is correct, it should be possible to promote the use of the imaginal system by having subjects image the prime items of each pair of words, prior to naming the target item. The pattern of priming and recall effects that were hypothesized to be due to imagery in Experiment 1 should hold for Experiment 2. Accordingly, the procedure for Experiment 2 was the same as for Experiment 1, except that subjects were instructed to form a mental picture or image of what the prime word represented. Only after they had successfully generated some form of image (even for the low-imagery words), were subjects to press a button which was then immediately followed by the presentation of the target item for naming.

In general, the similarity in the pattern of results for Experiment 1 and 2, despite the instructions to image in Experiment 2, lends credibility to the notion that imagery was involved especially in the processing of high-imagery words, and that imagery-verbal processing differences were responsible for the pattern of prime effects shown in Experiment 1. Dealing first with the associated condition, a comparison of Figs. 9.2 and 9.4 shows that in Experiment 2, as in Experiment 1, there were significant priming effects for the homogenous word pairs (Newman Keuls C.D. for high-high = 16.3; for low-low = 19.2, p's < .05), but not for the mixed high-low imagery pairs (Newman Keuls C.D. for high-low = 13.5, p > .05). Instructions to image the prime word of each pair

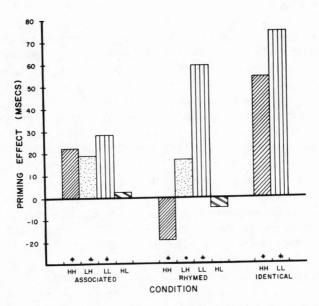

FIG. 9.4.   Priming effects in milliseconds for associated, rhymed, and identical word pairs with high and low imagery primes and targets (* designates significant priming effect, all p's at least .05; Experiment II.)

altered only the low-high imagery condition, producing a significant priming effect that had not occurred in Experiment 1 (Newman Keuls C.D. for low-high = 18.0, $p < .05$). If, as the results of Experiment 1 suggested, priming effects occur only within either the verbal or imaginal system, then the appearance of priming effects for the low-high associated pairs in Experiment 2 suggests that the low-imagery prime words and the high-imagery target words were being processed in the same system. Inasmuch as instructions to image the prime word were the only changes in procedure introduced between Experiment 1 and 2, it seems likely that the instructions may have induced subjects to process even the low-imagery prime words in some form of imaginal representation. As a result, both the low-imagery prime words and the high-imagery target words would be processed imaginally, giving rise to the priming effects for the low-high imagery condition.

Because low-imagery words are, by definition, difficult to image, the earlier explanation, which was based on the assumption that low-imagery items were imaged, might be discounted. However, it should be noted that low-imagery words are difficult, but not impossible, to image and, furthermore, that subjects were strongly encouraged to formulate some kind of image to represent the meaning of the word, no matter how difficult. In fact, mean latency from the onset of the prime word until the button was pressed causing the onset of the target item was significantly greater for low imagery than high imagery prime words (low imagery word $\bar{x} = 2197.7$ msec vs. high imagery word $\bar{x} = 1681.5$ msec, $F(1,15) = 22.3$, $MSe = 538,380$, $p < .01$). Although this does not prove that subjects sucessfully imaged low-imagery items, longer latencies for low-imagery prime words are at least consistent with such an explanation, and are also consistent with subjects' reports of successfully imaging low-imagery words although it was more difficult than imaging high-imagery words. Moreover, if subjects successfully imaged low-imagery prime words in the low-high imagery condition, then incidental cued recall of the low-high pairs should be increased as it was for the high-high and high-low pairs. In fact, recall for the associated low-high pairs was not significantly different from recall for the high-high and high-low pairs (Newman Keuls C.D. = 10.6 and 12.7 for low-high vs. high-low and high-high respectively, see Fig. 9.5).

By the same reasoning, the low-high rhymed pairs should show increased cued recall if the low-imagery prime words were successfully imaged. Figure 9.5 illustrates that recall for the rhymed condition was similar to that of the associated condition, with high-high, low-high, and high-low imagery pairs being better recalled than low-low imagery pairs (p's $< .05$).

In Experiment 1, however, rhymed pairs with high-imagery primes (i.e., high-high and high-low conditions) did not show priming effects, whereas, pairs with low-imagery prime words did. It was suggested that the phonemic code was not as salient for high imagery as for low-imagery prime words, with resultant poorer priming effects for the former than the latter conditions. The significant

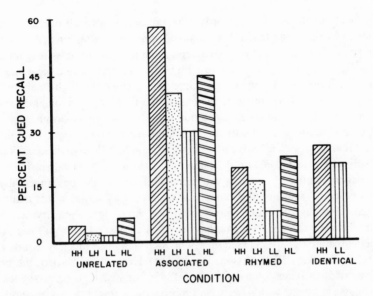

FIG. 9.5.   Percent cued recall for unrelated, associated, rhymed, and identical word pairs with high and low imagery primes and targets (Experiment II).

priming effects for the low-high rhymed pairs (Newman Keuls C.D. = 16.3, $p <$ .05), as well as for the low-low rhymed and associated pairs in Experiment 2 (Newman Keuls C.D. for low-low = 22.9, $p < .05$), suggests that even although low-imagery primes may have been imaged (as was argued earlier), the verbal/ phonemic code remained salient for the low-imagery prime words to the extent that they remained effective primes for their target words. Overall, the implication of the data is that high-imagery concrete and low-imagery abstract words are basically processed differently. Not only are high-imagery words apparently more amenable to processing by the imaginal system than low-imagery words, but also high-imagery words seem less reliant on verbal/phonemic encoding as compared to abstract words — even abstract words that have been imaged.

But the line of argument thus far raises at least two questions. First, if prime words in low-high imagery word pairs were imaged, then prime words in low-low imagery pairs also must have been imaged, since subjects had no way of knowing the relationship of the upcoming target to the prime. It has been argued that the successful imaging of prime words in low-high pairs caused the increased recall of the pairs in both the rhymed and associated conditions. By extension, it might be expected that the successful imaging of prime words in the low-low pairs also should have resulted in increased recall for the low-low pairs, which it did not. A *post hoc* explanation for this may be simply that for low-imagery words the verbal/phonemic code and the newly generated imaginal representation coexisted, but that the verbal/phonemic code was most salient. Consequently, when the low-imagery target words were presented as recall cues, the verbal/phonemic associations to the low-imagery prime words dominated rather than associations with the newly imaged representations of the low-imagery prime words. By contrast, recall for the low-high imagery pairs would have benefitted from the instructions to image the prime words since the high imagery target items would have been imaged, increasing the likelihood of imaginal associations to the newly imaged representation of the low-imagery prime.

A second question is why rhymed low-high pairs showed significant priming effects. It was suggested above that high-high and high-low rhymed pairs do not show priming effects because the phonemic code was not as salient for high-as low-imagery words. Following the same logic, it might be argued that the phonemic code would not be salient for high-imagery target words and, therefore, that low-high imagery pairs should not show significant rhyme priming effects. However, recent research has provided evidence that both imaginal and phonetic features are processed for both high and low imagery words (e.g., Nelson & Brooks, 1973; Nelson, Reed, & McEvoy, 1977). Also, the present findings of significant rhyme priming effects for low-high pairs suggest that high-imagery target words were not processed without the formation of a phonemic code. This conlusion seems valid even for Experiment 2 in which the low-imagery prime items were imaged. Overall, the evidence supports Paivio's contention that high-imagery words may be encoded verbally/phonemically or imaginally. Not surprisingly, evidence for either verbal/phonemic or imaginal encoding appears to depend on task conditions.

Summary and integration of Experiments 1 and 2.

The consistency of findings between Experiment 1 and 2 for the associated condition lends support to the notion that there are two separate semantic systems; one verbal, and the other imaginal. Although high-imagery words are linguistic units, the data suggest that semantic processing of high-imagery words occurs primarily within the imaginal system, whereas, semantic processing for low-imagery words occurs primarily within the verbal/phonemic system. As would be expected if high-high pairs were processed imaginally in Experiment 1, instructions to image in Experiment 2, which presumably encouraged imaginal processing, did not change the pattern of results for homogenous high-high imagery word pairs. Likewise, homogenous low-low word pairs showed the same pattern of results between experiments, as would be expected if their processing remained predominantly verbal in both experiments. The main difference between the two experiments was that there were no significant priming effects for associated low-high imagery pairs in Experiment 1, but there were significant effects in Experiment 2 when the low-imagery primes were imaged. Also, unlike Experiment 1, in Experiment 2 the associated and rhymed low-high imagery pairs were recalled to the same level as high-high and high-low pairs, as might be expected if low-imagery words were successfully imaged. The significant associative priming effects and higher recall for low-high pairs suggests that while low-imagery words may be primarily processed in a verbal semantic system, imagery encoding instructions make them subject to referential recoding from verbal to imaginal representation. The presence of significant rhyme priming effects for low-high and low-low pairs suggests, however, that even with imaginal representation, the verbal/phonemic code remains dominant for low-imagery words. The absence of rhyme priming effects for high-high and high-low pairs in both Experiments 1 and 2, suggests that the imaginal code was dominant for high-imagery prime words. Nonetheless, significant priming effects for low-high rhymed pairs implies that verbal/phonemic representation is available for high-imagery words when processing of the preceeding prime word has been primarily verbal/phonemic.

IMPLICATIONS FOR MODELS OF MEMORY

The present findings clearly favor a dual-coding model such as Paivio's rather than favoring common coding propositional models such as that of Seymour (or Bransford & Franks, 1971; Anderson & Bower, 1973). High-imagery words may be encoded verbally or imaginally, and low-imagery words are processed mainly verbally. Whereas Paivio's model maintains that abstract, low-imagery logogens are largely denied referential relationship to imagens, the present data suggest that, under loose time constraints, even low-imagery words may gain access to imaginal representation.

Paivio's model does not specify whether high-imagery words will be processed predominantly verbally or imaginally. The present findings suggest that, at least for naming latency tasks, it is predictively valid to assume that high-imagery words are processed primarily as imaginal representations unless preceeded by a verbally/phonemically processed word. The latter reasoning would also lead to the expectation of picture-word and word-picture priming effects, as reported by Sperber et al. (1979), since both pictures and words would share a common, imaginal semantic base.

The lack of rhyme priming effects for word pairs with high-imagery primes has been interpreted in the present chapter as evidence that phonemic encoding is less salient for high- than low-imagery words. However, although the verbal system may be closely linked with phonemic representation, as Paivio (1971) has argued, verbal and phonemic encoding are by no means synonymous. Although it probably is not possible to have phonemic encoding without verbal encoding, it is highly likely that verbal encoding occurs without phonemic representation; reading being the most cogent example (e.g., Bradshaw, 1975; Kleiman, 1975).

Lack of rhyme priming effects, then, may have reflected an absence, or decline in saliency, of phonemic encoding without logically necessitating that the words were not processed via the verbal system. It may be that initial processing for both high- and low-imagery words must be verbal, prior to either semantic or phonemic encoding.

In fact, a verbal-semantic-phonemic processing sequence for words is embodied in Seymour's adaptation of Morton's logogen model. The logogen system is a feature recognizer for linguistic units and, as such, is a verbal system. Only after the logogens have been incremented beyond their criterial threshold level, are storage addresses made available for access to the appropriate semantic descriptors. Following this, a second higher logogen threshold level must be reached before access is granted to the phonetic encoding store. Paivio's model, too, maintains that words, whether high- or low-imagery, initially must be processed via the verbal system. However, if high-and low-imagery words are processed by a common logogen (verbal) system, then why do rhyme priming effects, that are arguably logogen based, not occur when the prime word is high imagery? One possibility is that while both high- and low-imagery words access a common logogen system, the semantic storage addresses associated with high- and low-imagery logogens reference the imaginal and verbal semantic systems respectively. High-imagery words access imaginal semantic representation, whereas, low-imagery words access verbal semantic representation. If the verbal and imaginal semantic systems are inherently more closely related to phonemic and visual information respectively, then when semantic information is retrieved, the information for low-imagery words, by virtue of its intrinsically close phonemic tie, may lead to lowered criteria for phonemic feature analysers. On the other hand, because semantic representation for high-imagery words is not inherently tied to phonemic representation, criteria for high-imagery word feature analysers would not be lowered. The overall effect would be a greater sensitivity to phonemic features, and perhaps a faster retrieval of phonemic descriptors from the phonemic data store, for low-imagery as compared to high-imagery words.

Unfortunately, the foregoing explanation of why pairs with high-imagery prime words do not show rhyme prime effects rests on the assumption that logogens for high- and low-imagery words give access to the imaginal and verbal semantic systems respectively. As soon as the logogens are distinguished in terms of whether they address the verbal or imaginal systems, the logogen system becomes functionally separable into two systems — a verbal and an imaginal one. Thus, the foregoing explanation contradicts the original premise that both high-and low-imagery words are initially processed in a common verbal/logogen system. An alternative explanation, contrary to the models of both Seymour and Paivio, would be that, depending on variables such as task demands and context, high- and low-imagery words may not be processed initially in the same verbal input system.

Marcel and Patterson's dual-input model.

Marcel and Patterson (1979) have presented a model that meets the criterion of having two verbal input systems. In addition, the model maintains that there are two semantic systems, Sem1 and Sem2. Sem1 is based on sensorimotor experience, whereas, Sem2 is structured around logical-linguistic information. The distinction between Sem1 and Sem2 obviously parallels the distinction between the imaginal and verbal systems made by Paivio.

The model holds that at early developmental stages, before hemispheric specificity of function occurs, Sem1 becomes represented bilaterally, with Sem1 in both the right and left hemispheres having equal access to speech production. At later ontological stages, presumably after left hemispheric speech production specificity has started, Sem2 develops bilaterally. Left hemispheric Sem2 has direct access to speech production, whereas, right hemispheric Sem2 must access speech production indirectly via left hemispheric Sem2. Each hemisphere has an independent lexical address system through which Sem1 and Sem2 may be addressed.

Word imageability as a right hemisphere effect.   Marcel and Patterson suggest that word imageability effects are mainly right hemisphere effects resulting from differential access to speech production by high-imagery words (Sem1 processed) as compared to low-imagery words (Sem2 processed). Evidence from studies with deep dyslexics, as well as with normals, is relevant to their suggestions. Among other characteristics, deep dyslexics tend to be poor at naming low-imagery words as compared to high-imagery words (Richardson, 1975; Shallice & Warrington, 1975). Because deep dyslexics are known to have damaged left hemispheres, it may be that their deficient naming ability for low-imagery words actually reflects the processing of their intact right hemispheres (see also Coltheart, 1980; Saffran, Bogyo, Schwartz, & Marin, 1980). The implication is that processing in the right hemisphere normally favors high- over low-imagery words.

Saffran, Bogyo, Schwartz, and Marin (1980) sought to answer the question "Does deep dyslexia reflect right-hemisphere reading?" by using split-field studies of dyslexics. One study indicated that two out of the three deep dyslexics tested showed left visual field (right hemishere) lexical decision superiority when four-letter words were presented unilaterally. More convincing support for a "right hemisphere hypothesis" was provided by a second study employing bilateral stimulation with the same three dyslexics. It was argued that presentation of a lexical decision stimulus (either a word or nonword) to one randomly selected hemifield, with simultaneious presentation of a single letter to the other hemifield, should cause processing conflict between the hemispheres and result in enhanced lexical decision superiority for words presented to the favored right hemisphere. Indeed, all three dyslexics showed the predicted right hemispheric superiority under the bilateral presentation condition, implicating right hemisphere involvement in reading for deep dyslexics.

The "right hemisphere hypothesis" suggests that the processing superiority for high-over low-imagery words which dyslexics display should be reflected in normals in the form of right hemisheric advantage for-high imagery words. Saffran et al. (1980) report two split-field tachistoscopic recognition studies with normal subjects. The first study failed to show superior recognition performance for concrete (high imagery) as compared to abstract (low imagery) words presented to the left visual field. The second study resulted in the predicted right-hemispheric recognition superiority of concrete over abstact words. However, contrary to predictions, concrete-abstract word differences were greater for left than right hemispheric presentation.

Marcel and Patterson (1979) were more successful than Saffran et al. (1980) in extending the implication of split-field work with dyslexics to normals. Normal subjects were required to name masked high-and low-imagery words that were randomly presented to the right and left visual fields. High-imagery words were reported equally correctly whether presented to the left or right visual field, whereas, low-imagery words were correctly reported less often when presented to the left visual field (right hemihere) than when presented to the right visual field (left hemisphere). Similar results have also been reported by others using tachistoscopic identification, lexical decision, and semantic classification tasks (see Coltheart (1980) for a review). Although there have been failures to replicate, overall, the results from studies with normal subjects support the studies with dyslexics in suggesting that high-imagery words may be equally well processed by either the left or right hemispheres, but that low-imagery words are processed more efficiently by the left than the right hemisphere.

Imageability as a production effect. On the basis of a lexical decision experiment which required that neither the prime nor target word be named, Marcel and Patterson (1979) argue that right hemispheric imageability effects rely entirely on more efficient production access for high-as compared to low-imagery words in the right hemisphere. Normal subjects were presented, within and across hemifields, with high-and low-imagery prime words, followed by a pattern mask (to prevent awareness), in turn followed by associated or nonassociated words, or nonwords. Neither the latency of lexical decision nor the magnitude of the associative priming effect were affected by either word imageability or hemifield of presentation. The authors suggest that the lack of imagery and hemispheric effects were due to the removal of the requirement for an aware response output which circumvented the problem of indirect access to production processes by low-imagery words in right-hemishperic Sem2.

The production effect explanation of imageability effects needs further testing. Marcel and Patterson (1979) manipulated imageability only for prime words, not for target words. Imageability and hemispheric effects might have been significant if both prime and target word imageability had been varied factorially. In Experiment I, reported earlier, there were no imageability differences in either raw latency or priming effect measures for associated pairs when prime word imageability alone was taken into account, collapsing across target word imageability. Imageability effects became evident only when both prime and target word imageability were considered. It is possible that, aside from production processes, the right hemisphere may not process low-imagery words as efficiently as high-imagery words due to incomplete or impaired lexical entries for low-imagery words (see Patterson, 1979). Notwithstanding the issue of the locus of imageability effects, whether lexical, production, or even hemisphere specific processes, the data and models such as Marcel and Patterson's suggest two verbal input systems. One system is apparently impartial to imageability, whereas, the other system favors high-over low-imagery words.

As noted earlier, the evidence suggests that high imagery words are processed equally well by the right and left hemispheres and that low-imagery words are processed more efficiently in the left as compared to the right hemisphere. Given the assumption of separate input systems, it is conceivable that high-imagery words will be processed primarily in one system (the right hemisphere) when the context makes imagery desirable, and primarily in the other system (the left hemishphere) when phonemic processing is important. Low-imagery words might be processed primarily in the left hemisphere except in the unusual event that imagery is required for their processing. Under conditions such as those in the studies reported here, imaginal processing of high-imagery words may take place primarily in, or at least processing may be focused in, one system and linguistic processing of low-imagery words may occur mainly in the other system. Then if priming effects are restricted to input systems, as Morton (1979,1980) argues, merely sharing a common output system would not result in priming effects. Hence, consistent with the findings of the two studies reported in this chapter, associative priming between high-and low-imagery words would not be expected. Moreover, if graphemic-to-phonemic conversion is a function of one of the input systems (the left hemispheric system), and if high-imagery words are processed primarily in the other system (right hemispheric), then rhyme priming effects that rely on graphemic-to-phonemic conversion processes would not be expected for high-low and high-high imagery pairs.

It is tempting to speculate that high-imagery words may be processed directly from graphemic to semantic stages, whereas, low-imagery words must follow a graphemic-phonemic-semantic sequence. Such sequencing would explain why high-low and high-high imagery pairs showed no rhyme priming effects, presumably because high-imagery prime words were not encoded phonemically prior to semantic processing. The debate concerning the role of phonological encoding in reading has generated much controversy, but there seems to be a growing consensus that phonological recoding generally is not necessary prior to semantic access (e.g., Baddeley, 1979; Bradshaw, 1975; Coltheart, Davelaar, Jonasson, & Besner, 1977; Levy, 1978). Moreover, deep dyslexics may know the meaning of low-imagery words although they are unable to name them (Patterson, 1979), suggesting that phonological recoding may not be necessary prior to semantic processing even for low-imagery words.

A related possibility is that high-and low-imagery words may be processed in a manner that is similar to Japanese Kanji and Kana scrips respectively. Kanji is a logographic script that represents lexical phonemes, whereas, Kana is a phonetic alphabet that represents syllables or "mora." In tachistoscopic recognition tasks, Kana characters are more accurately reported when presented to the right visual field (Sasanuma, Itoh, Mori, & Kobayashi, 1977), as compared to Kanji characters that are favored by the left visual field (Hatta, 1977; Sasanuma et al., 1977). Because Kanji is logographic and favored by the right hemisphere, it has been suggested that Kanji may be processed visually or imaginally in a manner similar to pictures and other nonverbal stimuli that are also favoured by the right hemisphere (e.g., Hatta, 1977). Japanese Kanji, then, parallels English high-imagery words in that both show right hemispheric processing superiority, and in that both are purportedly associated with imaginal processing.

Further similarities between Japanese scripts and high and low imagery words also have been found in work with Japanese aphasics. Sasanuma (1975) classified Japanese aphasics into three types. Type I display characteristics that are similar to those described for English speaking deep dyslexics, Type II are similar to English speaking surface dyslexics, and Type III Japanese aphasics seem to be a mixture of Types I and II. The selective impairment for Kanji and Kana characters among Japanese aphasics Types I and II is reminiscent of the selective impairment for high-and low-imagery words among English speaking dyslexics, and supports the notion that high-and low-imagery words may have counterparts in Japanese Kanji and Kana script. If so, it may be that in the same way that Kanji scripts are thought to be processed as visual symbols and relatively directly translated into imaginal equivalents, likewise, high-imagery words may be very efficiently translatable. For example, the letter configuration *cat* might function like an ideographic representation that arouses nonverbal (although not necessarily conscious) images associated with the animal itself.

A note of caution regarding the possibility of ideographic processing of high-imagery words arises from a consideration of studies such as Saffran and Marin's (1977). They showed that a deep dyslexic patient was capable of reading words that had been physically altered in such a way that the words could not possibly have been matched directly to their orthographic images (e.g., the word HOUSE may have been presented as H+O+U+S+E). Clearly, words altered in this manner are not being processed in a simple ideographic fashion without the intervention of some mediating process. Rayner and Posnansky (1978) have provided evidence that visual and phonemic feature analyses mediate the extraction of meaning from visually presented high-imagery picture labels. They reported shorter labeling latencies for pictures that were superimposed either with their labels (e.g., horse), or by nonwords that were orthographically or phonemically similar to their labels. However, nonwords that preserved the first letter and general shape of the picture label (e.g., honre) facilitated picture naming more than nonwords that preserved either the identity of the label's middle letters in a randomized order (e.g., grsod), or the shape of the label's middle letters (e.g., scnrd). These findings suggest that, for recognition of high-imagery words, the overall configuration of the word may be more important than the identity of the individual letters. The notion that overall configuration is important for the processing of high-imagery words supports the argument being made here that high-imagery words may be processed in holistic, Kanji-like fashion.

For concrete words to be perceived as holistic ideographic symbols, it might be maximally efficient for orthographic images of the words to be stored so that word stimuli can be compared holistically with the orthographic images during recognition. Ehri (1980) has provided evidence that such orthographic images may play an essential role in both reading and writing, and that orthographic forms may be amalgamated with semantic, syntactic, and phonological identities. When a word is seen, it may be matched to its orthographic image, making its semantic, syntactic, and phonological identities simultaneously available. If a high-imagery word's semantic identity involves imagery, then Ehri's amalgamation theory serves to explain how a concrete, high-imagery word could function as an ideographic symbol to elicit imaginal representation.

An ideographic view of high-imagery word processing suggests a close alliance between the orthographic image and associated imaginal, semantic identity. Because both the orthographic and imaginal representation involve imagery, it might be expected, therefore, that congruity effects should be observed between the visual size of a word stimulus and the imaginally encoded size of what the word represents. However, Paivio (1975) demonstrated that word size has no effect on comparative judgment of animal size, whereas, the size of pictures of animals does affect size judgements for those animals. By contrast, Reich and Cherry (1979) reported a significant size congruity effect in a picture-sentence verification task, such that, for example, the congruent sentence ("JOHN is taller than Sue" was verified more rapidly than the incongruent sentence "John is taller than SUE" when the sentences were verified against the pictures of a boy and girl who represented John and Sue. Obviously, the verdict is not in on the issue of congruity effects, but the difference between Paivio's (1975) work as compared to that of Reich and Cherry (1979) suggests that context (in this case sentential context) may be an important determinant of congruity effects.

An ideographic view of high-imagery word processing ties in with Marcel and Patterson's (1979) suggestion that an enduring graphemic representation is necessary for a word to be consciously processed or output. Deep dyslexics probably suffer left hemisphere damage, leaving the right hemisphere as the primary word processor (Coltheart, 1980). Following the ideographic notion, perhaps for deep dyslexics, as for normals, high-imagery words have intact graphemic representations in the right hemisphere, whereas, low-imagery words do not, so that high-imagery words can be output more readily than low-imagery words.

More generally, the referents of high-imagery words are imageable and, therefore, it seems reasonable that their orthographic images could be more closely allied with their imaginal representations than low-imagery words that presumably have few imaginal representations. A closer alliance between orthographic and semantic imaginal representation would suggest greater processing efficiency for high-imager words, especially for the right hemisphere that seems to specialize in processing of nonverbal information. Moreover, there might be a feedback loop between orthographic lexical entries and imaginal semantic entries, perhaps similar to those posited by Morton (1969, 1978) to exist between the logogen and the semantic store, such that imaginal semantic representation would feedback to strengthen the orthographic images of the original word stimuli. In the case of low-imagery words, even if orthographic images occurred at the outset of right hemispheric processing, the orthographic images for those words might become functionally inoperative for lack of feedback from a closely allied imaginal semantic representation. Moreover, if phonemic features are initially used in the identification of high-imagery words, the persistence or usefulness of phonemic features may be limited by lack of verbal/phonemic feedback from the imaginal semantic system.

A MODEL

In terms of the arguments made in this chapter, the main features of the proposed model are, first, distinct verbal and imaginal semantic systems and, second, dual verbal input systems (see Fig. 9.6). Marcel and Patterson's (1979) model has been cited as an example of a model that postulates a dual verbal input system, and research has been referenced to support the dual verbal input view. However, their model incorporates hemisphericity assumptions that are extraneous for our present purposes. For example, the model assumes that the two input systems are hemispherically distinct (which they may be), but the assumption is not critical to the basic argument presented here for dual verbal input systems. Likewise, their model proposes redundant Sem1 and Sem2 systems, duplicated in both left and right hemispheres. Given the assumption that Sem1 and Sem2 are analogous to imaginal and verbal systems respectively, then a more parsimonious model might eliminate the redundancy by including only one each of a verbal and imaginal system. In addition, elimination of hemisphericity assumptions has the advantage of making it more likely that a model will generalize to, for example, the processing of left-handed individuals, members of both sexes, and Orientals whose hemispheric deployment of processing faculties may differ. Finally, Mar-

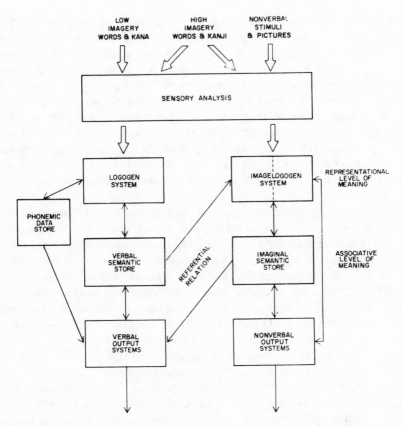

FIG. 9.6.   Revisitation of Paivio's dual coding model of representational, referential, and associative levels of meaning.

cel and Patterson's model is concerned with reading and makes no statement about processing for nonverbal material. The model proposed here is closer to Paivio's dual-coding formulation than to Marcel and Patterson's in that it is more explicit about the processing of nonverbal material.

According to the proposed model, verbal and nonverbal stimuli first enter sensory analysis. Following the lead of more detailed models such as Seymour's (1976), sensory analysis for visual stimuli might include iconic representation and entry into a graphemic/pictorial register. For auditory stimuli, sensory analysis could include echoic representation and entry into a phonemic register. After sensory analysis, processing for high-imagery words and Kanji might be focused in either the logogen or imagelogogen system, depending on context, task demands, and the part of speech of the word (e.g., Elman, Takahashi, & Tohsaku, 1981). Low-imagery words and scripts such as Japanese Kana would be processed for the most part, or at least most efficiently, in the logogen system, whereas, pictures, objects, and other nonverbal stimuli would be processed in the imagelogogen system. The logogen system is identical to that proposed by Morton (1969), acting as semantic and phonemic address system. As word features are detected, logogen feature counts increment until criterion levels are reached, allowing the addresses of, first, semantic, then phonemic information to become available from the verbal semantic and phonemic stores respectively.

As its name implies, an imagelogogen system would combine the properties of logogen and imagen (iconogen) systems as described by Seymour (1976) and Paivio and Begg (1981). Whereas logogen and imagen systems act as feature recognizers for words and pictures respectively, an imagelogogen system would have the capacity to process both words and nonverbal information such as pictures.

Alternatively, it would be consistent with the dual verbal input notion to substitute for the imagelogogen system a second logogen system and a separate imagen system on the right side of the model. It is mainly in deference to the notion that concrete, high-imagery words may be processed in a holistic, Kanji-like fashion, that the imagelogogen system is proposed. But whether a single imagelogogen system, or separate imagen and logogen systems are postulated, the main aspect of the model is that the verbal input system which favors high- over low-imagery words is more closely linked to the imaginal than the verbal semantic system. The verbal input system on the right is distinct from the logogen system on the left that processes high- and low-imagery words equally well and that readily accesses both verbal semantic and phonemic information.

Whereas the notion of dual verbal input systems represents a reconceptualization of the representational level of meaning as presented in Paivio's model, Paivio's notions of referential and associative levels of meaning are retained intact in the proposed model. The referential level of meaning would correspond to the links between the imagelogogen system and the verbal semantic store and between the imaginal semantic store and the verbal output system. High-imagery words initially may be processed verbally (and phonemically) if the task demands or context so dictate, and subsequently, via the verbal semantic store-imagelogogen link, the words may be imaged in the imagelogogen system. On the other hand, once again depending on task demands or context, high-imagery words processed in the imagelogogen system might be processed as visual, ideographic symbols and, subsequently, be recoded into phonemic format via the imaginal semantic store-verbal output system link. Likewise, the associative level of meaning would be retained in the form of associations between verbal and imaginal entries in the verbal and imaginal semantic stores respectively.

It was suggested earlier that high-imagery words processed by the right side of the system might benefit from orthographic imagery. Presumably the orthographic imagery would be generated in the imagelogogen system and might be more persistent for high-than low-imagery words on the right side of the model by virtue of feedback from the imaginal semantic store that presumably specializes in visual/imaginal information. Persistent orthographic images for high-imagery words might serve as the basis for a high-imagery word production superiority from the right side of the model. Whether orthographic images play an important role on the left side of the system is unclear.

Conclusion.   In this chapter, the nature of semantic representation and memory was at issue. The model that has been proposed was intended to integrate and clarify most of the conclusions and some of the speculations that arose throughout the chapter. The novel aspects of the model are, first, a dual verbal input system at what Paivio would call the representational level of meaning and, second, the introduction of an imagelogogen system. Because the approach in this chapter owes so much to Paivio's dual-coding model, it is perhaps not surprising that the proposed model retains the concepts of referential and associative levels of meaning, in almost pristine form. The model, and especially the novel aspects of the model, are admittedly tentative. Nonetheless, the model represents a gestalt that seemed to emerge both from the results of the naming latency studies reported here, and from a review of the literature. When ideas are systematized in a model, they tend to be more precise than they would be otherwise. Precision makes the ideas vulnerable to disproof, but if the ideas are worthwhile, they may become heuristically valuable and withstand the acid test of time. Although the novel ideas contained in this chapter may not last, Paivio's dual-coding model that inspired this work has already proven its ability to pass the test.

ACKNOWLEDGMENT

This research was supported by a grant from Trent University's Research Committee which, in turn, was funded by Canadian NSERC. I wish to thank Corinne Haley and Cathy Blom for their spirited assistance with data analysis, and Professor Douglas Lowe for contributing to initial pilot work and discussions of the data.

REFERENCES

Anderson, J. R., & Bower, G. H. *Human associative memory.* Washington, D.C.: Winston, 1973.

Baddeley, A. D. Working memory and reading. In P. A. Kolers, M. E. Wrolstad, & H. Bouma, *Processing of visible language Vol. I.* New York: Plenum Press, 1979.

Bradshaw, J. L. Three interrelated problems in reading: A review. *Memory and Cognition,* 1975, *3,* 123–134.

Bransford, J. D., & Franks, J. J. The abstraction of linguistic ideas. *Cognitive Psychology,* 1971, *2,* 331–350.

Coltheart, M. Deep dyslexia: A right hemisphere hypothesis. In M. Coltheart, K. E. Patterson, & J. C. Marshall (Eds.), *Deep dyslexia.* London: Routledge & Kegan Paul, 1980.

Coltheart, M., Davelaar, E., Jonasson, J. T., & Besner, D. Access to the internal lexicon. In S. Dornic (Ed.), *Attention and performance, VI*. Hillsdale, N.J.: Lawrence Erlbaum Assoc., 1977.

Ehri, L. C. The development of orthographic images. In U. Frith (Ed.), *Cognitive processes in spelling*. London: Academic Press, 1980.

Elman, J. L., Takahashi, K., & Tohsaku, Y. H. Asymmetries for the categorization of Kanji nouns, adjectives, and verbs presented to the left and right visual fields. *Brain and Language*, 1981, *13*, 290-300.

Hatta, T. Recognition of Japanese Kanji in left and right visual fields. *Neurophychologia*, 1977, *15*, 685-688.

Kleiman, G. M. Speech recoding in reading. *Journal of Verbal Learning and Verbal Behavior*, 1975, *14*, 323-339.

Levy, B. A. Speech processing during reading. In A. M. Lesgold, J. W. Pellegrino, S. D. Fokkema, & R. Glaser (Eds.), *Cognitive psychology and instruction*. New York: Plenum Press, 1978.

Marcel, A. J., & Patterson, K. E. Word recognition and production: Reciprocity in clinical and normal studies. In J. Requin (Ed.), *Attention and performance VII*. Hillsdale, N.J.: Lawrence Earlbaum Assoc., 1979.

Meyer, D. E., Schvaneveldt, R. W., & Ruddy, M. G. Loci of contextual effects on visual word recognition. In P. Rabbit & S. Dornic (Eds.), *Attention and performance, V*. New York: Academic Press, 1975.

Morton, J. The interaction of information in word recognition. *Psychological Review*, 1969, *76*, 175-178.

Morton, J. Word recognition. In J. Morton & J. C. Marshall (Eds.), *Psycholinguistics Series II*. London: Elek Scientific Books, 1978.

Morton, J. Facilitation in word recognition: Experiments causing change in the logogen model. In P. A. Kolers, M. E. Wrolstad, & H. Bouma, *Processing of visible language Vol. I*. New York: Plenum Press, 1979.

Morton, J. The logogen model and orthographic structure. In U. Frith (Ed.), *Cognitive processes in spelling*. London: Academic Press, 1980.

Nelson, D. L., & Brooks, D. H. Independence of phonetic and imaginal features. *Journal of Experimental Psychology*, 1973, *97*, 1-7.

Nelson, D. L., Reed, V. S., & McEvoy, C. L. Encoding strategy and sensory and semantic interference. *Memory and Cognition*, 1977, *5*, 462-467.

Paivio, A. U. *Imagery and verbal processes*. New York: Holt, Rinehart, & Winston, 1971.

Paivio, A. U. Perceptual comparisons through the mind's eye. *Memory and Cognition*, 1975, *3*, 635-647.

Paivio, A. U. A dual coding approach to perception and cognition. In H. L. Pick Jr., & E. Saltzman (Eds.), *Modes of perceiving and processing information*. Hillsdale, N.J.: Lawrence Erlbaum Assoc., 1978.

Paivio, A. U., & Begg, I. *Psychology of language*. Englewood Cliffs, N.J.: Prentice-Hall, 1981.

Patterson, K. E. What is right with deep dyslexic patients? *Brain and Language*, 1979, *8*, 111-129.

Piaget, J. La naissance de l'intelligence chez l'enfant. Neuchatel: Delachaux & Niestle, 1936. As cited by H. Ginsburg & S. Opper, *Piaget's theory of intellectual development: An introduction*. Englewood Cliffs: Prentice-Hall, 1969.

Rayner, K., & Posnansky, C. Stages of processing in word identification. *Journal of Experimental Psychology: General*, 1978, *107*, 64-80.

Reich, S. S., & Cherry, C. A direct access from graphics to meaning: A study of the stroop effect in sentences. In P. A. Kolers, M. E. Wrolstad, & H. Bouma, *Processing of visible language Vol I*. New York: Plenum Press, 1979.

Richardson, J. T. E. The effect of word imageability in acquired dyslexia. *Neuropsychologia*, 1975, *13*, 281-288.

Saffran, E. M., Bogyo, L. C., Schwartz, M. F., & Marin, O. S. M. Does deep dyslexia reflect right-hemisphere reading? In M. Coltheart, K. E. Patterson, & J. C. Marshall (Eds.), *Deep dyslexia*. London: Routledge & Kegan Paul, 1980.

Saffran, M., & Marin, O. S. M. Reading without phonology: Evidence from aphasia. *Quarterly Journal of Experimental Psychology*, 1977, *29*, 515-525.

Sasanuma, S. Kana and Kanji processing in Japanese aphasics. *Brain and Language*, 1975, *2*, 369—383.

Sasanuma, S., Itoh, M., Mori, K., & Kobayaski, Y. Tachistoscopic recognition of Kana and Kanji words. *Neuropsychologia*, 1977, *15*, 547-553.

Seymour, P. H. K. A model for reading, naming, and comprehension. *British Journal of Psychology*, 1973, *64*, 35-49.

Seymour, P. H. K. Contemporary models of cognitive processes: II. Retrieval and comparison operations in permanent memory. In V. Hamilton & M. D. Vernon (Eds.), *The development of cognitive processes*. New York: Academic Press, 1976.

Shallice, T., & Warrington, E. K. Word recognition in a phonemic dyslexic patient. *Quarterly Journal of Experimental Psychology*, 1975, *27*, 187-199.

Sperber, R. D., McCauley, C., Ragain, R. D., & Weil, C. M. Semantic priming effects on picture and word processing. *Memory and Cognition*, 1979, *7*, 339-345.

10

Representational Memory: Paivio's Levels of Meaning as Experiential Model and Conceptual Framework

James M. Clark
College of Cape Breton

Ten years ago, Paivio (1971) completed a review of human symbolic processing, a review that attempted to accommodate diverse findings from perception, memory, and language within a common conceptual framework. Central to that effort was a proposal about symbolic representation. The succeeding decade of cognitive psychology can be characterized as one of intensive concern with the nature of mental representation and the processes which operate on those representations. This conference provides a timely opportunity to reconsider Paivio's general conceptualization and to examine not only its adequacy as a specific theory about mental representation but also the appropriateness of his perspective as a more general scheme within which to interpret current issues and findings in cognitive psychology.

This chapter focuses upon Paivio's basic hypothesis that there are distinctive modes of representation for different types of information. This hypothesis is fundamental to the more complete theory that has evolved through the work of Paivio and others. Although a discussion of this basic premise and its import to cognitive psychology may prove valuable, the complete theory is more extensive and well developed than suggested by this chapter alone. Other sections in this volume will give a more accurate idea of the scope and specificity of the dual-coding theory.

I use the phrase "representational memory" to refer to the collection of memories which encode symbolically external or internal events. These representations and their mutual relationships provide the basic mechanism by which events assume significance or meaning. It is more common to refer to this collection of representations as "semantic memory" after Tulving (1972) but there is a danger that the label semantic will unduly constrain the scope of theories of meaning because of the term's prior association with the meaning of words in particular. Representational memory appears more appropriate especially in light of views of meaning, such as Paivio's, which recognize the contribution of nonlinguistic factors.

The purpose of this chapter is primarily to articulate the issues raised by Paivio's model of meaning and is not to review the evidence pertinent to each of the issues. However, concrete examples will be introduced to make the discussion explicit. The illustrations will be drawn from my own work on free association to synonyms (Clark 1978) and some pilot data on synonym judgment reaction times. The study of equivalence relationships in general (synonyms, translation-equivalents, and picture-word correspondence) is central to an understanding of symbolic processing. Similarity and identity play important roles in both perceptual and conceptual processes. The free association task provides a vehicle for the direct examination of certain aspects of representational memory and, in my view, warrants renewed investigation by cognitive psychologists.

Paivio's Levels of Meaning

The basic premise of Paivio's theory is that representational memory is comprised of distinguishable codes associated with different classes of information. Two coding systems have been emphasized: verbal representations which correspond to words, and imaginal representations which correspond to nonverbal elements of experience. There is uncertainty about the molecular constitution of both verbal and imaginal representations and about the perceptual processes involved in their elicitation. However, at the molar level, it is possible to conceptualize distinctive representations for the two classes of events, verbal and nonverbal. Essentially, the model postulates a separation in memory which parallels an intuitively plausible distinction between linguistic and nonlinguistic events. Much research has been directed toward the identification of different functional properties of the verbal and imaginal systems but a consideration of even the basic premise leads to some insights into theories about representational memory.

Paivio (1971, Chapter 3) articulated the immediate implications of his fundamental premise about representational memory. In particular, he noted that meaning or comprehension is determined by the total reactions of an individual to an external event and that these reactions can be classified as one of three types: representational, referential, or associative. Each of these aspects of meaning is described briefly in the following paragraphs and discussed at greater length in subsequent sections of the chapter.

The first level of activity involves a representation that maintains a perceptual correspondence with the actual event and is termed a representational reaction. A familiar word elicits activity in a specific verbal representation because the word belongs to a certain category that is defined primarily in terms of perceptual characteristics. In a similar manner, a familiar object initiates activity in a specific imaginal representation. The activation in both cases is based on a pattern recognition process and may be considered a direct and relatively unmediated reaction.

In contrast to the direct elicitation of representational reactions by perceptual processes, referential and associative reactions are mediated by the representational reaction. Initial activation of the verbal or imaginal representation results in second-order activation of other representations which are connected to the stimulus less directly. Given two different classes of representation, verbal and imaginal, one can identify two types of second-order reactions.

One second-order level of meaning involves a subsequent reaction in which mediated activity is initiated in a representation of a different type than the initial representational reaction. Paivio termed such activity referential. A verbal representation, once activated, stimulates related imaginal representations and an imaginal representation stimulates related verbal representations. The former correlates with imaging to a word and the latter with naming an object. Presumably, the strongest connections exist between words and images of the objects for which the words are labels so the availability of connections between verbal and

COMPONENTS

REPRESENTATIONS: V–VERBAL
                    I–IMAGINAL

CONNECTIONS: 〜〜 –REPRESENTATIONAL
              – – – – –REFERENTIAL
              ——— –ASSOCIATIVE

MODEL

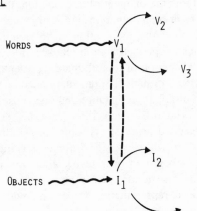

FIG. 10.1. Schematic representation of Paivio's levels of meaning model.

imaginal representations depends primarily on the concreteness of the word, although other factors are also important.

Another second-order level of meaning was identified by Paivio (1971). Associative meaning refers to the activation of representations of the same type as the original representational reaction. The activation of a verbal representation arouses other verbal representations and the activation of an imaginal representation arouses other imaginal representations. These second-order effects depend on associative connections determined by the prior experience of the individual.

Paivio referred to these different dimensions as levels of meaning because the ultimate significance or meaning of the external event is the composite of these representational, referential, and associative reactions. Figure 10.1 schematizes this view of representational memory and meaning. External events combined with two types of representation generate three kinds of relationships, each depicted by a distinct arrow. Subsequent discussion will examine more closely the implications of this general conceptualization, in particular the theoretical issues raised by each of the levels of meaning and the degree to which Paivio's scheme captures important considerations for a model of meaning.

Representational Meaning

The representational level of meaning forces deliberation about the basic elements of representational memory. As one of the major goals of cognitive psychology is to characterize the ultimate representations in semantic memory, there has been considerable discussion and controversy in this area. Paivio's first level of meaning provides an effective conceptualization of one major issue, the degree of abstractness of semantic representations. Dual-coding theory also offers one view about semantic coding, a view which contrasts with that endorsed almost universally by other workers and without which there may have been considerably less controversy.

From the moment of transduction, the encodings of external events undergo a series of transformations until, ultimately, activity is initiated in a representation that maintains associations with terminal representations of other events and which is operated upon by higher-order symbolic processes. Processing prior to the elicitation of this ultimate representation may be considered perceptual and the transformations momentary encodings. Processing subsequent to the elicitation of this representation may be considered more conceptual in nature and the representational state more enduring. The dichotomy between perceptual and conceptual processes is somewhat arbitrary but helps to emphasize the point at issue: to what level of abstractness is information encoded before semantic processes begin to operate or, alternatively, how abstract are permanent representations in associative memory? At an intuitive level, Paivio (1971) has equated representational meaning with a sense of familiarity about external events, words or objects.

Most theories of representational memory maintain that transformations proceed to extreme levels of abstraction prior to the initiation of semantic processes. That is, it has been argued or assumed that external events that constitute a single "idea" (e.g. object, picture, word, synonym, translation-equivalent) converge upon a common, amodal representation and higher-order cognitive processes operate upon these abstract elements. Encodings tied more directly to experience (i.e. verbal or imaginal representations) constitute temporary states whose primary significance is in mediating the ultimate activation of abstract, conceptual representations.

In contrast, Paivio maintains that representational memory is based upon elements that are closely tied to experience. Verbal and imaginal representations, although themselves quite abstract, are more perceptual or experiential than are the conceptual representations endorsed by most theorists. Experiential representations are more similar to the actual stimulus (word or object) than are abstract representations.

This fundamental issue is schematized in Fig. 10.2 which illustrates several possible levels of representation along an abstractness dimension. Representations to the left are experiential and representations to the right are concep-

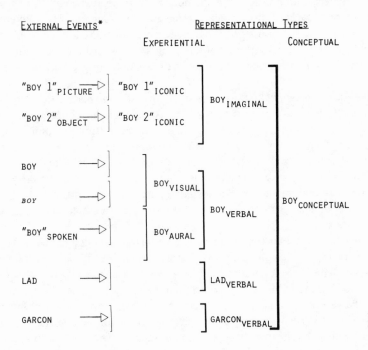

FIG. 10.2.   Abstractness dimension of representational elements.

tual. Intermediate levels of representation, verbal and imaginal, are relatively abstract even though they can be distinguished from the more fully abstracted conceptual representations. A conceptual representation of "boy" (if such existed) would be directly activated by any of a large set of alternative words or objects, alternatives which could differ from one another in substantial ways. For example, either a picture of a boy or the spoken word "boy" would terminate in activation of a common conceptual representation. Even a verbal or an imaginal representation would have a large set of elements by which it would be directly activated. However, in this case, the set would not be as extensive as that for the conceptual representation and the rules of membership would be based more on perceptual similarity than are the rules for conceptual representations. Some differences of a nonperceptual nature would be permitted (e.g. a word could be written or spoken) but these are of a more concrete order than the differences ignored by conceptual representations.

Wickelgren's (1972) characterization of a concept provides an alternative statement of the basic issue. Wickelgren proposed that a concept could be described as a disjunction of conjunctions. Any of many nonidentical events (A or B or . . .) could be classified as an instance of a common concept. Applied to the issue of representation in semantic memory, this conceptualization would restate the problem of level of abstractness as one about the degree of inclusiveness of the disjunctive rule. Abstract or conceptual representations assume highly inclusive disjunctions (e.g. object or word or picture) whereas experiential representations permit only more constrained disjunctions (e.g., spoken or written word).

The issue is made explicit if we consider how different classes of model would represent synonymity (see Fig. 10.3). According to conceptual models, synonyms would activate directly a common abstract representation. This convergence is identified in Fig. 10.3 as a representational process (wavy lines) to indicate that the verbal representations are merely transient states occurring on route to the underlying conceptual representation. The conceptual representation then activates other nodes in an associative manner. Synonymity or, more properly, any equivalence relationship is encoded in the representational structure of such models.

Two classes of experiential model are illustrated although the differences between these models will be discussed more fully in the following section which focuses on the referential dimension of Paivio's theory. Some experiential models of meaning include only verbal representations and do not consider nonverbal aspects of experience. According to such verbal models, synonyms would elicit distinct verbal representations which would be associated with one another and with other verbal representations. Synonymity would be based not on a shared representation but on associations between the two representations and/or on the similarity of the associative patterns elicited by each of the verbal representations.

ASSOCIATIVE–RELATIONAL
NETWORK

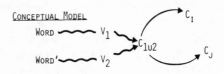

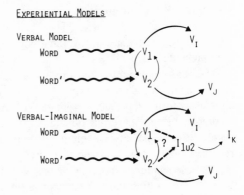

FIG.   10.3.   Alternative   representational models of synonymity.

The second experiential model, dual-coding theory, includes imaginal representations as well as verbal ones and, as schematized in Fig. 10.3, demonstrates
structural similarities with both the conceptual and verbal models. All synonyms
activate verbal representations which maintain associations with one another and
with other verbal representations. In addition, verbal representations for concrete
synonyms may initiate activity in a common imaginal representation. Synonymity will be based on verbal associative relationships and/or shared referential
reactions.

The main issue raised by the representational dimension of meaning is
whether semantic memory should be viewed as constituted to abstract conceptual
representations or more concrete perceptual entities whether verbal, imaginal, or
both. Most theories endorse the former view and assign experiential representations secondary roles in encoding or decoding phases not integral to the
central semantic processing. A few theorists, including Paivio (1971), have
argued that experiential representations are the primary form of representation in
semantic memory and that it may be unnecessary to include abstract representations at all. The critical difference is demonstrated in Fig. 10.3. Conceptual
models hypothesize many-to-one relationships between external events and internal representations but experiential models hypothesize one-to-one relationships,
at least at the representation level.

There is considerable evidence pertinent to this question but I mention only
the results of several free association studies that were completed several years

CLARK

ago (Clark, 1978). The rationale for the studies was provided by the models in Fig. 10.3 and paralleled reasoning of Kolers (1963) in several studies on translation-equivalents. The design and results should serve to clarify the issue at hand.

One group of subjects was asked to free associate to 200 words made up of 100 synonym pairs. The 200 words were individually randomized and the dependent variable was the amount of overlap in responses to members of synonym pairs. The overlap measure counted both shared common responses and synonym responses. A second group of subjects free associated to one member of each synonym pair presented twice. The order of presentation was again randomized and the dependent measure was the number of responses which were identical on both presentations.

The reasoning behind the predictions should be apparent from Fig. 10.3. According to the conceptual model, the separate presentation of synonyms is equivalent to the repeated presentation of the same word. Words converge on a common abstract representation in semantic memory, a representation that ignores differences between elements with equivalent meaning. This common representation mediates associations with other representations and, ultimately, the free-association response. One is led by this model to expect that subjects will be as likely to give the same response on both occasions when the stimuli are synonyms as when the same word is repeated, with one qualification. The qualification is necessary because when synonyms are presented subjects may give the synonym as a valid response but repetition of the same item does not permit the earlier presented item as a response since free-association instructions specify a response other than the word presented. For this reason, the percentage of shared or synonym responses to synonyms was contrasted with the percentage of identical (shared) responses to repeated items.

Experiential models lead to a different prediction. Verbal representations maintain separate associative networks in semantic memory and, although these networks will be similar to one another, there is no requirement that they be identical, a condition that appears to follow from conceptual models. The experiential models predict lower levels of associative overlap to synonyms than to repeated items. More specific predictions of the verbal-imaginal model are discussed in the following section.

Overall, the results favored the experiential models over the conceptual model. The associative overlap to synonyms was quite low (31%) suggesting that different associative networks were being addressed by different members of a synonym pair. This result would have been more compelling, however, had the repeated items led to a higher level of overlap than they did. Even though subjects responded to all items within a 30-min period, the reliability of responses to repeated items was also low (45%) although substantially and significantly greater than the overlap level of synonyms. Associative networks as measured by the free association task appear susceptible to strong sources of variability. Interpretation was further confounded by the different scoring procedures adopted for synonym and identical repetitions.

Despite these complexities, the study does illustrate the basic issue implied by Paivio's representational level of meaning: Are semantic representations highly abstract with only remote connections to external events or are they quite concrete with fairly immediate and direct relationships to the external world. Paivio has suggested in at least one paper that these alternatives might not be mutually exclusive and that both experiential and conceptual representations may be necessary to accommodate certain phenomena (Marschark & Paivio, 1977). The possibility of a more complex representational memory which includes verbal, imaginal, and conceptual representations introduces additional issues. For example, it seems likely that one would find reliable individual differences in the dominance of different coding systems as has been reported for imagery ability. Some individuals may operate more abstractly than others. Situational demands may also be associated with the arousal of one system rather than another.

In summary, representational memory may be viewed either as a system of highly abstract conceptual representations or as a collection of more experiential verbal and/or imaginal representations. Paivio's representational level of meaning provides an effective conceptualization of the issue and the dual-coding position one of several alternative positions. We turn now to several issues associated with the hypothesis that memory representations are experiential rather than abstract. These issues are raised explicitly by Paivio's referential level of meaning.

Referential Meaning

The first of Paivio's second-order reactions which we examine involves the subsequent arousal of representations which are of a different type than the initial representational code. In the case of words, referential meaning involves the activation of appropriate imaginal representations, if available. Conversely, in the case of objects, referential meaning involves arousal of appropriate verbal representations, names of the objects. Nodes of one form have relationships with nodes of another form, in both cases.

The present chapter focuses on nonverbal images as referential components of word meaning. The primary goal of models of semantic memory has been to understand verbal behaviour and an emphasis on the contribution of imaginal representations may serve to counteract somewhat the dominance of verbal/linguistic information in models of meaning. Much of Paivio's work has attempted to redress this inequity. The emphasis upon the comprehension of verbal units is also warranted by the importance of verbal communication in human experience. These arguments do not deny either the significance of comprehension of nonverbal events or the contribution of verbal referential reactions to the understanding of such events.

There are a number of issues implicit in the hypothesis of a referential level of meaning. These issues are only paritially independent of the level of abstractness of the representations, the major issue raised by the representational level of meaning. It is appropriate, therefore, to begin with a consideration of the relationship between the representational and referential levels of meaning. Essentially, the question is whether some theoretical positions on the level of abstractness issue are associated with specific hypotheses about the availability of referential levels of meaning.

Theorists who assume that representations are highly abstract are constrained, perhaps, to a single type of representation and the referential dimension is irrelevant or undefined according to such models. There is thought to be a single mode of representation for all information and, therefore, it is meaningless to talk about connections among different types of representation. There would be rich interconnections among the representations (i.e., associative meaning) but the representations would all be of a common, highly abstract type.

Homogeneity of coding may not be a necessary consequence of abstractness although the two appear to be closely associated. It may be possible to articulate qualitatively different conceptual codes, each of which conforms to the requirements of an abstract level of representation but it is not clear how such models would be discriminable from more experiential models. This possibility will not be considered further and abstract models are assumed to ignore the following issues or, rather, to maintain positions which are implicit within the hypothesis of abstract representations.

The hypothesis of experiential representations, on the other hand, raises questions that are separate from the question of level of abstractness. The issues concern the number of distinct coding systems which are required to account for human conceptual behaviour and corollaries such as, for example, the degree of interrelatedness of the various coding systems. Clearly the second question implies a particular answer to the first. We consider, in turn, models that hypothesize a single homogeneous code and models that incorporate multiple codes.

Although the dominant hypothesis in cognitive psychology has been that representational memory consists of abstract representations, several writers have noted that models based solely on verbal representations can account for many findings and that conceptual models are usually abstract in name only (Anderson, 1976; Hayes-Roth & Hayes-Roth, 1977; Potter, Valian, & Faulconer, 1977). Adherents of such verbal models argue that findings which appear to support conceptual representations are also consistent with the hypothesis of verbal representations connected by an associative-relational network. Effects accounted for by a common abstract representation are explained by associative connections among related verbal representations.

Verbal models perpetuate the emphasis upon linguistic units which has been characteristic of the conceptual models. Paradoxically, verbal models, although experiential, may be even less able to cope with nonverbal information than conceptual models. Conceptual models allow for nonverbal information even though coded in abstract form while verbal models would not generally be able to account for any but the most trivial sort of nonverbal information.

Purely verbal models do not consider referential meaning since only one type of code is involved in the processing of linguistic information. Meaning is based on the activation of the verbal representation and the subsequent arousal of other verbal representations in the associative network. Verbal and conceptual models, then, share the assumption that homogeneous coding is characteristic of semantic memory and, with respect to verbal materials at least, that it is unnecessary to postulate multiple types of code. This assumption is quite explicit in the characterization of these models in Fig. 10.3. A single type of code, either conceptual or verbal, is available and associations always connect nodes of the same type.

Despite this grouping of the verbal and conceptual models, there is at least one difference between the two with respect to the issue of referential meaning. The omission of nonverbal information from current verbal models may be a temporary exclusion that should be attributed more to the preliminary development of present theories than to a denial of the existence or the importance of such information. Verbal models may later incorporate other codes thus being modified into multiple-code theories. The conceptual models appear inherently less compatible with the hypothesis of multiple coding systems associated with experiential levels of representation and may require more radical modification if other codes are to be included.

In contrast to the uniform coding position, other experiential models state explicitly that distinct representational codes exist for different types of information. Paivio's dual-coding theory identified verbal and imaginal codes that are associated with linguistic and nonlinguistic information, respectively. Even though not elicited directly by verbal events, imaginal codes play an important role in verbal behaviour because of the availability of referential connections which result in the indirect or second-order activation of the imaginal representations. These connections are illustrated in Figs. 10.1 and 10.3. Considerable research has demonstrated that variables associated with the availability of imaginal representations (e.g. concreteness, instructions, individual differences) influence a variety of verbal behaviours.

The present issue can be made more explicit by reconsidering the models of synonymity presented in Fig. 10.3. Differences between the unitary and multiple-coding theories lead to differential predictions in the free association task outlined in the previous section. According to dual-coding theory, concrete synonyms converge upon a common imaginal code which may mediate responses in the free association task whereas abstract synonyms lack this common referential connection. This difference leads to the prediction that one should find differences in overlap between concrete and abstract synonyms. The hypothesis of a unitary verbal code, on its own, leads to the prediction of identical overlap for concrete and abstract synonyms. These predictions could be contrasted in the free association study because half of the stimuli were concrete and half were abstract in both the synonym and identical-repetition studies.

The results supported the dual-coding prediction. There was greater associative overlap for concrete synonyms (37%) than for abstract synonyms (25%) due both to more shared responses and to greater likelihood of eliciting the other member of the pair. Although there was also a difference for identical repetitions between concrete (48%) and abstract (41%%) words, the difference between synonym and actual repetitions was significantly greater for abstract words as opposed to concrete. This finding was predicted by dual-coding theory and is more difficult to account for on the basis of unitary coding theories. A second study demonstrated comparable concreteness effects on associative overlap when different subjects responded to each member of the synonym pair. This latter finding suggests that differences between concrete and abstract materials can properly be attributed to representational memory and are not simply a phenomenon of episodic memory.

The hypothesis of multiple-coding raises additional questions, two of which will be considered briefly: the degree of integration of different codes and the number of distinct coding systems. Both of these issues are in need of more careful articulation.

One issue associated with referential meaning concerns the degree of integration of different types of symbolic code. The distinct systems may be conceptualized as internally coherent with relatively weaker connections between systems than within systems. Recent box-model characterizations of dual-coding theory (Paivio & Begg, 1981, Fig. 5–11; Paivio & Desrochers, 1980, Fig. 1) are consistent with the idea of separate systems. An alternative conceptualization of bilingualism based on integrated representations appears in Fig. 10.4. In this representation of the model, codes of different types are thought to constitute a relatively integrated network with little difference in connectivity within and between systems. This is not to deny the anatomical or functional distinctiveness of different coding systems but simply to recognize that referential connections can be as rich and facilitative as associative connections within systems. The implication of concreteness in a wide variety of verbal tasks would seem to call for this integrated approach whereas the differential activation of systems by instructional sets, for example, suggests that the systems can be accessed independently. Additional research needs to be addressed towards this question.

A second issue concerns the number of distinct coding systems necessary to account for human conceptual behaviour. Dual-coding theory is somewhat ambiguous about this question. Paivio (1971, p. 8) stated explicitly that verbal and imaginal codes were not the only modes of representation and that affective meaning, for example, was excluded. However, Paivio and Begg (1981, p. 115) indicated that emotional and motor components were included in a dual-coding approach. The essential question appears to center about the inclusiveness of the

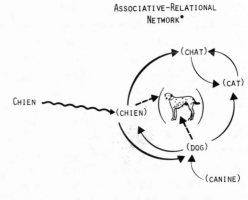

FIG. 10.4. Integrated network representation of dual-coding theory.

*() Representations

term imagery which is used sometimes to refer to visual imagery in particular and on other occasions to include other sensory codes. Much of what has been claimed for the imaginal system appears more characteristic of the visual system than of other sensory and motor systems and is based predominantly on operations involving visual imagery. The emphasis upon visual-imaginal codes is natural given the relevance of these to traditional cognitive concerns, especially memory, language, and thought. As cognitive psychology addresses broader psychological domains such as emotion, other classes of experience will receive greater attention and evidence will be forthcoming about the functional distinctiveness of different representational systems. Evidence has been reported recently, for example, that motoric imagery and visual imagery produce independent interference effects (Saltz & Donnenwerth-Nolan, 1981).

In summary, representational memory may be viewed as a system of homogeneous codes or as a collection of multiple codes working interactively to effect meaning, a distinction captured by Paivio's notion of referential meaning. Dual-coding theory, as a specific hypothesis about referential meaning, endorses the second view and has been supported by a number of findings such as concreteness effects in verbal tasks. Unitary coding theories attempt to account for such effects in terms of auxiliary premises about aspects of semantic memory other than referential meaning. One mechanism which has been invoked is associative meaning, the relationships among representations of a common type. We turn now to a consideration of this third level of meaning.

Associative Meaning

Paivio's associative level of meaning results from second-order arousal of representations of the same type as the initial code. The occurrence of a familiar word activates not only the verbal code which represents that word but also verbal codes for other words with which it has been associated. A similar chain of activation occurs among imaginal representations upon the presentation of an object or a picture. The issues raised by associative meaning concern relationships among codes of a common type.

Of the three levels of meaning, verbal associative meaning has received the greatest amount of attention in semantic research. One reason for this emphasis is the relative unanimity among theories of representational memory about the existence of associative meaning. As illustrated by all three models in Fig. 10.3, words arouse mental representations that stimulate additional representations of the same class. The models differ with respect to the degree of abstractness of the representations and the availability of nonverbal codes but not about the essentially associative character of the network.

A second reason for the emphasis upon associative meaning is the omission of nonverbal representations from conceptual and verbal models of meaning. The absence of a referential level of meaning leaves associative meaning to account for most semantic memory phenomena. Later discussion will articulate some of the difficulties with this approach even for the study of verbal associative memory.

These factors in conjunction with the availability of appropriate memory and decision tasks stimulated investigation of verbal associative memory. Some of the topics which have been addressed are: the organization or structure of associative-relational networks, processes that operate on the underlying associations to initiate or influence the spread of activation across nodes in the network, and ontogenetic questions about the development of associative structures and processes.

The associative level of meaning embraces these and related questions so that much of standard thinking about representational memory can be accommodated within Paivio's framework. However, dual-coding theory goes beyond these questions about verbal associative memory and raises additional concerns that have received less attention.

Indeed, the model can be said to multiply the number of issues that must be resolved since theories about representational memory would need to explain the structure and functioning of nonverbal associative networks as well as verbal. Imaginal networks may operate according to quite different laws than the verbal and may require novel methods of investigation.

A second complication introduced by dual-coding theory is that the more specific questions that have come to be asked of associative meaning must be asked also about referential meaning. Many cognitive tasks can be expected to initiate referential activity as well as associative and it may be difficult to develop situations in which associative networks of one type or another operate in isolation of other coding systems.

However, even if it were possible to observe purely verbal networks in operation, the investigator cannot ignore safely the implications of dual-coding theory. Consider the verbal and verbal-imaginal models presented in Fig. 10.3. According to dual-coding theory, the verbal model is appropriate for abstract words and the verbal-imaginal model appropriate for concrete words. The availability of a referential level of meaning for concrete words but not abstract suggests that verbal associative networks play a greater role in the meaning of abstract words. Verbal associative networks might reasonably be expected to evolve differently for concrete and abstract words. These differences would be displayed even in a task which required only the operation of verbal associative processes. The greater the number of separate codes in representational memory, the more difficult it is to consider distinct associative networks in isolation and the more important it is to examine interactions among different codes at all possible levels.

The associative and referential levels have been linked in a fourth but less direct manner related somewhat to the immediately preceding arguments. Adherents of verbal and conceptual models of representational memory have attempted to account for concreteness and related effects by postulating associative differences between concrete and abstract words. Although legitimate, these efforts often beg the question of the origin of the associative differences which may themselves be evidence for dual-coding theory, as argued in the preceding paragraph.

Associative meaning will be examined in the context of the representation of synonymity as were previous levels of meaning. Despite the likely interaction between referential and associative levels of meaning, the emphasis will be upon associative meaning per se although several references will be made to the contribution of nonverbal representations.

It has been noted that abstract representations account structurally for identity relationships so conceptual models seem to have little need of an associative mechanism to explain synonymity. Verbal models, on the other hand, do use associative relationships to account for synonymity whereas verbal-imaginal models appeal to similar verbal processes for words in general and to referential relationships for concrete words. The following analysis is more pertinent to the experiential models and largely irrelevant to conceptual models, at least with respect to synonyms.

Two approaches to verbal associative meaning can be identified. One standard approach emphasizes the formal nature of relationships and generally appeals to single, labelled associations to represent relationships such as category inclusion in associative memory. A second approach treats relationships as less well specified and considers the overall pattern or configuration of associative connections. Although synonymity could be represented as a single association, a less formalistic approach is adopted in the following discussion. If only first- and second-order associations are considered, there could be three patterns of connection involving two synonyms.

One type of connection is a direct association between each of the verbal representations. Each member of the pair elicits the other with some probability

DIRECT CONNECTIONS

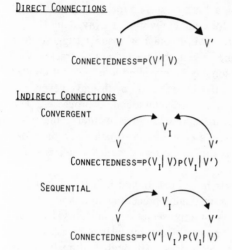

CONNECTEDNESS=P(V'| V)

INDIRECT CONNECTIONS

CONVERGENT

CONNECTEDNESS=P(V_I| V)P(V_I|V')

SEQUENTIAL

CONNECTEDNESS=P(V'| V_I)P(V_I| V)

FIG. 10.5. Types of associative connections between synonyms.

or strength. Two types of indirect connection are possible. A convergent pattern occurs when both synonyms elicit a common verbal representation which represents a third word. A sequential pattern involves a single mediator which creates a chain linking one synonym to its mate; one synonym elicits a response which itself has some probability of eliciting the other synonym. In both indirect cases, the strength of the connection is the product of the probabilities associated with each of the single associations in the pattern. More complex associative networks could be developed by the combination of these basic patterns which are illustrated in Fig. 10.5.

Standard free association methods elicit both synonym and shared responses which provide measures of direct and convergent patterns. Sequential pathways cannot be identified from the standard associations because first-order responses are not normally presented as stimuli, a step which is necessary to determine the probability that the initial response is in fact a mediator for the other synonym.

A pilot study was undertaken to determine if the difference between direct and convergent connections has any consequences for facilitation of synonym judgments. Associative relatedness measures were derived from the responses in the free association studies described previously. Four types of synonym were selected: high on both synonym and shared responses, high on synonym but low on shared, low on synonym but high on shared, and low on both measures. Given the low levels of overlap generally, the terms "high" and "low" should be interpreted only relatively. The two factors were made orthogonal to one another although considerable item selection was necessary to effect independence of the two variables. The final 24 synonym pairs were combined with 24 unrelated pairs matched on several variables and block randomized for presentation to 16 subjects. Subjects were instructed to press one key if the two words were synonyms

TABLE 10.1
Mean Reaction Times (sec) for Synonym
Judgments as a Function of Associative
Connectedness

		Shared Associations	
		High	Low
Synonym Associations	High	1.27	1.23
	Low	1.22	1.54

and another key if they were not. Reaction times were recorded and the means for synonym pairs are presented in Table 10.1.

Both main effects were significant but qualified by an interaction that was reliable when analyzed by subjects or by items. Reaction time was approximately 300 milliseconds slower when the synonyms had neither direct nor convergent connections as measured by the free association task. The presence of either type of association was enough to facilitate synonym judgments but the two types of connection were not additive.

A minimal amount of associativity appears to be necessary for facilitation to occur but beyond that threshold no further benefit seems to be derived. There are several sites at which the facilitation effect could operate. The facilitation could occur at a peripheral level in that activation of one synonym leads to arousal and faster recognition of the other member of the pair. Alternatively, the associative connections could be involved in the actual synonym judgment in which case the facilitation would occur at a deeper level. Less interesting explanations include confoundings of the associative variables with other attributes of either single words or synonym pairs. At the present time, such alternatives remain viable.

The study illustrates the sort of issue raised by an associative level of meaning. The pattern of associations among verbal representations has implications for the semantic processing of each of the individual nodes in the network. The occurrence of a word indirectly activates a number of representations and either individual associative responses or the entire pattern of responses may be involved in understanding and related processing of the presented item.

The study also demonstrates the possibility for systematic study of associative networks as patterns. However, a number of characteristics of associative networks are likely to hamper any such investigation on a more ambitious scale. Three problems are discussed briefly: the covert character of associations, the complexity of associative networks, and the variability inherent in such networks.

The first obstacle to the investigation of associative networks is the covert nature of the underlying individual associations. The informativeness of the free

COVERT NETWORK

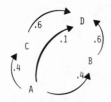

APPARENT CONNECTIONS

A→B   .40= P(B|A)
A→C   .40= P(C|A)
A→D   .49= P(D|A) + P(D|B)P(B|A) + P(D|C)P(C|A)

FIG. 10.6.   The nonequivalence of apparent and covert associative networks.

association task may be more apparent than real. Any given pattern of overt responses can be accounted for by a number of underlying, covert associative structures. Consider the hypothetical example presented in Fig. 10.6. Representation A has stronger direct connections with C and B than with D but the overall pattern of associations suggests that activation of A will elicit a higher level of activity in D than in either C or B. The free association task may provide a reasonably direct measure of the ultimate relative amount of activity at some node but this activation need not translate into an identifiable associative structure, as the example illustrates.

One approach to the first problem would be to examine clusters of associations rather than single connections in the hope that the underlying pattern of connections would be more determined as more nodes were observed. However, the mapping of networks can become quite complex even when relatively few nodes are considered. Figure 10.7 presents a simple example involving only four nodes and discrete connections. Mapping the ultimate consequences of activation

NETWORK REPRESENTATION

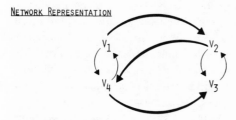

MATRIX REPRESENTATION

		SUCCEEDING NODE			
		V_1	V_2	V_3	V_4
	V_1	0	1	0	1
ANTECEDENT	V_2	0	0	1	1
	V_3	0	1	0	0
	V_4	1	0	1	0

FIG. 10.7.   Alternative representations of a simple associative network.

of any one node is still quite difficult and systematic approaches such as the matrix representation also included in Fig. 10.7 may be necessary. The initial entries in the matrix provide the direct connectedness and it is possible to compute both convergent and divergent connectivities by the application of operators to the matrix. However, massive data on free associations must be collected to provide the initial entries and, even then, computations can become restrictive when paths of two or three degrees of remoteness are followed (Kiss, 1973, 1975).

A third difficulty with associative structures, variability, leads one to wonder whether any static representation of such networks will be adequate. Even when the second presentation of the identical stimulus was within 30 min of the first, subjects in the free association studies described previously repeated their first response only 45% of the time. Similar levels of reliability have been reported by other researchers which suggests that variability may be an intrinsic characteristic of associative meaning. The instability may be due to spontaneous changes of a dynamic system, intentional factors, or contextual effects on momentary associative strengths. In any case, variability within subjects makes more complex the investigation of associative structures. There is an additional dimension of variability associated with individual differences. Elaborate associative networks based on composite responses from many individuals may not mimic the individual networks from which they are derived. For example, multidimensional scaling solutions for groups may indicate several dimensions underlie judgments even though individual patterns suggest unidimensional solutions are more appropriate. One might expect similar problems with associative aggregate data perhaps especially on the basis of experiential models which would predict considerable personal idiosyncrisy based on the different experiences of people. Mental networks should reflect the richness of these differences.

To return to an earlier point in closing this section, it should be noted that dual-coding theory hypothesizes that the preceding problems will probably be compounded by the need to consider coding systems in addition to the one of primary interest. Any effort to examine one system in isolation can be misleading. This point is illustrated by the issue of variability of associative structure. Verbal associations to concrete words tend to be more stable than associations to abstract words, a finding which can be accounted for on the basis of either differences in underlying associative structures or the implication of referential meaning in the free association task. However, the issue may be more complex. I examined synonym responses separately from other associations and found that there was no difference in the stability of concrete (66%) and abstract (67%) words. The difference between concrete and abstract words may reflect differences in the kinds of responses elicited rather than stability *per se*. That synonym responses were more stable than nonsynonym responses for both concrete and abstract words was also intriguing and suggests that the synonymity relationship focused upon in this chapter may have some special role in representational memory.

In summary, the associative level of meaning introduces a host of questions concerned with the organization, activation, and development of associative networks. Paivio's hypothesis of verbal and imaginal associative networks which are connected to one another provides a context for standard verbal association studies and, more importantly, suggests some shortcomings in any approach which ignores other coding systems. Several factors intrinsic to associative networks were identified as potential barriers to investigation of associative memory. These difficulties were raised, not to sound a note of pessimism, but to emphasize the importance of a conceptual framework to the constructive investigation of representational memory, a point argued briefly in the following conclusion.

Conclusions

The title suggests that the ideas developed in this chapter operate at two levels, as model and as framework. I would like to reinforce that impression and articulate more clearly the distinction, with special consideration of the second level.

At one level, the distinction among three levels of meaning becomes realized as a specific model of representational memory. Dual-coding theory hypothesizes that experiential representations of two types exist in memory. Verbal and imaginal representations, once aroused, stimulate additional activity in representations of the other class and in representations of the same class. Many deductions derived from this model have received empirical support.

However, the distinctiveness of dual-coding theory can be appreciated best by a consideration of the dimensions along which dual-coding and other theories about representational memory differ. Levels of meaning provide at least some of these dimensions. Representational meaning raises questions about the abstractness of elements in semantic memory. Dual-coding theory falls at the experiential or perceptual level of this dimension while other theories hypothesize more abstract forms of representation. Referential meaning raises questions about the number and connectedness of distinct representational systems. Dual-coding theory is a multiple-code theory in contrast to unitary coding models. The associative level of meaning considers relationships among codes of a common type. Although sharing many characteristics with other models, dual-coding theory generates some original concerns about associative memory because of the interconnectedness of different symbolic systems. Other theories focus upon purely associative networks, an ideal not likely to be realized according to dual-coding theory.

What is the significance of this distinction and Paivio's contribution at the second level, the conceptualization of representational memory? There is considerable debate among philosophers of science about whether science progresses through bottom-up or top-down processes. However, few would deny the importance of conceptual frameworks whether these be viewed as originating in the data or in the mind of the perceiver. Conceptual frameworks are essential to the progress of science and this may be particularly true in immature sciences such as psychology. The sheer complexity of our scientific worlds demands some order that will help to interpret known events and also raise additional questions for investigation. Levels of meaning and dual-coding theory provide powerful mechanisms for the ordering of much thinking about representational memory; they are both integrative and suggestive.

Perhaps the most significant feature of this conceptual scheme is that it is articulated. Many metatheoretical constructs within which researchers function remain implicit. Such implicit conceptual frameworks are seldom tested while Paivio's explicit scheme leads naturally to empirical testing allowing for disconfirmation. Its persistence as a viable model of symbolic processing in spite of its explicitness provides strong testimony to its strength.

In conclusion, Paivio's ideas, first drawn together over a decade ago, provide more than simply a competing model of representational or semantic memory. The ideas, once understood, provide a mental schema within which much of contemporary cognitive psychology can be situated.

REFERENCES

Anderson, J. R. *Language, memory and thought.* New York: Wiley, 1976.

Clark, J. M. *Synonymity and concreteness effects on free recall and free association: Implications for a theory of semantic memory.* Unpublished doctoral dissertation, University of Western Ontario, 1978.

Hayes-Roth, B., & Hayes-Roth, F. The prominence of lexical information in memory representation of meaning. *Journal of Verbal Learning and Verbal Behavior,* 1977, *16,* 119–136.

Kiss, G. R. *An associative thesaurus of English: Structural analysis of a large relevance network.* Paper presented at the Conference on Current Research in Aspects of Long-Term Memory, University of Dundee, July 1973.

Kiss, G. R. An associative thesaurus of English: Structural analysis of a large relevance network. In A. Kennedy & A. Wilkes (Eds.), *Studies in long-term memory.* New York: Wiley, 1975.

Kolers, P. A. Interlingual word associations. *Journal of Verbal Learning and Verbal Behavior,* 1963, *2,* 291–300.

Marschark, M., & Paivio, A. Integrative processing of concrete and abstract sentences. *Journal of Verbal Learning and Verbal Behavior,* 1977, *16,* 217–231.

Paivio, A. *Imagery and verbal processes.* New York: Holt, Rinehart & Winston, 1971.

Paivio, A., & Begg I. *Psychology of language.* Englewood Cliffs: Prentice-Hall, 1981.

Paivio, A., & Desrochers, A. A dual-coding approach to bilingual memory. *Canadian Journal of Psychology,* 1980, *34,* 388–399.

Potter, M. C., Valian, V. V., & Faulconer, B. A. Representation of a sentence and its pragmatic implications: Verbal, imagistic, or abstract? *Journal of Verbal Learning and Verbal Behavior.* 1977, *16,* 1–12.

Saltz, E., & Donnenwerth-Nolan, S. Does motoric imagery facilitate memory for sentences? A selective interference test. *Journal of Verbal Learning and Verbal Behavior,* 1981, *20,* 322–332.

Tulving, E. Episodic and semantic memory. In E. Tulving & W. Donaldson (Eds.), *Organization of memory.* New York: Academic Press, 1972.

Wickelgren, W. A. Coding, retrieval, and dynamics of multitrace associative memory. In L. W. Gregg (Ed.), *Cognition in learning and memory.* New York: Wiley, 1972.

11

Expectancy, Equilibration, and Memory

Marc Marschark
University of North Carolina at Greensboro

The discussion and research to be presented here focus on an integrative approach to psychological investigations of language and memory. Several experimental paradigms are considered in terms of what appear to be commonalities in the questions they address and the implications of the results they typically obtain.

Current research in human cognition tends to focus on either the nature of mental representation (e.g., Anderson, 1976; Kosslyn, Pinker, Smith, & Schwartz, 1979) or processes that characterize performance in particular task situations. While investigations of this sort have been fruitful in revealing some aspects of language comprehension, thinking, and memory, they also involve some important limitations. In particular, because of the inherent flexibility of cognitive processes, studies involving static or time-limited viewpoints are unlikely to yield sufficient information for complete theoretical interpretation of them. Rather, such research is likely to leave the investigator with only a partial explanation of the observed performance or, if unaware of this incompleteness, an erroneous conclusion.

An excellent parallel to this situation is the magician's sleight of hand. The maxim that "the hand is quicker than the eye" is clearly false, but the magician's "hand" need not be where the audience's eyes look for it. Observers of a sleight of hand routine typically attend closely to the central display and to proximal movements of the magician. On the basis of their experience in the world outside of the magic show, observers assume that they can ignore commonplace movements and objects. They also "know" that the phenomenon of interest (i.e., and trick) is potentially discernable in the routine and must occur in the temporal vicinity of the "magical" visual effect produced. The usual assumption is that a properly timed snapshot or slow-motion view of the magician from the observer's perspective would reveal the sleight of hand.

Fortunately for the world of imagination, however, all of these assumptions are false. The manipulation enabling a sleight of hand illusion, be it the exchange of a bogus coin for a real one or the removal of a to-be-vanished silk, typically happens long before the observed result and as part of a seemingly irrelevant action. The observer's difficulty thus lies not in the fact that the deceptive act happened too quickly, but that it occurred other than in the expected location and at a time when attention was elsewhere. This time- and space-limitation in perspective is a sort of functional fixedness that leaves one with either an incomplete understanding of how the trick was done or accepting the phenomenological data and concluding that magic, in fact, has occurred.

Researchers in cognitive psychology appear to be vulnerable to the same pitfalls as the magic show audience. In particular, it generally is assumed that a snapshot-like view of a subject's behavior is an adequate indicator of the mental event of interest. As in the magic show, however, knowledge of the preparatory processes involved in the performance may be essential for the unambiguous and correct attribution of a behavior to a particular cognitive process. Otherwise, an observed effect may be attributed to an ultimately incorrect process viable only within the limited empirical view of the investigator. In this event, no amount of convergent evidence from similar perspectives will yield additional, enlightening information (just as the magician can perform the same trick many times before the same or collaborating observers with little fear of discovery).

One means of avoiding such difficulties is to adopt broader perspectives on both the phenomenon of interest and the experimental task(s) in which it is observed. This would entail, for example, consideration of mental events temporally contiguous to the phenomenon, experience with related tasks, and the development of cognitive skills presumed to underly performance (cf. Paivio, this volume). This does not necessarily require a shift from current methodologies, as suggested by Neisser (1973) and Yuille (this volume), or theoretical considerations, as suggested by J. R. Anderson (1978; cf. Yuille & Marschark, 1982). It does require, however, the elaboration of current paradigms and theoretical views of some empirical phenomena. The remainder of this paper describes a general framework and some specific methods for conducting research of this sort.

A Strategy for Cognitive Investigation

The idea that cognition and memory are extremely flexible is not new, having been implicit or explicit in most information processing research. Seldom, however, has it served as a focal point in theories of cognition. A major exception is Piaget's notion of *equilibration* underlying his equilibrium model of cognitive development (e.g., Inhelder & Piaget, 1958). Equilibration is seen as the dynamic component of intellectual functioning by which the individual attempts to maintain equilibrium between its internal states and the environment through the assimilation of new information and the accomodation of existing cognitive structures. This process is of interest here not so much at the level of ontogenetic development discussed by Piaget, as one of "day-to-day" or, more precisely, second-to-second behavior. In this sense, equilibration essentially refers to the interfacing of ongoing cognitive processes and memory through a flexible and adaptive semantic priming system. The result is that cognition is continuously under the guidance of expectancies (i.e., knowledge of the world) that, in turn, are altered by their consequences (Neisser, 1976, pp. 52–53). Neisser (1976) made a similar suggestion, but in terms of a somewhat more externally-based model than the present position which emphasizes the internal components of the subject-environment interaction. The focus of the research in the following discussion concerns the hierarchical and probalistic nature of expectancies, the ways in which they affect performance, and how they change with context, experience, and development (cf. Flavell, 1963, pp. 244–249).

Beyond the extensive theoretical discussions of Piaget (Inhelder & Piaget, 1958; Piaget, 1952) and Neisser (1976), the flexibility of cognitive processes has been examined in several areas of empirical study, particularly those concerning the effects of context, knowledge of language, and knowledge of the world in comprehension and memory. Equilibration-like considerations, for example, have motivated the recent proposal of a number of schema-based theories of memory (e.g., R. C. Anderson, 1978; Bower, Black, & Turner, 1979; Rumelhart & Ortony, 1976). A common assumption of these models has been that the encoding of new information from the stimulus environment is guided by the organization of information already in memory. Encoding thus is seen as an active, integrative process rather than a passive recording of traces. Similarly, recent language comprehension studies have indicated that language processing involves a context-dependent knowledge base that operates in an integrative and elaborative manner (R. C. Anderson & Orotony, 1975; Barclay, 1973; Bransford, Barclay, & Franks, 1972; Marschark & Paivio, 1977). Such findings appear to implicate a flexible cognitive system in which internal (memorial) and external (stimulus) information interact in a cyclical fashion to yield interpretations consistent with the individual's knowledge of the world.

Unfortunately, most of the evidence from language comprehension (as well as schematic memory) studies relevant to the present position has been based on recall data. As such, it provides only an after-the-fact, static perspective on this dynamic process. Several other areas of current research, however, are more directly revealing. Investigations concerning Stroop effects, lexical ambiguities, lexical decisions, and congruity effects in symbolic comparisons are of particular interest here because all involve reaction time measurement of the activation of memorial information by a stimulus context. Congruity effects and symbolic comparisons will be considered in the most detail below, but examinations of the other phenomena first will be worthwhile insofar as they evidence a common underlying mechanism (also to be found in symbolic comparisons).

Stroop Effects, Semantic Priming, and Memory

Consider first Stroop and Stroop-like tasks. In the classic paradigm, the stimuli are printed color names presented in incongruent ink colors; the word "RED," for example, might be printed in green ink. The subject's task is to ignore the identity of the word and name the color of the ink. The typical finding is that response times tend to be longer than when the stimuli are color names printed in congruent colored inks or simply color patches to be named (Dalrymple-Alford, 1972). More generally, any stimulus having two or more discrete components can be presented and subjects requested to respond selectively to one component. Longer response times relative to control conditions without irrelevant dimensions are assumed to reflect interference in some phase of processing the relevant dimension, due to conflict or competition within the processing system. Equivalent response times are assumed to reflect independent, or different-system processing (Lupker, 1979).

One interpretation of the Stroop effect attributes it to a stage of perceptual encoding. That position suggests that response interference arises during the encoding of the stimuli when the subject divides his attention between the relevant and irrelevant stimulus components. Processing of the irrelevant word is assumed to delay processing of the color due to a limitation on processing capacity (Hock & Egeth, 1970). This interpretation, however, is unable to account for a number of Stroop-like results (see Lupker, 1979; Seymour, 1979 for details). The most common alternative is the response competition hypothesis (e.g., Klein, 1964; Lupker, 1979; cf. Seymour, 1979, pp. 264–265). This interpretation suggests that active, intentional processing of a relevant stimulus dimension is accompanied by automatic processing of the irrelevant dimension. Interference arises when task-related information about the irrelevant component (e.g., a color word's name) becomes available simultaneously with or before the necessary information about the relevant component. The observed increase in reaction times is accounted for by the assumption that the two responses complete for a single output channel and the subject must devote both cognitive effort and time to suppress a response to the irrelevant dimension.

The role of semantic priming in Stroop-like tasks is evidenced by the fact that performance is influenced by the relationship between relevant and irrelevant stimulus dimensions. Klein (1964), for example, demonstrated that color names interfered with color naming more than did color-related words such as "lemon." These, in turn, were more interfering than words that were not color-related. Rosinski (1977) found that words superimposed on a picture of an item from the same semantic category caused more interference than did words from other categories. These findings all appear to indicate that preexperimental (i.e., memorial) relationships between stimulus components may be automatically activated during cognitive processing, even when irrelevant to the task at hand.

An examination of Stroop-like interference pertinent to this suggestion was presented by Lupker (1979). He examined the nature of stimulus component conflict in a word-picture interference task like Rosinski's (1977). In his first three experiments, Lupker found semantic interference to be restricted to situations in which the word and picture were related by semantic category membership. Response times were unaffected by manipulations of associative relatedness (Experiment 1), semantic distance (Experiment 2), or typicality (Experiment 3) between word and picture components of stimuli. Lupker (1979) interpreted his results within the response-competition framework as due to the *relevance* of the irrelevant stimulus dimension to the appropriate response. That is, "[t]o the extent that the information about the word disqualifies it as an appropriate response, the word will be easier to suppress [and] the shorter the reaction time will be [p. 491]." To test this hypothesis, Lupker presented concrete and abstract words superimposed on unrelated, to-be-named pictures. His assumption was that abstract words would be more easily "identified" as irrelevant to the picture-naming task than (image-evoking) concrete words and thus should lead to less interference. The results of his Experiment 4 supported that hypothesis.

The interference effects observed in Lupker's experiments clearly resulted from interactions of stimulus characteristics and memorial information. Insofar as these involved pragmatic relationships based on the subjects' knowledge of the world, rather than logical relationships, Lupker's findings are consistent with an equilibration-based interpretation of Stroop phenomena. According to this position, the observed interference effects observed in such tasks are essentially semantic priming phenomena. It is assumed that when a subject in the Stroop task, for example, first attends to a compound stimulus, both the (relevant) color and the (irrelevant) word serve as primes or cues to semantic memory. Initially, the orthographic pattern automatically activates the identity of the word (Dalrymple-Alford, 1972) and its referential meaning. If that activation is consistent with the concurrently aroused name of the ink color, a response will be facilitated (cf. Becker, 1980, described below). If the initial activation is inconsistent with, but relevant to the judged dimension, responding is delayed while the conflict is resolved. Generally, the degree of interference produced will be related to the specificity (Marschark & Paivio, 1980), strength (Becker, 1980), or relevance (Lupker, 1979) of the priming relationships within the particular task.[1]

---

[1]Note that "priming relationships" differ from associative relatedness as manipulated by Lupker (1979). "Black" and "white," for example, are high in associative relatedness by virtue of their paradigmatic relationship, but they do not have the experiential contingency of word pairs like "turkey" and "carve" or "snooker" and "potting." The role of such relationships in Stroop tasks could be assessed vaying the strength of those contingencies just as Lupker varied typicality and associative relatedness.

This explanation of Stroop effects differs somewhat from Lupker's interpretation, since it assumes interference to result directly from the activation of incongruent (color and word) information in the encoding stage. This creates a delay in the response-decision process, but is completed by the response stage implicated in Lupker's analysis (cf. Lupker & Katz, 1981).[2] The difference between these positions is highlighted by the Stroop task situation in which subjects have to name an ink color that is in the form of a semantically-related word; for example, "BLOOD" written in red ink. In this case, the response competition hypothesis would predict an interference effect, because responses of "blood" and "red" both would be competing for the output channel. From the priming position, in contrast, no interference would be expected, since the referential information activated by both the irrelevant word and the color would overlap just as in the case of a color name printed in that color. Dalrymple-Alford (1972), in fact, found facilitation of color naming under these conditions, supporting the priming prediction.

A Stroop-priming relationship also was suggested recently by Logan (1980; see also, Logan, 1979) in the context of his investigation of automatic and attentional processes in the Stroop task. He accounted for both his empirical Stroop-like results and parallel priming results (e.g., Neely, 1976, 1977; Posner & Snyder, 1975) in terms of a model derived from Posner and Snyder's (1975) two-factor theory. According to Logan's (1980) model, both Stroop and priming tasks initially involve automatic processing that subsequently can be altered or superseded by attentional processes. The two paradigms also are assumed to involve similar decision processes in that "they both entail a temporally extended blend of evidence from past associations and current contingencies [p. 542]"; cf. Marschark & Paivio, 1981, Experiment 6). Both of these suggestions are consistent with the priming/equilibration position and are discussed in the following section.

Lexical Decisions, Equilibration, and Memory

One area of empirical research accounted for by Logan's (1980) model involves the *lexical decision task*. Subjects in this task are visually presented a letter string and are asked to judge whether it is a word or nonword. Decision times have been shown to decrease as congruent, or semantically-consistent word or sentence contexts are provided and to increase with incongruent or semantically-inconsistent contexts (e.g., Becker, 1976, 1980; Fischler & Bloom, 1979; Neely, 1976, 1977; Schuberth & Eimas, 1977; Schuberth, Spoehr, & Lane, 1981). Facilitation and interference effects are measured by comparing decision laten-

---

[2]The priming position also differs from Hock and Egeth's (1970) perceptual encoding hypothesis, since the former attributes the Stroop effect to automatic, but incongruent priming by the "cue" of the irrelevant word, rather than a capacity limitation (see Lupker & Katz, 1981).

cies following related and unrelated primes, respectively, to latencies obtained with nonword, neutral "primes."

A recent lexical decision study by Becker (1980) is particularly relevant to the previous discussion of Stroop effects as priming phenomena. Becker examined facilitative and interfering effects of semantic context and found a consistent pattern of their relative dominance. Facilitation was found to predominate when the semantic relations between primes and targets were consistently of about the same strength (cf. Neely, 1976), whereas interference predominated when the strengths of those relationships were more varied (cf. Fischler & Bloom, 1979; Neely, 1977). Becker accounted for those results in terms of a verification model of the lexical decision process (Becker, 1976, 1980; Schuberth et al., 1981). Although Becker's model is more akin to Morton's (1969) logogen model than the two-factor theory (Posner & Snyder, 1975) underlying Logan's (1980) model, it appears to provide an interesting complement to the latter.

Becker's model suggests that a semantic context provides a subject with "an expectancy set" of predictions for potential stimuli, based on experential and situational contingencies (cf. Marschark & Paivio, 1979, 1981). Lexical decisions are facilitated when a related word is presented subsequent to the context because it is likely to be a member of the preactivated set. Greater consistency in the range of prime/target relationships, increases the likelihood of relevant preactivation becuase priming can be more "focused." Interference effects, according to the model, are produced when a presented word is not a member of the expectancy set. The subject then has to reject the set and consider alternatives unrelated to the context. The model thus indicates relationships between semantic attributes of the materials and prior experience with them as a primary determinent of the usual lexical decision findings (Becker, 1980, p. 494).

As in the Stroop task, the relationships between judged (word vs. nonword) and unjudged (context) aspects of lexical stimuli affect the time course of the lexical decision process (Fischler & Bloom, 1979; Schuberth & Eimas, 1977). Without violating any assumptions of Becker's (1980) model, it could be assumed that the contents of expectancy sets are automatically determined by the probabilistic priming of information in semantic memory. Either automatic or intentional processing could operate in the subsequent rejection of a set and consideration of alternatives beyond the "probability threshold" relevant for the initial activation (cf. Logan, 1980). This phase would still be directed by experiential and situational contingencies, however, as would be its "blend" of automaticity and intentionality. In general, then, the interfacing of expectancy sets and the strategies and mechanisms related to them would be under the control of equilibrating processes. The mechanisms assumed to be operating in the lexical decision task thus would be exactly the same as those suggested to be functional in the Stroop task.

This suggestion is also consistent with findings from recent lexical decision studies indicating that high-frequency words are verified more quickly than low-frequency words (Becker & Killion, 1977; Schuberth et al., 1981). This effect generally is assumed to arise during the verification process as items are activated or sampled in an order determined by their frequency of occurence in the language (Schuberth et al., 1981). The effect of frequency in the lexical decision task is directly predicted from the priming/equilibration assumption of a hierarchical and probabilistic organization of memory, and it is consistent with findings to be discussed next from a recent study of congruity effects in number comparisons. Frequency also appears to play a role in the priming component of Stroop and Stroop-like interference tasks, as Klein (1964) found that interference produced by common (irrelevant) words in the Stroop task was greater than that produced by rare words.

Ambiguity, Expectancy, and Memory

An area of research closely related to the lexical decision task involves the comprehension of lexical ambiguities. The question of interest generally has been whether at some level, all possible meanings of an ambiguous word are accessed, one of which is eventually selected as appropriate, or whether context constrains comprehension so that only one, most probable interpretation is produced (Kess & Hoppe, 1979). The latter alternative is indicative of the priming/ equilibration position, and findings from a variety of studies have generally supported this prediction (e.g., Perfetti & Goodman, 1970; Swinney & Hakes, 1976). Recently, however, a study by Onifer and Swinney (1981) indicated that, at least initially, all meanings of an ambiguous word are activated regardless of any contextual biasing. Using a lexical decision task embedded in a sentence comprehension task, Onifer and Swinney found that lexical decisions to words related to both primary and secondary meanings of ambiguous words were facilitated when the lexical decision immediately followed the ambiguity. Differential facilitation of the decision was observed, however, when the decision was made 1.5 sec later. These findings were interpreted to reflect an automatic and exhaustive lexical access followed by an intentional, "post-access" process that provides a single reading of ambiguous word. Only the latter stage was assumed to be affected by context.

This interpretation contradicts the assumption of the priming position that a linguistic context should selectively bias activation of congruent, memorial information in comprehension. The finding itself, however, is not inconsistent with that position. Onifer and Swinney noted that 1.5 sec was likely an overestimate[3] of the time required for the decision process. This was based on Simpson's (1981) finding that selection of a single lexical meaning (or suppression of

---

[3]Given the context of their discussion, Onifer and Swinney's (1981) statement that 1.5 seconds "underestimates the time course of the decision" (p. 232) is assumed to be a misprint.

irrelevant meanings) for an ambiguous word occurs within 120 milliseconds. This, in fact, suggests an important caveat to Onifer and Swinney's interpretation of their results. In order to account for Simpson's finding within their framework, Onifer and Swinney concluded that his results reflected a conscious, post-access decision completed within 120 msec after presentation of the ambiguity. This interpretation is gratuitous, however, without some evidence that a process of such complexity could occur (consciously) within that time frame (cf. Posner & Snyder, 1975). Further, even if lexical access and semantic selection do occur sequentially, it does not necessarily follow that the earlier be automatic and the later intentional. Equally, if not more likely, would be the possibility that Onifer and Swinney's immediate-test subjects (at test) would have been still in a recognition state that automatically activated all meanings (or some probabilistically determined subset) of a word. This could have been followed by an equally-automatic integration state that would interpret the word in a manner most appropriate for the context.

In any case, it appears that a snapshot approach to the ambiguity question, regardless of when the picture is taken, cannot provide a wholly adequate understanding of the processes involved. The fact is that we do not know to what extent such experimental tasks are representative of comprehension "at-large," where every word is polysemous. The psychological generality of the findings from this task requires determination of contextual factors that do and do not effect subsequent restriction of meaning. Onifer and Swinney's (1981) generalization that "all meanings of a word are momentarily accessed" (p. 225), on the basis of a manipulation involving only primary and secondary meanings, may simply be a case of the sleight of hand observer beguiled into believing in magic.

Comparative Judgments, Expectancy, and Memory

The final empirical phenomenon to be considered in detail is the *congruity effect*. The congruity effect is obtained in bipolar symbolic comparison tasks when subjects are given a comparative term and have to decide which of two subsequently presented stimuli has a magnitude most congruent with that term. If given the term *smarter*, for example, the more intelligent of two animal stimuli must be selected. If given *dumber*, the less intelligent animal must be selected. In addition to bipolar comparatives, this task involves stimulus pairs that vary dichotomously in their relative positions on the dimension of interest, some being relatively high on the dimension and some being relatively low. The empirical result over all orthogonal pairings of comparative and relative magnitudes is the congruity effect: a statistical interaction of those two variables (see Fig. 11.1). Insofar as it appears to be a semantic priming phenomenon (Marschark & Paivio, 1981), the congruity effect presumably reflects equilibrative processes functional in the bipolar, symbolic comparison task. Before considering this further, however, several points should be made concerning the

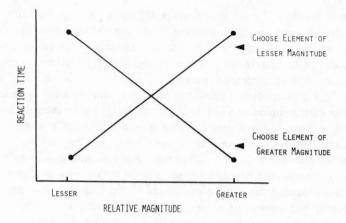

FIG. 11.1.   Schematic diagram of the congruity effect (comparative × relative magnitude interaction).

relevance of this position for the more common, single-pole comparative judgment task.

The symbolic comparison paradigm became popular with Moyer's (1973) study in which subjects were presented with pairs of printed animal names and were asked to decide which of the two was larger in real life. He found that the distribution of reaction times for such judgments followed a regular, inverse function of the actual size differences between the two animals. Moyer's findings were interpreted as indicating that size information about familiar objects is stored in memory in some analog format. This interpretation was later supported by Paivio's (1975) finding of a similar pattern of data but consistently faster reaction times with pictures as compared to words as stimuli.

Both the single-pole and bipolar symbolic comparison tasks involve a sequence of processes in which the stimuli are encoded (i.e., make contact with memorial information concerning relative magnitudes), those magnitudes are compared, and a response is executed. These tasks differ, however, prior to the so-called encoding stage. In the single-pole task, the subject typically awaits presentation of the stimuli in a state that is relatively passive compared to the bipolar task. In the latter paradigm, presentation of a comparative term prior to the stimuli can serve as a prime or cue for the creation of expectancies concerning possible stimuli or a range of stimuli congruent with that cue (Marschark & Paivio, 1979; see Becker, 1980). To the extent that priming is completed prior to the symbolic comparison itself, the congruity effect should prove independent of the symbolic distance effect. To the extent that both arise at the same stage (Banks & Flora, 1977; Holyoak & Mah, 1981), those effects should be interdependent (cf. Logan, 1979).

Congruity Effects in Symbolic Comparisons.   Potentially different sources of information operative in the single pole and bipolar paradigms provide an exemplary case for the "temporal" broadening of empirical investigation argued at the outset of this chapter. My own research in this area began with Al Paivio's suggestion that we interface his symbolic comparison research (Paivio, 1975) with my lexical marking research (Marschark, 1977). The *lexical marking effect* refers to the robust asymmetry observed in adults' and children's performance when the two members of a bipolar adjective pair such as *good-bad* or *big-little* are involved in a judgment task. A variety of studies have demonstrated that unmarked (usually positive) members of these pairs are acquired earlier and responded to faster and more accurately than their marked (usually negative) counterparts.

Paivio's suggestion was that we explore whether the markedness of comparative terms would make any difference to symbolic distance effects (as opposed to overall rection times). This was accomplished by presenting subjects with lists of comparative sentences like "a pencil is larger than a pumpkin" and "a horse is smaller than a desk" (Marschark & Paivio, 1979, Experiment 4). The subjects' task was to verify the sentences as true or false, as quickly as possible. Robust distance effects were obtained in that experiment for both comparatives, but another finding proved more interesting: the lexical marking effect obtained was reliable, as sentences with the adjective *larger* were compared faster than those with *smaller,* but the congruity effect was absent.

On the assumption that the failure to obtain a congruity effect was a consequence of differences between our verification task and the more typical two-choice comparative judgment task, the relevant literature was surveyed for similar findings. Few such cases actually were expected, since the purported joint occurence of congruity and marking effects, referred to as the *funnel effect,* was quite common. To our surprise, however, the reliable co-occurence of the effects was extremely rare and virtually always artifactual. Moreover, the studies we examined revealed a consistent pattern of congruity and marking effects as a function of the experimental paradigm employed (cf. Becker, 1980). Those studies in which the comparative preceded the stimulus pair (C-S paradigm) had obtained reliable congruity effects but not the typically-robust lexical marking effect (e.g., Banks, 1977; Banks, Clark, & Lucy, 1975; Holyoak & Walker, 1976). Conversely, those studies in which the comparative had followed the stimuli (S-C paradigm), or was presented simultaneously with them, had obtained the lexical marking effect but not the congruity effect (e.g., Glushko & Cooper, 1978, Experiment 2; Moyer & Landauer, 1967).

This pattern of effects was verified in two of our own experiments (Marschark & Paivio, 1979; Experiments 1 and 2), in which we varied the presentation order of stimuli and comparatives with both word and picture stimuli (between subjects). A C-S presentation order obtained a congruity but not a lexical marking effect, whereas an S-C order showed the reverse. Picture and word stimuli produced identical patterns of effects in the two experiments and symbolic distance effects were obtained in all conditions. The latter finding is particularly important for interpretation of the S-C results insofar as it indicated that subjects did not simply make a comparison between the first-presented stimuli and then preset themselves to respond to one stimulus if the comparative *larger* appeared and the other if *smaller* appeared (cf. Holyoak & Mah, 1981).

On the basis of our initial investigations, we arrived at an *expectancy hypothesis* (Marschark & Paivio, 1979). According to that position, the C-S paradigm, but not the S-C paradigm, provides an opportunity for the subject to create expectancies for particular stimuli or ranges of stimuli consistent with the preceding comparative (see also, Becker, 1980). The mechanism responsible for production of expectancies themselves initially was suggested to be a matter of theoretical preference (Marschark & Paivio, 1979, p. 176), but eventually, one construct emerged that was consistent with all of the empirical findings (Marschark & Paivio, 1981, pp. 306-307). That interpretation entailed the comparative term in the C-S paradigm acting as a cue for the priming of semantic memory. Over trials, priming would sometimes be correct, facilitating rapid responses, and sometimes incorrect, leading to relatively longer response latencies. The congruity effect thus would be obtained. Further, the usual presentation of the comparative term .5 to 1.0 sec prior to the stimuli also would provide sufficient prime time to offset the lexical marking effect. The C-S paradigm thus was found to yield congruity but not marking effects (see Glushko & Cooper, 1978).[4] The corresponding situation produced by the S-C paradigm differs from that produced by the C-S paradigm in two respects. First, no stimulus expectancies are created in the S-C paradigm since the to-be-compared stimuli are not preceded by a potential cue. Unlike the C-S paradigm, however, this paradigm has the requirement of a speeded response immediately after presentation of a comparative, a situation that typically produces a lexical marking effect. The S-C paradigm thus was found to produce marking but not congruity effects.

It should be noted here that a ''reverse congruity effect'' would be possible in the S-C paradigm if the association between a stimulus pair (e.g., *elephant–whale*) and a particular comparative were sufficiently strong to be activated prior to presentation of the comparative (Marschark & Paivio, 1981, p. 291). The

---

[4]A dichotomous stimulus pool is standard in the bipolar comparative task and is assumed in this interpretation. If a pool is constructed so that all of the stimuli lie toward one end of the continuum of interest, expectancies based on the opposite-pole comparative will never be correct (Marschark & Paivio, 1981, pp. 294-295). Those comparisons thus will always produce relatively long response times and funnel-type congruity effects will occur. These will not be the consequence of a lexical marking effect, however, but of the bias in stimulus selection. Two acknowledged cases of this are studies by Audley and Wallis (1964, Experiment 3) and Banks and Root (1979; Experiments 1-2).

speeded response required after the comparative, however, would still produce a lexical marking effect. Although this situation would provide a counterexample to the mutual exclusion (of lexical marking and congruity effects) prediction that follows from the expectancy hypothesis, the fact that this was not observed in any of our S-C paradigm experiments supported the hypothesis that S-C and C-S paradigms typically involve somewhat different processing schemes. Recently, in fact, Holyoak and Mah (1981) demonstrated that the S-C paradigm can yield a congruity effect as well as the lexical marking effect under particular, S-C task situations.

From its original publication, the expectancy hypothesis was quite robust in accounting for the presence and absence of congruity and lexical marking effects in symbolic comparison tasks. With the possible exception of Holyoak and Mah's (1981) recent findings (which are currently being reinvestigated with regard to the priming interpretation described above), in fact, virtually all of the relevant symbolic comparison literature appears to be consistent with the original formulation of the hypothesis. The hypothesis also recently has been shown to account for findings from perceptual comparison studies involving dimensions such as height or size (Marschark & Paivio, 1981) even though it was not originally intended or expected to do so.

Congruity Effects in Perceptual Comparisons. The expected difficulty in accounting for perceptual congruity findings had two sources. First, the perceptual congruity effect was quite variable in the literature (Banks, 1977). Some studies had obtained the effect and others had not, with no apparent systematic pattern. Second, it was unclear how a semantic priming mechanism of congruity effects could account for comparisons that did not involve a semantic memory component. A comparative presented, for example, prior to a pair of circles would be meaningless as a cue since circle size is not bounded by any experiential or logical regularity. These considerations guided a review of the literature that resolved much of the apparent variability in perceptual congruity findings (Marschark & Paivio, 1981). In essence, those "perceptual" studies that had obtained congruity effects all had entailed symbolic or memorial components despite using nonsymbolic stimuli. The earliest demonstration of a congruity effect with perceptual stimuli, for example, entailed decisions as to which of two colors (previously rated for preference) was "most preferred" or "least preferred" (Shipley, Coffin, & Hadsell, 1945; Shipley, Norris, & Roberts, 1946). This manipulation yielded a reliable congruity effect but not a lexical marking effect. Insofar as the task involved subjective judgments of colors rather than decisions on perceptual dimensions, however, the task was clearly more symbolic than perceptual.

Another relevant study was reported by Banks, Clark, & Lucy (1975). They presented subjects with line drawings similar to those depicted in Fig. 11.2.

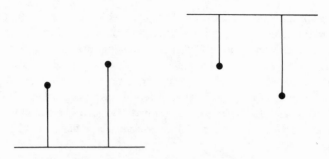

FIG. 11.2.   "Balloon" (left) and "yoyo" (right) stimuli used by Banks et al. (1975) and Marschark and Paivio (1981, Experiment 6).

Subjects were told that the stimuli represented (a) balloons and (b) yoyos. There were two within-subject test conditions, one in which subjects chose the higher or lower balloon or yoyo, and one in which they chose the longer or shorter strings of the same stimuli. Consistent with the expectancy hypothesis, Banks et al. did not obtain reliable marking effects in either of their C-S presentation conditions. The most interesting aspect of their results, however, was their demonstration of a congruity effect for the *higher/lower* comparisons but not for the *longer/shorter* comparisons. Although Banks et al. described this task as purely perceptual, their congruity findings could have resulted from semantic processing. The effect obtained in their *higher/lower* condition could have been a consequence of the interfacing knowledge about balloons and yoyos with the requirements of the task. Subjects would know that (helium filled) balloons tend to move higher when not restrained and that yoyos tend to move lower. They thus may have "naturally" expected balloons to be relatively high and yoyos to be relatively low. *Longer/shorter* judgments of string lengths, in contrast, would not have been as likely to create such expectancies. The lengths of strings attached to balloons and yoyos vary widely and there is no reason why one particular length or range of lengths would be expected on any given trial.

A final study of interest is that by Audley and Wallis (1964), the most widely cited study purported to have obtained perceptual congruity effects. They obtained congruity effects in four experiments in which the subjects chose the brighter or darker of two stimulus lights. Their materials, however, required judgments of only one stimulus pair at each level of display luminance. The experiments of interest (1–4) therefore involved comparisons of only two or three stimulus pairs, a total of 48 times, and subjects thus should have been well aware of the entire stimulus set. Rather than being a product of processes involved in symbolic comparisons, therefore, the observed congruity effects may have been the uninteresting result of perfect or near-perfect memory for the pairs. In terms of the expectancy hypothesis, these effects would reflect expectancies for particular stimuli on the basis of particular comparatives (see also, Banks & Root, 1979).

An extension of the expectancy hypothesis to perceptual comparisons was examined by Marschark and Paivio (1981). One goal of that study was to determine whether simple perceptual congruity effects were obtainable in the absence of symbolic or memorial task components. Their first five experiments therefore involved stimuli that were simple geometric figures presented on a constant-luminance background. A C-S presentation paradigm was employed to facilitate demonstration of a perceptual congruity effect; the expectancy hypothesis therefore predicted the absence of lexical marking effects in those experiments.

The first experiment involved a pool of 14 stimuli. Subjects were tachistoscopically presented with "larger" or "smaller" followed by a pair of either relatively large or relatively small stimuli at one of three levels of arithmetic difference. In all, subjects made 120 test judgments. As expected, no lexical marking effect was obtained, but neither was a congruity effect. In further attempts to produce a congruity effect, the differences between large and small stimuli were increased (Experiment 2), a preview of the to-be-compared stimuli was provided (Experiment 2–5), the number of test trials was extended to 192 (Experiment 4), and subjects were even explicitly instructed to memorize the preview stimuli for a later recognition task (Experiment 5). None of these manipulations, however, produced a reliable congruity effect (or lexical marking), and it appeared that the effect was unlikely to be obtained in any simple perceptual comparison task.

Marschark and Paivio (1981) therefore conducted a sixth experiment to determine whether the involvement of semantic memory or knowledge of the world is *necessary* for the production of congruity effects in the bipolar comparison task. The study was patterned on that by Banks et al. (1975) described earlier. One condition was a replication of their experiment, in which subjects were shown "balloon" and "yoyo" stimuli similar to those in Fig. 11.2 and were asked to decide which of a pair was higher or lower. The second condition employed the same stimuli, but the lines from the stimulus circles to the reference lines were omitted, and they were referred to as "circles." The third (and critical) condition involved the complete "balloon" and "yoyo" stimuli also referred to only as "circles." The primary prediction for that experiment was that if the congruity effect depended on semantic memory or knowledge of the world, it would be obtained only where such information could be activated: in the one condition where the stimuli were referred to as "balloons" and "yoyos." Because relative height is not a typical characteristic of circles, congruity effects were not expected in the other two conditions. Consistent with these predictions, a reliable three-way interaction of condition with the congruity effect was obtained; only the "balloons" and "yoyos" condition yielded a reliable congruity effect. Most striking was the difference between the 28 msec effect obtained in that condition and the 4 msec effect in the condition involving the identical stimuli but labeled as "circles."[5]

Marschark and Paivio's (1981) findings supported the proposal that the congruity effect is essentially a priming phenomenon. Moreover, their finding that the activation of subjects' world knowledge was the primary determinant of the effect parallels findings from Stroop tasks, lexical decision tasks, and comprehension of ambiguities. In order to further examine the characteristics of this memory interface, several recent investigations have explored the effects of stimulus characteristics on the comparative judgment task. Rather than focusing on representation questions, where symbolic distance effects are informative (Moyer, 1973; Paivio, 1975, 1978a, 1978b), these studies instead have examined how congruity effects are affected by the composition of the potential stimulus pool and subjects' knowledge and expectancies concerning those stimuli. The questions of interest therefore have concerned the way in which the organization of semantic memory, rather than the form of the information represented in it, affects subject performance in the comparative judgment task.

It is clear from some of Paivio's work (1978a, 1978b; Paivio & Marschark, 1980) that individual differences in verbal and imaginal abilities influence performance in comparative judgment tasks. The ability of subjects to optimize their processing through processes akin to equilibration may also be a skill, affected by relevant practice and experience with the materials (cf. Logan, 1979; Logan & Zbrodoff, 1979). To examine this possibility, stimulus characteristics have been manipulated in ways that would be expected to facilitate or interfere with semantic priming. In essence, these studies have addressed the possibility that some effects typically obtained in symbolic comparisions may be constrained by the particular types of stimuli involved. Congruity effects, in particular, may change as a function of stimuli being more or less amenable to equilibrative activation for particular subjects or in particular experimental designs.

Number Comparisons. A recent series of experiments in our laboratories investigated congruity effects in judgments of number magnitude (Marschark, 1981). Previous studies involving this task have used a symbolic comparison paradigm in which pairs of numbers are presented and subjects are asked to decide which of the two has the greater or lesser magnitude (e.g., Buckley & Gillman, 1974; Moyer & Landauer, 1967, 1973; Parkman, 1971). It is notewor-

---

[5]Reported lexical marking effects are the overall difference between "smaller" and "larger" comparisons. The reported magnitudes of congruity effects are the average distance that the four data points would have to be moved to remove the comparative × relative magnitude interaction (Banks et al., 1976, p. 439). In some cases, this per point calculation makes congruity effect magnitudes artificially appear small. In the three experiments involving the numbers 1–9, for example, the range in mean effects is only 16 msec. Calculation according to Holyoak & Mah's (1981) formula, in contrast, would yield a range of 64 msec.

thy, however, that most of these studies and *all of those involving bipolar comparisons* have required comparisons of the highly familiar digits 1–9. Insofar as digits are among the most familiar and overlearned of all symbolic stimuli, digit comparisons might not be representative of other number comparison tasks in all respects.

A priori, there is no theoretical reason to expect that comparisons of number pairs like 1 3 would involve any different *processes* than pairs like 41 43. Comparing the digits intuitively seems easier, but this would be expected to effect only overall reaction times, either linearly (Moyer & Landauer, 1967; Parkman, 1971) or according to some other function (Holyoak, 1978; Moyer & Landauer, 1973). However, the digits may be so overlearned that they might be functionally "descriptions" of the numbers they represent rather than symbols for them. This would facilitate the access of magnitude information prior to a comparison, similar to the observed advantage in comparing pictures relative to words in symbolic judgment tasks (Paivio, 1975, 1978a, 1978b). As a consequence of this facilitation, however, specific expectancies for digit stimuli would have a high probability of being generated, and the congruity effects obtained for digits therefore would be relatively large compared to other number stimuli. Further, an accessability-congruity effect relationship would also account for the heretofore unexplained findings that congruity effects in symbolic comparisons tend to be larger when subjects preview the stimulus set prior to the comparison task and when "finite" rather than "infinite" set ranges are used (Banks, 1977; Banks & Flora, 1977). Both of these manipulations would increase the probability that specific memory information will be activated by the comparative prime (cf. Collins & Loftus, 1975).

The number comparison experiments to be described all involved C-S presentation paradigms and symbolic (i.e., nonanalog) stimuli. According to the expectancy hypothesis, therefore, they should yield congruity but not lexical marking effects. One of the experiments was an attempt to replicate the digit comparison findings of Banks, Fujii, and Kayra-Stuart (1976). They had obtained congruity and lexical marking effects in a digit comparison task. This was inconsistent with the mutual exclusion prediction of the expectancy hypothesis and findings from other comparison tasks. The reason for Banks et al.'s (1976) result, however, was unclear. Although there was a potential confound in their materials (see Marschark, 1981), insufficient information was available to know whether it could have been responsible for the lexical marking finding. In any case, that confound was removed in this experiment. Subjects saw 60 digit pairs with arithmetic differences (distances) of 1, 2 or 3. Half of the pairs were composed of digits from 1 to 5 (i.e., relatively small magnitudes) and half of digits from 5 to 9 (i.e., relatively large magnitudes). On each tachistoscopic trial, subjects chose the larger or smaller digit of a pair. Banks et al.'s (1976) congruity finding was replicated insofar as a reliable, 18 msec effect was obtained, but a reliable lexical marking effect was not obtained.

Demonstration of a congruity effect in the above experiment was not surprising; a more interesting question concerned the extent to which that effect might have been a function of the familiarity of the *numerals* 1–9 as opposed to the *magnitudes* of the numbers they represent. In order to separate the effects of familiarity and magnitude of the digits, two other experiments were conducted in which subjects made relative magnitude judgments of the numbers 1–9, given their upper case (e.g., "SEVEN") of lowercase (e.g., "seven") printed names as stimuli. If the comparison process alone is sufficient to produce a congruity effect (Banks et al., 1976), both of those experiments would be expected to yield reliable effects comparable to the 18-msec effects obtained both in the preceding experiment and by Banks et al. (1976) with digit stimuli. If, however, the congruity effect is influenced by the familiarity of the to-be-compared stimuli (and thus the accessability of their relative magnitudes), congruity effects would vary across those experiments. Although no relevant normative data are available, it is obvious that upper case printed digit names are relatively infrequent and unfamiliar. The Kučera-Francis (1967) frequency norms do indicate, however, that lower case printed digit names are over three times more frequent (in print) than the digits themselves. From the priming position, therefore, the congruity effects in these experiments should increase from upper case printed digit names to digits to lower case printed names.

The findings were entirely consistent with the above predictions. Whereas the digit comparison task had yielded on 18-msec congruity effect, the upper case digit names yielded an unreliable effect of 13 msec and the lower case names a highly reliable effect of 29 msec (see footnote 5). Consistent with the mutual exclusion prediction of the expectancy hypothesis, a lexical marking effect was not obtained in the experiment involving lower case stimuli. The effect was reliable, however, in the experiment involving upper case stimuli. Although mutually exclusive with the congruity effect, this was not expected with the C-S paradigm. Further, the correlation between lexical marking and congruity effects was .17 ($N = 10$), indicating that mutual exclusion was not operating (cf. Marschark & Azmitia, 1981).

To further investigate stimulus and congruity effects in number comparisons, two-digit numbers were employed as stimuli in three other experiments. As in the two preceding experiments, these stimuli were not as familiar as the digits, and the priming position therefore would predict an attenuated congruity effect relative to the digit task. Stimulus pairs in the first of these experiments were numbers between 11 and 29 (smaller magnitude stimuli) and between 81 and 89 (larger magnitude stimuli). Numbers were paired only within decile to avoid comparisons based on the tens column only. The numbers from 30 to 80 were not used to ensure that subjects would recognize the dichotomous nature of the stimulus pool. As in the preceding experiments, pairs with arithmetic differences of 1, 2, and 3 were counterbalanced with relative magnitude and the comparatives *larger* and *smaller*. Consistent with the hypothesized accessability-congruity effect relationship, neither the lexical marking effect nor the -6 msec congruity effect was reliable.

Although the above finding appeared attributable to the relative unfamiliarity of two-digit numbers as compared to digits, there was another aspect of the design that could have reduced the congruity effect according to the priming position. If the comparative terms in this task serve to prime some range of number magnitudes, knowledge about the size and composition of the stimulus pool should facilitate that process (cf. Banks & Flora, 1977). In the digit comparison task, subjects would have been aware that there were only nine possible stimuli. Subjects in the two-digit comparison task, however, were not informed as to the stimulus ranges and any numbers between 11 and 99 (given two-digit training trials) thus would have seemed possible. Another experiment therefore was conducted that was identical to the preceding one except that subjects were informed of the stimulus ranges. This was expected to be comparable to the preview manipulation used in symbolic comparison studies and increase the magnitude of the congruity effect. The resulting effect was 11 msec larger, but still was not reliable. As expected, a lexical marking effect was not obtained.

A probable explanation for this finding, based on the priming position, was that the size of the potential stimulus set, relative to that in the digit comparison task, also influenced the congruity effect. Even though subjects in this experiment were informed as to the range of numbers used, there were still 36 possible stimuli, whereas there were only nine in the digit comparison task. Assuming that better defined, more distinct stimulus sets would lead to more precise and facilitative priming (Collins and Loftus, 1975), the difference between the congruity effects obtained with digits and two digit numbers would not be surprising. A final experiment was therefore conducted in order to evaluate the effects of set size as a partial explanation of the congruity effects obtained in the preceding experiments. This employed a between-subjects design in which both groups compared stimuli from sets of nine numbers; half of the subjects compared the numbers 21–29 and the other half the numbers 81–89. The numbers 21 to 25 and 81 to 85 were the "smaller magnitude" numbers and 25 to 29 and 85 to 89 were the "larger magnitude" numbers; all subjects were informed of these ranges.

If set size were an important determinant of congruity effects in the magnitude comparison task, subjects in both groups would be expected to yield congruity effects greater than those in the two preceding experiments. If familiarity were the sole determinant of the effect, neither group would be expected to obtain a congruity effect since these stimuli did not produce one in the preceding experiments. The results, in fact, supported the former hypothesis. Both conditions yielded reliable congruity effects (18 and 26 msec with 20's and 80's stimuli, respectively), although neither yielded a reliable lexical marking effect.

One other finding from these experiments, involving a congruity effect/set-size relationship, is also noteworthy. The last experiment described involved nine-number stimulus sets, and the informing of subjects about the ranges of those numbers. The average congruity effect for that experiment was 22 msec. This was approximately four times the 5-msec congruity effect obtained for the experiment in which subjects were informed of a stimulus range approximately four times that size. This apparently linear relationship between the congruity effect and set size also was found by Marschark and Paivio (1980). In those experiments, we presented subjects with symbolic stimuli of printed object and animal names. The composition of the lists, between subjects, was either 25%, 50%, or 100% animal names. Congruity effects obtained for the 50% and 100% lists were 24 and 48 milliseconds, respectively, apparently a function of stimulus uncertainty and thus the specificity of priming. This conclusion was supported by the finding that within the 50% list, the salient animal pairs yielded a congruity effect of 42 msec compared to an effect of only 13 msec for the nonanimal pairs. In the 25% list, however, where the animal stimuli were not particularly salient, the congruity effect for those pairs was only 14 msec. The object pairs in that list yielded an effect of 37 msec, exactly the same magnitude as the congruity effect obtained by Marschark and Paivio (1979; Experiment 2) with a similarly heterogeneous stimulus pool.

In short, the results from the number comparison experiments clearly supported a priming-based, expectancy interpretation of the congruity effect. Set size was constant in the three experiments involving the numbers one to nine, and the magnitude of the congruity effect was shown to vary with stimulus familiarity. When familiarity was held constant in three subsequent experiments, however, the magnitude of the congruity effect varies with the size of the potential stimulus set. Both of these findings appear to implicate probabilistically determined priming. Moreover, the influences of subjects' knowledge of numbers and memory organization of them in these tasks appear to be functionally the same as those involved in other comparative judgment tasks as well as Stroop tasks, lexical decision tasks, and the comprehension of lexical ambiguities.

A Developmental Study of Semantic Priming in Comparative Judgments. The apparent similarities among the several areas of research discussed earlier indicate the need for a broader, but more integrative approach to investigations of cognitive processing. One direction in which these tasks could be expanded is toward the manipulation or control of subject as well as stimulus characteristics (cf. Ernest, this volume; Katz, this volume). It was noted earlier that equilibration or priming ability might be considered a skill comparable to imagery or verbal ability. The relationship of equilibrative processes to information organization and accessability may even indicate it to be more of a macroskill, perhaps comparable (if not identical) to "fluid intelligence." If this is the case, it should be possible to trace the development of such abilities using any of the tasks described above.

With this in mind, Margarita Azmitia and I recently did a series of bipolar comparison experiments (Marschark & Azmitia, 1981) in the hopes of elucidating the organization of children's memories and developmental changes in their abilities to effectively make use of that organization. Our first task was to determine whether the usual, tachistoscopic methodology of bipolar comparisons could be adapted to a pencil and paper test suitable for use with younger children. Using stimuli that would be familiar to children as young as 6 or 7, we created eight lists of 25 stimulus pairs each, with all lists equated for symbolic distance. Four of the lists were composed of animal pairs, and four of object pairs; within each set, two of the lists contained relatively large things and two lists contained relatively small things. Each list was paired with the comparative *larger* or *smaller,* counterbalanced over subjects, so as to yield a 2 (stimulus set) × 2 (relative magnitude) × 2 (comparative), within-subjects design.

In order to evaluate the procedure, we first tested a group of 60 university students. Before each list, subjects were given a comparative, and then had 30 seconds to circle as many appropriate pair members as possible. They were instructed to work as quickly as possible without making mistakes. We assumed that if the same processes and strategies were involved here as in the tachistoscopic task, this C-S design would yield a congruity effect but no lexical marking effect. On the basis of Marschark and Paivio's (1980) findings and the expectancy hypothesis, we also expected the congruity effect obtained with the animal stimuli to be greater than that obtained with the object stimuli, since animals compose a smaller, better defined set that would be more amenable to equilibrative activation.

Mean response latencies were obtained by dividing the number of correct answers into 30 sec. The results were clearly consistent with the predictions. The animal stimuli yielded a reliable congruity effect of .12 sec, but a nonsignificant (−.09 sec) lexical marking effect. The object stimuli yielded a reliable congruity effect of .10 sec, and a nonsignificant (.20 sec) lexical marking effect. An overall analysis revealed a significant three-way interaction of the congruity effect (relative magnitude × comparative interaction) with stimulus set.

We then proceeded to test students in the second, fourth, and sixth grades. Ten males and ten females in each grade were tested. In addition, a group of high school sophomores and juniors were tested in the context of a university-level, psychology of language course for gifted and talented public school students. This group was somewhat different from the others tested, primarily because the students were considerably brighter than others in their grades but also because they were tested in a university setting in which the demand characterisics would have been somewhat different than those for the other grades. All groups were tested using the same procedure as that employed for the university students except that second and fourth graders were given one min per list rather than 30 sec.

Generally, we had three expectations. First, those grades or particular children who obtained congruity effects were not expected to obtain lexical marking effects (Marschark & Paivio, 1979). Second, to the extent that children or particular grades obtained congruity effects, we expected that they would be greater, or more consistent (in terms of the number of subjects obtaining effects, cf. Marschark & Paivio, 1981) for animal as compared to object stimuli. Finally, assuming that congruity effects obtained with these subjects would indicate relevant memory organization for the task and the ability to access that organization appropriately, we also expected the magnitudes of congruity effects to change with age, but the direction of change was unclear. One possibility was that verbally-presented comparatives might not be sufficiently directive cues for the younger subjects. In this case, congruity effects would likely increase with age. Alternatively, a number of studies (e.g., McCauley, Weil, & Sperber, 1976) have shown priming and memory organization in children of these ages to be fairly well developed. If the comparative were sufficient to provide access to such organization in the present samples, congruity effects might decrease as such abilities became more flexible and adaptive with age.

Mean correct latencies were obtained by dividing the amount of time given per list by the number of correct responses. Mean latencies consistently decreased with increasing grade (means = 9.35, 5.48, 4.16, 2.38 sec/comparison for second grade through high school samples, respectively). Considering the second graders first, a reliable congruity effect of 1.06 sec was obtained for animal comparisons and a nonreliable congruity effect of −.20 sec for object comparisons. Consistent with the mutual exlusion prediction, the lexical marking effect was not reliable for animal comparisons (1.17 sec) but was for object comparisons (1.78 sec). These results suggested that the second graders were able to make use of a prime in activating memorial representations of potential animal stimuli but not of other "things-at-large." Because the object-list comparatives were not "used" at presentation, there was no initial processing to offset the lexical marking effect.

The results from the fourth graders presented a somewhat difficult pattern for interpretation. They obtained nonsignificant congruity effects in both animal (.09 sec) comparisons and object (.31 sec) comparisons. The lexical marking effects were unreliable in both animal (.22 sec) and object (.89 sec) comparisons as well. Although some of the findings from this group were consistent with our expectations (see following), the failure to obtain a congruity effect with either set of materials was at first puzzling. According to the fourth grader's teacher, however, those students' performance on a variety of tasks had been affected by a recent curriculum change. One aspect of the new curriculum was intended to increase reflective linguistic skills. This was evidenced in our task by the fact that many of the students were observed to first pronounce the stimulus words and then ask themselves which was larger or smaller. Some of these students, therefore used a strategy more akin to an S-C than a C-S procedure, and the washing out of congruity effects thus was not as surprising (Marschark & Paivio, 1980). On the other hand, we have no idea why the congruity effect with the object stimuli was larger than that obtained with the animal stimuli. These data are considered further below, but a complete resolution will have to await additional testing.

The sixth graders obtained a reliable congruity effect only for animal comparisons (.17 sec) and not for object comparisons (.18 sec). Although the object stimuli yielded a slightly larger overall congruity effect, only eight of the 20 subjects showed the interaction with the object stimuli as compared to 14 with the animal stimuli. Neither the animal stimuli (.29 sec) nor the object stimuli (.08 sec) yielded a reliable lexical marking effect.

Finally, the high school students obtained a reliable cogruity effect in animal comparisons (.59 sec) but not for the object stimuli (.05 sec); the three-way interaction was reliable. Contrary to the mutual exclusion prediction of the expectancy hypothesis, however, the lexical marking effect for the animal set was reliable (1.03 sec), although that for the object set was not (.15 sec).

The lexical marking and congruity effects obtained by the high school students, as with the fourth graders, appeared to indicate the possibility of mixed (C-S and S-C) strategies across subjects. This possibility was evaluated for each grade by computing separate Pearson correlations for animal and object stimuli between the lexical marking and congruity effects obtained. For the animal stimuli, all of the correlations were negative and reliable (r's = $-.52$, $-.81$, $-.37$, and $-.76$ for grades 2 through high school, respectively). It is noteworthy that the highest correlation obtained was that of the fourth graders' data, which failed to show a significant congruity effect with the animal stimuli. The reliable correlation supports the mutual exclusion prediction for those subjects. For the object stimuli, positive and nonsignificant correlations were obtained for the data from grades 2 through 6 (r's = $.25$, $.36$, and $.29$, respectively). This appears to indicate that priming relevant for these stimuli did not occur, but that the blocked (C-S) paradigm was sufficient to offset the lexical marking effect in some cases (cf. Wallis & Audley, 1964). Only the data of the high school students, who obtained a reliable congruity effect with object stimuli, revealed a reliable (negative) correlation of $-.58$, again supporting the mutual exclusion prediction.

In general, our initial predictions were supported. Congruity and lexical marking effects were, for the most part, mutually exclusive (Marschark & Paivio, 1979), and the correlational analyses showed that despite great variability in some grades, priming did offset the usual advantage of unmarked adjectives. The prediction that congruity effects should be greater for animal than object stimuli was also generally supported, even though all of the materials were equally familiar. Although the three-way interactions of the congruity effect and stimulus condition were reliable only for the high school and university groups, all of the results were in the predicted direction. Finally, we did find an age-related change in the congruity effect. With the exception of the high school students, the congruity effect decreased with age from second grade to university. Children as young as 7 years old thus apparently already have relatively sophisticated category-related priming abilities (McCauley, Weil, & Sperber, 1976; Nelson &

Earl, 1973). The data appeared to indicate, in fact, that our subjects were less constrained by their (prime-induced) expectancies with increasing grade, resulting in smaller but reliable congruity effects for the clearly defined animal stimulus set, decreasing lexical marking effects (again, except for the high school students), and a concurrent decrease in the difference between animal and object congruity effects. These findings thus appear to reflect an increasing flexibility of priming/equilibration abilities with increasing age and cognitive development (Inhelder & Piaget, 1958, p. 331). At the same time, however, children's knowledge about semantic categories clearly improves with age and the categories become larger as more exemplars are learned or become properly classified. It thus may be that priming abilities remain about the same with increasing age, but the nature of the to-be-primed information changes. This possibility intuitively seems dubious, but warrants further empirical consideration.

In summary, virtually all of the comparative judgment findings described earlier were consistent with a priming-based, expectancy model. Symbolic comparisons of picture, word, and number stimuli as well as perceptual comparisons all were shown to involve symbolic or memorial components in the production of congruity effects. Congruity effects, in turn, were shown to vary as to-be-primed magnitude information was made more or less accessible through manipulations of age, stimulus frequency, set size, and semantic category size (cf. Roediger, 1973). Moreover, the newer evidence presented here (Marschark, 1981; Marschark & Azmitia, 1981) provides firm support for the assertion that the typical symbolic comparison task represents but a snapshot of a larger, extremely flexible process operative in these tasks. One additional finding is also consistent with that position. Beyond the congruity and lexical marking effects already discussed, most of the earlier studies also obtained reliable distance effects as comparative times decreased with increasing differences between stimulus magnitudes (but see Marschark, 1981). In 14 of the 15 experiments in our labs that have involved distance manipulations, distance effects and congruity effects were statistically independent. This supports the hypothesis that these effects arise from different stages of the comparison process and the need for a broader approach to the empirical investigation of such phenomena. These findings also limit interpretations of the congruity effect that place the loci of it and the symbolic distance effect at the same stage (Banks et al., 1976; Holyoak, 1978; Holyoak & Mah, 1981).

SUMMARY AND CONCLUSIONS

It should be evident by this point that our research on congruity effects did not originate in any particular theoretical perspective. Rather, several early experiments had shown performance in the comparative judgment task to change dramatically with what were assumed to be subtle changes in materials and methodology. These results led us to question the generality of findings from other studies involving more "typical" paradigms and indicated the need to look at cognitive processes within a larger empirical context.

A semantic priming/equilbration framework appears well suited to this task. This framework emphasizes the flexible interaction of a subject's knowledge with ongoing events in the environment. It is assumed that the individual's understanding of a particular situation creates a set of operation-outcome expectancies for that context. To the extent that a series of events is consistent with these expectancies, subsequent performance (either cognitive or behavioral) will be facilitated. Inconsistencies between the expected and actual events, however, require examination of additional, relevant information to determine the best alternative "course of action." This recomputation presumably follows some hierarchical and probablistic sequence and clearly must be based on a flexible cognitive organization (Anderson & Ortony, 1975). Semantic priming, or equilibration, then appears to be essentially the stuff of problem solving (in a very broad sense) insofar as it represents the interfacing of internal (memorial) knowledge with the external world.

The notion of equilibration in cognitive processes, like Neisser's (1976) ecological framework, entails its virtually continuous operation. For the most part, this goes on automatically as experience (i.e., memory) allows navigation of hallways, reading of novels, and other well practiced routines. Such processes do become conscious, however, in situations where two sources of information are in conflict and in moderately novel contexts requiring the application of knowledge acquired in different but related situations. Subsequently, however, such inconsistencies may be no longer novel. As the cognitive structures or schemata change (i.e., accomodate), the new contingencies become part of the data base: expectancies are modified by their outcomes.

Logan and Zbrodoff (1979) and Logan (1980) have demonstrated this empirically in a Stroop-like interference task (see also, Kosslyn, Murphy, Bemesderfer, & Feinstein, 1977; Maki, 1981). They presented subjects with the to-be-named words ABOVE and BELOW, positioned either above or below a fixation point. When conflicting stimuli were relatively rare (20%), they were responded to more slowly than compatible stimuli. When conflicting stimuli occurred on 80% of the trials, however, they were responded to faster than compatible stimuli. These results evidence the probalistic nature and flexibility of equilibrative processes in much the same way as the comparative judgment findings of Marschark and Paivio (1980) and Marschark and Azmitia (1981) and the interference effects reported by Lupker (1979).

Consistent, cross-paradigm findings of this sort support arguments for a broader, more integrative approach to cognitive investigations. The research discussed here, in particular, has indicated that a number of empirical, cognitive phenomena, previously dealt with in isolation, are primarily a function of the single mechanism of subjects' expectancies or preactivation of memorial information to verbal information in particular stimulus contexts. Congruent and incongruent priming over a series of trials appears to account for Stroop effects, congruity effects, facilitation and interference effects in lexical decisions (cf. Logan, 1980, p. 543), and comprehension of lexical ambiguities. The opportunity to form such expectancies also appears to affect sentence-picture verifications (Glushko & Cooper, 1978; MacLeod, Hunt, & Mathews, 1978), letter matching tasks (McLean & Shulman, 1978), and language processing (R. C. Anderson, 1978; Bower, Black, & Turner, 1978; Yuille & Paivio, 1969). The commonalities among these phenomena clearly indicate a similarity in the processes underlying them. Hopefully, clarification of such relationships in other areas of cognitive research will facilitate the understanding of the psychological processes involved in them and provide a more comprehensive and integrated view of human cognitive abilities.

ACKNOWLEDGMENT

Preparation of this report was facilitated by a grant from the Research Council of the University of North Carolina at Greensboro. Cheryl Logan and Reed Hunt provided extremely helpful comments on the ideas expressed herein.

REFERENCES

Anderson, J. R. *Language, memory, and thought*. Hillsdale, N.J.: Lawrence Erlbaum Assoc., 1976.

Anderson, J. R. Arguments concerning representations for mental imagery. *Psychological Review,* 1978, *85,* 249–277.

Anderson, R. C. Schema-directed processes in language comprehension. In A. Lesgold, J. Pellegrino, S. Fokkima, & R. Glaser (Eds.), *Cognitive psychology and instruction*. New York: Plenum, 1978.

Anderson, R. C., & Ortony, A. On putting apples into bottles—A problem of polysemy. *Cognitive Psychology,* 1975, *7,* 167–180.

Audley, R., & Wallis, C. Response instructions and the speed of relative judgments: I. Some experiments on brightness discrimination. *British Journal of Psychology,* 1964, *55,* 59–73.

Banks, W. Encoding and processing of symbolic information in comparative judgments. In G. Bower (Ed.), *The psychology of learning and motivation* (Vol. 11). New York: Academic Press, 1977.

Banks, W., Clark, H., & Lucy, P. The locus of the semantic congruity effect in comparative judgments. *Journal of Experimental Psychology: Human Perception and Performance,* 1975, *1,* 35–47.

Banks, W., & Flora, J. Semantic and perceptual processes in symbolic comparisons. *Journal of Experimental Psychology: Human Perception and Performance,* 1977, *3,* 278–290.

Banks, W., Fujii, M., & Kayra-Stuart, F. Semantic congruity effects in comparative judgments of magnitudes of digits. *Journal of Experimental Psychology: Human Perception and Performance,* 1976, *2,* 435–447.

Banks, W., & Root, M. Semantic congruity effects in judgments of loudness. *Perception and Psychophysics*, 1979, *26*, 133-142.

Barclay, J. The role of comprehension in remembering sentences. *Cognitive Psychology*, 1973, *4*, 229-254.

Becker, C. Allocation of attention during visual word recognition. *Journal of Experimental Psychology: Human Perception and Performance*, 1976, *2*, 556-566.

Becker, C. A. Semantic context effects in visual word recognition: An analysis of semantic strategies. *Memory & Cognition*, 1980, *8*, 493-512.

Becker, C., & Killion, T. H. Interaction of visual and cognitive effects in word recognition. *Journal of Experimental Psychology: Human Perception and Performance*, 1977, *3*, 389-401.

Bower, G. H., Black, J. B., & Turner, T. J. Scripts in memory for text. *Cognitive Psychology*, 1979, *11*, 177-220.

Bransford, J., Barclay, J., & Franks, J. Sentence memory: A constructive versus interpretive approach. *Cognitive Psychology*, 1972, *3*, 193-209.

Buckley, P., & Gillman, C. Comparisons of digits and dot patterns. *Journal of Experimental Psychology*, 1974, *103*, 1131-1136.

Collins, A., & Loftus, E. A spreading activation theory of semantic processing. *Psychological Review*, 1975, *82*, 407-428.

Dalrymple-Alford, E. C. Associative facilitation and interference in the Stroop color-word task. *Perception and Psychophysics*, 1972, *11*, 274-276.

Fischler, I., & Bloom, P. A. Automatic and attentional processes in the effects of sentence contexts on word recognition. *Journal of Verbal Learning and Verbal Behavior*, 1979, *18*, 1-20.

Flavell, J. H. *The developmental psychology of Jean Piaget*. New York: D. Von Nostrand, 1963.

Glushko, R. J., & Cooper, L. A. Spatial comprehension and comparison processes in verification tasks. *Cognitive Psychology*, 1978, *10*, 391-421.

Hock, H. S., & Egeth, H. E. Verbal interference with encoding in a perceptual classification task. *Journal of Experimental Psychology*, 1970, *83*, 299-303.

Holyoak, K. Comparative judgments with numerical reference points. *Cognitive Psychology*, 1978, *10*, 203-243.

Holyoak, K., & Mah, W. Semantic congruity in symbolic comparisons: Evidence against an expectancy hypothesis. *Memory and Cognition*, 1981, *9*, 197-204.

Holyoak, K., & Walker, J. Subjective magnitude information in semantic orderings. *Journal of Verbal Learning and Verbal Behavior*, 1976, *15*, 287-299.

Inhelder, B., & Piaget, J. *The growth of logical thinking from childhood to adolescence*. New York: Basic Books, 1958.

Kess, J. F., & Hoppe, R. A. Directions in ambiguity theory and research. In G. Prideaux (Ed.), *Perspectives in experimental linguistics*. Amsterdam: John Benjamins, B.V., 1979.

Klein, G. S. Semantic power measured through the interference of words with color-naming. *American Journal of Psychology*, 1964, *77*, 576-588.

Kosslyn, S. M., Murphy, G. L., Bemesderfer, M. E., & Feinstein, K. J. Category and continuum in mental comparisons. *Journal of Experimental Psychology: General*, 1977, *106*, 341-376.

Kosslyn, S. M., Pinker, S., Smith, G. E., & Schwartz, S. P. On the demystification of mental imagery. *The Behavioral and Brain Sciences*, 1979, *2*, 535-581.

Kučera, H., & Francis, W. N. *Computational analysis of present-day American English*. Providence, RI, Brown University Press: 1967.

Logan, G. D. On the use of a concurrent memory load to measure attention and automaticity. *Journal of Experimental Psychology: Human Perception and Performance*, 1979, *5*, 189-207.

Logan, G. D. Attention and automaticity in Stroop and priming tasks: Theory and data. *Cognitive Psychology*, 1980, *12*, 523-553.

Logan, G. D., & Zbrodoff, N. J. When it helps to be misled: Facilitative effects of increasing the frequency of conflicting stimuli in a Stroop-like task. *Memory and Cognition*, 1979, *7*, 166-174.

Lupker, S. J. The semantic nature of response competition in the picture-word interference task. *Memory and Cognition,* 1979, *7,* 485–495.

Lupker, S. J., & Katz, A. N. Input, decision, and response factors in picture-word interference. *Journal of Experimental Psychology: Human Learning and Memory,* 1981, *7,* 269–282.

MacLeod, C. M., Hunt, E. B., & Mathews, N. N. Individual differences in the verification of sentence-picture relationships. *Journal of Verbal Learning and Verbal Behavior,* 1978, *17,* 493–507.

Maki, R. H. Categorization and distance effects with spatial linear orders. *Journal of Experimental Psychology: Human Learning and Memory,* 1981, *7,* 15–32.

Marschark, M. Lexical marking and the acquisition of relational size concepts. *Child Development,* 1977, *48,* 1049–1051.

Marschark, M. *Comparative magnitude judgments with digits and other number stimuli.* Manuscript in preparation, 1981.

Marschark, M., & Azmitia, M. M. *Stimulus set composition and congruity effects in the development of semantic priming abilities.* Manuscript in preparation, 1981.

Marschark, M., & Paivio, A. Integrative processing of concrete and abstract sentences. *Journal of Verbal Learning and Verbal Behavior,* 1977, *16,* 217–231.

Marschark, M., & Paivio, A. Semantic congruity and lexical marking in symbolic comparisons: An expectancy hypothesis. *Memory & Cognition,* 1979, *7,* 175–184.

Marschark, M., & Paivio, A. *Expectancy, Associative priming, and the locus of semantic congruity effects in comparative judgments.* Unpublished manuscript, 1980.

Marschark, M., & Paivio, A. Congruity and the perceptual comparison task. *Journal of Experimental Psychology: Human Perception and Performance,* 1981, *7,* 290–308.

McCauley, C., Weil, C., & Sperber, R. The development of memory structure as reflected by semantic priming effects. *Journal of Experimental Child Psychology,* 1976, *22,* 511–518.

McLean, J. P., & Shulman, G. L. On the construction and maintenance of expectancies. *Quarterly Journal of Experimental Psychology,* 1978, *30,* 441–454.

Morton, J. Interaction of information in word recognition. *Psychological Review,* 1969, *76,* 165–178.

Moyer, R. Comparing objects in memory: Evidence suggesting an internal psychophysics. *Perception & Psychophysics,* 1973, *13,* 180–184.

Moyer, R., & Landauer, T. The time required for judgments of numerical inequality. *Nature,* 1967, *215,* 1519–1520.

Moyer, R., & Landauer, T. Determinants of reaction time for digit inequality. judgments. *Bulletin of the Psychonomic Society.* 1973, *1,* 167–168.

Neely, J. H. Semantic priming and retrieval from lexical memory: Evidence for facilitory and inhibitory processes. *Memory & Cognition,* 1976, *4,* 648–654.

Neely, J. H. Semantic priming and retrieval from lexical memory: Roles of inhibitionless spreading activation and limited-capacity attention. *Journal of Experimental Psychology: General,* 1977, *106,* 226–254.

Neisser, U. *Cognition and Reality.* San Francisco: Freeman, 1976.

Neisser, U. *Strategies for cognitive psychology.* Unpublished manuscript, 1973.

Nelson, K., & Earl, N. Information search by preschool children: Induced use of categories and category hierarchies. *Child Development,* 1973, *44,* 682–685.

Onifer, W., & Swinney, D. A. Accessing lexical ambiguities during sentence comprehension: Effects of frequency of meaning and contextual bias. *Memory & Cognition,* 1981, *9,* 225–236.

Paivio, A. *Imagery and Verbal Processes.* New York: Holt, Rinehart, and Winston, 1971.

Paivio, A. Perceptual comparisons through the mind's eye. *Memory & Cognition,* 1975, *3,* 635–647.

Paivio, A. Comparisons of mental clocks. *Journal of Experimental Psychology: Human Perception and Performance,* 1978 *4,* 61–71. (a)

Paivio, A. Mental comparisons involving abstract attributes. *Memory and Cognition*, 1978, *6*, 199–208. (b)

Paivio, A., & Marschark, M. Comparative judgments of animal intelligence and pleasantness. *Memory & Cognition*, 1980, *8*, 39–48.

Parkman, J. Temporal aspects of digit and letter inequality judgments. *Journal of Experimental Psychology*, 1971, *91*, 191–205.

Perfetti, C. A., & Goodman, D. Semantic constraints on the decoding of ambiguous words. *Journal of Experimental Psychology*, 1970, *86*, 420–427.

Piaget, J. *The origins of intelligence in children*. New York: Basic Books, 1952.

Posner, M., & Snyder, C. Facilitation and inhibition in the processing of signals. In P. M. A. Rabbit & S. Dornic (Eds.), *Attention and Performance V*, New York, Academic Press, 1975.

Roediger, H. L. Inhibition in recall from cueing with recall targets, *Journal of Verbal Learning and Verbal Behavior*, 1973, *12*, 644–657.

Rosinski, R. R. Picture-word interference is semantically based. *Child Development*, 1977, *48*, 643–647.

Rumelhart, D. E., & Ortony, A. The representation of knowledge in memory. In R. C. Anderson, R. J. Spiro, & W. E. Montague (Eds.), *Schooling and the acquisition of knowledge*. Hillsdale, N.J.: Lawrence Erlbaum Assoc., 1976.

Schuberth, R. E., & Eimas, P. D. Effects of context on the classification of words and non-words. *Journal of Experimental Psychology: Human Perception and Performance*, 1977, *3*, 27–36.

Schuberth, R. E., Spoehr, K. T. & Lane, D. M. Effects of stimulus and contextual information on the lexical decision process. *Memory & Cognition*, 1981, *9*, 68–77.

Seymour, P. H. K. *Human visual cognition*. New York: St. Martin's Press, 1979.

Shipley, W., Coffin, J., & Hadsell, K. Reaction time in judgment of color preference. *Journal of Experimental Psychology*, 1945, *35*, 206–215.

Shipley, W., Norris, E., & Roberts, M. The effect of changed polarity of set on decision times of affective judgments. *Journal of Experimental Psychology*, 1946, *36*, 237–243.

Simpson, G. B. Meaning dominance and semantic context in the processing of lexical ambiguity. *Journal of Verbal Learning and Verbal Behavior*, 1981, *20*, 120–136.

Swinney, D. A., & Hakes, D. T. Effects of prior context upon lexical access in sentence comprehension. *Journal of Verbal Learning and Verbal Behavior*, 1976, *15*, 681–689.

Wallis, C., & Audley, R. Response instructions and the speed of relative judgments: II. Pitch discrimination. *British Journal of Psychology*, 1964, *55*, 133–142.

Yuille, J. C., & Marschark, M. Imagery effects on memory: Theoretical interpretations. In A. Sheikh (Ed.), *Imagery: Current theory, research, and application*. New York: Wiley, 1982.

Yuille, J. C., & Paivio, A. Abstractness and the recall of connected discourse. *Journal of Experimental Psychology*, 1969, *82*, 467–471.

12
The Crisis
in Theories
of Mental Imagery

John C. Yuille
University of British Columbia

INTRODUCTION

Imagery has been a component of epistemologies since philosophy evolved in Greece some 3000 years ago. Indeed, images were often the mental elements of prescientific psychologies. More recently, when the first laboratories devoted to the study of mental processes appeared, images remained a major focus of concern. In fact, a dominant controversy of the first three decades of the fledgling science concerned the role of mental images. For example, the focus of the debate between the University of Leipzig and Wurzburg University concerned the need for images in thinking—the former argued that images were essential, while the latter said they were not. The result of this and similar debates was a crisis in imagery theories during the early part of this decade. The crisis was primarily the result of the introspective methodology adopted by the first psychological laboratories. The introspective training that the subjects received predetermined the kinds of images they described, or whether they reported images at all. Such a fragile data base was bound to create theoretical problems. The arguments between the various schools became heated but nonproductive. It is only a slight exaggeration to state that little was learned about psychological phenomena (other than perception) during this period. The frustration of a young group of American psychologists was understandable. They rejected introspection and the mentalistic theories it produced, demanding a new method which would yield objective, replicable results. This methodologically-caused crisis brought about a new definition of the discipline, and North American psychology became Behaviorism.[1] One casualty of the behaviorist revolution was imagery, as it was rejected along with all mentalisitc concepts. Imagery virtually disappeared from research and theories in North America for over 40 years.

The dismissal of imagery remained effective while behaviorists had their opportunity to explain and predict behavior. Ultimately, behaviorism has proved ineffective at either task, and mental concepts have slowly returned to the vocabulary of North American psychologists. About 20 years ago, research concerning imagery reappeared (Holt, 1964). This chapter pays tribute to the work of a man who was a major force in giving new conceptual life to images. His theoretical contributions, particularly the dual coding model, continue to be the major heuristic in imagery research. A striking characteristic of Al Paivio's efforts is his concern for experimental precision. In contrast to the earlier dependency of imagery upon introspective data, current conceptions, particularly Paivio's stand on firm empirical ground.

In spite of improved methodology, there are some serious problems for imagery models. In the following pages I suggest that there is a crisis in contemporary psychology, similar in severity and importance to the one that lead to the appearance of Behaviorism, and that imagery once again plays a central role in the crisis. In spite of its current popularity, imagery may again disappear from psychology, unless there are changes in both the theoretical and methodological approaches to the concept. There is a further parallel with the earlier crisis in psychology: Unless solutions are found to the problems associated with imagery, there will again be a change in the definition of psychology. This change, if it happens, will have consequences as serious as the behaviorist redefinition did, and, I believe, the effects will be negative. To provide the framework within which to elaborate this thesis, it is necessary to examine some aspects of the past 25 years of experimental psychology.

The decline in the popularity of the S-R style of theory preferred by behaviorists happened rather slowly, beginning in the mid 1950s, and gathering momentum during the 1965–75 period. Many factors contributed to the growing dissatisfaction with behaviorism. Primarily, there was a need to describe mental states as something other than intervening variables. The brain stimulation research of Penfield (Penfield & Rasmussen, 1950) required mentalistic terms to correlate with neurophysiology. Similarly, researchers of verbal learning were finding that complex processes mediated even simple learning tasks (Bugelski,

---

[1] "Behaviorism" is capitalized to designate it as a school of thought, that is, a systematic theoretical approach to the study of psychology. At later points in this chapter, the term is not capitalized, indicating that a later period in the history of psychology is being discussed. During the 1930s, North American psychology moved away from strict Behaviorism when intervening mechanisms (drives, habits, etc.) entered the S-R formula. From this point on, behaviorism became descriptive of a loose set of assumptions about psychology rather than a theoretical stance.

1962; Tulving, 1962). Another major stimulus for change in psychological theorizing came from outside the discipline, with developments in computer science. The rapid, and unanticipated, improvements in computer technology demanded increasing sophistication in computer systems and programming languages. Accompanying these software developments was a new jargon. Programmers found it useful to refer to the storage of information, to its retrieval, and to varieties of processing. If this jargon was appropriate for the description of the internal events of the computer, why not use them for mental processes? Experimental psychologists rapidly adopted the computer jargon, and the information processing approach to psychology appeared. The intelligent machine quickly became a metaphor for mind in psychological theorizing.

This is not the first time that theoretical inspiration has been found in machines. In fact, the influence of computers on psychology is the latest example of a continuous fascination of mental theorists with technology. Both philosophers and psychologists have found rich metaphors in the technological and scientific achievements of their day. For example, the first modern epistemologist, Rene Descartes, proposed that animal spirits flowing in tubes (the nerves) were the functional agents causing behavior. His description of how these spirits moved through the body, and caused motion by filling the muscles mirrored a technological toy of Descartes' age: the water powered moving statue. Throughout the European continent, and particularly at Versailles, the nobility enjoyed sculptures and toys that were animated by water. The movement was achieved by alternating water flow through tubes inside the figures.

A second example is found in the late 19th century, when Wundt adapted the notion of mental chemistry, originally proposed by John Stuart Mill, to form the first psychological theory. According to Wundt, the mind was composed of elements: sensations, images, and feelings. The elements combined, following the principles of mental chemistry to form the contents of consciousness. Both Mill and Wundt had been impressed and affected by a major development of their day, atomic theory. The usefulness of the atomic model in accounting for diverse chemical phenomena, and the unity provided by the periodic table of Mendelev, offered a tempting metaphor to the emerging science of psychology, a metaphor that Wundt could not resist.

Behaviorism provides a final example of this thesis. The S-R theories of the 1930s and 40s are appropriately referred to as telephone switchboard models. The associative connections that were assumed to mediate behavior were articulated in the same fashion as the best technology of the day. Although each of these metaphors, the water tubes, atomism, the telephone switchboard, proved inadequate, the search for a technological solution to the nature of mind continues. The computer is the latest and most seductive metaphor, more appealing because the computer is capable of intelligent activity.

As S-R theory was discarded in the 1960s, experimental psychologists concerned with perception, attention, and memory sought a new identity, and required a new language to deal with mental phenomena. Many of them found an identity in calling themselves cognitive psychologists, and, as noted earlier, they found the language they needed in computer science. However, the computer metaphor, unlike previous technological models, has not remained a model. During the past 10 years, the computer has changed from metaphor to testing ground of theories. A number of theorists have proposed cognitive models in the form of computer programs (Anderson & Bower, 1973; Kosslyn, 1980; Norman & Rumelhart, 1975). If the program "runs," and the output simulates some aspect of human behavior, the theory is assumed to have been tested. Although the earliest versions of these programs were primitive, for example, simulating simple patterns obtained in verbal learning studies, more recently the programs have become quite elegant and capable of simulating some intelligent behavior.[2] Now, some theorists argue that any intelligent activity can ultimately be modeled on the computer. This assertion is not simply that machines can be a useful aid to human intelligence. By evoking the notion of the Turing machine, it is asserted that any notion about psychological processes, if stated with sufficient precision, can be simulated in a computer. This argument, simply stated, is that if any set of concepts is elaborated adequately, and the relationships among them are logically stated, then a program can be written to test the model. Some see the computer as the major testing ground of psychological theory. For the first time, technology has supplied not only the metaphor, but the language and the tools for psychology.

THE CURRENT IMAGERY DEBATE

The extent to which computer models may come to dominate psychology is reflected in a recent issue of the journal *The Behavioral and Brain Sciences* (Vol. 2, 1980). Papers by Chomsky, Pylyshyn, and Fodor attempted to provide converging definitions for what they, and others, wish to call "cognitive science," which represents a new definition of psychology. Fodor (1980) assumes that psychological concepts must meet a formality condition which severely constrains the mental state/environment relations permitted in psychological theory. All acceptable concepts must be capable of being expressed computationally. Fodor (1980) claims that a "computational psychology is the only one that we

---

[2]The use of the word intelligent in reference to machines is problematic. The term appears appropriate because computers mimic a variety of behaviors which we consider intelligent. However, the word intelligent is inappropriate because it implies a commonality of process in machine and human being. A fallacious assumption of the computational approach to psychology is that if the behavior of a machine is the same as the behavior of a person then the processes mediating the behavior must be the same (Hornstein, 1981). For the context of this chapter, the word intelligent is used to refer only to the behavior of machines.

are going to get [p. 66]." He admits that many traditional issues in psychology cannot be dealt with from the computational perspective, but Fodor believes that to operate as a science we must restrict ourselves to what he calls nontransparent concepts (ones which refer to mental states without reference to semantic properties).

> We can try to say what (a) mental representation is, and what the relation to a mental representation is.... But there's no practical hope of making science out of this relation [p. 91].

The parallel with the Behaviorist call of 65 years ago is not only obvious but ironic. In the search for precision, we are once again asked to accept a narrow definition of the domain of psychology.

Pylyshyn also supported the call for a cognitive science, offering different grounds than Fodor. Pylyshyn's (1980) approach has involved the reification of the computational approach to psychology. "Given that computation and cognition can be viewed in . . . common abstract terms, there is no reason why computation ought to be treated as merely a metaphor for cognition [p. 114]." The premise that cognition and computation can be dealt with in a common fashion is tenuous. However, if it is accepted, the rest of the argument follows. Symbolic language is appropriate for modeling any computation, whether instantiated in a human or in a machine, since any single computational system can be modified to emulate any other system. Given the premise, computational models are not only an acceptable approach scientifically, they are the most appropriate.

There are a number of assumptions, some unwarranted, about the nature of science, and more to the point, about the nature of psychology that characterize cognitive science. The criticisms I deal with concentrate on the implications of the computational approach to psychology for imagery theory and research. In fact, imagery research and theorizing have played a central, although negative, role in the development of cognitive science. Some of the strongest proponents of the computational position have referred to both imagery research and to models of imagery, like Paivio's dual-coding theory, as indicative of the ultimate superiority of computer based theories in accounting for empirical results (Paivio's chapter in this volume offers strong arguments against this claim). The computational adherents assert that the representational models that have grown out of imagery research are vague and/or redundant. Basically, the argument hinges on the issue of epistemology. The computational approach assumes that any information, regardless of its original form (e.g., pictorial, verbal, etc.), can be represented by a discrete code, like the binary system employed in contemporary computers. This epistemological perspective has also been labeled propositional, since the functional form of knowledge representation is frequently in the form of a propositional network. Thus, an image in such a network would be represented as a set of propositions concerning the information contained in the

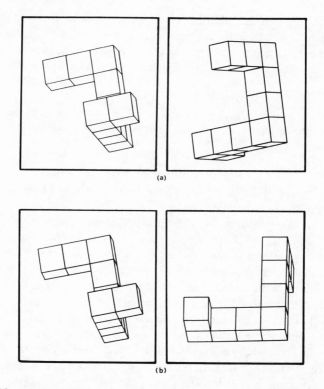

FIG. 12.1.   Standard block figures. Adapted from Shepard & Metzler (1971).

original image, and a set of connections reflecting the relationships among the propositional nodes. The essential point to note here is that the form of representation of the image is no different than any other type of knowledge.

Opposing the computational approach are the proponents of representational models, who argue that some aspects of knowledge, images in particular, have an analogue quality that makes such information unique, and not reducible to a propositional form. Pro-imagery researchers have developed a variety of experimental tasks that they believe demonstrate the analogue characteristics of images. Currently, the most popular of these are the "mental rotation" paradigm, and the mental size and distance comparison tasks. In the first task (cf. Shepard & Metzler, 1971), a subject views rotated versions of pairs of figures (see Fig. 12.1), and is required to make same/different judgements. The time required to correctly identify two figures as the same is a linear function of their angular disparity. Shepard, who developed the paradigm and has been its principal employer, has argued (Shepard, 1978) that this linear function reflects the fact that mental images mediate the solution of the task. Images have percept-like qualities, he claims, including the fact that they require time to rotate. Similar arguments are found in the other popular type of task. Moyer (Moyer & Bayer, 1976) has demonstrated that the time required to make "mental comparisons" of pairs of animals is an inverse logarithmic function of the size difference between them. This symbolic size effect "is assumed to reflect the analogue images mediating task performance" (Moyer & Bayer, 1976). This task can also ask for mental comparisons of distance rather than size, and the results are similar (e.g., Kosslyn, 1980). The time required to judge distances increases with the symbolic distance to be judged.

PROBLEMS ASSOCIATED WITH IMAGERY RESEARCH

The data resulting from this type of research seem to provide face validity for the proposed analogue nature of imagery. Intuitively, analogue images must mediate performance in all of these tasks. Shepard (1978) has argued that his results provide direct evidence for the quasi-perceptual properties of images. The image, he suggests, represents such properties as distance, size, and motion in a fashion analogous to reality (what he calls a secondary isomorphism). It is this type of conclusion that has drawn a strong, negative response from the propositional proponents. The latter claim that a propositional network can readily represent the kind of knowledge required to solve these "imagery" tasks. Further, they argue that the data from experiments employing these paradigms do not clearly support the pro-imagery position. It is this latter point that I examine first. I think that the critics of the imagery approach may be right, although for the wrong reasons. This type of imagery research may be misleading, and it reflects why there is a current crisis in imagery theorizing. The results of the mental rotation and mental comparison tasks do not and cannot support the imagery position. In fact, I would suggest that these paradigms do not offer a possibility of settling the imagery/propositional debate. In many ways, these are the worst possible tasks for the defenders of the imagery position to employ. In effect, they are attempting to win an epistemological debate using evidence and research that will ultimately assist the propositional perspective.

The elaboration and defence of this thesis requires a detailed examination of this type of research. However, because the points to be raised are basically the same for each of the research paradigms, an in depth look at one of them will suffice. The mental rotation paradigm has been selected primarily to reflect the importance assigned to the findings in the field. Shepard (Shepard & Metzler, 1971) developed the mental rotation paradigm in the late 1960s, using block figures like those in Fig. 12.1. The task for the subject is to determine whether the two figures are the same or different. They may be the same figures although differing in angular rotation, like the bottom pair in Fig. 12.1. The two figures may be different by virtue of one being a mirror image of the other, while still varying in rotational position (demonstrated by the top pair of figures in Fig. 12.1).

The assumption is that the subject must mentally rotate an image of one of the figures to determine whether it is the same as the other or a mirror image. This assumption appears to find support in the principal finding, noted earlier, that when the two figures are the same, the time required to make a correct response is a linear function of the angular separation of the two figures. The greater the difference in angle of rotation between the two figures, the longer the subject takes to respond.

As noted earlier, Shepard (1978) has concluded that the linear function relating reaction time and angular disparity reflects the time required to mentally rotate an image. He asserts that images have properties that are analogous to percepts, that during rotation the image passes through the intermediate steps between its initial and final position, and hence time is required to respond to the task. The results of research with this paradigm seem to offer such strong support to an imagery interpretation that the mental rotation results are found in introductory texts, and included in most discussions of imagery. Shepard was awarded a Distinguished Scientist Award of the American Psychological Association (1977) for this and related work.

The tenuous nature of Shepard's conclusions is demonstrated by the results of a series of studies carried out by a colleague, James Steiger, and myself during the past few years (see Steiger & Yuille, 1979; Yuille & Steiger, in press). Our research was prompted by acceptance of Shepard's conclusions rather than suspicion about them. Believing the mental rotation phenomena to be established, we sought to develop a memory analogue of the typical procedure. Simply, we wondered what pattern of results would be obtained if one of the figures of the pair was in memory rather than in view. We hoped to discover some properties of the memory image, and to compare those properties to the ones inferred by Shepard. In our first experiment, we presented each subject with a single block figure, labeled the standard figure, in one position. The rotational procedure was explained to the subject, and he/she was asked to commit the standard figure to memory. During this memorization phase, a mirror image of the standard was also present, for comparison purposes. In effect, the subject saw a pair of figures like those in the top of Fig. 12.1. After memorizing the standard, the subject was shown a series of block figures, one at a time. The task was to compare each presented figure with the memorized standard, and determine if they were the same, differing only in angular rotation, or different, by virtue of being mirror images. We were not surprised to find that subjects did this task faster than the typical Shepard task, since the memory form of the rotation task involves examining only one figure. However, as the curves in Fig. 12.2 demonstrate, the memorization procedure did not simply reduce the y-intercept, it also changed the slope relating angular disparity and reaction time. If one continues to accept Shepard's assertion that the slope of the curve reflects image rotation time, it appears that memory images can be rotated more rapidly than perceptual images. This conclusion was discomforting, and raises serious doubts about the validity

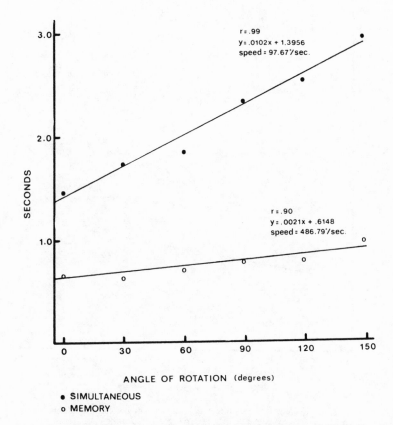

FIG. 12.2.   Reaction time for correct identification of same pairs of figures for simultaneous and memory conditions.

of the kind of inferences being drawn from this type of research. This prompted us to examine alternative interpretations of the mental rotation task.

In our second experiment, we determined the effect of the mirror image figure during memorization. Clearly, from an imagery perspective, the presence or absence of the second mirror image during the memorization phase should have no effect on subsequent performance in the comparison task. The purpose of the memorization phase is to create an image of the standard figure, the availability of the mirror counterpart should not affect image formation. However, if there are nonimaginal factors operating in this task, it is possible that the mirror image figure may supply information that is useful in solving the task. We repeated our first experiment, except that only the standard figure was present during the memorization phase. The results are displayed in Fig. 12.3. A comparison with Fig. 12.2 reveals that the memory condition continued to yield faster "rotation" times than the simultaneous procedure. However, the effect was substantially

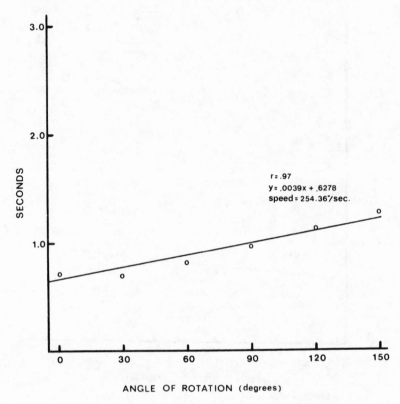

FIG. 12.3.   Reaction time for correct identifications in a memory condition, with no mirror image present during memorization.

reduced from that obtained in the previous experiment, with the slope roughly in between the two previously obtained values. Obviously, the absence of the mirror image substantially increased the slope of the reaction time function. The results of these two experiments do not support Shepard's analogue interpretation of mental imagery.

As our research on the mental rotation phenomena continued, we became aware that a variety of nonholistic problem solving strategies, some not involving imagery at all, could mediate the task. In fact, a close examination of the type of figure we have employed reveals a feature redundancy. It is necessary to examine only the bottom arm of each figure in order to make the same/different judgement. This fact is illustrated in Fig. 12.4, in which only the bottom arms of the block figures from Fig. 12.1 are displayed. Clearly, the "mirror image" pair can still be discriminated from the "same" pair. Informing subjects of this built in redundancy provides for a direct test of Shepard's holistic mental rotation hypothesis. He has argued that mental rotation is holistic, and unaffected by the

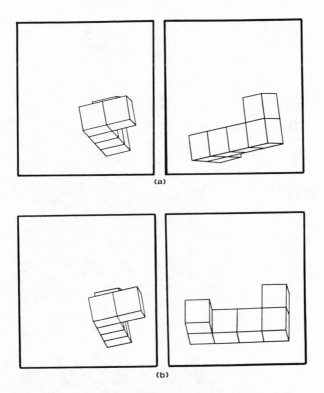

(a)

(b)

FIG. 12.4.   Bottom arms of the block figures of Fig. 12.1.

complexity of the object to be manipulated. Thus, whether a subject rotates the whole figure, or only part of it should not affect the slope of the reaction time curve. However, if subjects are using some other strategy, which is not holistic, manipulating only part of the figure should take less time than the whole object.

The experiment contrasting these predictions involved the employment of the standard Shepard task. Each subject saw pairs of figures like those in Fig. 12.1, for 112 trials. After a short break, half of the subjects continued for an additional 112 trials. The remaining subjects were informed during the break of the redundancy in the figures, and they were informed that they need compare only the bottom arms of the figures to solve the task. They also received an additional 112 trials. The results for the control group are found in Fig. 12.5. There is some improvement in performance from the first set of trials to the second, indicating a practice effect in these relatively naive subjects. The comparable curves for the informed group are found in Fig. 12.6. Upon learning of the feature redundancy subjects' performance changed substantially. The holistic, mental rotation hypothesis was again disconfirmed.

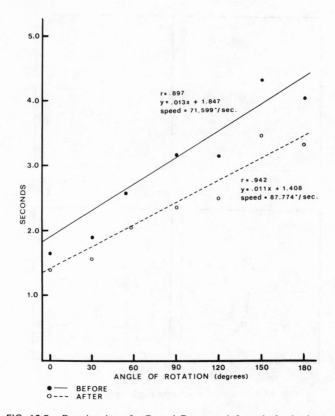

FIG. 12.5.   Reaction times for Control Group—uninformed of redundancy.

Although the results of this third experiment further muddy the interpretive waters, the results also raised an intriguing puzzle. Why had it taken us so long to notice the figural redundancy? Why had none of our subjects spontaneously noticed the simplifying solution? In Shepard's case, the redundancy might have escaped attention because he mixed different figure sets together, with each set incorporating a different kind of redundancy. But we used only one set, and the results of the experiment seemed consistent with a piecemeal comparison of figures. That is, apparently subjects compare parts of the figures, sequentially. This would make it even more likely that the redundancy should be discovered. We felt that the effect of figure complexity should be further researched to aid the interpretation of the findings of the first three experiments. Is there, perhaps, something about the standard Shepard figures that does not encourage task simplification?

To investigate the effects of figural complexity we constructed more complex block figures from the standard ones. The examples of these figures found in Fig. 12.7 reveal that arms of blocks have been added to the top of the standard

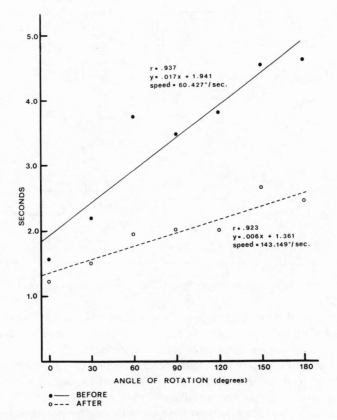

FIG. 12.6. Reaction times for Informed Group—informed of redundancy.

figures. Note that the bottom arms are still all that the subject need compare in order to solve the task. Our fourth experiment employed these figures, with the same type of instructions as employed in the standard task. Subjects saw pairs of complex figures, and made same/different judgements for each pair.

Before considering the reaction time results another aspect of the experiment must be reported. When presented with the standard figures, about 90% of our subjects are able to do the task (i.e., meet a criterion of less than 10% errors). The majority of our subjects were unable to meet this criterion with the more complex figures. In this case, the subjects fell into two distinct groups. The first, about half, were unable to perform the task. They had very high error rates, usually required many seconds, and often, minutes to respond to each pair. They reported that the task was very frustrating. None of their responses could be used. The second group were able to do the task, at a relatively low error rate. These subjects all reported, in post experimental interviews, that they had spontaneously discovered the built-in redundancy in the figures. The data for these sub-

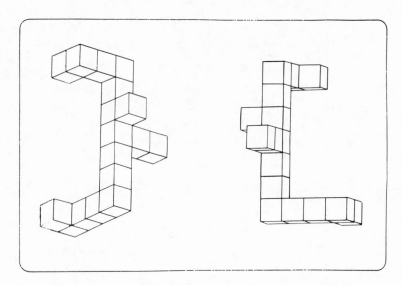

FIG. 12.7.   Complex block figures. From Yuille & Steiger (in press).

jects are graphed in Fig. 12.8, together with a comparison curve (from Fig. 12.2) for the standard size figures. For those subjects who discovered the redundancy, the complex figures became equivalent to the standards.

Apparently, these complex figures exceed whatever short-term attentional demands are required for the performance of the rotation task. For some people, these excessive demands lead to failure. They couldn't deal with the task, and were unable, or unwilling, to find a way of reducing the processing demands. Other subjects responded to the excessive demands by simplifying the task. They discovered some aspect of the built-in redundancy. As a result, the task no longer exceeded their attentional capacity. The conclusion from this experiment is that the standard Shepard figures are of the "right" level of complexity, in that they do not demand too much attention. As a consequence, the subjects are not prompted to simplify.

A fifth experiment completes this survey of mental rotation paradigm research. We wished to create complex figures that did not contain a redundancy. To this end, some of the figures used in the previous experiment were modified by twisting segments of each figure (demonstrated in Fig. 12.9). The resulting twisted figures were included with the untwisted versions, and the fourth experiment repeated. However, in this experiment subjects saw one of three types of pairs: figures that were the same, differing only in angular rotation, figures that were different, by virtue of being mirror images, and figures that were different, by virtue of one segment of one of the figures being twisted out of alignment.

This task proved to be very difficult, and again about half of the subjects could not perform the task. For those who were able to complete the task, a rejection

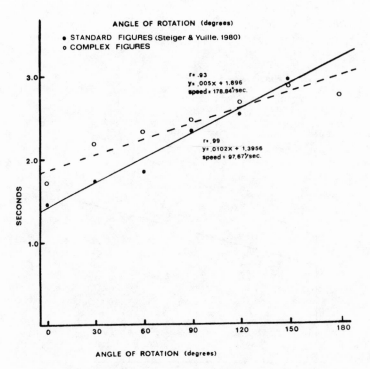

FIG. 12.8. Reaction times for complex block figures compared to standard figures. From Yuille & Steiger (in press).

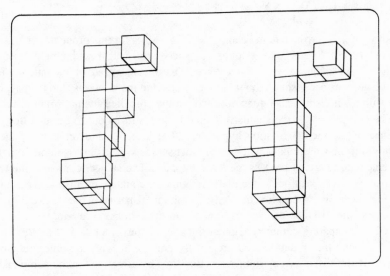

FIG. 12.9. An example of a complex figure with a "twisted" section. From Yuille & Steiger (in press).

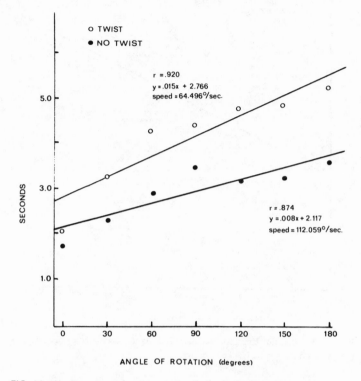

FIG. 12.10.   Reaction times for complex figures, with and without twisted segments. From Yuille & Steiger (in press).

criterion of 25% errors had to be adopted. The results for this group are presented in Fig. 12.10. Subjects took longer to successfully deal with this "twisted-complex" task than any we have tested. Estimated speed of mental rotation was 65 degrees per second, about ½ that obtained in the previous study. Imagery, in a simple, holistic sense does not mediate the so-called mental rotation task.

The complexity of the standard Shepard figures turns out to be ideal for the defence of the mental rotation hypothesis. The task demands created by these figures suit the attentional capacities of most subjects. It is our assumption that a piecemeal comparison process mediates the task. The subject compares the two figures section by section, sequentially looking for a match (or mismatch depending, on the strategy employed). As the angular disparity between two figures increases, the distance of eyemovements and the number of eyemovements required to compare a common segment increases. Carpenter & Just (1978) have reported oculometer data which are totally consistent with this interpretation. Thus, angular disparity determines reaction time by affecting feature comparison and not because of mental rotation of a holistic image. If there are too many segments to be compared in the figures (e.g., the complex figures employed in the research outlined above), subjects must either simplify the task, or fail to perform it. If some segments are rotated differently from the rest of the figure (e.g., the twisted figures used in our research), the task becomes even more complex. The generality of these conclusions is reinforced by Pylyshyn's (1979) demonstration of a complexity effect in this type of task with very different figures.

Some modifications of the Shepard figures and procedures revealed the tenuous nature of an imagery interpretation of findings using this paradigm. This demonstrates why this type of research is inappropriate for imagery theorists. This approach to research reveals nothing about the nature of representational processes. Rather, it provides yet another demonstration of implicit task demand effects in psychological research. Either position in the analogue/computational debate can find empirical support by employing the appropriate combination of figure type, instructions, and feedback. If Shepard had employed simpler or more complex figures, his findings would have been different, and he would not have proposed his holistic rotation interpretation. However, the outcome of this research is not ultimately indeterminate in the epistemological argument, as ultimately it favors computational interpretations. If it can be demonstrated that a computational interpretation is viable for some rotation task results, cognitive scientists will evoke parsimony to claim that their approach is appropriate for all such results.

The task demand effects in the mental rotation paradigm provide another parallel with the earlier crisis in psychology. At the turn of this century, one of the issues to grow out of imagery research concerned the *Aufgabe,* the effect of set on performance. Imagery experiments became increasingly concerned with the issue of task demands, helping to establish the circumstances that prompted the Behaviorist reaction (the behaviorists believed that their "objective" definition of psychology removed the concern for the Aufgabe). We seem to be acting this scene out again in contemporary research, and unless some changes are made in the type of theorizing and research, the cognitive scientist will be justified in demanding a new definition for psychology.

This negative picture of the current state of the imagery concept is amplified by research employing other popular paradigms. For example, the mental comparison technique developed by Moyer (1973) revealed an inverse relationship between the time required to compare the size of named objects and their normal size difference (related research is reviewed by others in this volume). Like the rotation results, this finding suggested the intuitive interpretation: The comparison task is mediated by representing the object pairs as analogue images. The more similar the two images are in "size," the harder it is for the "mind's eye" to discriminate them, and, hence, the longer the time required to make a decision. However, other researchers have cast doubt about the appropriateness of this interpretation. A symbolic size or distance effect has been obtained with abstract dimensions. Friedman (1978) found that paired comparisons on the evaluative dimension of the semantic differential yielded a similar pattern to the size comparisons: The closer a pair of words were on the "good/bad" scale, the longer time subjects needed to differentiate them. Friedman (1978) concluded that "it is entirely possible for memorial comparisons to yield these (linear) functions without recruiting the mind's eye [p. 443]."

Other difficulties were created when Holyoak (1978) reported that subjects explicitly encouraged to use imagery to mediate the size comparison task took longer than uninstructed subjects. Imagery theorists have responded in a confusing manner to these empirical challenges. Paivio (1978a, 1978b) suggested that even abstract qualities such as pleasantness and value must be represented imaginally, since these attributes produce symbolic distance effects, and interact with other variables assumed to affect imagery. Alternatively, it has been proposed (Marschark & Paivio, 1977; Yuille & Catchpole, 1977) that two systems exist, one which represents information propositionally or amodally (abstract knowledge), and a second, imagery system for analogue knowledge. The same trap is laid for the imagery theorist: Once a computational approach is permitted to account for some of the data, why restrict it's application? Friedman (1978) noted this explicitly: "there seems no need, at this point, to propose a data base which is structured propositionally for some types of information and analogically for others" (p. 443).

Kosslyn's (1980) imagery research is more obviously guilty of manipulating task demands rather than assessing mediating processes. For example, when he asks his subjects to mentally scan a map that they have committed to memory, he is providing them with virtually explicit task demands to take as much time as they believe would be required to mentally scan the scene.

To summarize, these cognitive problem solving tasks, i.e., mental rotation, mental size and distance comparisons, cannot provide evidence about the nature of imagery, as they primarily reflect task demands and expectation effects. On straightforward empirical grounds, this is not an appropriate arena for comparing imagery and propositional models. Anderson (1978), in a thoughtful review of the attempts to contrast these two positions, concluded that both types of models could be accommodated to fit the data base. He argued that a theoretical resolution is not possible, a conclusion with which the current analysis is in full agreement (contrast with Pylyshyn, 1981).

CONCLUSIONS

However, there is a stronger, more important conclusion being offered here: that a continuation of the current type of theorizing and research related to imagery will improve the likelihood of success of the computational approach, and that approach will be disasterous, not only for imagery models, but for psychology as a whole. The current crisis in imagery research stems from the weak theoretical concepts which characterize the field. For the most part, definitions of imagery seem to be based upon intuitive notions of mental processes, and the interpretation of research results appears to originate from the same intuitive source. This is not an argument that intuition is not a useful heuristic, but rather that it is not a sufficient basis for an empirical science. What is required from aspiring theorists is a solid definition of imagery, and its relationship to other cognitive processes. My preference for solidity is that a concept meets the criterion of falsifiability. Psychology may not have achieved a maturity that allows such complete testability, but this should be our goal. The loose, flexible, contemporary conceptions about imagery are so far from this goal that they result in the kind of research problems outlined earlier in this chapter.

In contrast with the conceptual difficulties associated with the imagery approach to epistemology, the computational models have the potential of great precision. Their approach to theory necessitates full definition of concepts and their interrelationships. The term potential is used because the accomplishments of this approach have been modest to date. There is no question, however, that the capacity of cognitive science to provide empirically testable (or should this read computer testable?) concepts is secure. If testability remains our major criterion, cognitive science will be the psychology of the future, unless imagery theorists make some changes. The next section of this chapter examines the changes necessary to meet the cognitive challenge.

The primary concerns are two: (1) to achieve greater precision in theory; and (2) to broaden imagery theory to demonstrate the unacceptability of the cognitive approach. Kosslyn's (1980) attempt to outline a theory of imagery is laudable in relation to the first of these concerns, although, due to an inherent self-contradiction, it fails badly on the second. Kosslyn has presented a computer based model of imagery, in which the analogue information that he believes images possess is displayed on a CRT. Thus the screen display simulates the hypothesized imaginal processes that mediate size comparisons, distance judgements, and mental rotation. Although this model is a step in the right direction concerning precision, the problem is that the CRT display is not relevant for the computer solution of the cognitive tasks. The screen display exists solely for the convenience of the human observer. The information that the computer uses to generate the display is in a computational form. The machine could solve all of the distance size and rotation problems without reference to the analogue information. By concentrating on these types of problems, Kosslyn has narrowed the definition of imagery so that it can be dealt with computationally.

Paivio's dual coding model is the exemplar in the field as far as precision of definition is concerned. His delineation of three levels of meaning within two types of codes (outlined in a number of chapters in this volume) has proved to be the most persistent and successful heuristic in the field. This aspect of his contribution is continued by his chapter in this volume. He clearly demonstrates that a variety of experimental findings have been predicted from dual coding theory, whereas no other approach can make this claim. Furthur, he argues that for the paradigms of concern, the results favor dual coding theory. The problem with dual coding theory is with its lack of breadth. The relationship of his hypothesized verbal and imaginal processes to other aspects of cognition has not been elaborated. In particular, it appears that there are amodal aspects to cognition, at least this is a common theme linking such diverse writers as Piaget (1952), Fodor (1975), Bransford (1979), and Chomsky (1968). While Paivio has entertained the possibility of a third code (Marschark & Paivio, 1977), this has not been elaborated. The imagery/computational disagreements would be substantially reduced if a model incorporating both dual coding theory and an amodal coding system were developed (for a more extensive discussion of this point, see Yuille & Catchpole, 1977; Yuille & Marschark, in press).

Dual coding theory, as well as any other approach to imagery, would benefit by accommodating another aspect of mind: emotions. It would be useful to extend imagery models to experimental areas where the computer can play no role. There is no arena that displays the limitations of a cognitive science more affectively than that of human emotions. For example, the research of Peter Lang (1980) has effectively combined imagery and emotions in a common research situation. He has compared high and low imagers in their capacity to generate images of emotionally neutral scenes, fear provoking scenes, and physically stressful scenes. The physiological responses that Lang monitored proved sensitive to interactions involving emotionality, imagery training, and individual differences in imagery. The results suggested a complex role for imagery in the mediation of emotions.

The recent, impressive research by Rogers (reviewed in his chapter in this volume) is a further example of the empirical investigation of emotion. Rogers provides a more detailed and convincing argument for incorporating emotion as a third coding system in Paivio's model than can be provided here. Suffice it to say that this writer is in full agreement with Rogers' thesis, this approach to the study of imagery would avoid the wasteful concerns caused by computational critics.

This chapter has attempted to raise concern about the proposed redefinition of psychology to a computational cognitive science, based on the assumption that such an approach would be detrimental to the discipline. This reflects an agreement with Heil (1980) in his reaction to the marriage of computation and cognition: "the internal states of a computing machine may be treated as symbolic only because they are connected to the representational activities of (the) agents who . . . give sense to the output [p. 139]." The computer cannot advance our understanding of human thought. By attempting to redefine psychology, the cognitive scientist is assuming that a narrow aspect of cognition, that which can be represented computationally, can be adequately dealt with in isolation. This assumption is wrong. Whatever processes are involved in thought, they form a mental Gestalt which must be approached in context. If the only way to make psychology a science is to practice cognitive science, psychology ought to seek an alternative status. Cognitive science proposes to make psychology a sterile and trivial discipline.

Once before the call for objectivity lured psychologists to an inappropriate definition of psychology. If we are not careful, this will happen again. Imagery researchers and theorists must respond to this challenge by expanding both their models and their paradigms to deal with other aspects of mind, particularly abstract, amodal thought, and emotions.

REFERENCES

Anderson, J. R. Arguments concerning representations for mental imagery. *Psychological Review,* 1978, *85,* 249-277.

Anderson, J. R., & Bower, G. H. *Human associative memory.* Washington, D.C.: Winston, 1973.

Bransford, J. D. *Human cognition.* Belmont, Calif.: Wadsworth, 1979.

Bugelski, R. R. Presentation time, total time, and mediation in paired associate learning. *Journal of Experimental Psychology,* 1962, *63,* 409-412.

Carpenter, P. A., & Just, M. A. Eye fixations during mental rotation. In J. Senders, R. Monty, and D. Fisher (Eds.), *Eye movements and psychological process II.* Hillsdale, N.J.: Lawrence Erlbaum Assoc., 1978.

Chomsky, N. *Language and mind.* New York: Harcourt Brace Jovanovich, 1968.

Chomsky, N. Rule and representation. *The Behavioral and Brain Sciences,* 1980, *3,* 1-61.

Fodor, J. A. *The language of thought.* New York: Thomas Crowell, 1975.

Fodor, J. A. Methodological solopsism considered as a research strategy in cognitive psychology. *The Behavioral and Brain Sciences,* 1980, *3,* 63-109.

Friedman, A. Memorial comparisons without the minds eye. *Journal of Verbal Learning and Verbal Behavior,* 1978, *17,* 427-444.

Heil, J. Computation, cognition, and representation. *The Behavioral and Brain Sciences,* 1980, *3,* 139.

Holt, R. R. Imagery: The return of the ostracized. *American Psychologist,* 1964, *19,* 154-264.

Holyoak, K. Comparative judgments with numerical reference points. *Cognitive Psychology,* 1978, *10,* 203-243.

Holyoak, K., & Walker, J. Subjective magnitude information in semantic orderings. *Journal of Verbal Learning and Verbal Behavior,* 1976, *15,* 287-299.

Hornstein, N. Book review of philosophical perspectives in artificial intelligence (M. D. Ringle, Ed.). *Journal of Philosophy,* 1981, *77,* 408-415.

Kosslyn, S. *Image and mind.* Cambridge, Mass.: Harvard University Press, 1980.

Lang, P. *Emotional imagery.* Colloquium presented at the University of British Columbia, April, 1980.

Marschark, M., & Paivio, A. Integrative processing of concrete and abstract sentences. *Journal of Verbal Learning and Verbal Behavior,* 1977, *16,* 217-231.

Moyer, R. Comparing objects in memory: Evidence suggesting an internal psychophysics. *Perception and Psychophysics,* 1973, *13,* 180-184.

Moyer, R. S., & Bayer, R. H. Mental comparison and the symbolic distance effect. *Cognitive Psychology,* 1976, *8,* 228-246.

Norman, D. A., Rumelhart, D. E., & the LNR Research Group. *Explorations in cognition.* San Francisco: Freeman, 1975.

Paivio, A. Comparisons of mental clocks. *Journal of Experimental Psychology: Human Perception and Performance,* 1978, *4,* 61–71. (a)

Paivio, A. Mental comparisons involving abstract attributes. *Memory & Cognition,* 1978, *6,* 199–208. (b)

Penfield, W., & Rasmussen, T. *The cerebral cortex of man.* New York: Macmillan, 1950.

Piaget, J. *The child's conception of number.* New York: Humanities Press, 1952.

Pylyshyn, Z. W. The rate of "mental rotation" of images: A test of a holistic analogue hypothesis. *Memory & Cognition,* 1979, *7,* 19–28.

Pylyshyn, Z. W. Computation and cognition: Issues in the foundations of cognitive science. *The Behavioral and Brain Sciences,* 1980, *3,* 111–169.

Pylyshyn, Z. W. The imagery debate: Analogue media versus trait knowledge. *Psychological Review,* 1981, *88,* 16–45.

Shepard, R. N. The mental image. *American Psychologist,* 1978, *33*(2), 125–137.

Shepard, R. N., & Metzler, J. Mental rotation of three-dimensional objects. *Science,* 1971, *171,* 701–703.

Steiger, J. R., & Yuille, J. C. *Long term memory and mental rotation.* Paper presented at the annual meeting of the Psychonomic Society, Phoenix, Arizona, 1979.

Tulving, E. Subjective organization in free recall of 'unrelated' words. *Psychological Review,* 1962, *69,* 344–354.

Yuille, J. C., & Catchpole, M. J. The role of imagery in models of cognition. *Journal of Mental Imagery,* 1977, *1,* 171–180.

Yuille, J. C., & Marschark, M. Imagery effects on memory: Theoretical interpretations. In A. Sheikh (Ed.), *Imagery: Current theory, research, and application.* New York: Wiley, in press.

Yuille, J. C., & Steiger, J. H. Nonholistic processing in mental rotation: Some suggestive evidence. *Perception and Psychophysics,* in press.

13

Emotion, Imagery, and Verbal Codes: A Closer Look at an Increasingly Complex Interaction

T. B. Rogers
The University of Calgary

INTRODUCTION

In February of 1966 I had a short, but significant conversation with Dr. Paivio. As a new recruit to the discipline of psychology, coming from a mathematics undergraduate degree, I was in the throes of grappling with the emerging dual-coding theory. When Al was finally able to drum his ideas into my thick skull I was still struck with a sense of incompleteness. I felt that something was missing in this evolving view of the human cognitive machine, but wasn't really able to articulate what it was. With some trepidation I approached Al and tried to voice my concerns. We talked for a while and several points emerged from our conversation. The general conclusion was that the emotional aspects of memory were not currently part of the theory, and that this might be a next step in its development once the imaginal and verbal codes had been sorted out. More specifically, three points were made: (1) It is certainly conceivable that there may be more than two codes, and that the choice to consider only two at that point was more a matter of convenience than being fact-based. (2) The idea of emotions or feelings being part of the model is clearly needed, as these were not directly addressed in the formulation. (3) It is possible that one could look at emotion as a "third code," acting in a similar interactive way with the other two codes, obeying its own rules, and adding the things I thought were missing from the then-new dual-coding formulation. I left the meeting feeling a lot better about the research enterprise, and with the distinct feeling that emotion was going to emerge as a central construct in cognitive work generally—if not specifically in Paivio's work.

Now 15 years later, it is possible to look at what has transpired in the area and decide if that conversation was the harbinger of things to come in human experimental psychology. What I propose to do in this chapter is harken back to the ideas Al and I discussed in the Rotunda so long ago with reference to some of the work that I have been doing in the last 5 years or so. I hope to explore the phantom "third code" of emotion in cognition—to determine whether such a distinction is necessary, to look at some relavent data, and to develop a metaphor for describing the interaction between the various components. To attain this goal it will be necessary to touch on some "hot" areas of current psychological debate. These areas relate rather closely to aspects of the 1966 conversation and include: (1) The suitability of strictly associationistic models of cognition as they apply to "hot" cognitions (Bower & Gilligan, 1979 vs Rogers, 1980a); (2) The need for revising our currently cold models of man by including sensitive treatments of emotional characteristics (Zajonc, 1980; Rogers, 1980b); and (3) We'll also confront some of the current shortcomings of current model building in physiological psychology and the hemispheric debate (e.g. Springer & Deutsch, 1981) as we cast about for a metaphor to help organize how the "third code" might be best handled.

The foregoing should make it clear that I have not opted for a conservative or safe approach in this chapter. My presentation is more speculative than data-tied, is intentionally provocative, will end up in raising more questions than it answers, and will probably brand me as a maverick from the neo-mentalistic fold. So be it. The field of emotion is rife with controversy, and a noncontroversial paper in the field would be of questionable utility and ecological validity. A comment by Mandler (1975) is appropriate: "I do know one fact about (current) systems of 'emotion'—they are all, to some extent, wrong. The joy is to try to be a little less wrong next time around [p. 66]."

Some Background Data

My return to the issue of emotion in cognition (following sabbaticals in the areas of personality assessment and social psychology) was facilitated by some research I did in Cape Breton and Calgary about 4 years ago. In Rogers, Kuiper and Kirker (1977) we used a slight variation of the then-popular incidental recall paradigm that Craik and Tulving (1975) had exploited in the depth-of-processing debate. The stimuli we used were personal adjectives of the kind you would expect to find on an adjective checklist designed to assess self-concepts of normal subjects (e.g. successful, tolerant, organized, determined, curious). They represented a broad spectrum of personal characteristics being chosen from the set of scales designed by Jackson (1967) for the Personality Research Form.

These adjectives were used in the incidental recall context with the standard structural, phonemic and semantic rating tasks *as well as* the addition of another rating task. The new task involved having the subject decide if the adjective described him/her. Thus with the addition of the Self-Reference rating, the Rogers et al. (1977) experiments involved four orienting tasks. Items were appropriately counter-balanced and incidental recall assessed in terms of the proportions of adjectives given Yes or No ratings as a function of Rating Task that were recalled. Results indicated the typical Craik and Tulving configuration for the three standard Rating Tasks with recall greatest for the Semantic and least for the Structural judgments. The Self-Reference task showed some unexpected results with incidental recall being very much greater than Semantic (13% of the Semantic rated items were recalled compared to 30% of the words rated in the Self-Reference task). Although we were expecting some superiority for the Self-Reference task, we certainly did not expect this great a difference. More Self-Reference rated words were recalled than the other three tasks combined (2.84 Self-Reference items compared to 2.35 for the other three tasks together). At the very least, these data suggested that the self imparts a very rich and strong aspect to the encoding environment, thereby facilitating recall.

The initial theoretical formulation that both generated and explained the Rogers et al. (1977) data revolved around the notion that the self is a cognitive structure not unlike those currently popular in the cognitive domain. We defined the self as:

> a list of features that have been derived from a lifetime of experience with personal data. More than likely a portion of the list contains general terms not unlike traits—that represent the abstracted essentials of a person's view of self. In addition to these general terms, there are also some more specific entries in the self. These relate to less salient and more situation specific aspects of self-perception as well as to specific behaviors [p. 677–678].

The self-referent memory enhancement was thought to be due to the involvement of this large and complex cognitive structure in the encoding environment.

At the time, there were a number of possible alternate explanations of these data. Probably the most important one was that the Semantic task we used was did not involve a person (it was a synonym task) whereas the Self-Reference task did. Perhaps, it could be argued, it is the involvement of a person—not the self—that has induced the tremendous recall advantage. In subsequent studies by ourselves and others (e.g. Hull & Levy, 1979; Keenan & Baillet, 1980; Kendzierski, 1980; Kuiper & Rogers, 1979) it has been clearly shown that the Self-Reference memory enhancement documented in Rogers et al. (1977) is indeed the result of the self being involved in the encoding environment.

Another emerging line of data speaks directly to aspects of dual coding theory and the self-referent memory enhancement. About (1980) replicated the Rogers et al. study using adjectives varying in concreteness. She generated a series of abstract personal adjectives that were similar to those we used. Furthermore she also gathered a set of more concrete descriptors (e.g. sunburned), that were matched on the usual word attributes with the abstract set. Her data clearly indicated that the self-referent memory enhancement was restricted to the abstract adjectives. These data suggest some interesting boundary conditions for the self-referent memory enhancement effect, but do not challenge our interpretation involving the self as the ephemeral characteristics that emerged as the concrete adjectives would not be part of the durable self concept we are considering.

Other possible explanations have also received considerable scrutiny in the literature, and the self still remains as a tremendously powerful adjunct to the encoding of words in this experimental paradigm (see Rogers, 1980a for a review).

The initial documentation of the self-referent memory enhancement spawned a series of other studies applying this idea to some most intriguing areas. Of note is the finding that the size of the enhancement is greater with increasing age, suggesting a more stable self with older subjects (Rogers & Rogers, 1981). Also, considerable work has been done using this approach to zero in on aspects of depression, with the self-referent memory enhancement interacting with a series of experimental variables (e.g. Davis, 1979; Kuiper & Derry, 1981) to suggest that the depressive's self concept is not an overly effective encoding aid for them. The task has also been used in some demonstration work on the emerging "new look" in the area of psychophysiology with lip EMG acting as an a good index of verbal involvement in the Self-Referent task (Cacioppo & Petty, 1981). In sum, our initial demonstration of the self-referent memory enhancement and the rather simple cognitive model we advanced to account for the data did generate considerable interest and research (you might prefer the word "heat" here) in the area broadly defined as social cognition.

Two Cognitive Explanations

Researchers with less concern for the social psychological aspects of cognition began to look carefully at the enhancement effect. In particular, Bower and Gilligan (1979) argued that the Rogers et al. (1977) data could be readily rationalized into a HAM-type formulation. They saw the enhancement effect as an example of the general rule that "any well differentiated cognitive structure can serve as a 'hitching post' for evaluation and attaching to the items to be remembered [p. 429]." Data were provided to indicate that recalling episodes related to one's self or one's mother produced comparable levels of incidental memory. These data satisfied Bower and Gilligan that the general form of semantic memory model could accomodate the self-referent memory enhancement effect.

At a very basic level, we were forced to reject Bower's argument. First, it seemed clear to us that no matter how hard we tried we could not rationalize the self as "just an ordinary" cognitive structure. Apart from some convergent data that suggested unique properties for the self (e.g. Rogers, Kuiper & Rogers, 1979), the Bower proposition seemed unnecessarily restrictive in its explanation of something as rich and significant as the self. Beyond this, however, the Bower formulation couldn't handle all of the data that were available at the time he made his suggestion. In particular, one aspect of the HAM-type model is a phenomenon called the "fanning effect." Basically, the amount of time spent in the nodal network during a search operation should be dictated by, among other things, the complexity of the network. A net that contains a great amount of information should require more time for a search to be executed. It seems clear that the self is a complex and large (if not *the* most complex and large) structure in our cognitive arsenal. It follows, then, that search times should be longer for Self-Referent decisions. This prediction has not been confirmed in a large number of earlier studies, as well as in some of our work (e.g. Kuiper & Rogers, 1979), thus calling into question a simple explanation of the HAM-type variety.

On another front, Keenan and Baillet (1980) conducted a series of very interesting studies involving self-reference in a cognitive context. Their concern was toward explicating models of the enhancement effect, and they were able to accomodate both their and our data with an "Availability/Computational" formulation. This formulation suggested that words that are a part of the self concept are processed differently from those that are not. Words compatable with the self concept would be processed fast and effectively as the relevant cognitive dimensions would be "ready for action" or available in the Tversky and Kahneman (1973) sense. On the other hand, words that are not part of the self concept would require more extensive processing, involving intelligent guesses and various other kinds of "computations" to reach an output stage. This computed response would be slower, which is indeed the results found by Keenan and Baillet (1980) and Kuiper and Rogers (1979). Furthermore, some of the effects of target familiarity on response time documented in these two experimental series are nicely rationalized by Keenan's approach. Although there are some aspects of the available data that the Availability/Computational model cannot handle (see Rogers, 1980a, p. 205), from a strictly cognitive perspective this formulation seems the best current candidate as far as the published work is concerned.

What About Affect?

Although these cognitive models are adequate in a strict sense of the word, they leave a lot to be desired as far as being reasonable models of the complete cognitive system, particularly with respect to an event as complex as self-reference. Zajonc (1980) has addressed this issue and offers some useful insights into the shortcomings of a strictly cognitive stance. He offers an impressive amount of data to suggest that we *need* to include affect into our models. As a sampler, Argyle, Salter, Nicholson, Williams and Burgess (1970) found that 22 times more variance is accounted for by voice tone (a known aspect of emotional behavior) than content in studies attempting to encode degraded verbal utterances. Zajonc (1980) goes on to suggest that affect is: (1) basic, representing the first link in the evolution of adaptive behaviours; (2) inescapable, being very hard if not impossible to control; (3) irrevocable, being very hard to change or even to doubt subjectively; (4) difficult to verbalize; and (5) not dependent upon and separable from cognitions. An essential part of Zajonc's argument is that the moment we move out of the sanctity of our labs into the real world of valuing, evaluating, liking, rejecting (what Abelson, 1963, labeled as ''hot'' cognitions), we find an increasing need to begin to inject some aspect of emotion into our theories. Combine this with Neisser's (1976) proclamations on ecological validity, and the handwriting is on the wall regarding the emergence of a renewed interest in emotional processes and their place in cognition.

Another aspect of dissatisfaction with purely cognitive (read ''cold'') models of cognition is the (unnecessarily) restrictive nature of a linear, mechanistic approach to human psychology (see Rogers, 1980b for an extended discussion). Of concern, is that adopting a strictly cognitive position will begin to define some topics in psychology as inappropriate for study. If we restrict ourselves to questions that are (easily) answerable using current experimental techniques one really has to wonder about the possibility of meaningful progress. If we reject the study of affect because it is not easily accomodated in our current models of cognition, surely we have a classic example of the tail wagging the dog. This is not to deny the tremendous advantages that accrue properly scientific approaches (again see Rogers, 1980b), but serves to underscore the need for careful scrutiny of our macro models and techniques to ensure we aren't being subtly seduced into addressing less important problems because they easily fit within the current models and methods.

In all fairness, it should be noted that Keenan did consider affect in aspects of her work. This consideration was cut short, however, when she concluded: ''for now . . . the data can be adequately explained using only cognitive constructs; they may raise the possibility of a motivational account, but they do not compel one'' (Keenan & Baillet, 1980, p. 25).

A Model Encorporating Affect

What follows is a model of cognition that can handle aspects of emotional activity in the human information processing system. While some time will be spent looking at the self-referent data with this model, it should be emphasized that the proposed formulation has generality beyond this specific data set. The self-reference material serves to illustrate the origin of my concerns, but the goal is to develop a general model that can be used to think about a large number of different areas in the study of psychology considered broadly.

Before proceeding it is necessary to do a bit of semantic housecleaning. Thus far in the presentation I have been using the words "affect" and "emotion" as synonymous. This trend is also apparent in the literature on the topic. Various dictionaries offer a distinction between these two words that proves to be rather useful in developing a model. Emotion is a generalized state of the organism typically defined in terms of some kind of bodily state. According to Merriam (1961) emotion is "a psychic and physical reaction subjectively experienced as strong feeling and physiologically involving changes that prepare the body for immediate vigorous action." Affect, however, tends to be considered in terms of the cognitive system. For example Drever (1952) views affect as "any kind of feeling or emotion attached to ideas or idea-complexes [p. 10]." It seems, then, that affect can be considered as postcognitive emotional experience. With this distinction in mind the construction of a model of emotion in human cognition can be redefined as the attempt to determine how the cognitive system transforms emotion into affect. Not only is this transformational approach compatable with contemporary information processing language, but it also stresses the fact that the cognitive aspects of emotional experience are fundamental to understanding the generalized area of emotion (e.g. Schachter & Singer, 1962). It even telegraphs a tacit agreement with Zajonc's (1980) point that cognitions are—at least in part—post-emotional.

As a code, the emotional system has some noteworthy characteristics. Probably the seminal property of the system is its verbal ineptitude. Generations of researchers have attempted to pin down this aspect of emotion, and success rates have not been particularly good. Clearly, the emotional system is vague and undifferentiated, and efforts to analyse it verbally can lead to all sorts of interesting findings (e.g. Schacter & Singer, 1962). Beyond this, the system is pervasive, powerful as well as being subjectively rich. It is most important to be careful in how one defines the emotional system at this point, as too precise an approach will no doubt limit the utility of the eventual model. With this caveat in hand, let's develop a model.

Per the 1966 conversation a convenient (and very over-simplified) starting place is to consider that emotion can serve as a third code, and develop a triple-coding theory. The evocation of a response in this third code at the Representational level of processing would be raw emotional experience (the emotogen?). As processing proceeds through the Referential and Associative stages this raw emotional experience is transformed into affect by virtue of its contact with the other two codes and their interaction. Although this is a very crude starting place, it does give us some purchase on explaining some of the data that is available. As a demonstration, let's examine the self-reference data and see where this triple code leads us.

The self-reference work can be seen as the study of the interaction of the Verbal and Emotional codes, as the Aboud (1980) study has shown that concrete adjectives (e.g. sunburned) do not induce the enhancement effect, indicating that the Imaginal code is not active. The affective aspect of reacting to the stimulus (as translated through the Referential and Associative stages) becomes part of the encoding environment in the incidental recall context. If we assume that the intensity of this emotional reaction varies as a function of degree of self-reference of the stimulus, with highly self-descriptive terms producing intense reactions, we begin to get some explanatory power. As processing continues through the latter stages of encoding the emotional reaction has a number of implications. Foremost among these is that it becomes part of the encoding environment. Thus, highly self-descriptive terms are characterized by a highly emotional encoding environment. Put another way, the emotional code is very strong for these items. But there is also a very strong Verbal code for these items as they are compatable with the self, which is a large and complex (Verbal) cognitive structure. In sum, without even considering the interaction between the Verbal and Emotional codes, the memory trace for highly self-descriptive terms is rather strong, distinctive, and (probably) retreivable. Certainly the data support this with the continual finding in our and other labs that items answered Yes during the Self-Referent task (which means they are self-descriptive) are recalled (or recognized) better than those receiving a No response. When we realize that the Verbal and Emotional codes can interact in any number of ways, and thereby produce even stronger effects during input, it is not surprising that the self-referent memory enhancement effect is so large.

The interactions between the Emotional and other codes are no doubt complex and most intriguing. A full-blown discussion of these is clearly beyond the scope of this chapter. Just to indicate the flavor of some of the possibilities this section presents a brief summary. Four types of interactions will be discussed: Interruption, Amplification, Diversion and Cognitive Short-Cuts. These four are by no means inclusive, but rather serve to indicate the kinds of processes and structures that could be involved when the Emotional code interacts with the rest of the cognitive system.

Interruptions.   Mandler (1975) spent a considerable amount of time discussing Interruptions in his exposition on emotion. He defines interruption as a disruption of an organized and ongoing response. He is very explicit about the emotional quality of such interruptions, and indicates that they cause autonomic arousal. From the current perspective, interruptions can be the cause *and/or* the result of activity in the Emotional code. A strong input into the Emotional code can cause an interrupt and alert the cognitive system that something important is occurring (e.g. hearing one's own name in the cocktail party effect). Further, an interrupt can cause more activity in the Emotional code by frustration or blocking types of behaviors.

Amplification.   A second type of interaction involving the Emotional code is amplification. Here the Emotional code injects extra effort or energy into the cognitive system thereby creating a very embellished cognitive analysis of an emotional stimulus (see Rogers, 1980a for a discussion of this re self-reference).

Diversions. A third form of interaction with the Emotional code can involve attention changes or diversions. Significant activity in the Emotional code can either overload the cognitive system, or cause the cognitive system to divert attention away from a highly emotional input. Anecdotally, the classic ''look away'' response to a gory scene is an example of this kind of activity. This also bears some resemblance to the classic Repression-Sensitization dimension, indicating the potential for a rich theoretical link up.

Cognitive Short-Cuts. A fourth class of Emotional interaction is its involvement in cognitive short-cuts. The idea of intuitive leaps, where a person is unaware of how he arrived at a particular solution, has always been an intriguing and hard-to-explain phenomenon in psychology. One possible approach to this is to suggest that the Emotional code, with all its power and verbal ineptitude, becomes involved in the cognitive process. The portions of the process where the Emotional code is highly active may constitute the phenomenological event of intuition or insight.

Before proceeding to some other data it is important to relate this triple-code structure to some of Paivio's later work. Of particular relevance here is his finding that paired-comparisons judgments of pleasantness are faster for pictures than for words (Paivio, 1978). His interpretation of these findings was: ''the analog information involved in pleasantness ... judgments is more closely associated with the image system than with the verbal system [p. 207].'' In elaborating this he argues that the Verbal and Imaginal systems process information derived from any of the sensory modalities, and that the Imaginal representation includes the affective component. He also suggests that some of the affective attributes are stored as associative information. At first blush, these data and the attending interpretation seem to go against the formulation being presented here. Paivio seems to have chosen to place emotion squarely in the Imaginal system, thereby finessing the need for introducing a third code. However, if the Emotional code is constantly aroused during the pleasantness task—as it is likely to have been—it is possible that the data presented in Paivio (1978) reflect a situation where the Emotional code is active, but not differentially, over the course of the experiment. Hence, these data represent a case where the three codes are active, but with Emotional coding contributing more to the overall levels of performance rather than to some differential aspect of the performance of the paired-comparison task. The issue of whether the affective component is restricted to the Imaginal system will be addressed more fully later in this presentation.

Several other researchers have provided data and arguments that are consonant with the three-code approach. Zajonc (1980) suggests that: ''feeling accompanies all cognitions . . . arises early in the process of registration and retrieval, albeit it weakly and vaguely, and . . . derives from a parallel, separate, and partly independent system in the organism [p. 154].'' He provides a considerable array of data that speak to the independent affective code he posits to be basic to an understanding of ''hot'' cognitions. These data prompt him to consider: ''This review suggests that a separation between affect and cognition may well have a psychological and a biological basis [p. 169].''

One particularly relevant study has come out of Posner's lab in Oregon. Using an impression-formation-type of task, Posner and Snyder (1975) explored affective processing in a tightly controlled chronometric context. Subjects were shown an input display consisting of a person's name and a series of personal adjectives (e.g. James is honest, loyal, mature). All of the adjectives were either of a positive (as in the example) or a negative emotional tone. Following a 2 sec blank interval a probe adjective was presented and the subject had to indicate whether the probe adjective had been in the adjective set just seen. The emotional tone of the probe either matched or mismatched the tone of the adjective set. The number of items in the adjective set was also varied from one through four. Two important results emerged: (1) Reaction time (RT) was faster when the emotional tone of the probe was opposite the stimulus set; (2) Error probability was enhanced with increasing set size for the matching trials only. These data were interpreted by suggesting two independent memory structures, one associated with the adjectives (a la serial memory) and the other with the impression abstracted during the study phase of the experiment. The first structure would be negatively influenced by set size to additional items by loading it up, providing an anology to the Verbal system. The other structure, based on the impression created of the target, represents the abstracted emotional information. This structure was seen as responsible for the matching data. In cases of mismatches between the emotional tone of the adjective set and the probe, the addition of items would enhance certainty about the response, thereby facilitating RT and decreasing errors. This structure is a functional analogue of the Emotional code discussed earlier.

Posner and Snyder (1975) conducted a second study where they were able to verify the predictions from this two-factor formulation. In summing up, they argued that the current data do not substantiate the notion that the Emotional structure is in any way different from higher-order semantic structures, suggesting that: ''evaluations are handled very much like other semantic decisions [p. 80].'' They also noted that Emotional information and its storage is pretty much the same as the findings attending dot patterns. This is particularly interesting in light of the Rogers, Rogers and Kuiper (1979) demonstration of the traditional ''dot pattern'' data configuration for personal adjectives. Although Posner's analysis does not provide distinctive evidence for a separate third code, it does go a long way toward substantiating some aspects of the functional independence of Emotional and Verbal codes. It is clear that further work along the lines of this study would be very useful in further elucidating this aspect of emotion in memory.

Kirker (1981) attacked the Emotional code a bit more directly by designing a procedure that permitted the collection of idiographic ratings of the Affectivity of personal adjectives. These adjectives were used in the incidental recall paradigm, with Structural, Semantic and Self-Referent orienting tasks. It was expected that words rated by the subject as highly affective would produce considerably greater recall, particularly with the Self-Referent task. Surprisingly, the predicted interaction did not emerge. However, the main effect of Affectivity was significant, indicating that the implications of Affectivity generalized across all three rating tasks. In addition, it was found that RT to make the orienting judgment did interact with Rating Task and Affectivity, with the more complex tasks showing faster RTs for the high Affective words. These data suggest that, in this particular context, Affectivity of stimulus words produces a somewhat generalized facilitation reflected in recall scores and RT data. Presumably the high Affective words have a stronger Emotional code, and the results from Kirker (1981) reflect, in part, this increased aspect of the processing environment.

In sum, a review of the work by Zajonc, Posner and Kirker indicates some degree of support for the utility of considering a third code. These data, in no way, make an open-and-shut case for this proposition. Rather they begin to offer a convergent data set *that is compatable with* such a formulation. As cognitive researchers have tended to shy away from considering Emotion in their formulations (see footnote 3 in Zajonc, 1980 for a particularly refreshing demonstration of this), it is not surprising that it is difficult to marshall a strong case for the current proposal.

It seems clear in my review of the literature that there has been a real hesitancy on the part of strongly experimental researchers to come to grips with the Emotional code. This is due, in part, to our desire for mechanistic explanations. In fact, the typical pattern is for researchers to make one or two forays into the area of Emotion and then abandon it (Posner [Posner & Snyder, 1975] is a good case in point). The upshot of this is that there is a paucity of hard-headed (neomentalistic) studies that speak directly to the issues of emotion in cognition. The literature is rife with theories, and occasional demonstrations, but in the main there are very few extensive experimental programs that can be cited in this domain.

Our Metaphors

Although there are a large number of reasons why the study of emotion in cognition has not proceeded apace with other aspects of current work, I believe two reasons are foremost. First, as I will show later, we have tended to underestimate the complexity of the emotional system by taking unidimensional and frequently uni-physiological approaches. Second, I believe we have tended to adopt the wrong metaphors in our scientific fantasies. During those delicate, creative moments when we are trying to make sense our of our data, we often fall back on the wrong analogy, the wrong metaphor, we look to the wrong place for our inspiration.

When I first became involved in psychology at Western I was struck by the way in which the natural sciences seemed to be leading us around by the nose. The natural scientists would invent electricity, the engineers would develop it into something as exciting as the telephone, and *then* we'd come along and (if we were Clark Hull) adopt the switchboard as an explaining metaphor for learning. Kinetic theory, and hydraulics served valiantly as Freud's metaphor. And of course, today the computer has us all seduced into adopting it as the pre-emminent metaphor in current experimental psychology. I don't mean to ridicule the power of the computer metaphor—nor do I intend to devalue the utility of the work that has stemmed from using it—*but* I do wish to ask why we feel so obliged to use inferior machines such as the computer for our metaphor? There is one machine around these days that has the computer beaten—hands down—as far as being an astounding accomplishment. Why don't we use this better machine for our metaphor? The machine I'm referring to is the human body. It makes no sense to me that we should use a creation of the human body such as the computer to model it. Why not use the real McCoy? Why not have a close look at the living computer we all inhabit and use this when we're trying to figure how best to make our science work? With respect to the current presentation, it is very clear that we must abandon the computer metaphor if we hope to make any progress what-so-ever in the understanding of emotion. Computers don't have emotions (with occasional exceptions like Clark's HAL in *2001 A Space Odyssey*), people do. Computers don't have adrenal cortices, or reticular formations, or right hemispheres, people do. And most important, computers don't have rich inner mental lives that direct their behavior and are deeply effected by what we call emotions. The computer, for all its utility, is a very poor candidate for our prevailing metaphor.

In proposing that we use the human body for our metaphor I am not—in the least—suggesting that we all should become physiological psychologists. Nor am I suggesting that we need the presence of a specific physiological structure to validate a theoretical proposition. What I am suggesting is that we should look—quite carefully—at the functional divisions within the human nervous system when we begin to develop our models of human behavior. There is no need to physiologize, but there is a need to pay heed to the machine in which the behavior we are studying unfolds. I am also arguing that even when dealing with ''pure'' cognition, where the computer seems to be so effective a metaphor, we should be spending more time using the human nervous system as our metaphor. It is clear that we have shied away from using the human machine as an anology in the development of our science. Whether this is due to our desire for machinistic explanations, or a curious kind of ethnocentrism (e.g. our accomplishments are so good they are all we need) is irrelevant. What matters is that we have erred in our propensity for avoiding contact with this aspect of the human being.

Perhaps an example would help. Paivio has for some time now drawn a parallel between the Verbal system and the left hemisphere, as well as the converse Imaginal/right hemisphere relationship. His concern for hemispheric function emerged again in the 1978 paper with pleasantness judgments. In these data (described earlier) aspects of the Affective task seemed to reside with the Imagery code, and prompted him to cite some data indicating that affective activity seems to be right hemisphere, as is Imagery, and—apparently—as is affect. Missing in this use of the metaphor is discussion of the intrahemispheric organization, and how it might be part of the dual code system. Several recent authors (e.g. Springer & Deutsch, 1981) have indicated that the current zeitgeist regarding hemispheric research is somewhat misplaced. Both structurally and behaviorally the most impressive feature of cortical function is the intrahemispheric organization. In both hemispheres visual centers are rather far away (in cortical distance) from the "association" areas. Transfer of information from visual to association areas must either pass through verbal and motor areas or move through lower order structures. This suggests some interesting thoughts on how the Verbal and Imaginal codes may interact, with three basic possibilities suggesting themselves: (1) Visual information could pass directly to the frontal lobe (although it would be modulated by quite a few lower structures on its way), (2) it could pass from the occipital areas through Broca's (verbal) area, or (3) it could pass from the occipital area through subcortical structures. There seems to be no reason why *all three* of these patterns couldn't exist, and thereby suggest some interesting extensions for the interaction of verbal and imaginal information. Although the hemispheric differences alluded to by Paivio (1978) are topical and interesting, they figuratively, at least, restrict verbal/imaginal interaction to the corpus callosum, rather than looking to the more salient aspect of cortical organization. This brief discussion has not been intended to be a definitive statement of how to conceptualize the verbal/imaginal interaction. More accurately, the attempt has been to show how looking at even a crude aspect of the physiology of the animal can begin to translate into useful thinking that can be taken into the lab and given thorough testing. This, of course, is exactly what a metaphor should be doing for us.

Emotion and the New Metaphor

With our "new" metaphor in hand, it soon becomes abundantly clear that emotion is going to be an immensely complex topic. Not only are there a number of possible avenues for this input of emotional information to the cognitive system, but also the cognitive system (read cerebral cortex) is overlaid on a complex subcortical system. All of this will have to be considered in developing a model of affect using the "new" metaphor.

For starters, consider the possible avenues through which emotional information can be conveyed to the cognitive system. While there are a number of ways to cut the cake here, I will, for simplicity, only talk about FIVE possible highways. It should be noted that five is considerably more than most theorists in emotion talk about with one being the mode and (roughly) 1.01 being the mean. The five are: (1) autonomic nervous system, (2) reticular formation, (3) subcortical structures, (4) right hemisphere, and (5) left hemisphere.

Autonomic Nervous System (ANS).   A considerable number of thinkers (see Mandler, 1975 for a summary) suggest that ANS arousal represents the totality of emotional expression in the human. There is considerable debate and disagreement currently about the nature of this information when it arrives, but most feel this is the essence of emotional information. All agree that the ANS information is crude, but some suggest that it is differentiated along some basic evaluative lines before contacting the cognitive system (e.g. Bowlby, 1973; Cacioppo & Petty, 1981). Others, in particular Mandler (1975), disagree and suggest that the only thing that arrives at the cognitive site is intensity—totally undifferentiated in terms of evaluation. The evaluation is a function of the cognitive system. In Mandler's view it might be best to characterize ANS arousal as generalized excitement. The jury is still out on this debate, but even if the simpler version is true, the presence of the other four sources of information forces considerable revision into a theory such as Mandler's that assumes that only ANS arousal is indicative of emotion.

Going back as far as the Cannon/Lang controversy brings us to an area that relates, in an important way, to the ANS aspect of emotion. One of Cannons' critiques of James' position was that the ANS was too slow to account for the experience of emotion. It takes from 1 to 2 sec for the autonomic responses to occur, and clearly emotional events are cognized and acted on much faster than that. Mandler had to confront this with his unitary view, and postulated that the speed of emotional processing was actually cognitive. He suggested that the cognitive system receives the information and by association with previous affective experience, a kind of "autonomic imagery" emerges. For a person with a phobia of dogs the concept dog contains affective information, and when the cognitive system identifies a dog this stored affective information is released in the form of an image. This image is sufficient to sustain the emotional experience across the ANS response time lag, thereby explaining the response speed.

There is a much more parsimonious explanation of the speed issue that indicates some difficulty for the unitary view. The ANS is indeed slow, but the marker neurons that are involved in stimulating the system are very fast. There is no reason to believe that these neurons feed only to ANS output sites. In fact, there is evidence that they do indeed enter into the CNS rather rapidly. Thus the speed of emotional information processing could be ANS mediated, but due to neuronal input to the central processor, not to the preception of ANS arousal symptoms. This approach finesses the need to postulate "autonomic imagery" and several other aspects of Mandler's view. Furthermore, autonomic imagery could evolve as the cognitive and emotional data is in the cognitive system concurrently if the cognition persists long enough to accompany the emergence of ANS symptoms.

In sum then, it is unclear whether the ANS input is evaluated before it arrives at the cognitive system. However, it seems certain that there are at least two kinds of ANS input to the cognitive site: (1) The neuronal input from the marker neurons which is fast, and (2) the input from the visceral system that is slow, but an important concommitant of ANS arousal. These latter inputs are those responsible for the subjective experience of emotional states.

Reticular Formation.   The so-called arousal center of the central nervous system has a number of facets that are germane to a theory of emotion. This component of the brain has major involvement in the sleep/awake distinction, as well as being related to attentional variations. Within the Reticular Formation several structures, with most interesting properties, exist. Zajonc (1980) describes the locus coerulus, and its relevance to emotional activity. Raphe's structure, which is more central than locus coeruleus, shows different chemical properties, and is also deeply involved in attention. Both of these structures are rapid and have numerous connections with the upper and lower parts of the central nervous system, which makes them important candidates for our model. It should be stressed here that the Reticular Formation contributes *different* kinds of information to the emotional system than does the ANS. The central point, then, is that looking at the Reticular Formation—even in this most shallow manner—indicates the need for multivariate considerations of emotional input.

Perhaps a more romantic conceptualization of this area of the nervous system is MacLean's (1973) R-complex. Some subcortical areas are included in this region, but the functional distinction is that the phylogenetic properties associated with the reptiles are embedded in the R-complex. Aggressive behavior, territoriality, ritual and social hierarchy behavior are thought to have deep-seated representations here. These kinds of behaviors have clear emotional properties, and are differentiatble from ANS activity—although there will be a meaningful interaction between the two input sources.

Whether one talks in terms of the Reticular Formation or the R-complex the crucial point is that these regions clearly relate to important components of our evolutionary heritage. As such, their involvement in emotion is very strong and should not be overlooked.

Subcortical Structures.   There are a number of structures in the subcortex that have been explicitly linked to emotional behavior. Pre-eminent here is the limbic system, in particular the amygdala. At a very basic level, these structures are responsible for the generation of strong and vivid emotional experience. While attached to the Reticular Formation and having implications for the ANS, the subcortical structures add yet another dimension to the emergence of emotional experience in the intact human.

Right Hemisphere.   As indicated earlier, several theorists have suggested that the usually-mute right hemisphere of the brain is an ideal candidate for the seat of emotion in the human. This link is made not only because of the verbal ineptitude of both the emotional system and right hemisphere, suggesting a kinship, but also because of some data suggesting emotional deficits with some types of right hemisphere damage. For example, Heilman, Scholes & Watson (1975) found right hemisphere patients were very poor at judging the mood of a speaker compared to left hemishpere patients. More directly, Kolb, Taylor and Milner (1980) found right hemisphere patients were very poor at matching facial photographs to emotions. These, and other data, suggest that the right hemisphere is involved with processing the emotional tone of meaningful stimuli. Combined with other data suggesting that the right hemisphere is implicated in musical perception and processing, recognition of faces and a number of other "affect-laden" tasks, it is possible to make a strong case for its involvement in emotion. The important point is whether the right hemisphere is the *sole* cortical seat of emotion.

Left Hemisphere.   It seems clear that the left hemisphere is not as extensively involved in emotional behavior as the right. But it is involved. The primary involvement relates to the literal analysis of the emotional experience. In a way, this is similar to the definition of affect (in contrast to emotion) given earlier, wherein affect is seen as the postcognitive experience of emotion. The left hemisphere is deeply implicated in this aspect of emotional experience.

Of particular pertinence to our model is the manner in which the left hemisphere "bullies" the entire cognitive system into thinking that it is the only focus of activity. It is as though the left hemisphere over-writes all the activity of the other systems in an effort to gain credit for their actions. The demonstration that most effectively speaks to this is Gazzaniga's celebrated interrogation of Paul's right hemisphere (Gazzaniga, Le Doux & Wilson, 1977; Le Doux, Wilson & Gazzaniga, 1977). Because of early damage, Paul had developed some language capability in his right hemisphere before having his corpus callosum cut to alleviate epilepsy. Like most split brain patients he was able to perform simultaneous picture matching tasks when targets were presented separately to the two visual fields (hence to the separate hemispheres), using the lateral hands to indicate the conceptual match to the target. In one example the left hemisphere was presented a chicken's foot, and with his right hand Paul indicated a picture of a chicken from a set of four available pictures. Simultaneously he indicated (with his left hand) a picture of a snow shovel that matched the picture of a snow scene presented to his right hemisphere. Apart from his ability to perform this task with no apparent problem, the most interesting aspects of this demonstration were Paul's explanations of why he had chosen the particular pictures. When asked why his right hand was pointing to the chicken he very correctly indicated that it matched the foot that had been shown him. However, when asked why his left hand was indicating the shovel he gave a highly confabulated response relating to the use of the shovel to clean out the chicken coop. The reason for selecting the shovel (being related to the snow scene) was apparently unavailable to Paul, so the dominant left hemisphere system made up a seemingly reasonable explanation. This kind of "bullying" seems to be a characteristic of the left hemisphere, and probably is a key to some of the problems that have been plaguing emotion researchers for years.

For the emotion theorist, it is clear that emotional experience is very undifferentiated, vague, and hard to verbalize. I submit that the dominant left hemisphere system, as with Paul, moves in and offers a confabulated (seemingly reasonable) interpretation of the internalized emotional events. Whereas in most cases these confabulations may indeed be accurate, there can be numerous times when they are very much off the mark. The important thing is that the cognitive system *believes* them to be correct, in the same way that Paul was positive that the shovel was for use in the chicken coop. This indicates that the left hemisphere has a highly important—and amazingly complex—role in the emotional system. Efforts to suggest that emotion resides in the right hemisphere are clearly incorrect from this view. In fact, it seems as though the left hemisphere is a focal key in understanding emotional experience as it can send out numerous false alarms and incorrect interpretations of internal events.

Integrating the Emotional Inputs

The foregoing indicates that there are multiple avenues for the entrance of emotional information into the cognitive system. The ANS, Reticular Formation, Subcortex, Left and Right Hemisphere all have significant involvement in emotional experience, and each of these avenues provide input into the central processing of the emotional event. Undoubtably, while there is considerable redundancy and time-frame stability among the five avenues, the review suggests that a significant amount of variation in the signals—as they arrive at the cognitive stage—is possible. Presumably the cognitive system is able to integrate and differentiate these various signals, and thereby glean significant amounts of information from the emotional data as it arrives. This formulation is a far cry from Mandler's idea that a single, unidimensional response is the emotional input to the cognitive system. Rather, the argument here is that subtle variations in the patterning and intensity of the various inputs convey very important information to the cognitive system. Whether this is best conceptualized as "primitive evaluative information" (à la Bowlby (1973)) is not answerable at this time. It is quite possible that a new form of calculus will be necessary to describe and determine the nuances of this multiple input. For now, the important thing is that the Emotional code as we've talked about it before, needs to be considered in a multivariate framework. The day of simple, unidimensional approaches to emotion seems to be coming to a close.

The next issue is now the Emotional information interacts with the Verbal/ Imagery or cognitive systems. A detailed explication of the numerous possibilities here is clearly beyond the scope of this chapter. However, one major point must be made in this context. Without doubt, the Emotional code can have impact *at any point in the information processing stream*. Using the traditional macro-model of information processing, the Emotional code can inject input at any point between (and including) sensory registration and responding. Further, the effects can be interactive with other codes *and* highly disruptive to the total system (see Interrupts above). Involvement of emotion early in the processing sequence could relate to the various vigilance phenomena that have plagued theorists for some time now (e.g., Erdelyi, 1974). Emotion in the various encoding stages can cause various kinds of biases and "blind spots" in pattern recognition and attention processes. Once into short-term memory (and consciousness) the affective component can have any number of effects ranging from contributing to a rich inner phenomenology through perception of a slight blush. Emotionality can touch on rehearsal process and the movement of information into Long-Term Memory in any number of ways—some of which have been mentioned earlier in this chapter. Once in long-term memory the representation retains an aspect of the emotional and affective qualities aroused during input and storage, and these can serve as an aspect of the semantic network thought to underly our memory system. And finally, involvement of affect during responding can be highly complex, acting as an "energizer" or "inhibitor" and entering into various kinds of cybernetic loops with any of the three codes. Even this hand-waving summary gives a sense of the complexity—and richness—that attends the insertion of emotion and affect into the cognitive system.

Some Concluding Remarks

Let's return now to the 1966 conversation with Al in the Rotunda. How did we fare back then, compared to what seems to be going on in the area? As far as adding to the two codes is concerned, Paivio's published work does not seem to have moved in that direction. Zajonc (1980) has made the Emotional code suggestion, but, not unlike the present paper was stumped for definitive data— although he presented a most persuasive case. We still await the detailed and hard-nosed experimental program addressing this issue.

Back in 1966 we felt that emotion should be included in our models—the current review (along with Zajonc, 1980, and others) indicates that we haven't made a lot of progress along these lines. In this chapter I tried to pinpoint some of the reasons this might be so, and want to redraw your attention to the metaphor argument offered earlier. I found it most difficult to integrate the five-sided emotional input into the macro-model of information processing. The macro-model is computer-based. I believe that a significant portion of the difficulty I encountered in trying to integrate emotion in the present formulation rests with the cognitive model. The computer-based model does not have the flexibility or potential for handling something as complex as affective processes. Being as it is—left hemisphere—it is certain that significant revisions to the macro model will be forced as we zero to on affective processes. As above, hopefully a physiological or neurophyschological metaphor will guide this activity.

As far as the possibility of looking at emotion as a "third code" is concerned the present chapter uses this idea as a convenience for entering several issues. The utility of thinking in triplicate comes from sensitizing us to the pervasive effects of emotion throughout the entire cognitive system. It is most useful as a short-hand or cognitive convenience. I hold little hope, however, for a triple-coding hypothesis surviving rigorous empirical test. This reservation comes from the physiological metaphor, which tells us most clearly that information does not enter the system in nicely packaged bundles with three types of addresses on them. The work on memory doesn't hold great promise for some kind of triple-storage nodes either. Although this may be tempered by the emotion-phobia shown by some memory theorists, there doesn't seem to be an emerging ground swell for the inclusion of a third aspect at the storage nodes of current semantic memory models. (In fact, it seems they aren't that impressed with two—let alone three.)

What does seem to have been realized from the 1966 conversation is the emergence of the idea that emotion seems to play by a different set of rules compared to the Imagery and Verbal systems. I think that aspects of this chapter, Zajonc (1980), Mandler (1975) and some of the more recent work on emotion are converging quite rapidly on the relization that it will be necessary to rewrite the law books when we start to look at affect. What isn't certain is the time frame attending the realization of the need for this rewriting enterprise. For me, I hope it is sooner than later, and I sincerely hope that it will be based on an appropriate metaphor—the human nervous system.

REFERENCES

Abelson, R. P. Computer simulation of "hot" cognitions. In S. Tompkins & S. Messick (Eds.), *Computer simulation of personality.* New York: Wiley, 1963.

Aboud, F. Self-referent memory for concrete and abstract personal adjectives. Paper presented at Canadian Psychological Association meetings, Calgary, June 1980.

Argyle, M., Salter, V., Nicholson, H., Williams, M., & Burgess, P. The communication of inferior and superior attitudes by verbal and nonverbal signals. *British Journal of Social and Clinical Psychology*, 1970, *9*, 222-231.

Bower, G. H., & Gilligan, S. G. Remembering information related to one's self. *Journal of Research in Personality*, 1979, *13*, 420-432.

Bowlby, J. *Attachment and loss* (Vol. II). *Separation*. London: Hogarth Press, 1973.

Cacioppo, J. T., & Petty, R. E. Electromyograms as measures of extent and affectivity of information processing. *American Psychologist*, 1981, *36*, 441-456.

Craik, F. I. M., & Tulving, E. Depth of processing and the retention of words in episodic memory. *Journal of Experimental Psychology: General*, 1975, *104*, 268-294.

Davis, H. Self-reference and the encoding of personal information in depression. *Cognitive Therapy and Research*, 1979, *3*, 97-110.

Drever, J. *A dictionary of psychology*. Harmandsworth, B. B.: Penguin, 1952.

Erdelyi, M. H. A new look at the New Look: Perceptual defense and vigilance. *Psychological Review*, 1974, *81*, 1-25.

Gazzaniga, M. S., Le Doux, J. E., & Wilson, D. H. Language, praxis, and the right hemisphere: Clues to some mechanisms of consciousness. *Neurology*, 1977, *27*, 1144-1147.

Heilman, K., Scholes, M. R., & Watson, R. T. Auditory affective agnosia. *Journal of Neurology, Neurosurgery and Psychiatry*, 1975, *38*, 69-72.

Hull, J. G., & Levy, A. S. The organizational functions of the self: An alternative view to the Duval & Wicklund model of self-awareness. *Journal of Personality and Social Psychology*, 1979, *37*, 756-768.

Jackson, D. N. *Manual for the Personality Research Form*. Goshen, N.Y.: Research Psychologists Press, 1967.

Keenan, J. M., & Baillet, S. D. Memory for personally and socially significant events. In R. S. Nickerson (Ed.), *Attention and performance VIII*. Hillsdale, N.J.: Lawrence Erlbaum Assoc., 1980.

Kendzierski, D. Self-schemata and scripts: The recall of self-referent and scriptal information. *Personality and Social Psychology Bulletin*, 1980, *6*, 23-29.

Kirker, W. S. *Self-reference and emotion*. Unpublished master's thesis, University of Calgary, 1981.

Kolb, B., Taylor, L., & Milner, B. *Affective behavior in patients with localized cortical excisions: An analysis of lesion site and side*. Unpublished manuscript, 1980.

Kuiper, N. A., & Derry, P. A. The self as a cognitive prototype: An application to person perception and depression. In N. Cantor & J. F. Kihlstrom (Eds.), *Personality, cognition and social interaction*. Hillsdale, N.J.: Lawrence Erlbaum Assoc., 1981.

Kuiper, N. A., & Rogers, T. B. The encoding of personal information: Self-other differences. *Journal of Personality and Social Psychology*, 1979, *37*, 499-514.

Le Doux, J. E., Wilson, D. H., & Gazzaniga, M. S. A divided mind: Observations on the conscious properties of the separated hemispheres. *Annals of Neurology*, 1977, *2*, 417-421.

MacLean, P. D. *Triune concept of the brain and behaviour*. Toronto: University of Toronto Press, 1973.

Mandler, G. *Mind and emotion*. New York: Wiley, 1975.

Merriam, G. *Webster's Seventh New Collegiate Dictionary*. Toronto, Ont.: Allen, 1961.

Neisser, U. *Cognition and reality*. San Francisco: Freeman, 1976.

Paivio, A. Mental comparisons involving abstract attributes. *Memory & Cognition*, 1978, *6*, 199-208.

Posner, M., & Snyder, C. R. R. Attention and cognitive control. In R. L. Solso (Ed.), *Information processing and cognition*. New York: Wiley, 1975.

Rogers, T. B. A model of the self as an aspect of the human information processing system. In N. Cantor & J. Kihlstrom (Eds.), *Cognition, social interaction and personality*. Hillsdale, N.J.: Lawrence Erlbaum Assoc., 1980. (a)

Rogers, T. B. Models of man: The beauty and/or the beast. *Personality and Social Psychology Bulletin*, 1980, *6*, 582–590. (b)

Rogers, T. B., Kuiper, N. A., & Kirker, W. S. Self-reference and the encoding of personal information. *Journal of Personality and Social Psychology*, 1977, *35*, 677–688.

Rogers, T. B., Kuiper, N. A., & Rogers, P. J. Symbolic distance and congruity effects for paired comparisons judgements of degree of self-reference. *Journal of Research in Personality*, 1979, *13*, 433–449.

Rogers, T. B., & Rogers, P. J. *The self-referent memory enhancement as a function of age.* Unpublished manuscript, Calgary, 1981.

Rogers, T. B., Rogers, P. J., & Kuiper, N. A. Evidence for the self as a cognitive prototype: The "false alarms effect." *Personality and Social Psychology Bulletin*, 1979, *5*, 53–56.

Schachter, S., & Singer, J. Cognitive, social and physiological determinants of emotional state. *Psychological Review*, 1962, *65*, 379–399.

Springer, S. P., & Deutsch, G. *Left brain, right brain.* San Francisco: Freeman, 1981.

Tversky, A., & Kahneman, D. Availability: A heuristic for judging frequency and probability. *Cognitive Psychology*, 1973, *5*, 207–232.

Zajonc, R. B. Feeling and thinking: Preferences need no inferences. *American Psychologist*, 1980, *35*, 151–175.

14 The Empirical Case for Dual Coding*

Allan Paivio
University of Western Ontario

This seems an appropriate occasion for me to try to evaluate the current status of dual-coding theory. First, I review some relevant developments in imagery research and dual-coding theory since the publication of *Imagery and verbal processes* in 1971. I then assess the explanatory and heuristic value of the theory by summarizing the critical findings that have been predicted or explained by it, as well as those observations that are problematic for the theory. Finally, I identify some of the directions that theoretical development should take in light of the current factual knowledge in the area.

Developments Since 1971

There have been important developments over the last decade in virtually every area of research and theory that was covered in *Imagery and verbal processes*. We have new factual knowledge on such problems as the effects of the imagery value of items, imagery mnemonic instructions, pictures as compared to words in memory and other cognitive tasks, and so on. New methodological paradigms have also been invented and old ones refined. For example, Shepard's elegant experimental work on mental rotations and other transformations (reviewed in Shepard, 1978) had only begun at the time my book was published, so its impact on the field has occurred since that time. Another important advance was Moyer's (1973) reactivation of the symbolic comparisons procedure, which led to theoretically-relevant extensions of that approach in our own work and that of many others. A third innovation has been the development of various operational

*The author's research reported in this chapter was supported by grants (A0087) from the Natural Sciences and Engineering Research Council of Canada.

307

approaches to the measurement of integration of information in images and linguistic ideas. These empirical developments do not exhaust the list but they are representative of the more important ones. The notable theoretical developments include the increased general emphasis on analog representations; Kosslyn's (1980) development of a detailed theory of the structure and function of conscious mental imagery and the debate on the nature of the cognitive representations that underlie imagery and verbal phenomena, which is really a contemporary version of an old controversy, to which I return presently.

The changes are matched by the remarkable stability of many basic facts and issues. The earliest empirical conclusions concerning effects of imagery variables are completely valid today. A prominent example is the memorability of high-imagery items in various tasks, including their special potency as retrieval cues. No other attribute has yet been identified that has displaced imagery-concreteness empirically or provided a superior base for a theoretical explanation. The same conclusion is true of mnemonic instructions, which remain among the most potent procedures for augmenting verbal memory.

The most striking example of persistent theoretical issues is the debate concerning propositions and images as representations (e.g., Anderson, 1978; Kieras, 1978; Kolers & Smythe, 1979; Kosslyn & Pomerantz, 1977; Paivio, 1977; Pylyshyn, 1973). This closely parallels the opposition of verbal mediation to imagery and dual coding, which was one of the focal issues throughout the 1960s. The proponents of verbal mediation argued that a single mediating process suffices to explain the data and, that this process is essentially linguistic in nature. This traditional approach contrasted with the dual-coding emphasis on the mediating role of nonverbal images as well as verbal processes. Today, propositions are analogous to verbal mediators in their structural and functional properties. The main difference seems to be that propositions are assumed to be more abstract and amodal than the sentences they resemble. More generally, the proposition-imagery debate continues a dialectic that began at least as early as the 16th century in the work of Peter Ramus, who rejected imagery mnemonics in favor of a logical, lauguage-based method called "dialectical order." Those historical events are reviewed in more detail elsewhere (Paivio, 1977).

What about developments in the dual-coding approach itself? Most of the ideas I presented in 1971 still seem valid to me, although I have tried to express them more explicitly and precisely. This stability could be interpreted as conceptual rigidity, but I hope to show later that the basic assumptions are justified and reinforced by the accumulating empirical data. At the same time, there are some disquieting facts that must be considered. I get into that empirical review after summarizing the main assumption of dual-coding theory, with special emphasis on the recent modifications.

The main assumption still is that cognition consists largely of the activity of two partly interconnected but functionally independent and distinct symbolic systems. Partial interconnectedness was assumed from the outset, as reflected in research on imagery reactions to words and labeling reactions to pictures. These mirror-image responses are possible only if an association exists between representations corresponding to the verbal and nonverbal events. The incompleteness of the interconnections is revealed by the fact that the verbal and imaginal responses occur less readily to some classes of stimuli than others. For example, it is more difficult to image to abstract than concrete words. The independence assumption led to a search for additive effects of codes, as in the free-recall studies done with various collaborators (e.g., Paivio & Csapo, 1973; Paivio, Rogers, & Smythe, 1968), and experiments using the free-recall repetition-lag paradigm (Paivio, 1975a) to investigate directly the statistical independence of repeated pictures and words as well as instructionally-induced imaginal and verbal codings in memory.

Functional differences are also retained in the model. The earlier contrast (Paivio, 1971, Ch. 2) was between parallel and sequential processing capacities of imagery and verbal systems. More recently (e.g., Paivio, 1975b, 1978b), I have preferred to express the distinction in terms of synchronous and sequential processes, correlated with the contrast between analog and discrete representations. The idea of integration or unitization of information (Paivio, 1971, Ch. 3) also remains essentially the same in that visual images are assumed to be organized hierarchically in the manner of a visual nested set, so that smaller parts are embedded within larger ones, and structures at each level of complexity are functionally integrated for some purposes but separable for others. Memories of familiar structures such as faces and living rooms, for example, seem to have such properties. Conversely, the verbal system can be described in terms of symbolic representations that are functionally organized in a sequential or serial fashion. Those sequential verbal structures can also be functionally integrated in the sense that George Miller emphasized in 1956. For example, up to some limit, words of different length function as units in such tasks as memory span. The simple generalization, then, is that both nonverbal and verbal representational units are integrated, although the internal structure of the units differs. This implies that there are different constraints on the processing of the components of verbal and nonverbal compound representations, as well as differences in the ease with which new integrated structures can be cognitively constructed.

Another aspect of dual coding that has been only slightly modified is the analysis of the functional relations between different representational units, which I discussed in 1971 (Ch. 3) in terms of levels of meaning. The representational level refers to the relations between perceptual stimuli and their corresponding representations in the two symbolic systems. The referential level refers to relations between imaginal and verbal representations. The associative level refers to relations between units within each system. The last statement is a change toward descriptive consistency, since my earlier statement referred to the associative level as involving elaborative associations both within and between systems. It seems more appropriate now to restrict the conception to relations between representational units within each system and to describe more complex elaborative processing as a combination of referential and associative reactions. I have also adopted, rather timidly, a new terminological practice of referring to the representational units of the two systems as *logogens* and *imagens* (e.g., Paivio, 1978d; Paivio & Begg, 1981). The former corresponds in principle but not in detail to Morton's (1969) concept of the logogen, and the imagen is its nonverbal counterpart. Others have independently proposed concepts similar to the imagen, namely, *iconogen* (Attneave, 1974) and *pictogen* (Morton, 1979).

There is also no reason to modify the operational or empirical aspect of the dual-coding approach. I suggested originally that three general classes of empirical indicators or operations encompass the procedures used in the study of inner processes, including attributes of stimulus material, various experimental manipulations, and individual difference variables. These are used systematically to affect the probability of imaginal or verbal processes being involved in a given task. The three classes of empirical procedures are viewed as convergent operations with respect to the theoretical constructs, although even in 1971 I recognized the complexity of such an enterprise and the apparent lack of convergence of different operational indicators with respect to the concept of imagery. In particular, individual difference measures all too often seemed to stand apart from the other two. There is more consistency in some recent findings (see following), but the search for convergence remains a problem. At the same time, a systematic operational approach is essential in this area as in others that are based on inferred processes of whatever kind.

The clearest example of a specific advance in the dual-coding model is its recent extension to bilingual memory (Paivio & Desrochers, 1980). The principle assumptions of the unilingual dual-coding model are retained in the bilingual version, but the overall elaboration and new assumptions related to direct interverbal connections between two linguistic systems have important new implications that we have only begun to explore. I describe one set of results predicted from the bilingual model in the next section, in which I evaluate the factual evidence for and against dual coding.

EMPIRICAL EVIDENCE

It is generally accepted in science that an explanatory theory must have generality and integrative value. In addition, it should be predictive and heuristic if there are to be advances in knowledge. It is most important therefore to evaluate the dual-coding approach in terms of empirical criteria, and to compare it on those criteria against other approaches. I have done this in several articles (e.g., Paivio, 1977, 1978b), as have others (e.g., Kieras, 1978; Kosslyn & Pomerantz, 1977).

The empirical reviews have generally been selective and incomplete, however, especially on the part of the critics of imagery and dual coding. Pylyshyn (1973), for example, did not discuss any of the effects of imagery variables, saying that he did not dispute the observations. Instead, his arguments against mental imagery were primarily on logical grounds. He has concerned himself more recently (e.g., Pylyshyn, 1981) with mental rotations and some of the observations reported by Kosslyn, but these represent a very small proportion of the relevant data that are available. Similarly, John Anderson (1978) described some experimental findings that he felt were inconclusive and dismissed earlier ones on the grounds that reliance on such data is waning. To support the last contention, he cited only picture-word differences in memory tasks, suggesting that "further evidence has indicated that the pictorial material is not superior to verbal material. First of all, verbal material when 'deeply processed' can display similar high levels of memory. . . . Second, the good memory for pictorial material only seems to apply when that pictorial material can be meaningfully interpreted [p. 259]." However, he did not discuss several important qualifications of picture-word effects on memory, nor what exactly is meant by deep processing or meaningful interpretation. For example, could these involve imaginal or verbal elaborative processing quite in keeping with dual-coding theory (see Madigan, this volume)? Moreover, a wide range of facts related to concreteness effects, mnemonic instructions, and so on are missing from the review. So, there seems to be a need for a systematic review of the entire set of early and recent findings that are relevant to the current theoretical dispute.

The review shows that it is an unequal contest when it comes to empirical criteria. Dual coding and imagery based theories generally account for a wide range of findings, which cannot be handled by abstract descriptive approaches except by the addition of *post hoc* assumptions with each new turn in the data. Moreover, the imagery based theories have been productive in generating new observations, whereas proponents of the descriptive approach have mainly reacted to the data and the explanations produced by the imagery researchers. In other words, the vast majority of relevant facts that have fascinated propositional and imagery researchers alike have been generated by the latter.

Positive Evidence

I have identified about 60 reliable empirical findings of various levels of generality that are consistent with and often were generated by dual-coding theory. These facts are difficult for propositional theories to handle inasmuch as they all point to two or more kinds of modality specific information in long-term memory, whereas the propositional approaches assume a single, amodal representational base. The classes of findings include effects of item concreteness or imagery value, pictures as compared to words as stimuli, imagery instructions in various tasks, reaction time functions in such tasks as mental comparisons and figural transformations of various kinds, modality specific interference, perceptual and memory comparisons, effects of individual differences in spatial and verbal abilities, and functional differences in the two cerebral hemispheres.

TABLE 14.1
Positive Evidence for Dual Coding
(2 = Evidence for Independent codes; Q = Evidence for Qualitative
Distinctions)

Imagery-concreteness Effects of Language

2Q   1. Concrete > Abstract in item memory tasks (PAL, FR, VDL, etc.)

Q   2. C vs A effect reduced in sequential memory tasks (IMS, etc.)

2Q   3. Stimulus (retrieval cue) C effect > Responce C effect in PAL ("conceptual-peg")

2Q   4. C > A in secondary memory, effect reduced or absent in primary memory

      5. C = A in perceptual recognition

Q   6. Recall increment from FR to cued recall greater for C than A

Q   7. Recall is integrated for C phrases but not A phrases

Q   8. More synonym intrusions for C than A during recall

Q   9. Incremental effect of synonym repetitions on recall greater for C than A

Q   10. Higher associative overlap for C than A synonym pairs

2Q 11. Image RT increases with abstractness, verbal associative RT does *not*

Q   12. Sentence construction faster for sets of C than A words

Picture versus Word Effects

2Q 13. P > W in item memory tasks

Q   14. P > W reduced in sequential memory tasks

2Q 15. P > W difference greater on stimulus than R side in PAL

Q   16. Integrated (interactive) P pairs > separated Ps in PAL

2Q 17. P + W (P name) repetition effect is additive in FR (= independence)

2   18. Transfer of learning between P and W, when referential coding relevant

Q   19. Sentence construction faster for sets of P than W units

2   20. Naming RT faster for W than P

Effects of Coding Instructions

2   21. PAL higher under imagery than verbal or rote instructions with C items

Q   22. PAL higher under integrated than separated imagery

Q   23. FR to Cued R increment greater for integrated than Sep. Im.

2Q 24. W = P in incidental FR under imagery instructions

2Q 25. Imagery + Verbal codings have additive effect in FR

Q   26. Imagery + Verbal codings > bilingual coding in FR

2   27. Imaginal and Verbal codes can be independently forgotten (?)

Q Symbolic Comparisons

     28. Symbolic distance effect

     29. (a) Comparison RT faster for P than W for some concrete attributes

         (b) Comparison RT faster for W than P for linguistic attributes

         (c) P = W RT for associative relatedness judgments

     30. Stroop-like conflict for size-incongruent P but not W pairs

     31. Reversal of conflict with relative distance judgments

     32. Size comparison RT not affected by category membership

     33. Comparison RT affected by associative frequency of referents

Q Perception-Imagery Functional Similarities

     34. Functional isomorphism between perceived and imagined objects (shapes, colors, etc.)

     35. Appropriate preparatory image facilitates speed + accuracy of discriminative R to stimulus

     36. RT functions for spatially localized probes comparable for perceived and imagined figures

37. Takes longer to "see" properties of smaller than larger imaged objects
38. Image scanning time varies directly with distance
39. Larger objects "overflow" sooner than smaller ones when imaged as approaching
40. Acuity of visual imagery decreases toward periphery
41. Magnitude estimation functions are similar for perceptual and imaged objects

Q Mental Rotations
42. RT functions for mental rotations, especially for verbally-evoked images
43. Rotation rate relatively unaffected by stimulus complexity
44. Illusion of apparent movement in rotating images

Q Modality-specific Interference
45. Spatial task interferes with visual image processing
46. Interaction of reading *vs* listening × memory for spatial *vs* nonsense messages
47. Spatial *vs* verbal memory task × comprehension of C *vs* A sentences
48. Verification of C sentences selectively interferes with pattern memory
49. Tracking selectively interferes with imagery mnemonic effectiveness
50. Imagery selectively interferes with detection of perceptual signals in same modality

Individual Differences
2 51. Imagery and verbal abilities are factorially independent
Q 52. Imagery ability > verbal ability as predictor of mental comparison RT for attributes that also show P faster than W
Q 53. Imagery ability correlates with memory performance in some relevant tasks (e.g., incidental PAL)

Q Neuropsychological Evidence
54. LH *vs* RH temporal lobe lesions: verbal *vs* nonverbal memory disruption
55. RH (temporal) lesions disrupt image-mediated concrete word PAL but not sentence-mediated abstract word PAL
56. Imagery ability × materials × visual field interaction in perceptual recog.
57. LH > RH in perceptual recog. of A but not C words (?)

Q Subjective Report Data
58. Imagery reported with C-word PAL: verbal + rote with A-word PAL
59. Imagery recall associated with R recall in image-mediated delayed recall
60. Imagery reported as preceding word recall under imagery instructions

The specific findings are listed under relevant headings in Table 14.1. I comment briefly on some of these, with particular attention to their relevance to the theoretical debate. Several general features should be noted at the outset: First, a relatively small set of theoretical assumptions suffice to account for a wide range of independent phenomena. Second, these dual-coding assumptions sometimes predict specific changes and even reversals of effects as a function of task conditions. And finally, different classes of variables often produce parallel effects, presumably because the variables converge on the same underlying process. Some findings are consistent with the quantitative implications (e.g., additivity) of having the two independent coding systems (identified in Table 14.1 by the numeral 2, for dual coding); others are consistent with qualitative (modality-specific or structural) distinctions (identified by the letter Q); still others implicate both quantitative and qualitative distinctions simultaneously (2Q).

Imagery-concreteness Effects.   The effects of word imagery-concreteness in memory tasks are among the most familiar of the listed findings. It has been repeatedly shown that concrete materials are generally remembered better than abstract materials. These findings are consistent with the dual-coding idea that concrete items more easily evoke imagery than do abstract items, and that the imaginal representations serve as a supplementary memory code for item retrieval. We were concerned from the outset with the possibility that the effects could be explained in terms of some other confounding attribute. By 1971, more than 20 alternatives had been ruled out, but additional possibilities have been proposed from time to time. For example, Anderson and Bower (1973) suggested that the differences could be due to the greater number of dictionary meanings or the greater lexical complexity of abstract words, either of which might create uncertainty and confusion, hence poorer recall of abstract than concrete words. Neither interpretation stood up to empirical tests (e.g., Peterson & McGee, 1974; Richardson 1980), nor has any other attribute yet succeeded in accounting for the positive effect of word imagery, although some show independent relations with memory scores for items. It was once thought that concreteness itself might have some independent predictive value, but the chief proponent of this view, John Richardson (1980), recently concluded that the conventional imagery interpretation is probably correct in the case of memory tasks. Thus, imagery value remains the best single predictor of memorability of items within the range of meaningful verbal material.

The theoretically-relevant effects go beyond the simple generalization that high-imagery concrete items are remembered better than abstract ones. Some of the variations are as follows: First, the generalization is correct for item-memory tasks, such as free recall, recognition memory, and paired associates, but the effect is reduced or absent in sequential memory tasks such as immediate memory span. This differential effect on item and order memory was predicted from the dual-coding assumption that sequential information is more efficiently stored in the verbal system, whereas item information can be stored in both imaginal and verbal form (Paivio & Csapo, 1969). Second, the effect in paired-associate learning is greater among stimulus terms than response terms, or, to be more consistent with current terminology, the imagery value of the retrieval cue is particularly important. This was the first major finding in my research program and it was predicted from the conceptual peg hypothesis. A third qualification is that the concreteness effect holds for long term or secondary memory tasks and does so less strongly or not all for short term or primary memory tasks (e.g., Bleasdale, 1978; [Richardson,] 1976). The effect also appears to be absent in perceptual recognition, as O'Neill and I [Paivio & O'Neill,] 1970) expected on theoretical grounds, although the possibility remains that concreteness may interact with visual field when presentation is lateralized to one hemifield or the other. I return to this point later.

Table 14.1 lists a number of other predicted variations on the concreteness effect, such as the recall increment from free to cued recall being greater for concrete than abstract items, differences in associative overlap and recall for concrete and abstract synonyms, evidence for greater integration of concrete than abstract phrases, and so on, for a total of about 12 independent effects.

The important theoretical point is that all of these effects are consistent with dual-coding theory while at the same time straining the explanatory capacity of current propositional theories. Consider for example the suggestion by Anderson and Bower (1973) that the positive effects of concreteness in memory tasks might be explained in terms of a greater number of auxiliary propositions that are available in the case of concrete material. This *post hoc* hypothesis would not account for the interactions of concreteness with various task conditions. Moreover, it could just as easily generate the prediction that there should be more interference among concrete items than abstract in associative learning tasks, in a manner paralleling the interference paradox of meaningfulness that was a source of theoretical frustration in the early 1960s. In any case, the auxiliary propositions hypothesis has no independent empirical support.

Pictures Versus Words. Despite the operational distinctiveness of the two procedures, comparisons of pictures and words yield effects that are similar in many important respects to those described above for high- and low-imagery words. Thus, pictures are easier to remember than words in item memory tasks but not in tasks requiring immediate memory for item order, the facilitating effect of pictures is greater when they serve as retrieval cues than as responses, and pictures and words have additive (statistically independent) effects in free recall. These findings, although logically independent of verbal concreteness effects, are nonetheless consistent with predictions from the independence assumption of dual-coding theory and the added empirical generalization that the image code (generated in this case by pictures) is mnemonically superior to the verbal code (Paivio & Csapo, 1973). Other supportive findings include better associative recall of pictures than words, faster construction of sentences from pictures than words using two or more items, and faster naming latencies to printed words than to pictures. These findings are related theoretically to the synchronous versus sequential organizational properties of imaginal and verbal information, and the idea that representational responding (naming words) is more direct than referential responding (naming pictures) because the latter required a "crossover" between systems.

Effects of Coding Instructions. The effects of stimulus materials are matched by a series of conceptually related (though operationally distinct) effects of imagery and verbal coding instructions in memory tasks. The general superiority of imagery mnemonics over rote repetition and, at least sometimes, verbal mediation conditions in paired associate learning (Paivio, 1971, Ch. 12) is consistent with the idea that imagery instructions are relatively more likely to engage the powerful organizational properties of the image system along with additive effects of dual coding in the verbal learning task. The superiority of integrated over separated imagery instructions in associative learning (Bower, 1970; Rowe & Paivio, 1971) directly confirms the organizational hypothesis, as does the corollary finding that the increment from free to cued recall is greater under integrated than separated imagery instructions (Begg, 1973). Code independence is supported by the observation that imagery instructions wipe out the superiority of pictures over words in free recall under incidental conditions, and by the additive effect of image and verbal coding of repeated items in free recall (Paivio, 1975a). Also consistent with independence is the suggestive observation of differential forgetting of imaginal and verbal mediators used in associative memory tasks (Yuille, 1973).

A related but independent extension is our recent finding (Paivio & Lambert, 1981) that imaginal-verbal dual coding results in much higher recall than bilingual coding in incidental free recall. This finding is particularly interesting because the evidence suggests that both kinds of dual coding are additive in their effects and that the higher recall for imaginal-verbal dual coding therefore must be due to the mnemonic superiority of the image code over the second linguistic code.

Could the effects that I have reviewed so far be explained in terms of levels of processing or some semantic processing model other than dual coding, as John Anderson (1978) and others have suggested? The levels of processing approach suffers at the outset from its circularity (e.g., see Baddeley, 1978). This is specifically relevant to our bilingual memory data in that there are no a priori grounds for assuming that the tasks of naming pictures and imaging to words are any deeper than translating French words into English or vice versa, although the former tasks result in better recall. Even leaving that criticism aside, however, and relying entirely on the rule-of-thumb definitions of depth used by Craik and Tulving (1975), D'Agostino, O'Neill, and I (1977) showed that the effects of different processing operations applied to pictures, concrete words, and abstract words produced results more consistent with dual coding than with a levels approach that does not capitalize theoretically on the distinction between verbal and nonverbal memory codes.

The other semantic processing alternatives refer to models that include some kind of abstract semantic system, as distinct from the modality - specific imaginal and verbal systems that are the basis of semantic processing within dual-coding theory. For example, imaging to words is clearly a semantic task according to dual coding. Now, it is also true that some other semantic tasks, such as judging the pleasantness of words, can increase recall as much as imagery instructions (Paivio, 1978c), but this is not damaging to dual coding because the model does not suggest that only visual image or verbal elaboration can modify item recall. The criticism would be telling only if it could be shown that the other semantic variables can entirely account for the effects of variables identified most directly with dual coding. This has not yet been done.

I turn next to a series of findings bearing on qualitative distinctions, with particular attention to the modality-specific, analog properties of images.

Symbolic Comparisons. The symbolic comparison task has produced a number of critical findings. Recall that this task requires subjects to choose between stimuli according to their values on some symbolic attribute. For example, subjects might be asked to indicate which of two named animals is larger in real life (e.g., Moyer, 1973). One basic finding is that it takes less time to make the comparison as the difference on the compared attribute increases. The continuous nature of this *symbolic distance effect* (Moyer & Bayer, 1976) suggests that subjects are responding on the basis of analog representations of some kind. Thus the data are consistent with such theories as dual coding, which assume that cognitive representations are perceptual analogs of the objects they represent. However, the evidence is inconclusive because the effect can also be predicted from some verbal associative and propositional models.

The following results provide stronger support for the analog interpretation and dual-coding theory in particular. One critical contrast is that the reaction time for comparisons is faster with pictures than with words in the case of size and certain other attributes that are closely associated with the perceptual referents themselves, whereas reaction times are faster with words than with pictures when the comparison is on an intrinsic attribute verbal stimuli, such as pronounceability or frequency of usage (e.g., Paivio, 1975c, 1980). These contrasting findings follow directly from the basic assumptions of dual-coding theory, but each must be handled separately and in a *post hoc* fashion by propositional models. Thus, propositional theorists (e.g., Banks, 1977) account for picture superiority effects in reaction time tasks by suggesting that both pictures and words use a common semantic memory system, which is accessed more rapidly from pictures than words. The fact that sometimes the comparisons are faster with words than pictures would presumably require a further *ad hoc* analysis. Dual coding not only predicts both findings, it also suggests that pictures and words might not differ in some tasks because the relevant information is redundantly represented in imaginal and verbal systems. For example, associative relations are assumed to be dually represented because of contiguities of experiences involving objects and their verbal labels. John te Linde (Chapter 5 in this volume) in fact obtained equivalent reaction times for pictures and words using a variant of the symbolic comparison task in which subjects judged the degree to which items are associates of each other.

The next two findings are particularly strong evidence that mental comparisons are based on modality-specific representations. First, a Stroop-like conflict occurs between perceptual and symbolic information when the relative sizes of two pictured objects is incongruent with their real-life sizes (Paivio, 1975c)—for example, it takes longer to decide that a *zebra* is larger than a *lamp* when the items are presented as pictures showing the zebra smaller than the lamp than when the size relationship is congruent. Second, that function is reversed when subjects are asked to decide which pictured object appears to be further away; that is, the incongruent condition is now faster than the congruent one. The conflict and its reversal were both predicted from dual-coding theory on the assumption that size is represented in memory in an analog fashion and that such information will therefore interact with perceptual information in relevant tasks. Banks (1977) was able to provide a *post hoc* interpretation of the conflict in terms of his semantic coding model, but he did not discuss the reversed function when subjects judged relative distance. I can only infer that the latter finding could not be accomodated by Banks' model without further modification.

Dual coding is further supported by an additive effect of perceptual and symbolic information in a clock comparison task (Paivio, 1978a). Subjects are required to compare the sizes of the angles formed by the hands of two clocks when the clock times are presented either digitally or as analog clocks. The comparisons are of course faster for two analog than for two digital times, because the former simply require a perceptual judgment. The critical finding is that the reaction time is intermediate for the mixed case in which one clock is analog and the other digital. Dual-coding theory predicts this finding on the assumption that only the digital time needs to be transformed into analog form to complete the task. I can't see how propositional theories would predict that effect. In fact, Banks' (1977) analysis of a conceptually-related study leads to the reverse prediction that the two digital times would be faster than the mixed case.

Other relevant findings from comparison tasks are listed in Table 14.1, but they are less crucial theoretically than the ones already discussed because they are consistent with some semantic network models of long-term memory as well as dual coding. I turn now to some other findings that bear on the perceptual analog hypothesis of mental imagery.

Functional Similarities Between Perception and Imagery.   This section includes findings by Shepard, Kosslyn, and others, which seem to demonstrate strong functional equivalence of perception and imagery. Shepard's (1978) concept of second-order isomorphism refers to similarity in the functional relations among objects when they are perceived as compared to when they are imagined, as determined by the analysis of similarity rating data. The general finding was that the similarity data were statistically indistinguishable between the perceptual and imagery conditions for such objects as two-dimensional shapes, spectral colors, printed names, familiar faces, and musical sounds. Multidimensional analyses indicated further that, in both conditions, subjects based their judgments on the physical properties of the objects—irregularity and other dimensions for shapes, hue for colors, and so on.

Another paradigm used by Shepard and his colleagues is the reaction time to respond discriminatively to a test stimulus when the subject has or has not formed a preparatory visual image of the stimulus. The studies of Shepard and Metzler (1971) with perspective views of three-dimensional objects and Cooper's (1975) work with random polygons are examples of the paradigm. The typical result is that the discriminative response (for example, whether a numeral is correctly oriented or a mirror image) is fast and accurate when the preparatory image is appropriate, but considerably slower when no image or an inappropriate image has been formed.

Podgorny and Shepard (1978) demonstrated the comparability of imagery and perception even more directly using reaction times to spatially localized probes. A subject is shown a grid with a figure, such as a block letter F, or simply imagines such a figure on a blank grid. One or more small colored dots are presented and the subject must indicate whether or not at least one dot falls on the portion of the grid defined as figure. One result was that reaction time was only slightly slower (50 msec on the average) under the imagery than the perceptual condition. Also, error rates in both conditions were low, reaction times showed no consistent dependence on the position of the probe within the grid, off-figure responses in both cases decreased in reaction time with the distance of the probed square from the figural portion of the grid, and so on. I have not tried to list all of the specific findings using this paradigm and I simply conclude that all are consistent with the idea that the subject is responding to the same kind of information under perceptual and imagery conditions.

Kosslyn and his colleagues (see Kosslyn, 1981; Kosslyn, Pinker, Smith, & Schwartz, 1979) have similarly provided evidence of perceptual-like functional properties of visual images. The following four observations appear to be relatively independent of each other:

1. More time is required to "see" properties of smaller than of larger images;
2. image scanning time varies directly with the distance between points in a spatial image;
3. larger objects "overflow" sooner than small ones when the subject is asked to imagine the object approaching the viewer; and
4. the acuity of visual imagery decreases toward the periphery of the visual field, much as in visual perception.

Kosslyn has obtained a number of other interesting findings but they seem to be either predictable from the above or from other theoretical assumptions, so I have not included them here. Pylyshyn (1981) has criticized findings like Kosslyn's on the grounds that subjects have "tacit knowledge" of what happens to perceptual stimuli under conditions analogous to those described in the imagery instructions and that they adjust their responses accordingly. This is a plausible interpretation of some findings but experimental support for it is generally lacking and Kosslyn (1981) has been able to provide strong counterarguments.

A final relevant observation in this category is that recent studies of memory psychophysics by Kerst and Howard (1978), using magnitude estimation, have revealed similar functions for symbolic and perceptual stimuli, except that they differ in terms of the exponent of the power function. Kerst and Howard did not use imagery instructions nor did they obtain other evidence on the use of imagery in the task, but the findings are nonetheless consistent with the dual-coding interpretation that the judgments are based on imagens activated by the names of objects.

Mental Rotations. The results of mental rotation studies generally provide support for analog models, although Anderson (1978) and others have argued that propositional (computational) models could also account for the effect. The argument is plausible in the case of perceptual stimuli, as in the original study by Shepard and Metzler (1971). A propositional account is more difficult in the case of the rotation function for comparisons of imaged and perceptual stimuli in the Cooper and Shepard (1973) study, in which subjects were asked to image a letter or number and to rotate it through a series of 45° angles to the verbal cues "tip, tip" etc. The absence of a stimulus complexity effect, up to a certain degree of complexity, is also consistent with analog representations and difficult for propositional approaches. Robins' and Shepard's (1977) experimental demonstration of an illusion of apparent movement in rotating images, that is, evidence that the mental image moves through locations in space, is also powerful support for an imagery model and difficult for propositional models.

Modality-specific Interference. When a perceptual task selectively disrupts performance on a concurrent mental task or vice versa, it is generally accepted as evidence that common processing systems are involved. Dual coding is specifically supported by double selective interference between verbal (perceptual and mental) tasks on the one hand, and two nonverbal tasks on the other. Such effects were demonstrated in the now-classic studies by Brooks (1967, 1968), and numerous investigators have subsequently explored different variants of the basic problem. Successful demonstrations of such effects pose grave difficulties for propositional theories, which assume that mental tasks use amodal processing systems. However, the reliability and interpretation of the crucial effects are currently in dispute. Richardson (1980) noted that the findings are inconsistent in regard to interference between spatial tasks and memory tasks that are presumed to involve visual imagery. For example, Baddeley, Grant, Wight, and Thomson (1974) showed that a visual tracking task selectively intefered with memory performance under imagery mnemonic instructions but not with memory for concrete (as compared to abstract) items (cf. Warren, 1977). Richardson also argued that Brooks' experiments lacked certain important controls. Despite the inconsistency, however, there is enough positive evidence to conclude that some kind of selective interference can be demonstrated between perceptual and mental tasks. But what is the basis of the effect when it occurs? Some results (summarized in Richardson, 1980, p. 57) suggest that, in the case of the Brooks type task, the disruption involves a spatial processing system rather than a visual one. This argument is not damaging to dual coding, however, because visual imagery is assumed to include spatial information as an essential component. I have therefore included Brooks' findings in Table 14.1 as reliable examples of selective interference.

Other supporting findings have thus far avoided even the above criticisms. The Stroop-like conflict with size-incongruent pairs, already described in the section on symbolic comparisons, is equally relevant here as a demonstration of selective interference between perceptual and symbolic information processing. Table 14.1 lists a number of other observations that are logically independent from each other in that they involve different classes of independent or dependent variables, or differ in whether the direction of the interference is from perceptual to mental tasks or vice versa. Segal and Fusella (1970) showed that visual imagery interferes more with the detection of visual than auditory signals, whereas auditory imagery interfered relatively more with the detection of auditory signals, thereby demonstrating that imagery is modality specific and not amodal. Several investigators (e.g., Pellegrino, Siegal, & Dhawan, 1975; Warren, 1977) have found that verbal and nonverbal distracting tasks selectively interfere with memory for words and pictures in a manner consistent with dual-coding theory. The effectiveness of different mnemonic techniques is similarly disrupted by appropriate perceptual-motor tasks. Saltz and Nolan (1981) reported one of the most informative studies of this kind because it systematically compared the effects of visual, motoric, and verbal competition tasks on memory for sentences learned with the aid of visual imagery, motoric enactment, or verbal-only instructions. The results clearly showed that sentence recall was disrupted when the competition task and mnemonic technique matched (e.g., motoric competition and motoric imagery) but not when they differed.

Finally, some researchers have obtained theoretically-appropriate selective interference effects using concrete and abstract verbal materials. Janssen (1976) demonstrated such effects in recall of word lists. Klee and Eysenck (1973) showed that the comprehension of high-imagery sentences was selectively disrupted by a concurrent visual spatial memory task whereas abstract sentences were more disrupted by a verbal task. Glass, Eddy, and Schwanenflugel (1980) showed a converse effect: verification of high imagery sentences selectively interfered with memory for patterns. The precise limiting conditions for such effects remain to be determined, but the evidence as a whole again favors continuity between imagery and perception as well as the distinction between verbal and nonverbal symbolic modalities.

Individual Differences. This section deals with individual difference data that bear on the theoretical issues. Dual-coding theory is supported by the general observation that verbal abilities are factorially independent of imaginal and spatial abilities. This pattern showed up in Guilford's (1967) factor analytic research on his structure-of-the-intellect model. Our own work and that of others (e.g., Di Vesta, Ingersoll, & Sunshine, 1971; Forisha, 1975) has demonstrated such independence specifically for the most commonly used measures of imagery and verbal abilities. Although generally more variable in the literature, predictions of performance on relevant experimental tasks sometimes are consistent with theory. For example, we have recently found that relevant individual difference variables predict reaction time in mental comparison tasks (Paivio, in press). Clock comparisons in particular are nicely predicted by a battery of spatial and imagery ability tests but not by tests of verbal ability (Paivio, 1978a).

It is noteworthy, too, that the imagery ability tests correlate with reaction times in those tasks that also show faster comparison times with pictures than with words as stimuli (size, value, pleasantness), but not ones in which comparisons are faster with words than pictures (name frequency and pronounceability) or in which words and pictures do not differ (brightness and hue) (Paivio, in press). Thus, we find nice convergent evidence from the symbolic comparisons paradigm for dual-coding constructs using all three classes of operational approaches, that is, item attributes, experimental manipulations, and indiviual difference variables. Carole Ernest (1977), Ronald Finke (1980), and others have found similar predictive success for relevant individual difference tests.

Functional Differences Between the Cerebral Hemispheres. We have neuropsychological evidence that the two halves of the brain differ in the efficiency with which they can process verbal and nonverbal material, as revealed particularly by the well-known work of Brenda Milner (e.g., 1980) and her colleagues. Jones-Gottman and Milner (1978) recently extended the research to encompass imagery variables by showing that right temporal lobe lesions specifically affected the learning of imagery-linked concrete word pairs but not sentence linked abstract pairs. Concreteness has also been found to interact with visual field, so that right visual field (presumably left hemisphere) presentation results in superior tachistoscopic recognition of abstract words, but no hemispheric difference occurs in the recognition of concrete words (e.g., Day, 1977; Ellis & Shepherd, 1974; Hines, 1977). However, I am somewhat doubtful about the reliability of that finding because some researchers, including Brian O'Neill and I, have failed to obtain the interaction. Also in need of replication is the interaction that Carole Ernest and I (Paivio & Ernest, 1971) obtained between spatial ability, field of presentation, and materials: letters were generally recognized more accurately in the right field; pictures were correctly recognized better by high imagery than low imagery subjects, and geometric forms yielded an interaction so that high imagers showed a slight left-field superiority and low imagers showed a substantial right-field superiority. Even allowing for the tentativeness of some of the facts, however, the neuropsychological observations are generally consistent with the dual-coding idea of two separate cognitive systems that are specialized for dealing with different classes of information in a modality-specific fashion.

Subjective reports.   Finally, post-experimental subjective reports of learning strategies provide further convergent evidence for a functional distinction between imagery and verbal mediational processes in associative recall (see Paivio, 1971; Richardson, 1980). First, subjects report a "preference" for using imagery mediators with concrete (high imagery) pairs, whereas they prefer verbal or rote learning strategies with abstract pairs. Second, frequency of reported use of imagery correlates highly with recall of concrete words but not abstract words. Third, correct recall of a mediating image is associated with correct response recall under imagery instructions (Yuille, 1973), and image recall can precede verbal recall (May & Clayton, 1973). The subjective reports are not decisive in themselves, but when considered together with the experimental data, they provide compelling evidence for dual coding effects in verbal memory.

Negative Evidence

I now turn to evidence that presents difficulties for dual-coding theory. Three kinds of negative evidence appear in the literature. One consists of pseudonegative findings that are in fact based on misinterpretations of dual coding. A second group includes failures to find significant differences between conditions that should have produced differences according to predictions from dual-coding theory. Such findings can be taken as support for propositional models or, less generously, as failure to reject the null hypothesis. A third set of findings include differences that are not predicted by dual coding theory as it was initially formulated, but also are not consistent with propositional models.

The pseudonegative findings include ones that are simply oversights. For example, some studies have indicated that picture naming is not automatic and this was taken to be contrary to the dual-coding model of picture processing. In fact, automaticity was never claimed; instead picture naming like imaging to words was said to be probabilistic and modifiable by various experimental conditions, such as instructional sets (see Paivio, 1971, pp. 179–180).

Another example concerns the abstract functional characteristics of the verbal system. My statements on this have been interpreted by some to mean that tasks requiring processing of general information are verbal. Thus, for example, category decisions should be faster with words than pictures, contrary to what is found in experiments. However, the inference is not necessarily correct. General terms like furniture and insect are rated high on concreteness and imagery. Moreover, two possibilities were discussed in *Imagery and verbal processes* in regard to how general information might be represented in imagery. One is by a grouping of category instances, whereby a general category like fruit might be imaged as a basket containing different kinds of fruit. The other is representation of abstract information by schematic or symbolic images. Since then, studies published by Rosch (1975) and by Anderson and McGaw (1973) have provided empirical evidence that generic information might be represented in the form of nonverbal exemplars or prototypes.

Other examples involve incomplete interpretation of aspects of dual-coding theory. Thus, failing to find significant correlations between naming latency and memory for pictures, even at slow presentation rates, Intraub (1979) concluded that, "contrary to the dual-coding prediction, implicit naming apparently was not responsible for the improvement in picture memory at slower rates [p. 78]." The conclusion should be qualified because Intraub used free recall and recognition memory tasks whereas Kal Csapo and I had expected and obtained the biggest effects of rate of presentation in sequential memory tasks. It is nonetheless correct that I would have expected some interaction between rate and naming latency even in item memory tasks, so Intraub's negative findings remain somewhat embarrassing for the dual-coding model.

The second group of studies present greater difficulties for dual-coding theory. These involve failures to find picture-word differences where they would be theoretically expected. For example, Potter, Valian, and Faulconer (1977) required their subjects to decide whether a picture or a word probe was related in meaning to an immediately preceding sentence. They found no difference in response times to the two kinds of stimuli. The times tended to be faster to drawings than words in the case of high-imagery sentences whereas the reverse was true for low-imagery sentences, but this tantalizing interaction did not approach significance.

Guenther (1980) similarly required subjects to decide whether picture or sentence probes were true or false of some previously studied picture and prose episodes. True probes depicted events that were either explicitly or only implicitly part of one of the episodes. The results showed that response times to explicit probes were faster when they were in the same modality (picture or prose) as their episodes than when they were in the opposite modality, but response times to implicit probes did not differ for same and opposite conditions. Guenther interpreted these results to mean that conceptual memory is identical for pictorial and prose episodes and, moreover, that the conceptual memory is represented in an abstract form.

The data are generally consistent with Guenther's interpretation but other explanations are also possible. The sentences, like the pictures, depicted concrete episodes. Accordingly, subjects could easily image the events in the prose episodes and may have been prompted to do so by the fact that presentation conditions were mixed, so that picture episodes and prose episodes occurred alternately. Thus the conceptual memory may have been the same for all episodes, but imagistic rather than abstract in form. Alternatively, the mixed presentation may have encouraged subjects to verbalize to pictures and image to sentences, thereby resulting in dual coding of each episode. Either interpretation could account for the equivalence of picture and sentence probes under the implicit condition. The imagery interpretation is favored by the fact that response times were generally faster to picture than to sentence probes, but this could simply mean that reading time for sentence probes was longer than perceptual processing time for picture probes. In any case Guether's findings do not rule out a dual-coding interpretation.

The following observation is more troublesome for dual coding. John te Linde and I found that the reaction time to compare objects mentally on either brightness or hue did not differ for pictures and words. This was unexpected from a dual-coding viewpoint because color, being a perceptual attribute of things, should be more closely associated with imaginal than verbal representation in long-term memory. We were able to rationalize the findings because other behavioral and neuropsychological data have independently shown that color is a somewhat anomalous attribute but the precise nature of that anomaly remains to be determined.

Similarly problematic are the cases where concrete and abstract verbal material fail to differ in tasks where differences were expected. One of the most telling observations was the repeated failure by Marschark and myself (Marshark & Paivio, 1977) to demonstrate greater integration of memory for concrete than abstract sentences, although overall memory scores were always better for the concrete sentences. The latter is a common finding completely in accord with the dual-coding model, but the equivalent integration of what is remembered from concrete and abstract sentences seems to require an additional, amodal coding system. To date, we have not been able to come up with a more satisfactory specific interpretation. I will nonetheless continue to seek interpretations consistent with the basic assumptions of dual-coding theory because it is unparsimonious to postulate a third system unless it is absolutely compelling to do so. I don't believe that there is enough negative evidence to warrant such a modification at this time, particularly in light of the far greater range and number of successful predictions from dual-coding theory.

The final set of problematic findings include picture-word and other differences that were not predictable from dual-coding theory but which at the same time were inconsistent with common coding models. One is the finding of faster symbolic comparisons with pictures than with words and with concrete than with abstract words even in the case of such abstract attributes as pleasantness, monetary value, and animal ferocity (Kerst & Howard, 1978; Paivio, 1978c). I have suggested that the attributes in question, although abstract in the sense that they are less consistently correlated with specific perceptual attributes than is the case for more concrete concepts, nonetheless represent attributes of things and are therefore stored in the imagery system or at least in close association with the core representations of such things. The nature of the "core" is, of course, problematic in itself, although I did suggest that it might be patterned after the prototypical shape or form of the perceptual objects (cf. Rosch, 1975). Other associated attributes, such as pleasantness, might involve stored proprioceptive or interoceptive information that can vary in a continuous fashion and constitute the representational base for comparisons (but see Zajonc, 1980, for an alternative interpretation).

Another troublesome observation concerns picture-word transfer effects in the comparison task. Marschark and I (Paivio & Marschark, 1980) serendipitously obtained asymmetrical transfer effects with intelligence and pleasantness comparisons when subjects first completed a block of trials with one kind of material and then switched to comparisons of the same concept pairs with the other type of material. Switching from pictures to words appeared to have a negative effect whereas switching from words to pictures had a positive effect on subsequent reaction times. Marschark, te Linde, and I have pursued the problem in a series of unpublished experiments, with some surprising results. First, to explore the generality of the apparent transfer effect, we studied it with the attributes of size and brightness. These are interesting because both are concrete dimensions but differ in terms of the initial picture-word differences. That is, size comparisons are reliably faster with pictures than with words whereas brightness judgments do not differ. What we found was essentially no specific transfer in the case of size or brightness. That is, when materials were switched it is as though the subjects were starting the task from scratch. This was confirmed by the fact that the pattern of results was essentially the same when subjects were given completely new pairs along with the switch in materials.

These findings are puzzling because both dual coding and single code models would lead one to expect some positive transfer when materials are switched. In the case of dual coding, the assumption is that comparisons on such dimensions as size are based on information in the image system, which is accessed more directly by pictures than words. In the case of common code theories, the assumption is that both pictures and words access the same amodal representational system that contains the information on which the comparisons are based. Thus, even if we assume that switching materials is essentially like starting from scratch as far as encoding is concerned, we would nonetheless expect some positive transfer at the comparison stage. This apparently did not occur with the concrete dimensions of size and brightness.

We then explored the transfer problem in more detail with the more abstract dimensions of intelligence and pleasantness. Here we did find some evidence of concept-specific transfer, most clearly revealed by faster reaction times for conditions in which materials were switched with the same concept pairs than in the condition in which both materials and concepts were switched. Moreover, the differential effect seemed to be greatest when switching from words to pictures, at least in the case of intelligence. Assuming that encoding problems after the switch are equivalent for the experimental and control groups, it appears that the effect is attributable to comparison processes. The finding is consistent with the dual-coding interpretation that the image system has some priority in the task, since pictures had the advantage over words at least on posttransfer trials.

A final critical result occurred in John te Linde's study (see Chapter 5, this volume) of the effect of picture-word manipulations in judgments of associative relatedness of pairs of items. The original dual-coding position was that associative relations between concrete concepts are represented in both verbal and image systems. This implies that associative decisions could be equally fast for picture pairs and word pairs, which in fact was the case. The unexpected result, however, was that the decisions were just as fast with mixed picture-word pairs, which presumably would require the additional step of recoding one concept into the format of the other if associative relations are only represented within but not across systems. The results would seem to be more consistent with propositional models, which assume that associations are represented at an abstract conceptual level. However, the absence of picture-word differences is also troublesome for propositional theorists (e.g., Banks, 1977; Friedman & Bourne, 1976) who have suggested that the abstract representational system is more readily accessed from pictures than words. In addition, the te Linde finding may have limited theoretical generality in view of the fact that we now have results from an unpublished experiment showing that judgments of relatedness with picture-word pairs were faster when the pair members were referentially related (picture-name pairs) than when they were associatively related (a picture paired with the primary verbal associate of its name). This finding, which is described in more detail by te Linde (this volume), confirmed a simple prediction from the dual-coding model. These theoretically-contrasting observations remain to be resolved.

Theoretical Prospects

In this final section I briefly consider the kinds of theoretical developments that seem necessary to accomodate the anomalous findings, or are desirable for other reasons. I have argued that the dual-coding approach is supported by a wide variety of different findings whereas relatively few findings are inconsistent with it. Thus it would be unreasonable to abandon the dual-coding approach unless it can be replaced with a more general model that is capable of accomodating both the positive and negative observations within a single framework. It could be argued that propositional approaches are sufficiently general and flexible to do the job. In fact, they seem to have limited predictive power because they can only handle such findings as the differential effect of materials by constant recourse to *post hoc* assumptions that map onto those differences. Some propositional theorists (e.g., Anderson, 1978; Kieras, 1978) have sought to avoid that problem by distinguishing between perceptual and linguistic propositions, so that a propositional approach would account for exactly the same range of findings as dual-coding theory. The two approaches would then become indistinguishable because the propositional model would simply be a conceptual variant or paraphrase of dual coding. It seems to me, then, that the real challenge to dual-coding theory is the more specific one of explaining the discrepant findings in terms that are consistent with the general assumptions of the model, including the associationistic principles on which it is essentially founded.

One general possibility is to increase the emphasis on the variety and the strength of interconnections between imaginal and verbal systems in a way that would account for the absence of picture-word differences under some experimental conditions. Te Linde suggested such a possibility to account for his finding that association decisions were just as fast for mixed picture-word pairs as for homogeneous pairs. He proposed that connections between symbolic systems might occur at the associative level of meaning in addition to the referential level, so that the representation of, say, a mouse in the verbal system may be directly linked to the representation of cheese in the nonverbal system. By itself, however, this assumption would not explain the faster confirmation of referentially related than associatively related picture-word pairs in our unpublished experiment. Some additional assumption, such as variation in the associative strength as well as directness of different types of connections may be required. Speculations of that kind are gratuitous in the absence of relevant data and I shall not pursue them further here. The general point is that dual-coding theory may require additional assumptions if it is to account for differences in picture-word effects that result from relatively small procedural variations using the same experimental paradigm.

It would also be desirable for some purposes to elaborate on the theoretical details of the dual-coding model. I had already suggested this requirement in 1971 in relation to such problems as the modality-specific nature of verbal representations. Thus, I proposed (Paivio, 1971) that

> When the verbal representational process is activated by a visual rather than an auditory verbal stimulus, we must assume that intermodal association is involved. An auditory-motor verbal representation is already available in the case of the auditorily familiar word, and an association develops with a visual-word image (or visual representations of lower order units, such as letters and syllables) as the child acquires the grapheme-to-phoneme transformational skill involved in reading [p. 56].

Note that this statement anticipated later developments in Morton's (1969) conception of logogen as a word representation. Morton originally thought of the logogen as amodal in the sense that its excitatory potential would be augmented by visual or auditory word stimuli, as well as via the semantic system. More recently, however, Morton (1979) found that stimulus pretraining lowered tachistoscopic recognition thresholds for words only when the pretraining and target stimuli were in the same modality, but not when they were different. This led him to propose different logogens for different input modalities. His most recent version of the model in fact includes not only modality-specific input logogens but output logogens as well. Moreover, following Seymour's (1973) suggestion, he assumes separate representations ("pictogens") for pictorial stimuli. At the general level, these ideas are similar to the dual coding distinction between word representations (logogens) and nonverbal representations (imagens).

The details of the organizational structures of units within systems and of the processes involved in transforming or rearranging these structural units also require elaboration. For example, the verbal system must function according to syntactic principles of some kind, and these will need to be incorporated into the model. Thus far, I have simply assumed that associative processes play an important role in grammatical behavior along with whatever constructive process underlies the generative aspects of grammar. I have also assumed, like others in recent years, that nonverbal processes play an important role in grammatical behavior, so a detailed theoretical statement becomes especially difficult because it would need to distinguish between linguistic and nonlinguistic contributions to grammatical performance. Some general suggestions have been made (e.g., Paivio & Begg, 1981, Ch. 4), but no one has yet come up with a detailed hybrid model of that kind.

REFERENCES

Anderson, R. C., & McGaw, B. On the representation of meaning of general terms. *Journal of Experimental Psychology*, 1973, *101*, 301–306.

Anderson, J. R. Arguments concerning representations for mental imagery. *Psychological Review*, 1978, *85*, 249–277.

Anderson, J. R., & Bower, G. H. *Human associative memory*. Washington, D.C.: Winston, 1973.

Attneave, F. How do you know? *American Psychologist*, 1974, *29*, 493–499.

Baddeley, A. D. The trouble with levels: A reexamination of Craik and Lockhart's framework for memory research. *Psychological Review*, 1978, *85*, 139–152.

Baddeley, A. D., Grant, S., Wight, E., & Thomson, N. Imagery and visual working memory. In P. M. A. Rabbitt & S. Dornic (Eds.), *Attention and performance V*. London: Academic Press, 1974.

Banks, W. P. Encoding and processing of symbolic information in comparative judgments. In G. H. Bower (Ed.), *The psychology of learning and motivation*. Vol. 11, New York: Academic Press, 1977.

Begg, I. Imagery and integration in the recall of words. *Canadian Journal of Psychology*, 1973, *27*, 159–167.

Bleasdale, F. *Concreteness and imagery in long- and short-term recall*. Unpublished Ph.D. thesis, University of Western Ontario, 1978.

Bower, G. H. Imagery as a relational organizer in associative learning. *Journal of Verbal Learning and Verbal Behavior*, 1970, *9*, 529–533.

Brooks, L. R. The suppression of visualization in reading. *The Quarterly Journal of Experimental Psychology*, 1967, *19*, 289–299.

Brooks, L. R. Spatial and verbal components of the act of recall. *Canadian Journal of Psychology,* 1968, *22,* 349–368.

Cooper, L. A. Mental rotation of random two-dimensional shapes. *Cognitive Psychology,* 1975, *7,* 20–43.

Cooper, L. A., & Shepard, R. N. Chronometric studies of the rotation of mental images. In W. G. Chase (Ed.), *Visual information processing.* New York: Academic Press, 1973.

Craik, F. I. M., & Tulving, E. Depth of processing and the retention of words in episodic memory. *Journal of Experimental Psychology: General,* 1975, *104,* 268–294.

D'Agostino, P. R., O'Neill, B. J., & Paivio, A. Memory for pictures and words as a function of processing: Depth or dual coding? *Memory & Cognition,* 1977, *5,* 252–256.

Day, J. Right-hemisphere language processing in normal right-handers. *Journal of Experimental Psychology: Human Perception and Performance,* 1977, *3,* 518–528.

Di Vesta, F. J., Ingersoll, G., & Sunshine, P. A factor analysis of imagery tests. *Journal of Verbal Learning and Verbal Behavior,* 1971, *10,* 471–479.

Ellis, H. D., & Shepherd, J. W. Recognition of abstract and concrete words presented in the left and right visual fields. *Journal of Experimental Psychology,* 1974, *103,* 1035–1036.

Ernest, C. H. Imagery ability and cognition: A critical review. *Journal of Mental Imagery,* 1977, *1,* 181–216.

Finke, R. A. Levels of equivalence in imagery and perception. *Psychological Review,* 1980, *87,* 113–132.

Forisha, B. D. Mental imagery verbal processes. A developmental study. *Developmental Psychology,* 1975, *11,* 259–267.

Friedman, A., & Bourne, L. E., Jr. Encoding the levels of information in pictures and words. *Journal of Experimental Psychology: General,* 1976, *105,* 169–190.

Glass, A. L., Eddy, J. K., & Schwanenflugel, P. J. The verification of high and low imagery sentences. *Journal of Experimental Psychology: Human Learning and Memory,* 1980, *6,* 692–704.

Guenther, R. K. Conceptual memory for pictures and prose episodes. *Memory & Cognition,* 1980, *8,* 563–572.

Guilford, J. P. *The nature of human intelligence.* New York: McGraw-Hill, 1967.

Hines, D. Differences in tachistoscopic recognition between abstract and concrete words as a function of visual half-field and frequency. *Cortex,* 1977, *13,* 66–73.

Intraub, H. The role of implicit naming in pictorial encoding. *Journal of Experimental Psychology: Human Learning and Memory,* 1979, *5,* 78–87.

Janssen, W. H. Selective interference in paired-associate and free recall learning: Messing up the image. *Acta Psychologica,* 1976, *40,* 35–48.

Jones-Gottman, M., & Milner, B. Right temporal lobe contribution to image-mediated memory. *Neuropsychologia,* 1978, *16,* 61–71.

Kerst, S. M., & Howard, J. H., Jr. Memory psychophysics for visual area and length. *Memory & Cognition,* 1978, *6,* 327–335.

Kieras, D. Beyond pictures and words: Alternative information-processing models for imagery effects in verbal memory. *Psychological Bulletin,* 1978, *85,* 532–554.

Klee, H., & Eysenck, M. W. Comprehension of abstract and concrete sentences. *Journal of Verbal Learning and Verbal Behavior,* 1973, *12,* 522–529.

Kolers, P. A., & Smythe, W. E. Images, symbols, and skills. *Canadian Journal of Psychology,* 1979, *33,* 158–184.

Kosslyn, S. M. *Image and mind.* Cambridge, Mass.: Harvard University Press, 1980.

Kosslyn, S. M. The medium and the message in mental imagery: A theory. *Psychological Review,* 1981, *88,* 46–66.

Kosslyn, S. M., Pinker, S., Smith, G. E., & Schwartz, S. P. On the demystification of mental imagery. *The Behavioral and Brain Sciences,* 1979, *2,* 535–581.

Kosslyn, S. M., & Pomerantz, J. R. Imagery, propositions, and the form of internal representations. *Cognitive Psychology*, 1977, *9*, 52–76.

Marschark, M., & Paivio, A. Integrative processing of concrete and abstract sentences. *Journal of Verbal Learning and Verbal Behavior*, 1977, *16*, 217–231.

May, J. E., & Clayton, K. N. Imaginal processes during the attempt to recall names. *Journal of Verbal Learning and Verbal Behavior*, 1973, *12*, 683–688.

Miller, G. A. The magical number seven, plus or minus two. *Psychological Review*, 1956, *63*, 81–97.

Milner, B. Complementary functional specializations of the human cerebral hemispheres. In R. Levi-Montalcini (Ed.), *Nerve cells, transmitters and behaviour*. Vatican City: Pontificia Academia Scientiarum, 1980.

Morton, J. Interaction of information in word recognition. *Psychological Review*, 1969, *76*, 165–178.

Morton, J. Facilitation in word recognition: Experiments causing change in the logogen model. In P. A. Kolers, M. Wrolstead, & H. Bouma (Eds.), *Processing of visible language*, Vol. I. New York: Plenum, 1979.

Moyer, R. S. Comparing objects in memory: Evidence suggesting an internal psycophysics. *Perception & Psychophysics*, 1973, *13*, 180–184.

Moyer, R. S., & Bayer, R. H. Mental comparisons and the symbolic distance effect. *Cognitive Psychology*, 1976, *8*, 228–246.

Paivio, A. *Imagery and verbal processes*. New York: Holt, Rinehart, and Winston, 1971. [Reprinted by Lawrence Erlbaum Associates, Hillsdale, N.J., 1979.]

Paivio, A. Coding distinctions and repetition effects in memory. In G. H. Bower (Ed.), *The psychology of learning and motivation*. Vol. 9, New York: Academic Press, 1975. (a)

Paivio, A. Imagery and synchronic thinking. *Canadian Psychological Review*, 1975, *16*, 147–163. (b)

Paivio, A. Perceptual comparisons through the mind's eye. *Memory & Cognition*, 1975, *3*, 635–647. (c)

Paivio, A. Images, propositions, and knowledge. In J. M. Nicholas (Ed.), *Images, perception, and knowledge*. The Western Ontario Series in the Philosophy of Science. Dordrecht: Reidel, 1977.

Paivio, A. Comparisons of mental clocks. *Journal of Experimental Psychology: Human Perception and Performance*, 1978, *4*, 61–71. (a)

Paivio, A. Dual coding: Theoretical issues and empirical evidence. In J. M. Scandura & C. J. Brainerd (Eds.), *Structural/process models of complex human behavior*. Leiden: Nordhoff, 1978. (b)

Paivio, A. Mental comparisons involving abstract attributes. *Memory & Cognition*, 1978, *6*, 199–208. (c)

Paivio, A. The relationship between verbal and perceptual codes. In E. C. Carterette & M. P. Friedman (Eds.), *Handbook of perception. Vol. IX: Perceptual processing*. New York: Academic Press, 1978. (d)

Paivio, A. On weighing things in your mind. In P. W. Jusezyk & R. W. Klein (Eds.), *The nature of thought*, Honoring D. O. Hebb. Hillsdale, N.J.: Lawrence Erlbaum Associates, 1980.

Paivio, A. Individual differences in coding processes. In F. Klix, J. Hoffmann, & E. van der Meer (Eds.), *Cognitive research in psychology: Recent approaches, designs, and results*. Amsterdam: Elsevier, North-Holland, in press.

Paivio, A., & Begg, I. *The psychology of language*. Englewood Cliffs, N.J.: Prentice-Hall, 1981.

Paivio, A., & Csapo, K. Concrete-image and verbal memory codes. *Journal of Experimental Psychology*, 1969, *80*, 279–285.

Paivio, A., & Csapo, K. Picture superiority in free recall: Imagery or dual coding? *Cognitive Psychology*, 1973, *5*, 176–206.

Paivio, A., & Desrochers, A. A dual-coding approach to bilingual memory. *Canadian Journal of Psychology*, 1980, *34*, 390–401.

Paivio, A., & Ernest, C. Imagery ability and visual perception of verbal and nonverbal stimuli. *Perception and Psychophysics*, 1971, *10*, 429–432.

Paivio, A., & Lambert, W. Dual coding and bilingual memory. *Journal of Verbal Learning and Verbal Behavior*, 1981, *20*, 532–539.

Paivio, A., & Marschark, M. Comparative judgments of animal intelligence and pleasantness. *Memory & Cognition*, 1980, *8*, 39–48.

Paivio, A., & O'Neill, B. J. Visual recognition thresholds and dimensions of word meaning. *Perception & Psychophysics*, 1970, *8*, 273–275.

Paivio, A., Rogers, T. B., & Smythe, P. C. Why are pictures easier to recall than words? *Psychonomic Science*, 1968, *11*, 137–138.

Pellegrino, J. W., Siegel, A. W., & Dhawan, M. Short-term retention of pictures and words: Evidence for dual coding systems. *Journal of Experimental Psychology*, 1975, *104*, 95–102.

Peterson, M. J., & McGee, S. H. The effects of imagery instructions, imagery ratings, and the number of dictionary meanings upon recognition and recall. *Journal of Experimental Psychology*, 1974, *102*, 1007–1014.

Podgorny, P., & Shepard, R. N. Functional representations common to visual perception and imagination. *Journal of Experimental Psychology: Human Perception and Performance*, 1978, *4*, 21–35.

Potter, M. C., Valian, V. V., & Faulconer, B. A. Representation of a sentence and its pragmatic implications: Verbal, imagistic, or abstract? *Journal of Verbal Learning and Verbal Behavior*, 1977, *16*, 1–12.

Pylyshyn, Z. W. What the mind's eye tells the mind's brain: A critique of mental imagery. *Psychological Bulletin*, 1973, *80*, 1–24.

Pylyshyn, Z. W. The imagery debate: Analogue media versus tacit knowledge. *Psychological Review*, 1981, *88*, 16–45.

Richardson, J. T. E. Procedures for investigating imagery and the distinction between primary and secondary memory. *British Journal of Psychology*, 1976, *67*, 487–500.

Richardson, J. T. E. *Mental imagery and human memory*. MacMillan Press Ltd., London, 1980.

Robins, C., & Shepard, R. N. Spatio-temporal probing of apparent rotational movement. *Perception & Psychophysics*, 1977, *22*, 12–18.

Rosch, E. The nature of mental codes for color categories. *Journal of Experimental Psychology: Human Perception and Performance*, 1975, *1*, 303–322.

Rowe, E. J., & Paivio, A. Imagery and repetition instructions in verbal discrimination and incidental paired-associate learning. *Journal of Verbal Learning and Verbal Behavior*, 1971, *10*, 668–672.

Saltz, E., & Nolan, S. D. Does motoric imagery facilitate memory for sentences? A selective interference test. *Journal of Verbal Learning and Verbal Behavior*, 1981, *20*, 322–332.

Segal, S. J., & Fusella, V. Influence of imaged pictures and sounds on detection of visual and auditory signals. *Journal of Experimental Psychology*, 1970, *83*, 458–464.

Seymour, P. H. K. A model for reading, naming and comparison. *British Journal of Psychology*, 1973, *64*, 35–49.

Shepard, R. N. The mental image. *American Psychologist*, 1978, *33*, 125–137.

Shepard, R. N., & Metzler, J. Mental rotation of three-dimensional objects. *Science*, 1971, *171*, 701–703.

Warren, M. W. The effects of recall-concurrent visual-motor distraction on picture and word recall. *Memory & Cognition*, 1977, *5*, 362–370.

Yuille, J. C. A detailed examination of mediation in PA learning. *Memory & Cognition*, 1973, *1*, 333–342.

Zajonc, R. B. Feeling and thinking: Preferences need no inferences. *American Psychologist*, 1980, *35*, 151–175.

Author Index

Italics denote pages with bibliographic information.

Subject Index

DATE DUE